Collier's Gui

Night Photography

in the Great Outdoors

~ 2nd Edition ~

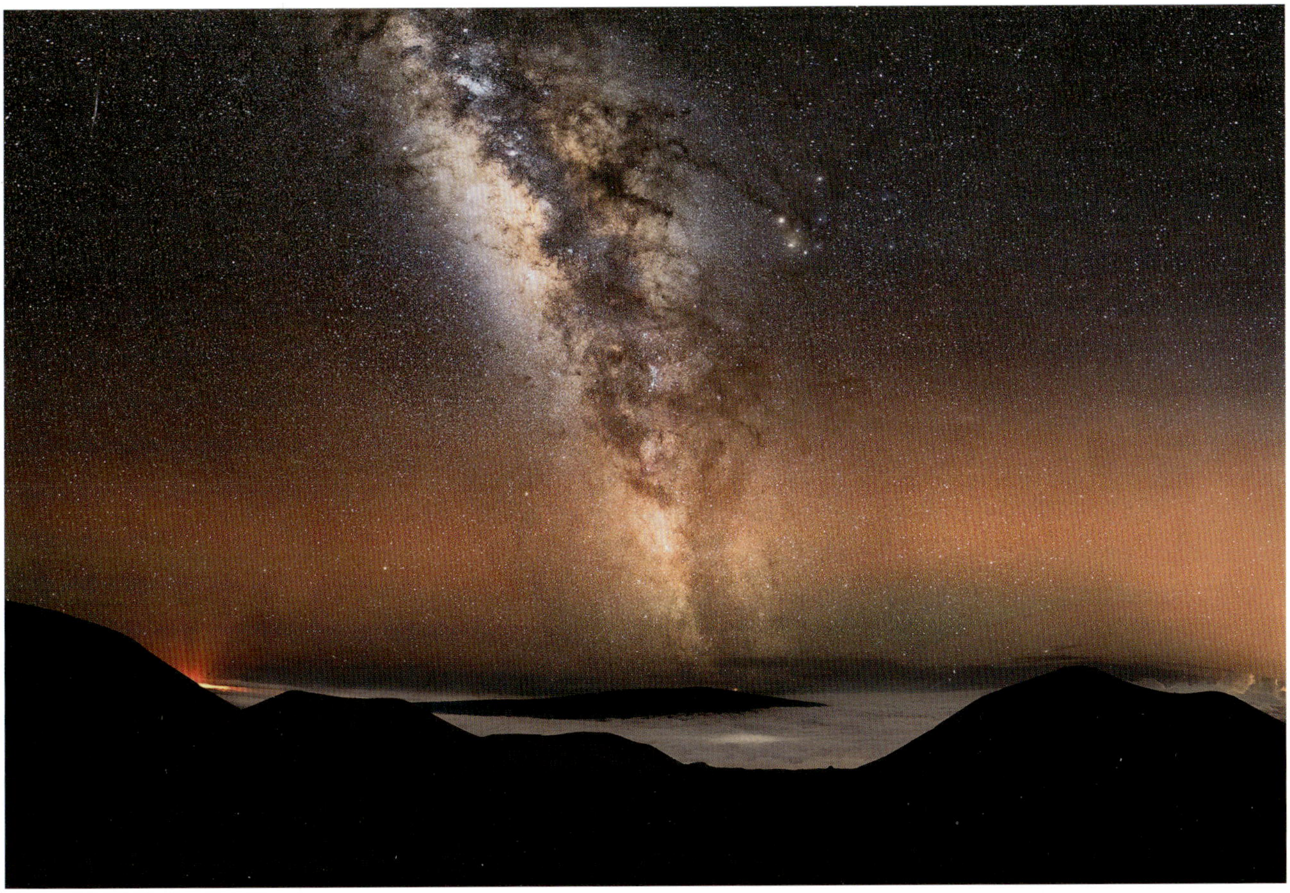

Text and Photography by Grant Collier

Collier Publishing LLC

Arvada, CO

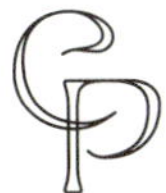

ACKNOWLEDGMENTS

I learned most of the information in this book by experimenting with different equipment, camera settings, and shooting techniques over 17 years. However, I wanted to ensure that this book was as thorough as possible, so I scoured the web for any other tips and pointers that might be useful. I would like to thank the following photographers for the advice they have provided to ensure that capturing a good shot in the dark is more than just a shot in the dark!

David Kingham, Tony Kuyper, Floris Van Breugel, Mike Berenson, Nat Coalson, Glenn Randall, Ian Norman, Steven Christenson, Allister Benn, John Mumaw, Mikko Lagerstedt, Jeffrey Sullivan, Brad Goldpaint, Phil Hart, Thomas O'Brien, Tony Prower, Marc Adamus, René Pirolt, Todd Salat, Aaron D. Priest, and Jason Hatfield.

RELATED MATERIALS FROM COLLIERPUBLISHING.COM

Collier's Guide to Post-Processing Night Photos (Instructional Video)
Collier's Guide to Photographing Arches National Park
Starry Nights Wall Calendar

Design by Grant Collier

ISBN # 978-1-935694-49-6
Printed in South Korea

Published by Collier Publishing LLC
https://www.collierpublishing.com

Cover Photo: The aurora borealis lights up the night sky over Vestrahorn mountain in Iceland.
Title Page: The Milky Way and a distant lava lake are seen from the summit of Mauna Kea in Hawaii.
Below Photo: The full band of the Milky Way is visible above Turret Arch in Arches National Park, Utah.
Author Page: Grant stands in the opening of Wilson Arch near Moab, Utah on an autumn night.
Back Cover: A large arch is seen from inside a cave in a remote part of Utah during twilight.

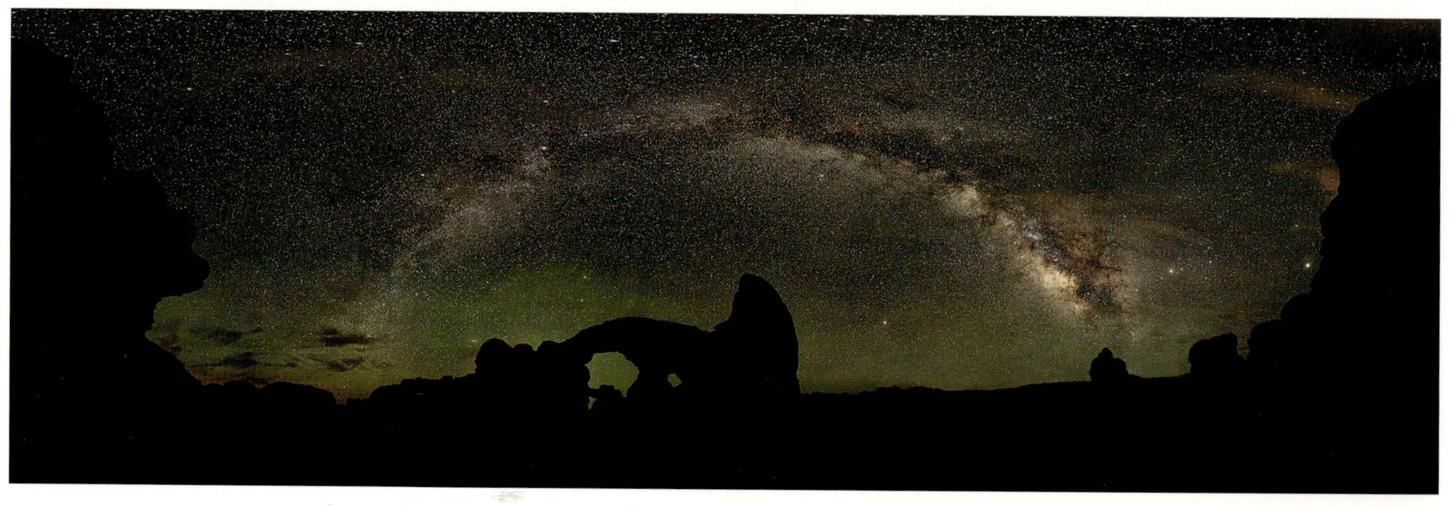

About the Author

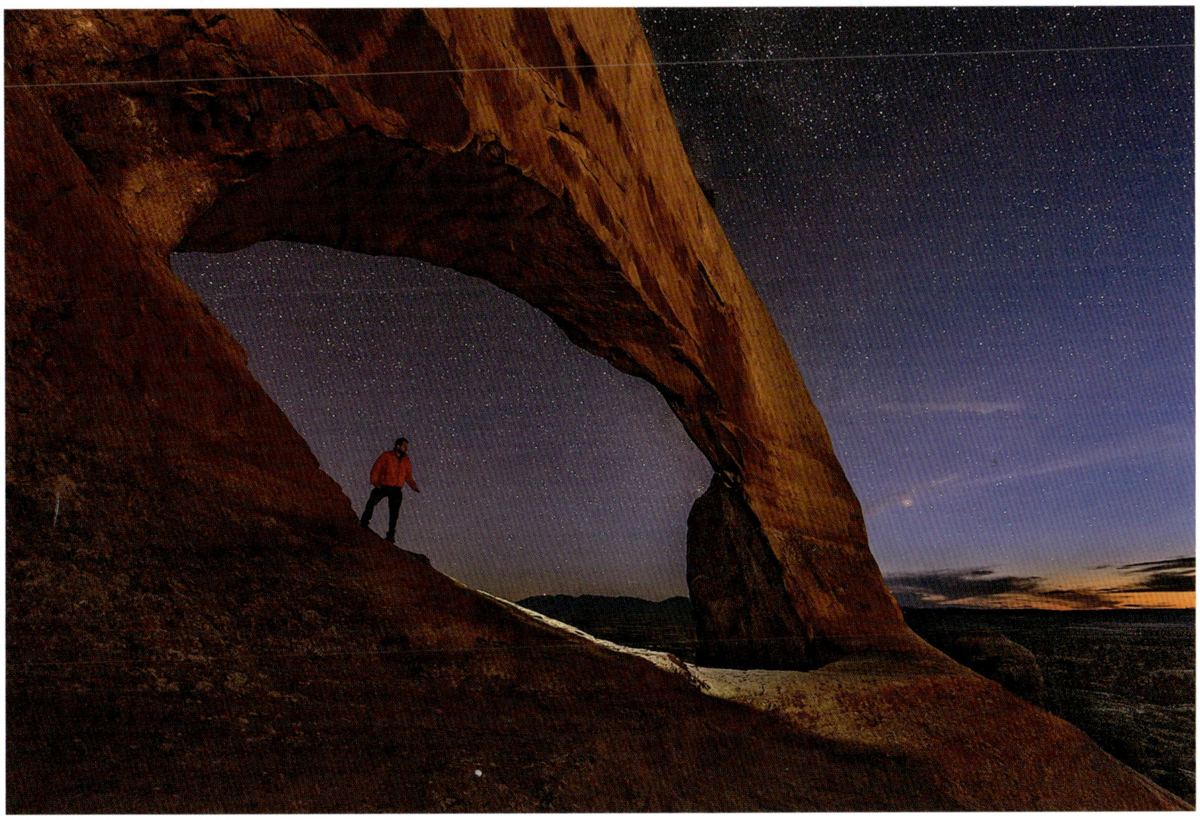

Grant Collier grew up in the foothills above Denver and spent much of his childhood exploring Colorado's Rocky Mountains. Grant took up photography while attending college in Los Angeles. He found endless photographic opportunities in the Desert Southwest while driving to and from L.A.

After graduating from college in 1996, Grant began a photographic career that had him following, quite literally, in the footsteps of his great-great-grandfather, the pioneer photographer Joseph Collier. Grant traveled throughout Colorado, taking photos from the exact same spots that Joseph had taken his images over one-hundred years earlier. These photographs were published in the book *Colorado: Yesterday & Today* in 2001. A sequel to this book called *Colorado Then & Now* was released in 2016.

In 2003, Grant began taking photos at night with his film camera. This quickly grew into an obsession, and a few years later, he began shooting night photos with a digital camera. These early cameras produced large amounts of noise at night, so Grant experimented with different techniques to minimize the noise and create high-quality images. Over the years, he learned new ways of shooting and processing photos that dramatically improved his images.

Grant produces the Starry Nights Wall Calendar, which features his night photography and includes dates of major astronomical events. He also publishes a Colorado calendar, a National Parks calendar, and a humorous Demotivational calendar.

Grant has authored numerous photography books, including *Collier's Guide to Photographing Arches National Park, Arches National Park by Day & Night,* and *Moab, Utah by Day & Night*.

You can see more of Grant's photos, books, calendars, and instructional videos at GCollier.com and CollierPublishing.com.

Contents

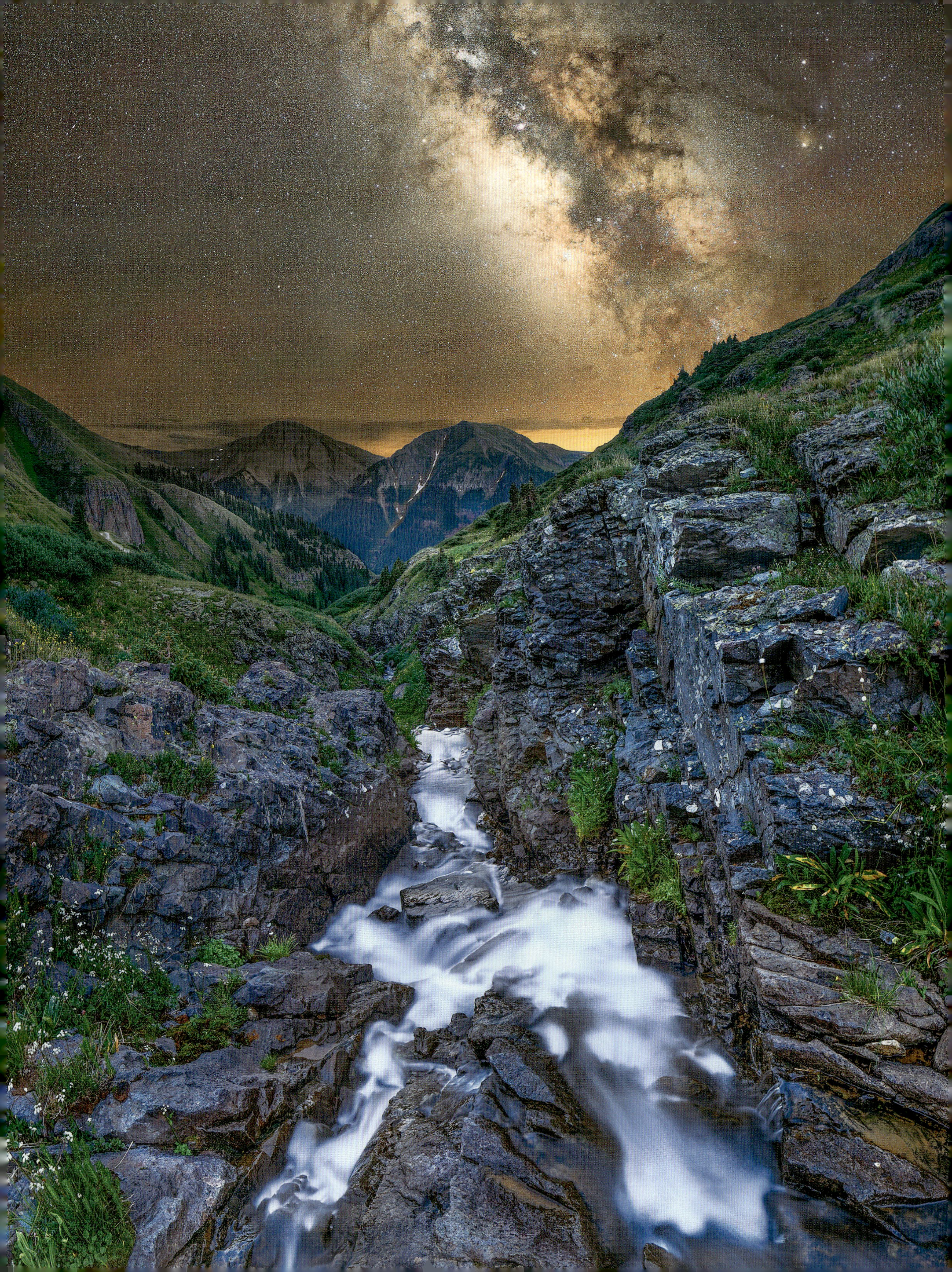

Introduction

We are literally blinded by the light. The sun is so bright during the day that we can see only a blue sky above us, giving the illusion that there is little else out there. Only when Earth rotates away from this light are we able to see the dazzling display of stars that surrounds our tiny planet.

For a long time, it was very difficult for the average photographer to capture good images of this celestial display. Film simply wasn't light-sensitive enough to capture high-quality photos with short exposures. The digital revolution has changed all of this. With a little practice, anyone can now capture stunning images of the night sky with relatively inexpensive equipment.

Astronomers with massive telescopes can still capture far more distant objects than we are able to with standard lenses on a standard camera. However, these lenses can do something that powerful telescopes cannot. They can include terrestrial objects in the foreground, giving context to the scene and tying everything back to our home planet.

When we take images of the night sky, we can capture objects spread out over immense distances. When shooting such distant objects, we are not just photographing different points in space; we are also capturing different points in time. The universe is so vast that some of the photons that reach the camera sensor have been traveling through space for hundreds, thousands, or even millions of years.

Our nearest celestial neighbor is the moon, which is a mere 240,000 miles away. Light from the moon takes a little over a second to reach us. So when you photograph the moon, you are peering back one second into the past. Light from Venus, which is the brightest planet in the sky and the closest one to us, takes between 3-13 minutes to reach us, depending on where it is in its orbit relative to Earth. The next brightest object in the night sky is Jupiter, the largest of all the planets. Light from this gas giant takes 35-52 minutes to reach us. The most distant planet in our solar system is Neptune. It appears as a tiny speck of light in the sky, indistinguishable from the stars around it. Light from this planet takes four hours to reach Earth.

While these distances are immense, they are nothing compared to the stars. Light from the nearest star, Proxima Centauri, takes a little over four years to reach Earth. Light from the most distant star we can capture using a wide-angle lens under relatively dark skies departed over 16,000 years ago. At this time in Earth's history, the great Egyptian pyramids had not yet been built. Earth was still gripped in the last ice age, and humans lived as primitive hunters and gatherers.

Since it takes so long for the light to reach us, there's a chance that one of the stars you capture in a photograph no longer exists. If it was large enough, it might have exploded in a massive supernova. The dazzlingly bright light from that supernova, however, may not reach Earth for many more centuries or millennia.

The stars that we can capture in a photograph make up only a small portion of the Milky Way Galaxy, which is 100,000 light-years across. We can, however, still peer much farther back in time. A standard camera can easily record light from the Andromeda Galaxy. This galaxy is an unfathomable 15,000,000,000,000,000,000 (15 quintillion) miles away.

Left: To capture this image of a mountain stream in Colorado, I used techniques discussed in Chapters VIII and IX to stitch and blend multiple exposures. Nikon D800e; exposure for land during twilight: 14mm, f/13, 3 seconds, ISO 100; 51 exposures for stitched image of sky: 50mm f/1.8, 10 seconds, ISO 6400.

When light left this galaxy 2.5 million years ago, Homo sapiens had not yet evolved. In fact, our most distant ancestors in the Homo lineage, known as Homo habilis, would not evolve for at least 100,000 more years.

The nearest galaxies are the most distant objects we can capture with standard camera gear. However, even this represents only a tiny fraction of the size of the universe. There are approximately 200 billion galaxies stretched over unimaginably vast spaces. Light from the most distant galaxy ever observed with the Hubble Space Telescope departed over 13 billion years ago. At this time, the universe was a mere 800,000 years old, and it would be billions of years before the sun and Earth formed.

Digital cameras allow photographers to capture detailed photographs of some of these unfathomably distant objects. However, it requires a lot of expertise to capture these images, as the rules of photography are often turned on their head.

When I first started taking photos at night in 2003, I was faced with the challenge of learning these rules with equipment that was fairly primitive compared to what we have today. I used a film camera with superfine grain ISO 100 film to capture very long exposures that resulted in star trails. If I had attempted shorter exposures to render the stars as points of light, the images would have been vastly underexposed and almost unusable. Film with an ISO of 800 or 1600 would have worked better for short exposures, as it is more light-sensitive. However, this film is very grainy and doesn't result in high-quality images.

In 2006, I started shooting night photos with my new Canon 5D digital camera. I was able to capture short exposures at night that were superior to what I could obtain with a film camera. However, these early digital cameras produced images with large amounts of noise at night, and it was still difficult to capture photos with a lot of detail. I had to experiment with many different camera settings and lenses to discover what worked best. Eventually, I began creating huge stitched images to minimize the noise that was so problematic with early digital cameras. I also experimented with equatorial mounts, which allowed me to take much longer exposures while still rendering the stars as round points of light. Any foreground in these images was blurred by the movement of the mount. However, digital imaging software had also improved to the point where I could blend a separate photo of the foreground with an image of the sky.

Once I captured the images with a camera, I was faced with the challenge of optimizing them on the computer using Adobe Photoshop or Lightroom. Night photos can be more difficult to process than daytime photos, as they often look very flat and have a lot of noise. Over time, I developed a workflow that helped me minimize noise and bring out the colors and details in the night sky.

With the improvement of digital cameras, night photography has become increasingly popular. Places that I once had to himself at night, like Arches National Park, are often filled with photographers trying to take dramatic images of the night sky. However, compared to daytime photography, there is still somewhat limited information on how to capture these nightscapes. Much of this information is scattered throughout the web. It's hard to know what information you can rely on since not all of it is accurate. So I decided to share just about everything I have learned over the past 17 years in this book.

This book is intended for people who have some experience using a digital SLR or mirrorless camera. You should know how to focus manually, how to get a proper exposure when shooting in manual mode, and how to view and interpret the histogram. I won't spend a lot of time going over the basics, as there are a lot of books that cover this. I want to focus on the things that are unique to shooting at night and that are not as easy to learn elsewhere. An excellent resource for learning the basics is Nat Coalson's book *Nature Photography Photo Workshop*.

My book is also intended for people who have some fundamental understanding of Photoshop and Lightroom. You should know how to import photos into Lightroom and adjust them in the Develop module (alternatively, you can make the same adjustments in Adobe Camera Raw). You should also know how to use layers in Photoshop and make selections and masks. Again, I will focus on specialized post-processing techniques that are geared towards night photography. There are a lot of good books that can introduce you to these programs.

Although instructional books can help you learn the basics, it's also essential to practice as much as you can. It's easier to learn when shooting during the day, as getting good quality images at night is more challenging. However, if you are new to photography and still want to jump right into night photography, I recommend starting with Chapters I-VI. These chapters mostly go over the basics of night photography. You can then skip to Chapter X on post-processing images at night. The section on Lightroom Adjustments in this chapter is fairly basic, but the section on Photoshop Adjustments is more advanced. Once you're comfortable with this material, you can tackle Chapters VII, VIII, and IX. These chapters cover more and more advanced topics, with Chapter IX being suitable for the most experienced photographers.

The last few chapters discuss advanced post-processing techniques. For those who want an in-depth demonstration of all of these techniques and a few new ones, I've created a series of videos on post-processing night photos. It is available at https://www.collierpublishing.com.

In both this book and the video, I discuss many different ways of capturing and processing photos, from taking single exposures to combining multiple exposures. Some people may object to combining multiple exposures, as they believe it makes the images "less real." However, you will often need to combine multiple exposures to reduce noise and increase the quality of the images. Since noise is an unnatural artifact, it is not "real." So it could be argued that some images from multiple exposures are more "real." Ultimately, it comes down to your definition of reality and how close you want to keep your photographs to that reality.

Some people may define reality as that which we can see with our own eyes. If a photograph doesn't closely match that, it is not "real." This is, however, nearly impossible to accomplish with night photos. The camera can capture far more stars than the eye can see. Just because the stars are not visible to the naked eye does not make them any less real.

Also, cameras are designed to create images that mimic how we see during the day. We see much differently at night. This is because we see mainly with rods in our eyes at night versus cones during the day. Rods are far more light-sensitive, but you can't see nearly as much detail with them. Rods are more sensitive to blue and green wavelengths of light than to reds. However, you cannot see color with rods, and unless you have a bright light source that can be seen with cones, the world at night appears black and white.

Cameras, on the other hand, still capture photos at night the way we would see them with cones. No camera can capture things as we see them with rods. In post-processing, we could try to dramatically subdue the colors and details in an attempt to mimic what we see with rods. This would produce rather dull, monochromatic images. Alternatively, we can bring out the colors and try to mimic how we would see if our cones were incredibly light-sensitive. I choose the latter, as I think it's fascinating to know all the colors and details the camera can "see" at night that we can't.

Ultimately, there is no fixed reality. We all have different ways of interpreting what exists at night. To some extent, we can only imagine what the night sky looks like, as we are half-blind to it. The camera can help bring our imagination to life.

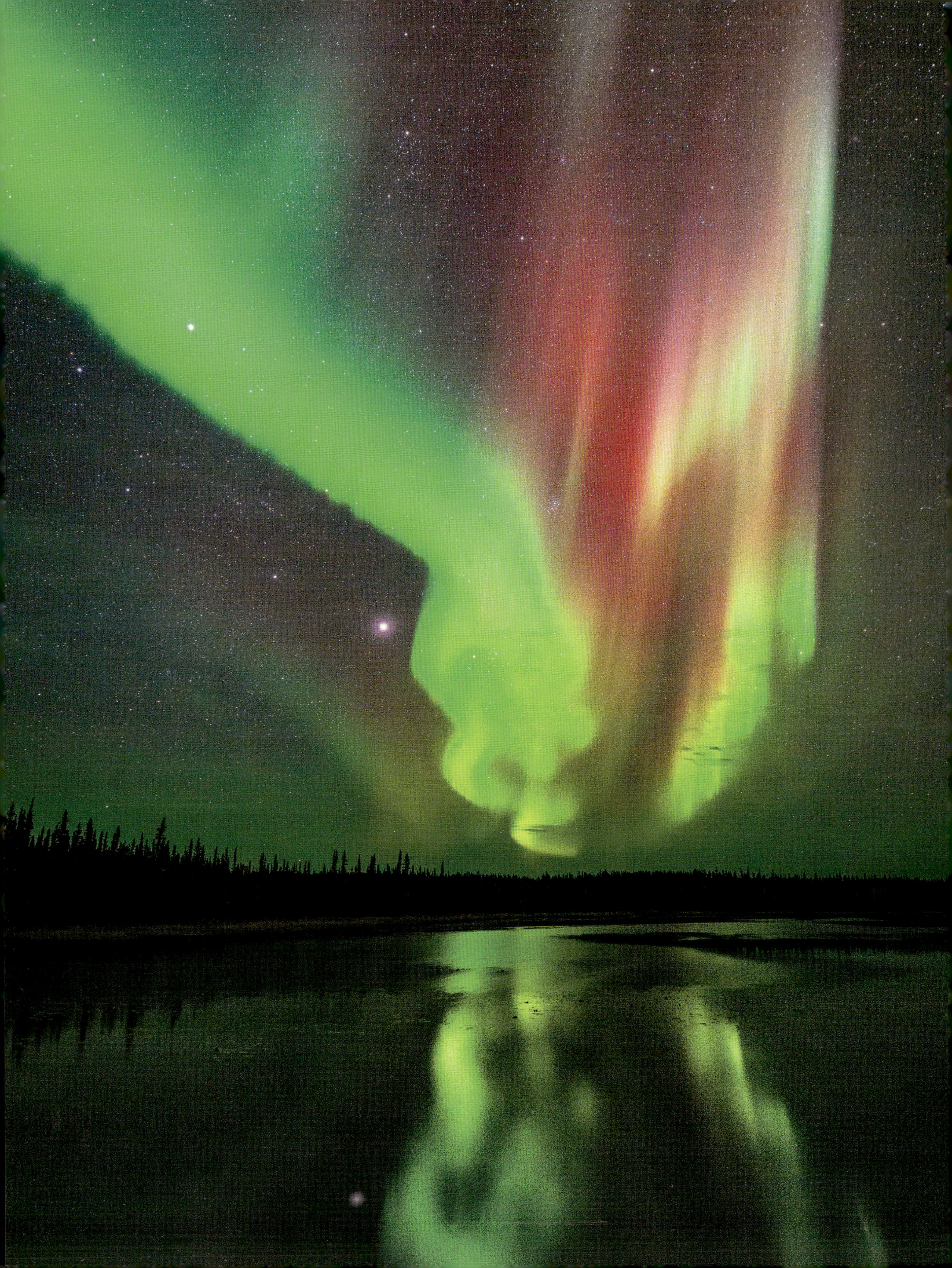

I. Equipment & Supplies

Today, photography equipment is so advanced that most modern digital cameras can produce excellent images when shooting photos during the day. Owning the right equipment is still of some importance and can increase the options available to a photographer. However, the quality of the images depends mostly on the talent of the photographer, not on the equipment they are using.

While the talent and knowledge of the photographer are still of great importance when taking photos at night, owning the right equipment becomes more valuable. The proper equipment can help minimize noise that is inherent in low-light images and make it possible to print these images at large sizes.

Image noise is an unnatural variation in the color or brightness of an image. It can be produced by the circuitry in a digital camera or by the random nature in which photons hit the camera sensor. It exists in all images but is mostly drowned out during the day because of the large number of photons hitting the sensor. At night, so few photons hit the sensor that the noise competes strongly with the signal and can significantly reduce the quality of the images. Minimizing this noise is one of the biggest challenges of night photography and is something that will be discussed extensively throughout this book.

The first step in the battle against noise is using the right equipment. You don't necessarily need to spend a fortune on this equipment. A newer digital camera and one or two fairly inexpensive lenses can be all you need to capture stunning images at night.

In this chapter, I'll provide a summary of the equipment that I find most useful for shooting at night. Since equipment is continually changing, I recommend that you do some research online before purchasing anything. DxOMark.com is one of the best sites for evaluating equipment, as it extensively tests and rates many different cameras and lenses. While this is my favorite site for evaluating equipment, the tests aren't designed specifically for night photography, so the ratings aren't perfect. Another useful website is DPReview's studio shot comparison, where you can compare images from different cameras using different ISOs. This can be seen at: https://www.dpreview.com/reviews/image-comparison.

To keep the information I provide current, I also have a list of equipment that I recommend for night photography at https://www.gcollier.com/gear/.

If you're unsure what camera or lens to purchase, you might want to rent one first to test it out.

CAMERAS

Digital cameras have improved dramatically in the past two decades, allowing you to capture high-quality images with relatively short exposures at night. I will mainly focus on using digital SLRs and mirrorless cameras in this book. However, film cameras can sometimes be useful for taking long exposures that result in star trails, so I will discuss them briefly as well.

Digital Cameras

In the table on the following page, I've listed most of the cameras I recommend for night photography, sorted by their DxOMark low-light rating. Unfortunately, the low-light rating isn't perfect, since DxOMark tests this with very short exposures using high ISOs. This can account for photon noise and some read noise in an image but not for the dark noise that is produced during long exposures (I discuss photon noise and dark noise in more detail on pages 62-64). In general, newer cameras handle dark noise better than older cameras. For example, I've found that my Nikon D850 usually produces a little better quality images at night than my old Nikon D800e, even though the D800e is rated higher on the next page. This is because the D850 produces less dark noise. Overall, though, dark noise is significantly less noticeable than photon noise in most night photos,

---

Left: A dramatic display of the northern lights is reflected in a lake near Yellowknife, Canada. By using a camera that is rated well for low-light ISO performance and a Nikkor 14-24mm lens, I was able to capture a high-quality image with a single exposure. Nikon D800e, 14mm, f/2.8, 15 seconds, ISO 2500.

Camera	Low-Light Rating	Overall Rating	Megapixels	Release Date	≈ Cost (as of 2020)
Sony A7 III	3730	96	24.2	2018	$2,000
Sony A7S	3702	87	12.2	2014	$650*
Panasonic Lumix DC-S1R	3525	100	47.3	2019	$3,700
Sony A7R III	3523	100	42.4	2017	$2,800
Sony A9	3517	92	24.2	2017	$3,800
Sony A7R IV	3344	99	61.2	2019	$3,500
Panasonic Lumix DC-S1	3333	95	24.2	2019	$2,500
Nikon Z6	3299	95	24.5	2018	$1,800
Pentax K-1	3280	96	36.4	2016	$1,700
Nikon Df	3279	89	16.2	2013	$1,200*
Canon EOS 5D Mark IV	2995	91	30.4	2016	$2,500
Nikon D600	2980	95	24.3	2012	$450*
Nikon D800E	2979	96	36.3	2012	$700*
Canon EOS RP	2978	85	26.2	2019	$1,000
Canon EOS 6D Mark II	2862	85	26.2	2017	$1,200
Sony A7R	2746	95	36	2013	$600*
Nikon D850	2660	100	45.7	2017	$2,900
Canon EOS 6D	2340	82	20.2	2012	$500*
Canon EOS 5DS R	2308	86	50.6	2015	$1,400*

*Table 1.1: The cameras I recommend for night photography are sorted by their DxOMark low-light rating. You can view a longer list at https://www.dxomark.com/Cameras/Ratings/List-view/Sports. I have included a variety of camera brands and some of the more affordable older models that perform well in low light. *For cameras originally released before 2016, I've the listed approximate cost for a pre-owned camera.*

so the DxOMark ratings are still quite informative.

As you can see from Table 1.1, Sony mirrorless cameras currently lead the way in terms of minimizing photon noise and read noise with high ISOs. However, there is a new Panasonic camera that is not far behind. Also, the Pentax K-1 has several features designed primarily for night photography. One of the most impressive is the Astrotracer, which works like an equatorial mount by rotating the camera sensor with the rotation of the stars. This lets you do much longer exposures of the night sky without getting star trails (I discuss equatorial mounts in detail on pages 132-134). Although the Pentax doesn't work quite as well as an actual equatorial mount, it is easier to set up and doesn't require carrying extra gear. The lens selection is a bit more limited with the Pentax. You can't use the Sony ART lenses, which are my favorite for night photography. However, you can get Rokinon lenses and some good lenses made by Pentax.

Nikon and Canon have fallen a bit behind in producing cameras that are optimized for night photography. However, if you already shoot with Nikon or Canon, it probably isn't worth the time and cost to switch over to a different brand. The camera quality from all the top brands is continually improving, and you can get high quality images from any of these cameras. The most important factor in getting good photos is knowing how to use the equipment properly. That being said, I did recently purchase a Sony A7 III, which I now use for my night photography. I still own a Nikon D850 for daytime images and for when I shoot with two cameras at night. For night photography, my primary lenses are the Sigma 14mm f/1.8, the Sigma 50mm f/1.4, and the Nikkor 14-24mm f/2.8, which I use on my D850 or on my Sony with an adapter.

There is usually some trade-off between the number of megapixels a camera has and the image quality at night. Cameras with fewer megapixels tend to perform a little better at night since each pixel is larger and able to collect more light. However, as sensors have improved, the difference in quality has diminished, and you can now get cameras with 40+ megapixels that perform very well at night. If you want a high megapixel count to print huge images of your daytime photos and still get high quality images at night, you can now have the best of both worlds.

If you're on a tighter budget, I've included several older cameras in the table that you can buy used on sites like eBay for under $1,000. These can all produce high quality images at night. A good, lower budget setup is the Rokinon 14mm f/2.8 lens paired with either a Sony A7S, Nikon D600, or Canon EOS 6D.

If you already own a digital SLR or mirrorless camera that is not rated as high for low-light ISO performance, I don't necessarily recommend buying a new camera. Most modern cameras can produce good results at night. If you use a fast lens and the techniques outlined in this book, you can still achieve excellent results. I took many of the photos in this book with the Canon 5D Mark II, which has a low-light rating of 1815. However, by stitching together multiple images, as described in Chapter VIII, I have made huge, high-quality prints of night photos taken with this camera. So it may be better to use the camera you currently own as you become proficient in night photography. If you decide your images have too much noise for your intended use, you can consider an upgrade.

Medium Format Cameras

Since medium-format digital cameras have significantly larger sensors than standard digital cameras, they can theoretically collect more light in a single exposure at night. The Pentax 645Z and Hasselblad X1D-50c have higher low-light ISO ratings than any other camera on DxOMark. However, these ratings are for the sensor only and don't factor in the lenses for the camera.

DxoMark has not yet rated the Fujifilm GFX 100 and GFX 50R medium format cameras. However, the Laowa 17mm lens, which is compatible with these cameras, is probably the most practical lens for night photography. This focal length is equivalent to 13mm on a 35mm format sensor. It is easily the widest lens currently available for a medium format camera. This is important for photographing something as expansive as the night sky. However, the widest aperture for this lens, and all other wide-angle medium-format lenses, is f/4.0. As a result, it can only let in half as much light as an f/2.8 lens on a 35mm camera and just 1/5 the amount of light of the Sigma 14mm f/1.8. This effectively negates any real advantage of a medium format camera for night photography. For this reason, I don't currently recommend medium format for night photography. If you happen to already own such a camera for daytime photos, then it can certainly be worth trying at night.

Film Cameras

Although few photographers still shoot with film cameras, they can potentially be useful with very long exposures that result in star trails. I'll discuss this in more detail in Chapter VII. 35mm film cameras will produce images with more grain, but I've found that the noise reduction software I discuss in Chapter X, called Topaz DeNoise, also does a good job with reducing grain.

LENSES

Owning the right combination of lenses is perhaps even more important for night photography than owning the right camera. You need lenses with wide apertures that can let in a lot of light. I recommend lenses that have apertures at least as wide as f/2.8. These lenses will help minimize noise, but there are also pitfalls you should be aware of when shooting with such fast lenses.

One issue with lenses with wider apertures is that they can produce coma in the corners of the images. In night photos, coma will make stars look like birds with wings rather than points of light. Lenses with aspherical elements are generally better at reducing coma. However, depending on their build quality, even these lenses can

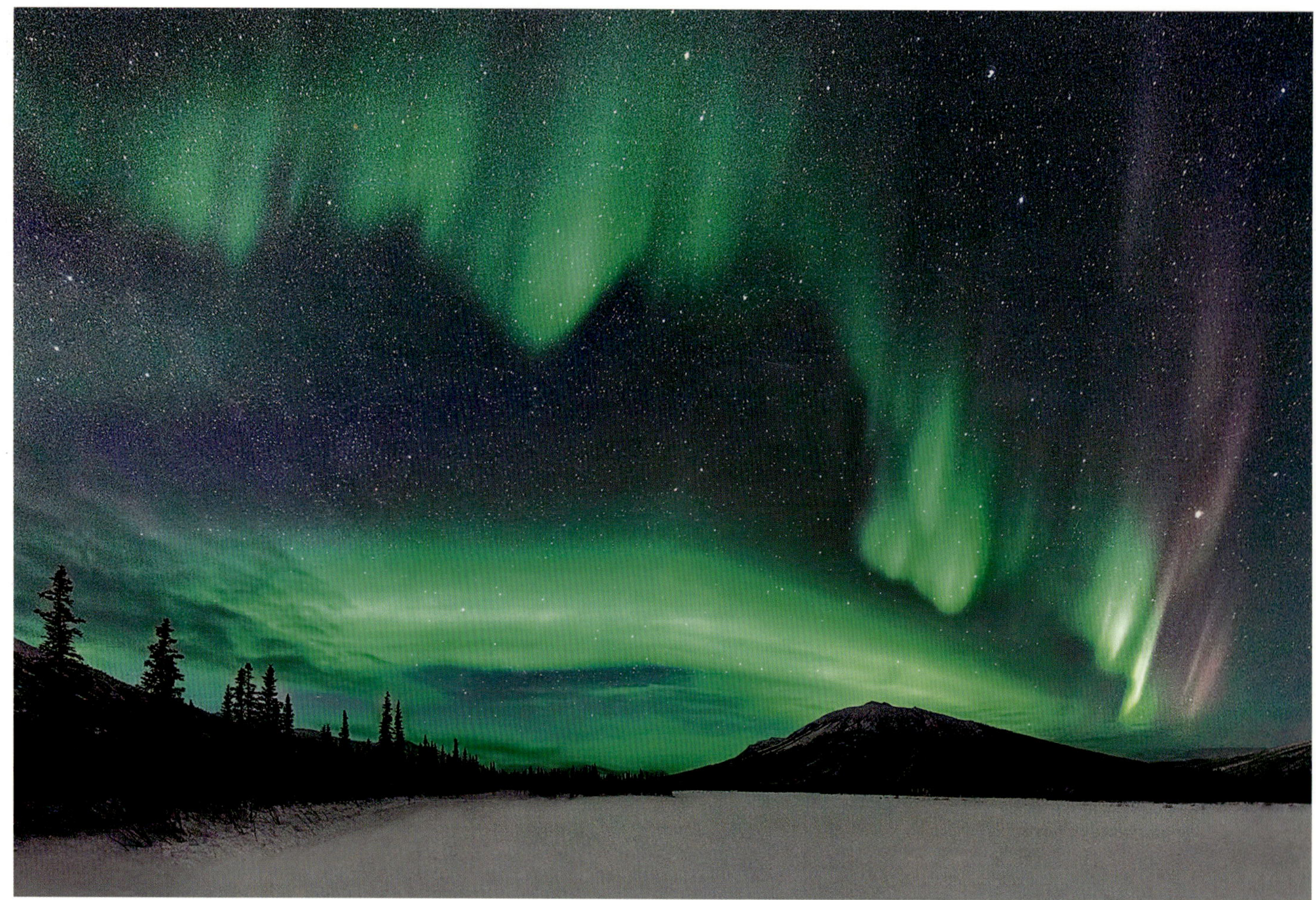

The northern lights dance in the sky above Wiseman, Alaska. My Nikkor 14-24mm lens was invaluable for capturing a large portion of the sky in a single exposure. Canon 5D II, 14mm, f/2.8, 15 seconds, ISO 6400.

produce a lot of coma. Also, the price of the lens is not always indicative of how well it will perform in low light with wide apertures. Some of the most expensive lenses will show a lot of coma, while a few of the less expensive options can produce superior results.

Other problems you may have with lenses when shooting at night are chromatic aberration and vignetting. In night photos, chromatic aberration will generally appear as an unnatural color fringe around the edge of stars. Vignetting will cause the corners of the image to appear darker than the rest of the image. These issues can be corrected more easily in post-processing than coma, but it is still best to find lenses that keep these problems to a minimum.

In Tables 1.2-1.4, I've listed lenses that work well for night photography and can help minimize coma, chromatic aberration, and vignetting. I've included a large number of lenses to include options for different camera brands and for those wanting as much versatility as possible. However, you only need one or two lenses to capture a wide variety of stunning night photos. If you're new to night photography and are looking to buy just one lens, I'd recommend starting with the Rokinon 14mm, Sigma 14mm, Tamron 15-30, or Sigma 14-24. If you want to try stitched images, I recommend one of the 35mm or 50mm lenses that I've listed.

I'll go over the advantages of lenses with different focal lengths below, followed by an overview of the best lenses that are currently available.

Ultra-Wide-Angle Lenses

When I am not stitching together multiple images, I usually shoot with an ultra-wide-angle lens at around 14mm. It is important to have a wide-angle lens when photographing something as vast as the night sky. These lenses also give you a lot of depth of field, even at the

Ultra-Wide-Angle Lenses	DxO Score	≈ Cost (as of 2020)	Camera Mounts
Rokinon 14mm f/2.8	31	$330	Nikon F / Canon EF / Sony E / Pentax K
Sigma 14mm f/1.8 Art	not tested	$1,400	Nikon F / Canon EF / Sony E / Panasonic L
Sigma 14-24mm f/2.8 Art	not tested	$1,200	Nikon F / Canon EF / Sony E / Pansonic L
Tamron 15-30mm f/2.8	32	$1,000	Nikon F / Canon EF
Tokina 11-20mm f/2.8 (crop sensor)	21	$450	Nikon DX / Canon APS-C
Rokinon 10mm f/2.8 (crop sensor)	not tested	$350	Nikon DX / Canon APS-C

Table 1.2: There is now a good selection of ultra-wide-angle lenses for night photography. The DxO score of a lens depends on the camera that is used. I've posted the highest score a lens had with any camera. The test is not done for night photography, so the ratings are not perfect. However, they give a general idea of the lens quality.

widest apertures. At f/2.8 with a 14mm lens, you can get objects in focus from about four feet to infinity.

Sigma 14mm f/1.8 Art

One of the newer fixed-focal-length, ultra-wide-angle lenses that is very well suited for night photography is the Sigma 14mm f/1.8. It lets in 2.4 times as much light as an f/2.8 lens, which had long been the widest option for an ultra-wide-angle lens. At f/1.8, you do start to get more coma and vignetting in the corners of the image. However, you get significantly less noise, so I believe the trade-off is more than worthwhile.

The Sigma can be especially advantageous if you have rapidly-moving objects in the sky, like the northern lights or clouds. In this situation, it is difficult to create stitched or stacked images to improve image quality. The objects in your photo may move too much between each shot to be able to combine multiple exposures.

The Sigma is quite expensive and costs around $1,400.

Rokinon 14mm f/2.8

The least expensive option for an ultra-wide-angle lens with an aperture of f/2.8 or wider is the Rokinon 14mm. It usually sells for a little over $300. The lenses made by this company are marketed under the names Rokinon and Samyang. Regardless of the name, you'll be getting the same lens. For simplicity's sake, I'll just refer to this brand as Rokinon. This lens can be used with many different camera models, including Canon, Nikon, Sony, and Pentax.

In my tests, this lens shows a bit more softness and coma in the corners than the other full-frame, ultra-wide lenses in Table 1.2 when used at f/2.8. Overall, though, it produces quality images at night. It is a great way to get started in night photography without breaking the bank.

The Rokinon can also be useful if you own two cameras and want a second, less expensive lens so you can shoot with both cameras at the same time.

Most Rokinon lenses are manual focus, but they have introduced some autofocus lenses, including a 14mm version. These cost around $650. They are probably not worth the extra cost for night photography since you'll often need to manually focus images anyway.

Rokinon has also introduced a 14mm f/2.4 lens that costs around $1,000. This lens is useful for night photography, as it can let in about 33% more light than an f/2.8 lens. However, the price is almost as high as the other three ultra-wide-angle lenses I recommend. I'm not convinced that it would be a better value than any of those lenses, especially given some quality control issues with Rokinon, which I'll go over later.

Tamron 15-30mm f/2.8

If you want an ultra-wide-angle lens, along with the versatility of a zoom lens, your main options are the Tamron 15-30, Sigma 14-24, and Nikon Nikkor 14-24. The Tamron sells for around $1,100 and performs similarly to the other two zoom lenses, which are more expensive. In comparison to the fixed focal length lenses, I think the Tamron surpasses the Rokinon 14mm for night photography, but falls short of the Sigma 14mm, due to the wider aperture of the Sigma.

The widest focal length of the Tamron is 15mm, versus 14mm for the other full-frame lenses I've listed. This is a pretty small difference, but it can be important for night photos, where you often want to include as much of the sky as possible.

An advantage of the Tamron is that it can zoom in to 30mm, whereas the Nikkor and Sigma only go to 24mm. This can be useful for creating big stitched images if you don't want to buy a separate lens specifically for that purpose. Occasionally, you may want to shoot single exposures at 30mm, but for me, this is somewhat rare.

Tamron has a new G2 version of this lens out for an extra $300. They mainly added better autofocus and vibration compensation, neither of which you'll need for night photography. So I recommend the less expensive, original version. You can buy versions of the Tamron for Nikon and Canon cameras.

Sigma 14-24 f/2.8 Art

The Nikkor 14-24 was my primary lens for night photography for many years, but I now recommend the Sigma 14-24 over the Nikkor. Both lenses perform exceptionally well at night. They are so close that I only recommend the Sigma because it costs about 35% less. It's also available for many different camera bodies, whereas the Nikkor can only be used on a Nikon unless you buy an adapter.

The price and quality of the Sigma is similar to the Tamron 15-30. So the main advantage of the Sigma is the wider focal length of 14mm. You can always stitch images to create even wider images with either lens. However, it's easier to take single exposures, so having a little wider lens is still useful.

If you choose to also purchase the Sigma 14mm f/1.8, the Tamron may be more useful, as you will then be able to cover a range of focal lengths from 14-30mm.

Tokina 11-20mm f/2.8 DX

If you own a crop-sensor camera and are looking for an ultra-wide zoom lens, I recommend the Tokina 11-20mm. You can also use any full-frame lens on a crop-sensor camera (but not vice-versa). However, because of the crop-factor, a 14mm lens will only have an effective focal length of around 21mm. This is not very wide for night photos. The Tokina will give you an effective focal length of around 16-30mm. If you also want a longer lens, I recommend getting a lens made for a full-frame camera. That way, if you ever upgrade to full-frame, you won't need to replace that lens.

Rokinon 10mm f/2.8

If you want a little wider lens for a crop-sensor camera and don't need a zoom lens, the Rokinon 10mm is a good option.

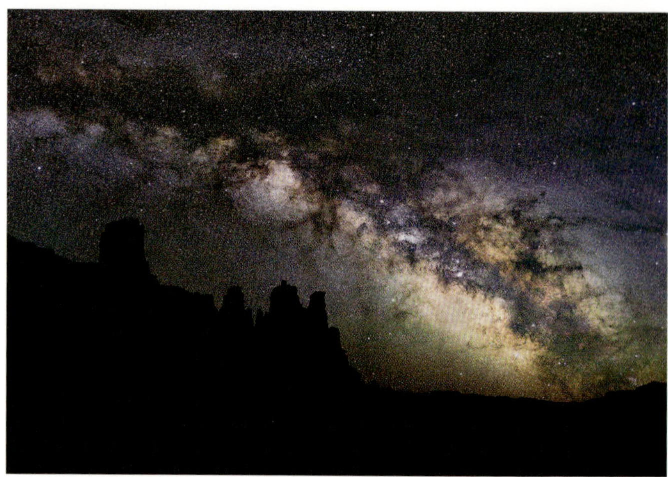

The Milky Way rises above Fisher Towers in Utah. I used a 50mm lens to take 28 images of this scene. I later stitched all of the photos together. Canon 5D II, 50mm, f/1.6, 10 seconds, ISO 6400.

20-55mm Lenses

If you initially only plan to purchase one lens for night photography, I recommend one of the ultra-wide-angle lenses discussed in the last section. However, if you want a second or even third lens, I recommend those in the 20-55mm range. For photos of the night sky, you'll find that lenses of this focal length are not all that wide. For single exposures, they can be useful for images of Orion or the Big Dipper, as well as close-ups of the bright, central portion of the Milky Way. However, the main reason I recommend a lens in this focal range is to create large stitched images. These photos can be of significantly higher quality than a single exposure. I'll

20-55mm Lenses	DxO Score	≈ Cost (as of 2020)	Camera Mounts
Sigma 20mm f/1.4 ART	41	$900	Nikon F / Canon EF / Sony E / Pansonic L
Sigma 24mm f/1.4 ART	39	$850	Nikon F / Canon EF / Sony E / Pansonic L
Rokinon 24mm f/1.4	37	$500	Nikon F / Canon EF / Sony E / Panasonic L
Sigma 35mm f/1.4 ART	43	$700	Nikon F / Canon EF / Sony E / Panasonic L
Rokinon 35mm f/1.4	37	$450	Nikon F / Canon EF / Sony E / Pentax K
Tamron SP 35mm f/1.8	42	$600	Nikon F / Canon EF / Sony E
Tamron SP 45mm f/1.8	37	$400	Nikon F / Canon EF
Sigma 50mm f/1.4 ART	46	$950	Nikon F / Canon EF / Sony E / Panasonic L
Rokinon 50mm f/1.4	not tested	$400	Nikon F / Canon EF / Sony E / Pentax K
Nikon Nikkor 50mm f/1.8D	31	$130	Nikon F
Canon EF 50mm f/1.8 STM	35	$125	Canon EF
Sony FE Carl Zeiss 55mm f/1.8	48	$1,000	Sony E

Table 1.3: There is a wide selection of lenses with very wide apertures with focal lengths between 20-55mm.

discuss how to create stitched images in Chapter VIII.

When shooting stitched images, longer lenses will produce higher-resolution photos. A 50mm lens will create an image that is a little over four times larger than a 24mm lens, assuming you're capturing the same scene with the same field of view. If both lenses are about the same quality and you use the same camera settings, you will be able to print the image taken at 50mm about four times larger than the one taken at 24mm, while getting the same print quality.

A disadvantage to using a 50mm lens is that you will have to take about four times as many images to capture a scene. If you want to capture an extremely wide panorama that includes the entire band of the Milky Way, you'll need to shoot around 80 photos. With a 24mm lens, you'd need to take around 20 images. With a 14mm lens, you could shoot one row with about 6 vertical photos.

It will also take longer to process the images on a computer. For very large stitched images, I recommend a computer with at least 16 GB of RAM and a steady-state drive.

Another disadvantage of a 50mm lens is that you will get less depth of field, meaning you won't be able to get both close and distant objects in focus in a single exposure. Table 4.1 on page 60 shows the depth of field you can achieve with different focal lengths using common camera settings for night photography. Since a 50mm lens can only get objects in focus from about 80 feet to infinity at f/1.8, it is best used if you have large foreground objects that are a long way away. Alternatively, you can blend separate exposures of the land and sky, as I'll describe in Chapter IX.

With the continual improvement in cameras, many night photographers may never need a 50mm lens, since a 24mm or 35mm lens can produce remarkably detailed stitched images that can be printed quite large. I personally still use a 50mm lens for many of my stitched images, as I want to have photos that I can print at very large sizes with superior quality.

Ultimately, the lens or lenses you want in this range depends on your shooting style and your budget. I suggest first deciding on an approximate focal length you want, as this will narrow down the choices considerably. Part of this decision may depend on which ultra-wide-angle lens you choose, as you may not want to have too big of a gap in focal range. If you use a Rokinon or Sigma 14mm, you may want a 24mm lens. If you use the Sigma or Nikkor 14-24mm, you might consider a 35mm lens. Owners of the Tamron 15-30 might prefer a 50mm lens. The ultra-wide zoom lenses can be used at their longest focal length to create smaller stitched images. One disadvantage of these lenses is that the widest aperture is f/2.8, whereas the longer fixed focal length lenses I've listed go as wide as f/1.4 and can let in 4 times more light. However, you can still get very good quality stitched images at f/2.8. The smaller aperture will also give you a little more depth of field.

Since there are a lot of lenses to choose from in the 20-55mm range, I won't discuss each lens individually. Instead, I'll discuss the advantages and disadvantages of the various brands of lenses that are available.

Sigma 20mm, 24mm, 35mm, and 50mm f/1.4 ART

Sigma produces some of the very best lenses for night photography. All of their lenses in this focal range typically sell for a little under $1,000. There are less expensive options, but the quality is not quite as good. If quality is your primary concern and the price is within your budget, I recommend the Sigma f/1.4 ART lenses.

Rokinon 24mm, 35mm, and 50mm f/1.4

Rokinon lenses are often priced lower than similar lenses made by other companies. This is, in part, because the least expensive Rokinon lenses do not support autofocus.

One issue with these lenses is quality control. Many lenses perform great, while some can be of poor quality. I recommend testing the lens during the day and night as soon as you get it, making sure to set the exposure and focus correctly. A little softness and coma in the corners are normal at night at f/2.8 or wider, but if you notice overall poor image quality, you should be able to return it for a replacement. You may want to look up test images taken with the same lens to make sure that

The Milky Way rises above Bryce Canyon in Utah. I used a 50mm lens to capture a large stitched image of the land during civil twilight and a second stitched image of the sky during astronomical twilight. I later blended the two stitched images in Photoshop. Canon 5D II, 50mm; exposures for land: f/18, 3.2 seconds, ISO 100; exposures for sky: f/1.6, 13 seconds, ISO 6400.

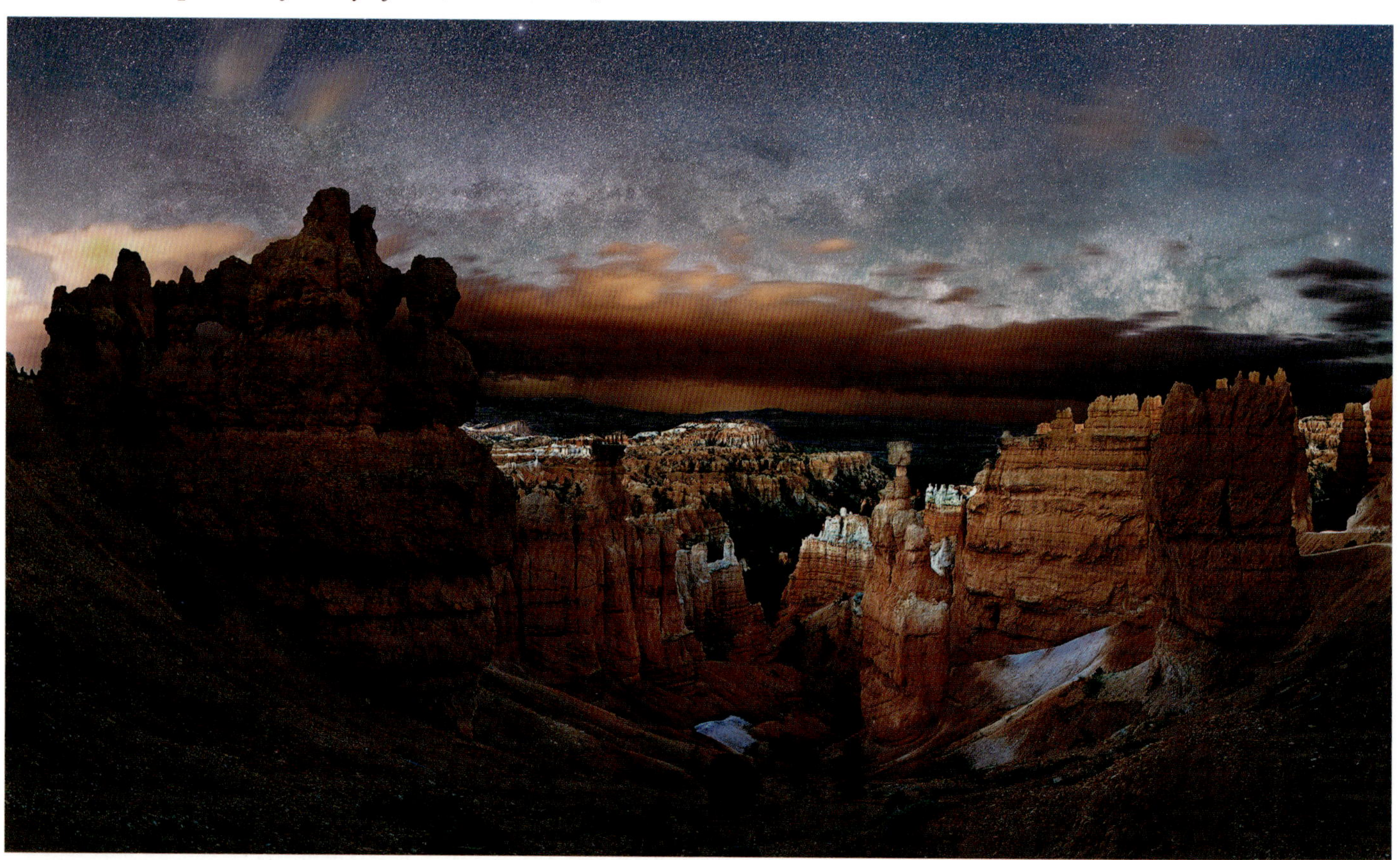

Fisheye or Telephoto Lenses	DxO Score	≈ Cost (as of 2020)	Camera
Rokinon 8mm f/3.5 Fisheye	not tested	$200	Nikon F / Canon EF / Sony E / Pentax K
Rokinon 12mm f/2.8 Fisheye	not tested	$450	Nikon F / Canon EF / Sony E / Pentax K
Sigma 150-600mm f/5.0-6.3 C	not tested	$900	Nikon F / Canon EF / Sony E

Table 1.4: Fisheye and telephoto lenses can be useful in special circumstances for night photography but should probably not be one of the first lenses you purchase.

the quality of your lens is noticeably worse.

You won't save quite as much by going with a Rokinon at these focal lengths as you will at 14mm. However, it could still be a good option for those not wanting to stretch their budget. As long as you get a good lens, you can get very high quality images, especially if you are creating large stitched images.

Tamron 35mm f/1.8 and 45mm f/1.8

The Tamron lenses strike a balance between the Rokinon and Sigma lenses. Overall, the quality is a bit lower than the Sigma for night photography, while the quality control is better than the Rokinon. They are also usually priced somewhere between these two lenses.

Nikkor 50mm f/1.8D

Nikon produces several good lenses for night photography between 20-50mm. However, they usually cost nearly as much or more than the Sigma ART lenses. I believe they slightly underperform the Sigma lenses, so I have not listed them in Table 1.3.

I have included the Nikkor 50mm f/1.8D since this a good, low-cost lens that retails for around $130. It can produce a lot of coma in the corners, but you can crop this out with stitched images. You do have to set the aperture on this lens manually.

Canon EF 50mm f/1.8 STM

Unfortunately, I've found that Canon lenses don't usually perform too well at night for the price you pay for them. However, the Canon EF 50mm f/1.8 II is a good, low-cost lens that sells for about $125. As with the Nikkor 50mm, it does show a lot of coma in the corners at f/1.8, but again you can crop this out if you are creating stitched images.

Sony FE Carl Zeiss 55mm f/1.8

This Sony lens, which was made with assistance from Zeiss, is superb. Among the lenses I've listed, it has the highest DxOMark score, slightly surpassing the Sigma 50mm. It also performs very well at night. This lens retails for about $1,000.

Sony also makes excellent 35mm and 50mm f/1.4 lenses, but the price is much higher than the Sony Art lenses, which are of nearly the same quality. Also, Zeiss makes some exceptional 55mm lenses for Canon and Nikon, but these currently retail for about $4,000. The quality is so high with 50mm stitched images taken with less expensive lenses that the extra cost probably won't be worthwhile for most night photographers.

Telephoto Lenses

If you want to capture dramatic images of the night sky that include foreground objects here on Earth, you may not have much use for a telephoto lens. However, telephoto lenses can be useful for capturing things like lava or forest fires, which you often can't get close to at night.

You can also use a telephoto lens with an equatorial mount to capture detailed images of a small part of the night sky. This can be useful when photographing lunar or solar eclipses. I'll discuss equatorial mounts in more detail on pages 132-134. You can capture even more distant objects by mounting a telescope onto a camera. This can allow you to capture some truly stunning images, but it takes a lot of expertise and is outside the scope of this book.

Telephoto lenses with wide apertures can be prohibitively expensive and probably aren't worth the cost to be used mainly for night photography. If you already own one for wildlife photography, it can be fun to oc-

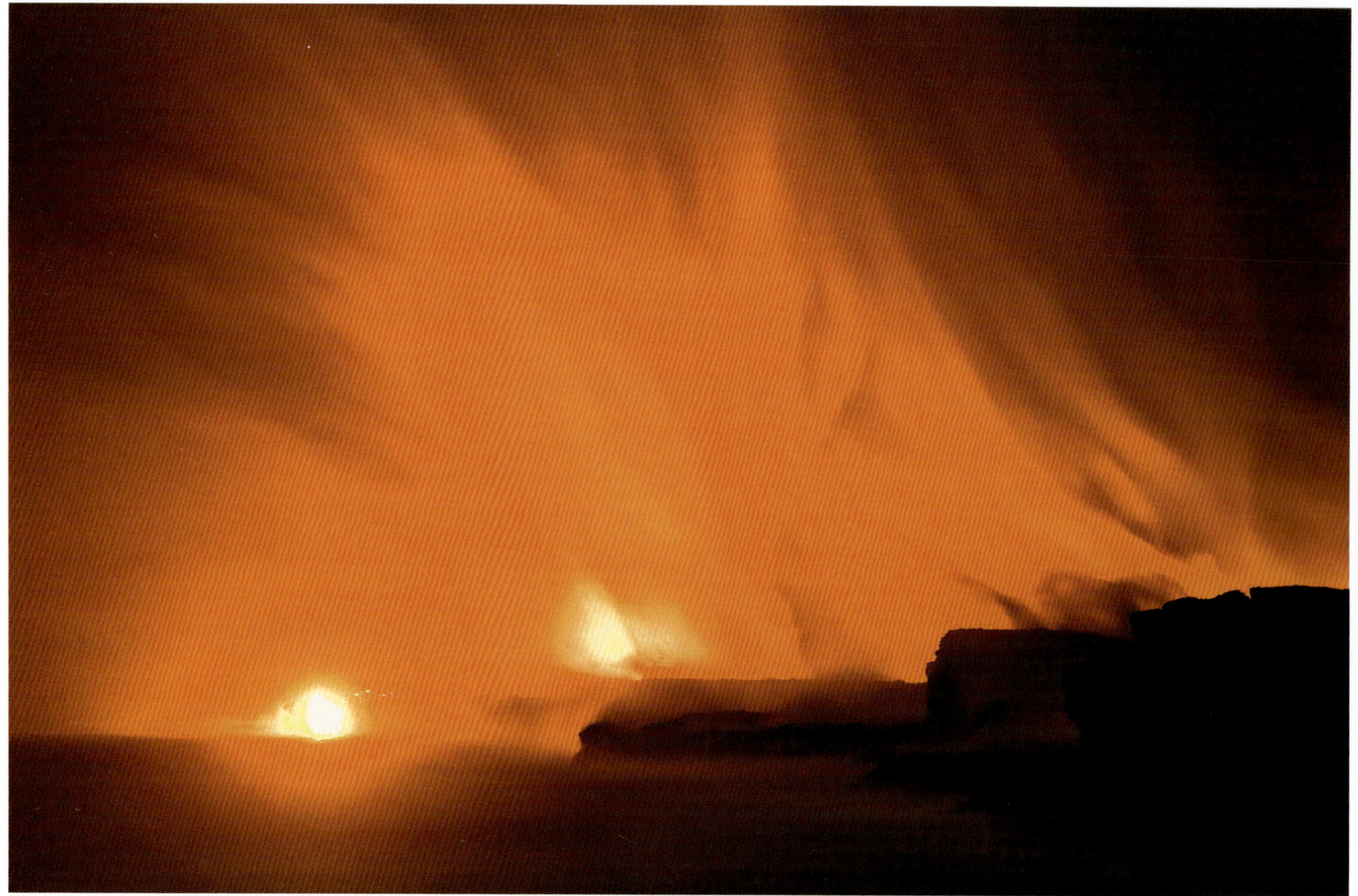

Since it was too dangerous to get close to the lava flowing into the Pacific Ocean from Hawaii's Big Island, I used a telephoto lens to capture this image. Canon 5D, 300mm, f/5.6, 30 seconds, ISO 400.

casionally use at night. Otherwise, there are less expensive options with smaller apertures that can still produce good quality images. One of the best options is the Sigma 150-600mm f/5-6.3 Contemporary.

Fisheye Lenses

Fisheye lenses can capture a more extensive view of the sky than a standard 14mm lens. However, they significantly distort the image and can turn a flat horizon into a curved horizon. I usually prefer a standard 14mm lens to capture broad swaths of the sky. These lenses can still distort an image but not nearly as much as a fisheye. If I want a wider field of view, I will create a stitched image rather than use a fisheye.

There are two types of fisheye lenses - a circular fisheye and a diagonal fisheye. A circular fisheye usually captures a full 180-degree field of view, though some can record an even wider field of view. This lens is called a circular fisheye because it renders the image as a circle with a black border around it. A circular fisheye I recommend is the Rokinon 8mm f/3.5 Fisheye.

One interesting use of a circular fisheye is that if you point the camera straight up, you can capture the entire night sky, and the horizon will be rendered as a circle around the edge of the image. This can produce some unique and compelling images.

A diagonal fisheye produces standard, full-frame rectangular images. It usually captures a 180-degree field of view diagonally from corner to corner but not across the entire photo. A diagonal fisheye I recommend is the Rokinon 12mm f/2.8 Fisheye.

TRIPODS

While you can sometimes get away with not using a tripod during the day, you need to use a tripod at night. You'll be shooting long exposures that cannot be handheld without blurring the image.

Tripod Legs

Carbon fiber tripod legs have become standard for most professional photographers since they are strong and lightweight. While they can be expensive, they are well worth the cost. Gitzo and Really Right Stuff produce some of the best and most durable tripod legs. For a lower-cost, mid-range option, I recommend the Feisol carbon fiber tripods. For a budget option, I recommend Bonfoto tripods.

If you are tall, I recommend searching for a tripod that is high enough to use without stooping over, even in uneven terrain. You should avoid relying on the center bar on the tripod to raise it higher, as this will make the camera significantly less stable. If possible, I recommend purchasing a tripod that doesn't have a center bar. This will allow you to also position the tripod very low without mounting your camera upside down.

Ball Heads

I recommend getting a ball head that has a rotating base with degree markings on it. This will make it easier to create stitched images at night. Acratech and Really Right Stuff both make excellent ball heads ranging in price from around $300-$500. I have used the Acratech Ultimate Ballhead for many years, and it still works very well. I've found that less expensive ball heads often don't last very long if you put them to heavy use.

A lower-cost option with degree markings is the Manfrotto XPRO Ball Head, which costs about $180. A low-budget option with degree markings is the Neewer Professional Ball Head, which sells for around $25.

L-Bracket

An L-bracket lets you mount your camera to your tripod from the bottom or the side. This allows you to quickly change from a horizontal composition to a vertical composition without changing the position of your tripod head. It can be significantly more stable than turning your ball head 90 degrees to get a vertical composition. This is very important when you are taking long exposures at night. You'll need to purchase an L-Bracket that is compatible with both your camera and your tripod head.

ACCESSORIES

In addition to the camera, lens, and tripod, there are many useful accessories for night photography.

Memory Cards

You can use up a lot of memory when shooting at night, especially if you are capturing large stitched images or taking repeated exposures throughout the night. Fortunately, the capacity of memory cards keeps rising while the prices keep falling. I recommend using 64 to 256 gigabyte cards so that you rarely need to change them during the night. If possible, you should back up all your images shortly after you shoot them. Alternatively, some cameras allow you to shoot with two memory cards at the same time, automatically creating a backup.

Batteries

Night photography involves taking a lot of long exposures, which can use up battery life much more quickly than when you are shooting during the day. Batteries also die faster in cold weather, which you'll often encounter when shooting at night. I recommend having a minimum of two fully charged batteries when shooting at night. If you plan to shoot all night long, you'll likely need more.

It can be useful to have a power outlet in your car to charge your batteries. If your vehicle doesn't have a built-in outlet, you can purchase a power inverter for your cigarette lighter. You can also plug some battery chargers into your USB port.

Battery Grip

A battery grip allows you to double your shooting time by adding a second battery to your camera. This can be useful if you'll be taking repeated exposures throughout the night like you do when photographing star trails or a meteor shower. The brand name battery grips from Canon and Nikon are expensive, so I recommend buying one from a third party, like Powerextra, Neewer, or Meike.

Remote Shutter Release

A remote shutter release (sometimes referred to as a remote switch or shutter release remote control) is useful for shooting at night. It allows you to take exposures longer than 30 seconds and to automatically take multiple photos in a row. Some remote releases have programmable timers that allow you to set the exact length of the exposure and the exact number of exposures. These releases are known as intervalometers or timer remotes, and they can be especially useful for night photography. I recommend owning at least one intervalometer. I also recommend having at least one backup release, whether it be a standard remote shutter release or an intervalometer. Most remote releases aren't overly durable, and I've occasionally had to turn to my backup when one stopped working.

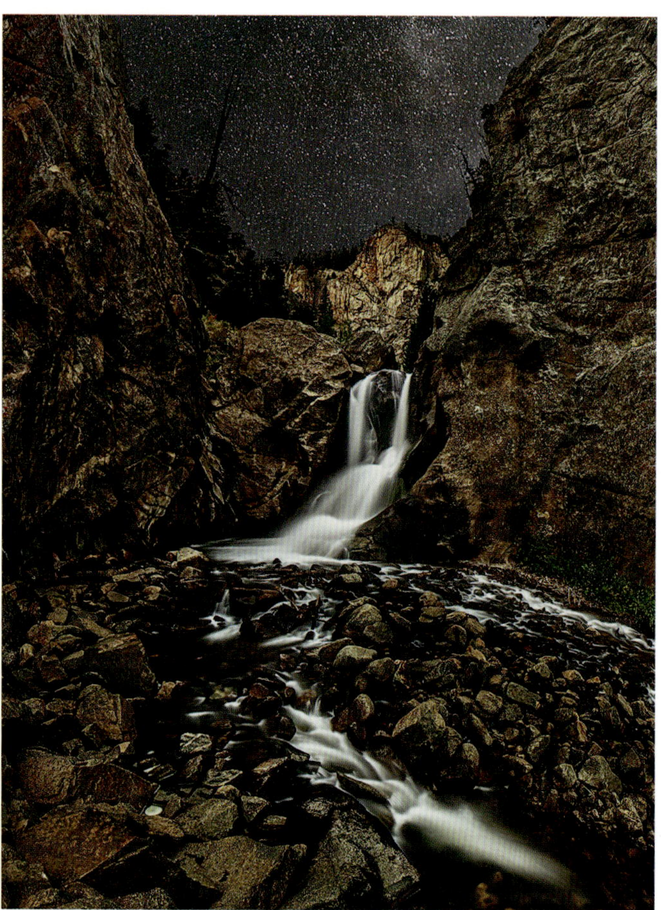

I used the interval timer on my Nikon to take repeated exposures of Boulder Falls. I later stacked the images to reduce noise. Nikon D850, 14mm, f/2.8, ISO 2000.

There are also wireless remote releases that allow you to trigger your camera's shutter release from a distance. This can be useful if you are light painting and want to shine your flashlight far away from your camera.

The brand name remote shutter releases from Nikon and Canon are rather expensive. I recommend buying the Vello or Neewer brand remote releases. The Neewer releases don't seem to be quite as durable, but they are less expensive. You can also find some inexpensive remote shutter releases on eBay.

If you don't have a remote release or if yours stops working while shooting, you can still capture exposures up to 30 seconds using the manual mode on your camera. This will be long enough for most shots you will take at night. To minimize camera shake when you hit the shutter release button, I recommend using the shortest self-timer setting on your camera, which is usually 2 seconds.

You don't always need a separate remote shutter release to take repeated exposures. Most newer Nikon cameras have built-in interval timers. These timers don't always act quite like you would expect, as I'll describe shortly. Some of the newer Canon EOS cameras also have built-in timers. For those that don't, you can add this feature using the free Magic Lantern software, which installs on your camera's memory card. This can be found at https://magiclantern.fm/. With some Sony cameras, you can add an interval timer using the Time-lapse camera app. Most of the interval timers in cameras still limit you to 30-second exposures, so you'll need an intervalometer if you want to do longer exposures.

When using an intervalometer, you first need to set your camera to Bulb mode. Most intervalometers have four programmable settings - Delay, Long, Interval, and Frames. I'll discuss each of these in turn. The built-in timers in cameras have similar settings.

Delay

If you set a time for the delay, the camera will wait that long before starting to take images. You'll usually want this set to zero and will only want a delay if you don't want to start shooting right away. This might be the case if you are light painting and want a delay so you can shine the flashlight a long distance away from the camera. It could also be useful if you are setting up two cameras at different locations. If it is still too light out to begin shooting when you are setting up the first camera, you can set a delay so that it starts shooting when it is dark and you are off setting up the second camera.

Long

This sets the length of each exposure. I'll discuss proper exposure lengths for different situations later in this book.

Interval

This tells the camera how long to wait between each

exposure. You'll usually want this set to one second, which is the shortest interval you can program on most intervalometers. It's particularly important to set the interval to one second if you are taking repeated exposures to try and capture star trails, meteors, or lightning.

You might want to program a longer interval if you are taking self-portraits at night. Since you'll have to stay as still as possible during the exposure, this will allow you to rest between each exposure. Another time you might want a longer interval is if you are doing light paintings. This will give you time between each exposure to move to a different position and try light painting from different angles.

If you are using a built-in interval timer on a Nikon camera, the interval time does not refer to the time that elapses between each exposure. Instead, it refers to the exposure length plus the time between each exposure. To achieve a one-second pause between each exposure, you'll need to set the interval to a time that is one second longer than the exposure length. But there's a catch. Your camera sometimes lies to you! Standard exposure lengths on a camera are 2, 4, 8, 16, and 32 seconds, but they are listed as 2, 4, 8, 15, and 30 seconds on your camera. When you set your camera to take 30-second exposures, it actually takes 32-second exposures. Likewise, when you set your camera to take 15-second exposures, it actually takes 16-second exposures. If you want a one-second pause between each exposure and your exposure length is set at 30 seconds, you will need to set the interval to 33 seconds. If your exposure length is set at 15 seconds, you'll need to set the interval to 17 seconds. For all other times, including 20 and 25 seconds, you can set the interval to one second longer than the exposure length shown on your camera.

To maximize my chances of capturing meteors above Brainard Lake in Colorado, I programmed my intervalometer to take repeated exposures throughout the night. I later combined all of the meteors I captured into a single image. Nikon D800e, 14mm, f/2.8, 30 seconds, ISO 1600.

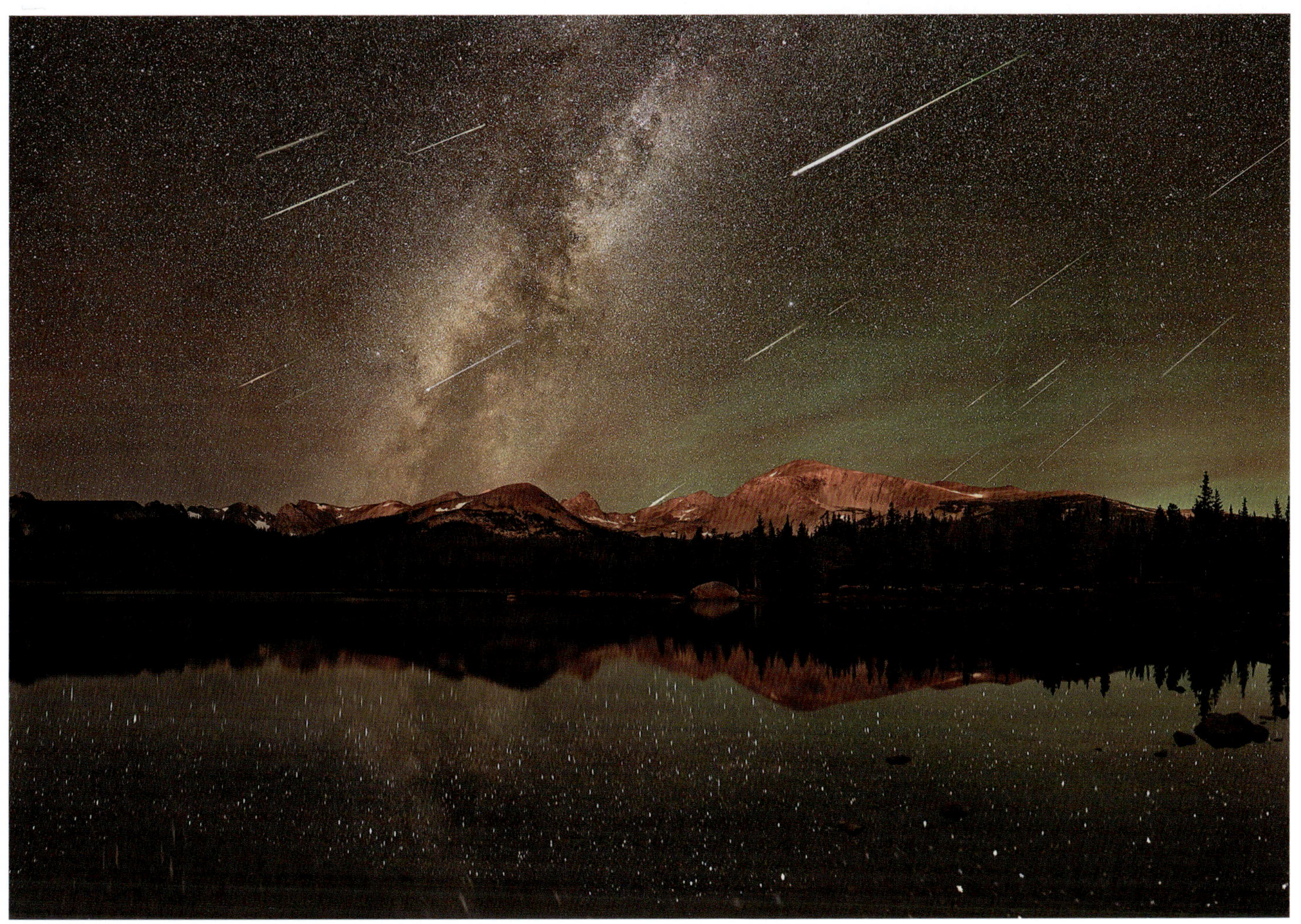

N or Frames

This tells the camera the total number of exposures you want to take. If you set this to --, your camera will keep shooting until you press stop on the intervalometer.

Filters

In general, I don't recommend using filters for night photography. They will decrease the amount of light that is let into the lens and therefore reduce image quality. However, the fog filter described below can potentially be useful.

The ultra-wide-angle lenses that I described earlier in this chapter do not accept filters. You would need to also buy a filter holder for these lenses.

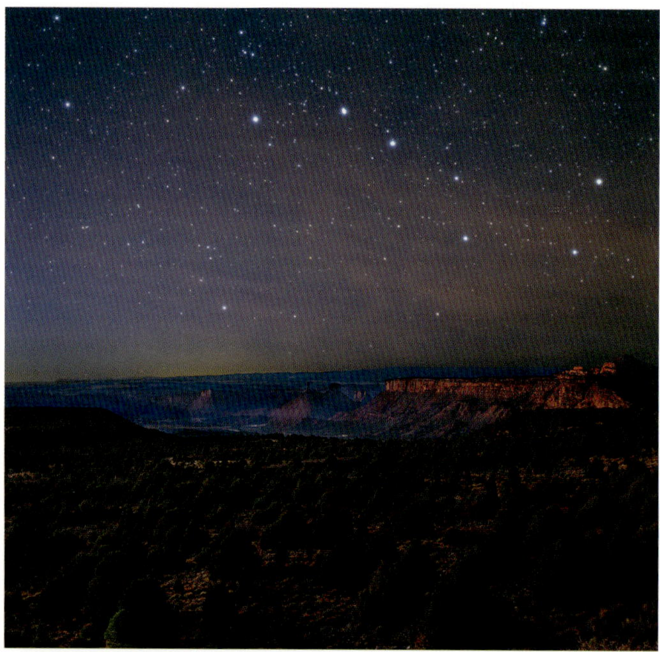

I used a fog filter to bring out the stars of the Big Dipper above Castle Valley, Utah. Nikon D800e, 35mm; exposure for land during civil twilight: f/11, 13 seconds, ISO 100; exposure for sky during astronomical twilight: f/2.2, 8 seconds, ISO 5000.

Fog Filter

A fog filter attempts to mimic the effects of fog by decreasing contrast and creating a glow around the highlights. It can be beneficial at night because it can create a strong glow around the brighter stars and make them appear larger. This can be especially useful if you want stars in a constellation to appear brighter so that the constellation is more easily identifiable.

Unless your foreground is a dark silhouette, a fog filter can cause the foreground to appear blurry in a night photo. Therefore, you will need to blend two exposures - one of the sky with the fog filter and the other of the foreground without the filter. Blending multiple exposures will be discussed in Chapter IX. This chapter is geared towards more advanced photographers, so I only recommend getting this filter if you are comfortable with blending exposures.

Some good fog filters are the Tiffen Double Fog 3 and the Hoya or Kenko Pro Softon Type-A.

Bubble Level

A bubble level is a simple but important tool for a night photographer. Since you often can't see what you're shooting, it is easy to forget to make sure the camera is level. Many tripod heads have built-in bubble levels, but most of these don't work for photos taken with a vertical orientation unless you're using an L-Bracket. You can instead use a two-axis bubble level that you mount on the hot shoe on top of your camera.

Many newer cameras have a built-in leveling feature, so a bubble level may not be necessary for all cameras. If you do use your camera's leveling feature, I recommend assigning a custom button to it, so you don't have to always scroll through the menu to find it.

Dew Heater or LensMuff

When shooting in cold temperatures at night, especially in humid locations, dew can start to build up on your lens. One way to prevent this is to store your camera equipment in an outdoor location, like the trunk of your car. Condensation can build up quickly on your lens when it is introduced to significantly different temperatures or humidity levels. You will, however, want to store your batteries in a warm location. Cold batteries do not last as long as warm ones, so this can help maximize battery life.

If you need to store your equipment inside when shooting in humid or frigid locations, make sure you have all of your gear in a tightly-zipped camera bag before entering. You could also put all of the equipment inside ziplock bags within your camera bag before coming inside.

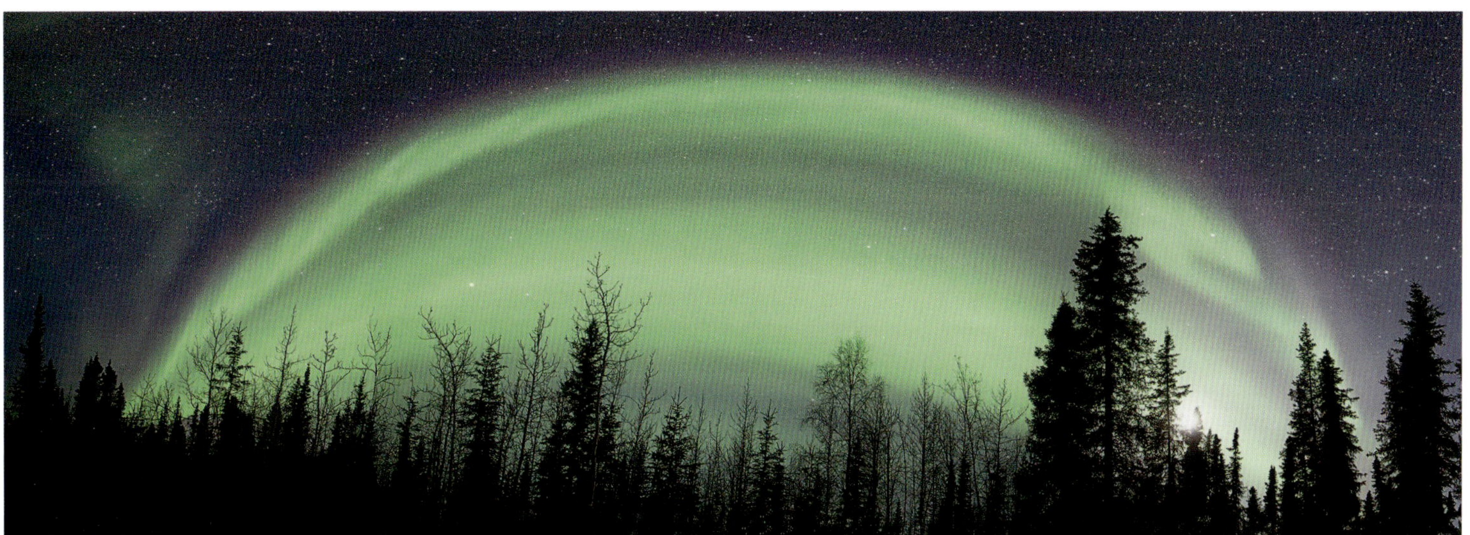

When I captured this image of the northern lights over Alaska, it was -15° F. In a situation like this, having the right clothing is of paramount importance. Canon 5D II, 20mm, f/2.8, 6 seconds, ISO 6400, five images stitched together.

Sometimes, your lens will still get dew or frost even if you take these precautions. You can predict whether this will happen by looking up the dew point. If the temperature is expected to fall to or below the dew point, you can expect moisture to build up on your lens. You can prevent this by keeping your lens warm. You can do this with a dew heater, though these can be expensive and require special batteries. A less expensive solution is to attach one or more hand warmers to the side of your lens using rubber bands. Or, you can get a LensMuff created by Kevin Adams, which holds the hand warmers in place. You can find this at https://www.kadamsphoto.com/shop/. Kevin has some other useful gadgets for night photography on this site.

Lens Cleaning Cloth

A lens cleaning cloth is useful for cleaning dust off of your lens. It can also be used to defog a lens. The lens will probably fog up again quickly, so this should only be done as a last resort. However, it is better than nothing and should give you time to get a few shots before you have to wipe it clean again.

CLOTHING & SURVIVAL GEAR

Photographing in the wilderness at night can be dangerous, but not because of wild animals or things that go bump in the night. Unless you're deep in grizzly country, the danger from wild animals is usually going to be minimal. The real danger is getting lost at night, getting hurt in a fall, or going out unprepared for the weather. Before you leave, you should tell someone where you are going and when you plan to return.

I've provided recommendations on clothing and survival gear that you should consider taking with you. This is just a basic list and is not intended as a thorough guide for all situations. If you haven't spent much time at night in the wilderness, I recommend taking your photos close to your car. There are countless photographic opportunities that don't require hiking.

Clothing

Even if it is warm out during the day, it can get cold at night. Be sure to always check the weather forecast beforehand and dress appropriately.

You should dress in layers so that you can remove some clothing if you're hiking and start to get hot. You don't want to start sweating, as the sweat can later freeze, making you much colder.

I recommend a base layer consisting of socks, bottom pants, a long-sleeve top, and a balaclava. The fabric I prefer for the base layer is merino wool. Not only is it very warm and comfortable, but it also remains remarkably stink-proof, even if you wear it for many days in a row. You should avoid using cotton as a base layer, as this fabric retains moisture and dries slowly, which can make you very cold.

If it is going to be below 45° F, I recommend having

at least two layers of clothing over most of your body. If it is going to be below 10° F, I recommend having at least three layers of clothing covering most of your body. Hand warmers and foot warmers are also essential, as these are parts of your body that are hardest to keep warm.

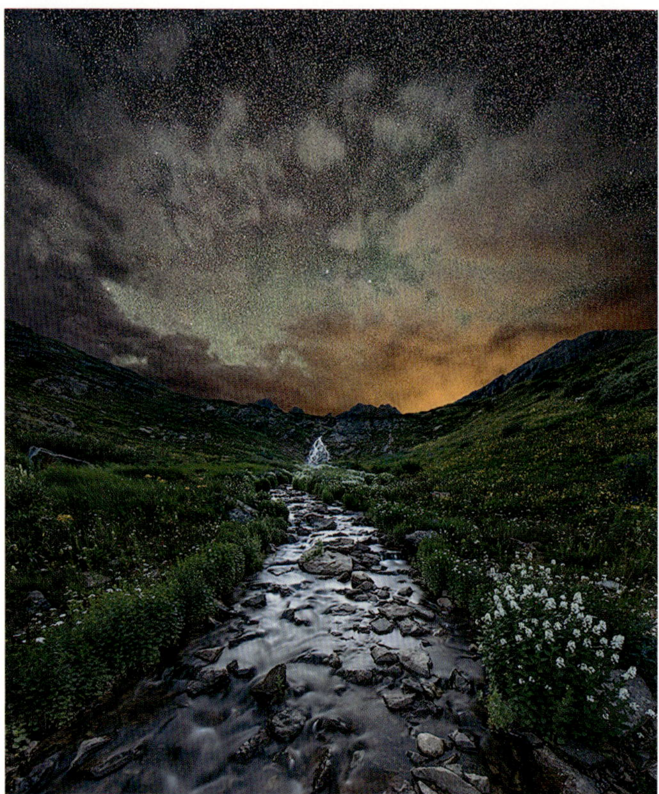

Picturesque clouds float above a waterfall and stream in the San Juan Mountains. Even on a summer night, it can get quite cold in the mountains of Colorado, especially if you're foolish enough to stand in the stream. Nikon D800e, 14mm, exposure for land during twilight: f/10, 13 seconds, ISO100; exposure for sky at night: f/2.8, 30 seconds, ISO 6400.

Some gloves I recommend for photography are Heat Factory Gloves with Pop-Top Mittens. The top of these mittens can be folded back so that you just have a glove over the fingers. The glove is thin enough to allow you to operate your camera. When you're not shooting, you can put the mitten top on to keep your fingers warm. You can also insert a hand warmer into the mitten top. If it's really cold, you can wear a glove liner under this or a large mitten over it.

Verseo makes battery-heated ThermoGloves that are thin enough to operate a camera with. One drawback is that the charge only lasts a couple of hours on full power. I've also found that the wires inside the fingers can easily become misaligned with the glove and pinch your fingers. However, these gloves can be an option if you are shooting in below-zero temperatures where other gloves may not provide adequate warmth. Even with these gloves, I do still recommend hand warmers if it is very cold.

Another option for frigid temperatures is to wear thick gloves and use the eraser on a pencil to operate your camera controls.

Some boots I recommend are the NEOS overshoes. They are worn over your regular shoes, which allows you to add an extra layer of warmth. It can be a little cumbersome hiking long distances in these. However, I typically don't venture far from my car in these circumstances due to the dangers of hiking in frigid temperatures at night. I own the STABILicers, which give excellent traction when walking on icy surfaces. They also have extendable gaiters, which are suitable for walking through, or standing in, deep snow.

Food & Water

Always bring plenty of food and water with you, especially if you plan to hike at night. Even if this isn't needed for survival, it can keep you motivated to stay out a little longer to get the shot you want.

Flashlights

If you're photographing and hiking alone at night, you should always bring at least two flashlights in case one stops working. For your primary light, a headlamp is very convenient, as it frees your hands up while hiking. As a backup for short hikes, most smartphones let you use your camera flash as a flashlight. For longer hikes, I recommend a real flashlight as a backup.

Flashlights are also useful if you want to do light painting to illuminate the object you are photographing. I will discuss what flashlights I recommend for this in Chapter VI.

Bright flashlights can significantly disrupt your night vision. It takes about 10 minutes for your cones to adapt to the dark and over 30 minutes for your rods to adapt. Anytime you shine a bright flashlight, you will lose most of your night vision, and your eyes will take the same amount of time to readapt. Some flashlights have red lights that are supposed to help preserve night vision since the rods in your eyes are less sensitive to red light. However, for somewhat complex reasons, this is largely a myth. Deep red lights can be beneficial at very low levels, but red lights can be more harmful than helpful at brighter levels.

The most significant factor for preserving night vision is not the color of the light but how bright it is and how long you use it. If you want a flashlight for night vision, the Proton Pro has both red and white lights and is dimmable to very low levels (approximately 0.3 lumens).

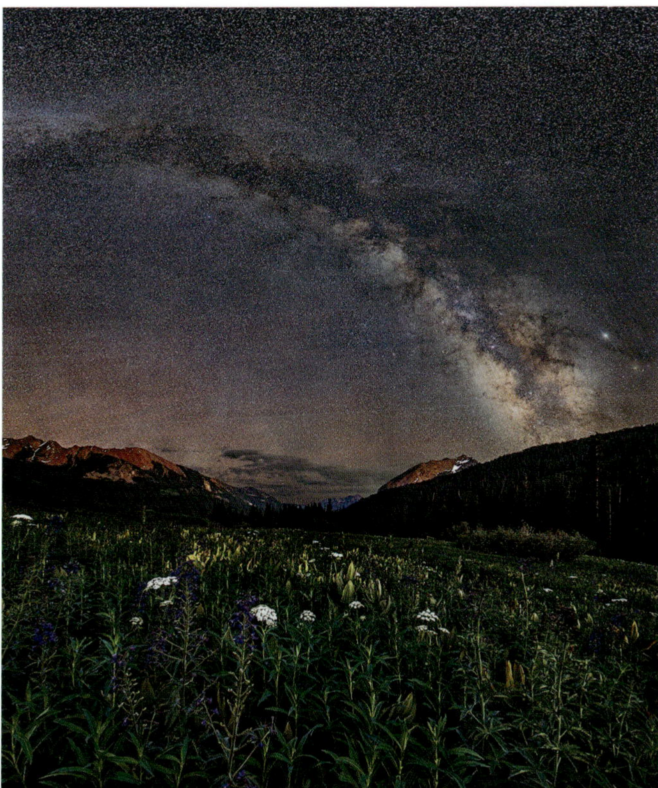

The Milky Way rises above mountains near Crested Butte, Colorado. When taking this shot, I could see the basic form and shape of the Milky Way before my eyes had adapted to the dark. The sky became a little clearer as my eyes adapted, but I still could not see the red colors from light pollution or the vast number of stars that the camera can pick up. Sony a7 III, exposure for land during twilight: 14mm, f/22, 30 seconds, ISO 100; 57 exposures for stitched image of sky: 50mm, f/1.6, 8 seconds, ISO 1600.

Personally, I find the Coast focusing headlamps, which I describe in more detail in Chapter VI, suitable for preserving some night vision. You'll need to make sure you get one that is dimmable down to just a few lumens, like the Coast HL7 Focusing LED Headlamp. One reason I recommend a focusing headlamp is that it can also be used for light painting.

I've gone into some detail about preserving night vision, as I know it is important to some photographers. Personally, though, I don't find preserving night vision to be all that important for photography. The camera can pick up far more detail and color than our eyes, regardless of how long they have had to adapt. You will need to learn how the camera will "see" at night and how images will look when photographing different parts of the sky. You simply can't get an adequate feel for this by viewing the scene with your eyes.

Survival Kit

You can create your own survival kit or buy one that comes prepackaged with many different items. Some things you should include in a survival kit are a fire starter, first aid supplies, a survival blanket, and a multipurpose tool or knife.

Map, Compass, & GPS Unit

Navigational tools are essential if you plan to hike at night. It's much easier to get disoriented at night than it is during the day. I recommend hiking to a location while it is still light out, so you can become familiar with the route for the hike out in the dark.

Personal Locator Beacon

A personal locator beacon can transmit your location to a satellite to alert rescue crews. One option is the SPOT Satellite GPS Messenger. With this device, friends and family can track your location in real-time, and you can send a pre-programmed message to let them know you are okay. The newer SPOT 2-Way Messenger allows you to send messages back and forth. Garmin also makes Satellite Communicators that include two-way messaging, topo maps, and navigation. These are more expensive than the SPOT but are also usually rated better. All of these beacons require a monthly service plan.

If you don't want to pay a monthly service plan, you can purchase the Fast Find Personal Locator Beacon. This unit costs a bit more than the SPOT, but you'll save quite a bit in the long run with no monthly fees. It can only be used in an emergency and can't be used to let friends and family know you are okay.

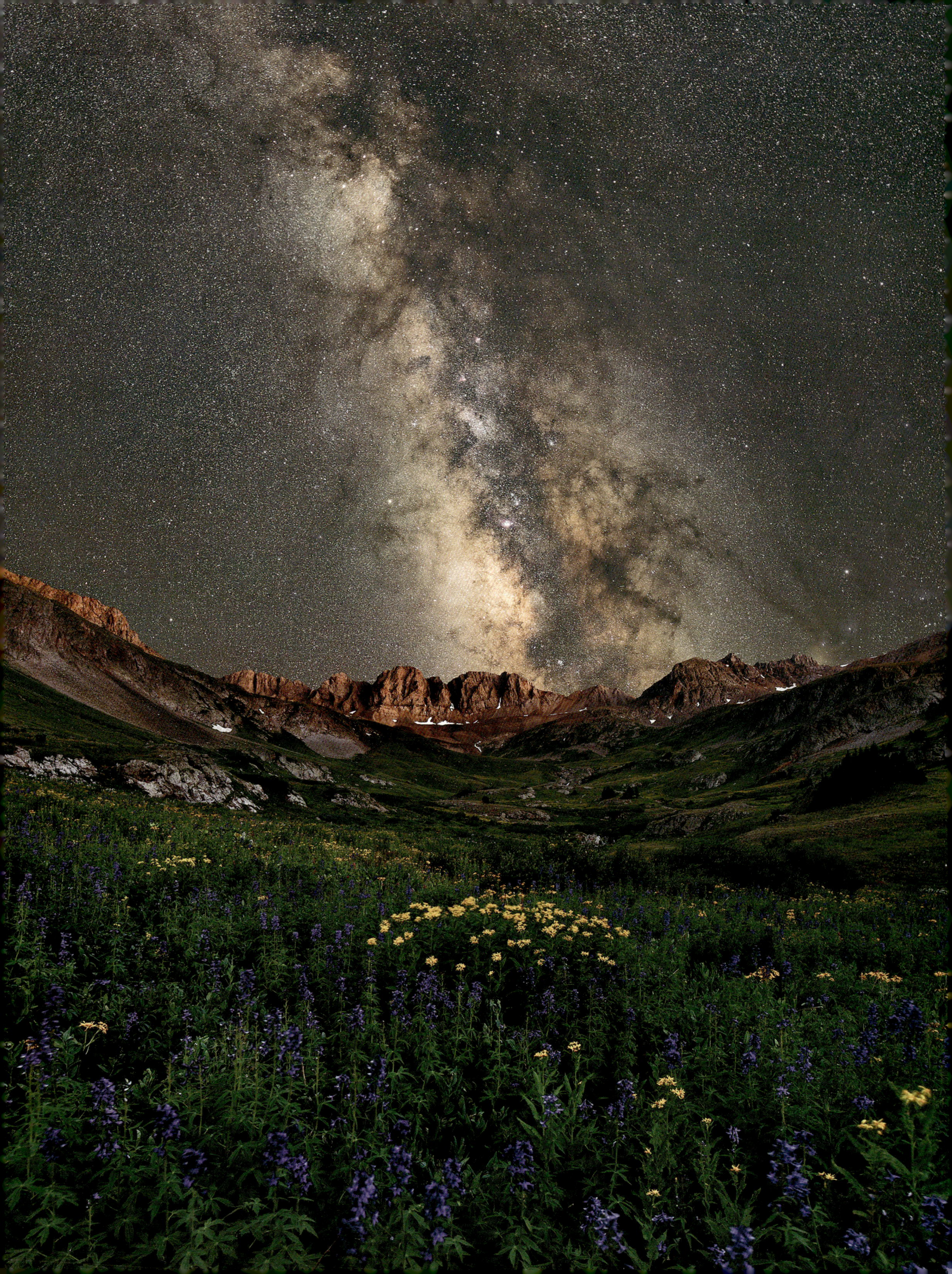

II. Planning Your Shots

If you take the time to plan when it will be best to photograph at a particular location at night, you will almost always get results that are superior to an unplanned shoot.

There are many things you need to consider before ever leaving your house. Do you want the Milky Way in the photograph? Do you want the foreground illuminated by the moon, or do you prefer to shoot the scene under no moon? Do you want any clouds in the sky? Do you want specific planets or constellations in the photograph? Do you want to try to capture meteors in your image?

By planning your photos, you gain much more control over the appearance of the final image. I'll discuss many of the things you can do to plan and previsualize your photographs in this chapter.

COMPUTER SOFTWARE PROGRAMS

There are many computer software programs that can help you plan a photo shoot at night. I'll describe two of my favorites below. A great thing about these programs is that they are free.

Stellarium

Stellarium is an exceptional software program that shows exactly how the night sky will appear from any location around the world at any date and time you choose. This program can be downloaded online at https://www.stellarium.org/. It can also be purchased as an iPhone or Android app at a low price.

When you open Stellarium, the first thing you should do is select a location close to where you will be photographing. You can do this by pressing F6. A dialog box will appear that will give you hundreds of locations around the world to choose from. Choose a medium to large city that is closest to the spot you will be photographing. Alternatively, you can enter the exact GPS coordinates where you plan to shoot and add that location to the list.

You will next want to change the time and date to see how the sky will look at different times. You can do this using the icons on the bottom left of the screen. Towards the right, you will see icons that look like the Play, Fast Forward, and Reverse buttons on a DVD player. Click on these icons to "fast forward" in time, "reverse" back in time, or hit the Play button to move forward in real-time. Alternatively, you can press F5 and enter an exact time and date.

Stellarium shows the location of the moon and the planets, which is very helpful as these objects constantly change position in the sky relative to the stars.

Stellarium is also useful for previsualizing the Milky Way. The Milky Way is one of the most spectacular objects to photograph in the heavens, and its location changes continuously throughout the night and throughout the year. By checking Stellarium to see where the Milky Way will be in the sky, you can plan for it to be over a specific object, like a rock formation or a mountain.

You can increase the brightness of the Milky Way to help previsualize it better. Press F4 to open the Sky panel. Make sure the Milky Way Brightness / Saturation box is checked and increase the number values in the leftmost box to increase the brightness. You could also check the box next to Light Pollution that says Take from Locations Database to simulate light pollution where you plan to shoot. I also recommend clicking SSO at the top left of this panel, enabling the Scale Moon option, and setting this value to 4. This will make it easier to spot the moon, and it will show the moon phase. You could also click on Landscape at the top and select Zero Horizon to prevent any foreground objects from blocking your view of the sky. There are a lot of other options in this panel that you can experiment with.

Left: The Milky Way rises over American Basin in Colorado. I used Stellarium to determine that the Milky Way would be over this scene shortly after sunset during peak wildflower season. Nikon D800e; exposure for land during twilight: 16mm, f/14, 30 seconds, ISO 100; 40 stitched images of sky: 50mm, f/1.8, 13 seconds, ISO 6400.

Google Earth

Most photographers are probably familiar with Google Earth at https://www.google.com/earth/. I prefer the original Earth Pro on Desktop version, but they also have a newer version that can be opened in a Chrome browser. It is also available for free as an iPhone or Android app.

Google Earth is an incredibly detailed mapping software that can help you discover places to photograph. You can drag the yellow Pegman to any spot in the desktop version to get an idea of what the terrain looks like from the ground. You can also view photos that other people have uploaded to get a better idea of what certain places look like.

If you go to View > Sun in the desktop version, it will show you how the sunlight will alter the light and shadows on the land throughout the day. It will also show how the stars will appear at night. The position of the stars isn't always accurate, so I still recommend Stellarium for precise planning. However, this is a way to get a rough preview of how the foreground and sky will look for any photo you want to take.

WEBSITES

There are many different websites you can use to plan your photos. I'll describe some that I frequently use.

The Photographer's Ephemeris

The Photographer's Ephemeris (TPE) is a valuable tool for planning night photos. You can use it for free online by going to https://www.photoephemeris.com/ and clicking on TPE Web App. There are also iPhone and Android apps available that have a lot of extra features, including Night Mode and Augmented Reality.

TPE shows the moon phase for any given day and shows the times of moonrise, moonset, sunrise, sunset, and twilight. It shows the exact direction in the sky from which the moon and sun will rise and set. TPE also has a built-in map, so you can figure out what direction you will be shooting at any location. This can be useful if you want to know where the moon will be relative to the direction you will be photographing.

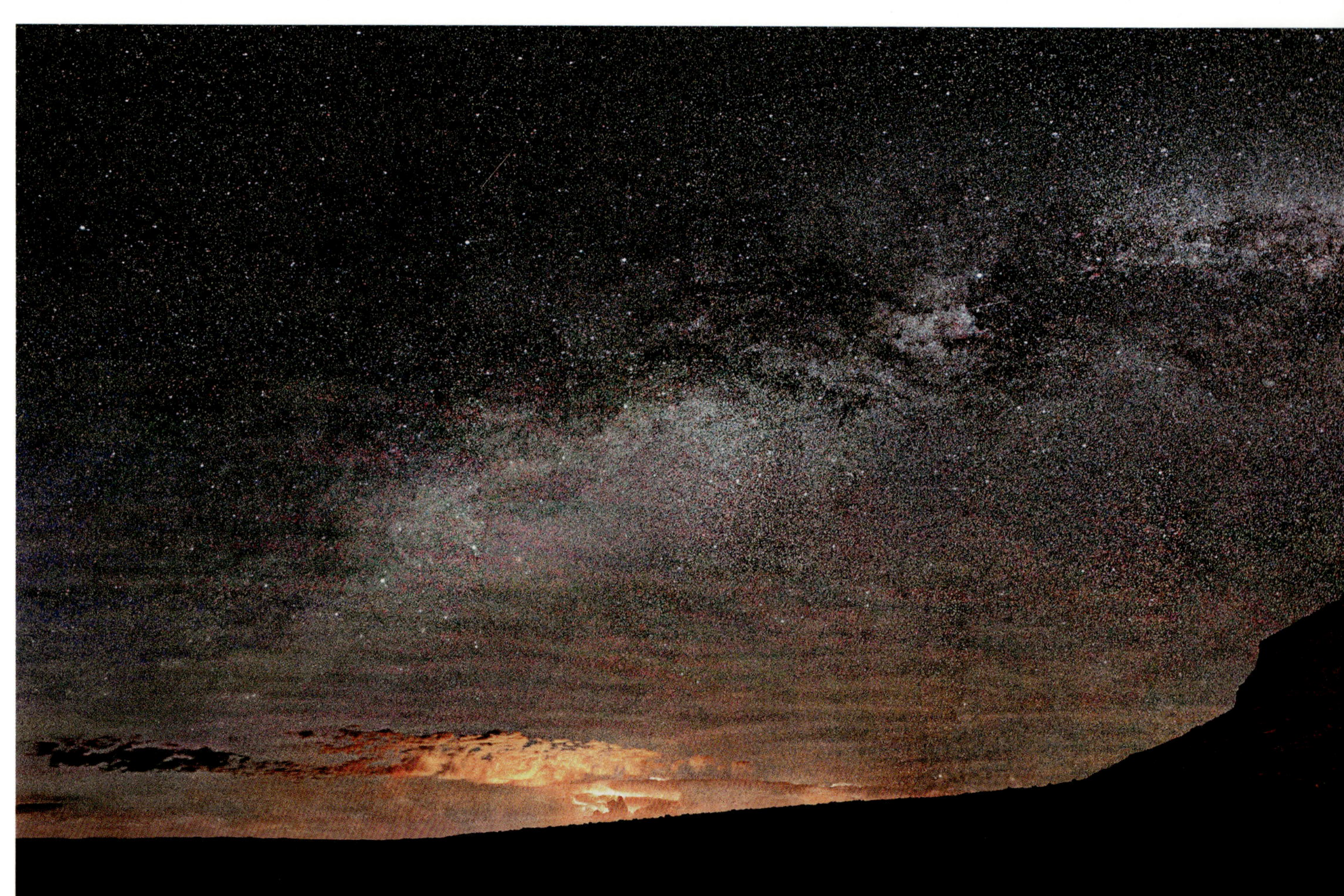

Weather Sites

You will need to shoot under clear skies or partly-cloudy skies to capture any stars in your image. I therefore recommend checking the weather forecast before heading out on a photo shoot.

Since there are a lot of weather sites to choose from, it can be hard to know which one to use. Fortunately, there is now a website called Forecast Advisor at https://www.forecastadvisor.com/ that can help you decide. If you enter a U.S. zip code, it will provide a basic forecast for that location. Towards the bottom of the page, it shows which weather sites have provided the most accurate forecasts for that location over the past month and the past year. I recommend using the website that had the best forecast over the past year, since there won't be enough data over one month for it to be as statistically significant.

Overall, The Weather Channel, Weather Underground, and AccuWeather are usually the most accurate sites studied by Forecast Advisor.

If you're able to leave on short notice or have flexibility in where you're traveling, the extended forecasts on weather sites can be useful. These forecasts aren't overly reliable if it will be partly cloudy or mostly cloudy during that time, as clouds are notoriously unpredictable. But if there's a forecast for nothing but clear skies for ten days, you can be pretty confident that it will be a good time for night photography.

Most sites also have short-term hourly forecasts that predict how much cloud cover there will be throughout the night. If the weather forecast calls for it to

I previsualized this image of East Pawnee Butte in Pawnee National Grasslands using Stellarium. This photo was taken on June 25, 2011, at approximately 10:30 p.m. If you go to this time and date on Stellarium, select Greeley, United States as your location, and look to the east, you will see that the Milky Way appears very similar to how it looks here. Canon 5D II, 50mm, f/1.6, 10 seconds, ISO 6400, 86 images stitched together.

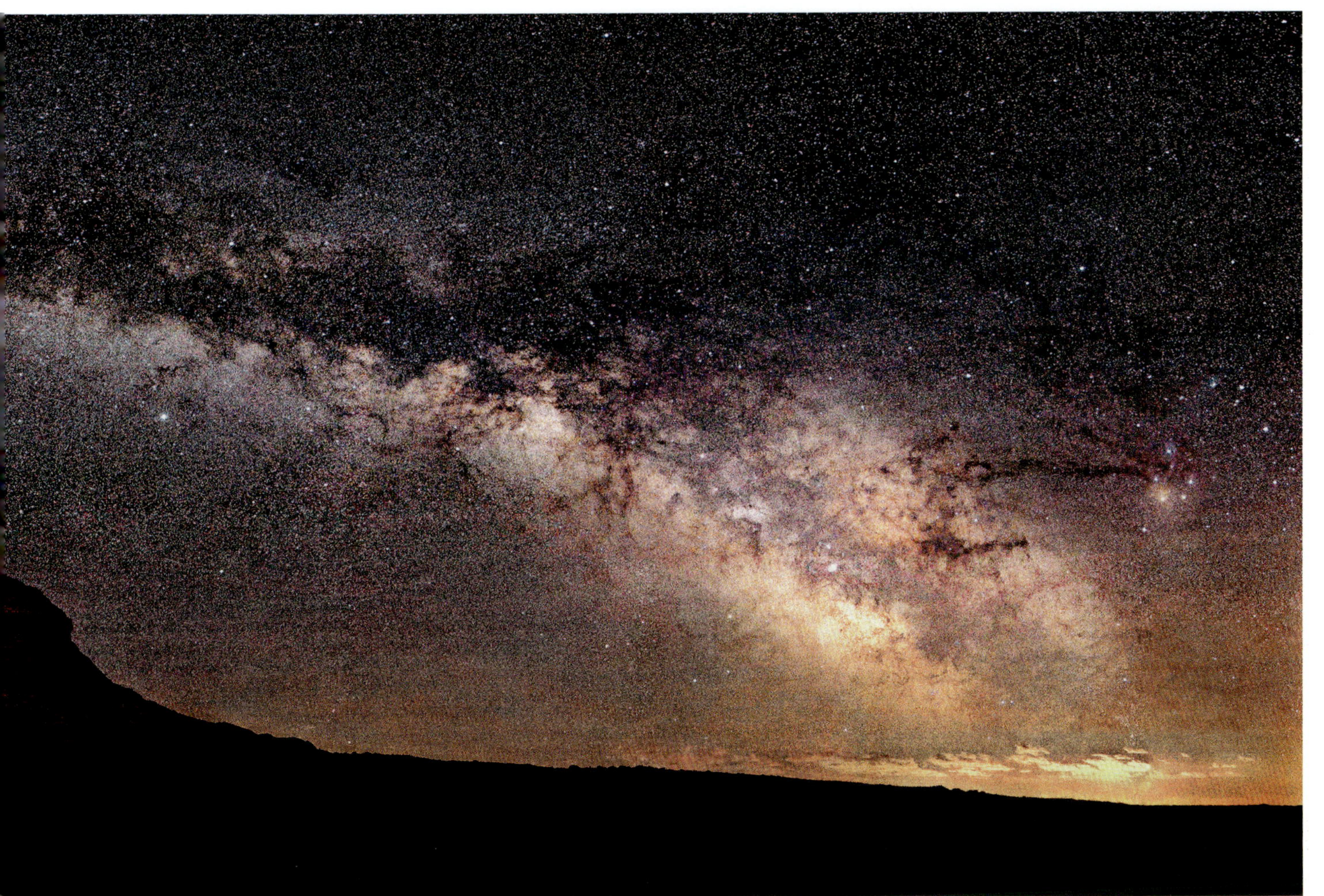

be mostly cloudy throughout the night, you probably won't have much luck. I usually stay home on nights like these. If the forecast calls for it to be partly cloudy, you might have more success, as you can get some dramatic images if you're able to get both the stars and clouds in an image.

I'll go over some of the more useful features for night photography on various weather sites below.

Weather Underground

Weatherground.com is my favorite weather site, as it has a wealth of information available. This can also make it a bit more difficult to use. However, it is easy to view cloud cover predictions. Just search for a specific town and click on Hourly near the top of the page. Near the center of the table, it will show an hourly forecast of the percentage of cloud cover that is expected.

This website also has an astronomy section on the Today tab of each town's forecast page. This section tells the twilight times, as well as the moon phase and the times of moonrise and moonset.

Weather Underground has free Android and iPhone apps, but the information they provide is more limited.

AccuWeather

On AccuWeather.com, you can also see cloud cover predictions by searching for a town and clicking on Hourly. When you click on any of the hours, it will display a drop-down list that includes the expected cloud cover at that location.

It was overcast at night during most of my trip to Maui, so I had to shoot primarily during the day. I also spent time scouting locations to shoot at night and kept a close eye on the forecast. On the one night it appeared the clouds would break, I headed to this spot and was fortunate to get some compelling clouds in the image, along with plenty of stars during astronomical twilight. Nikon D850, 14mm, f/2.8, 30 seconds, ISO 6400.

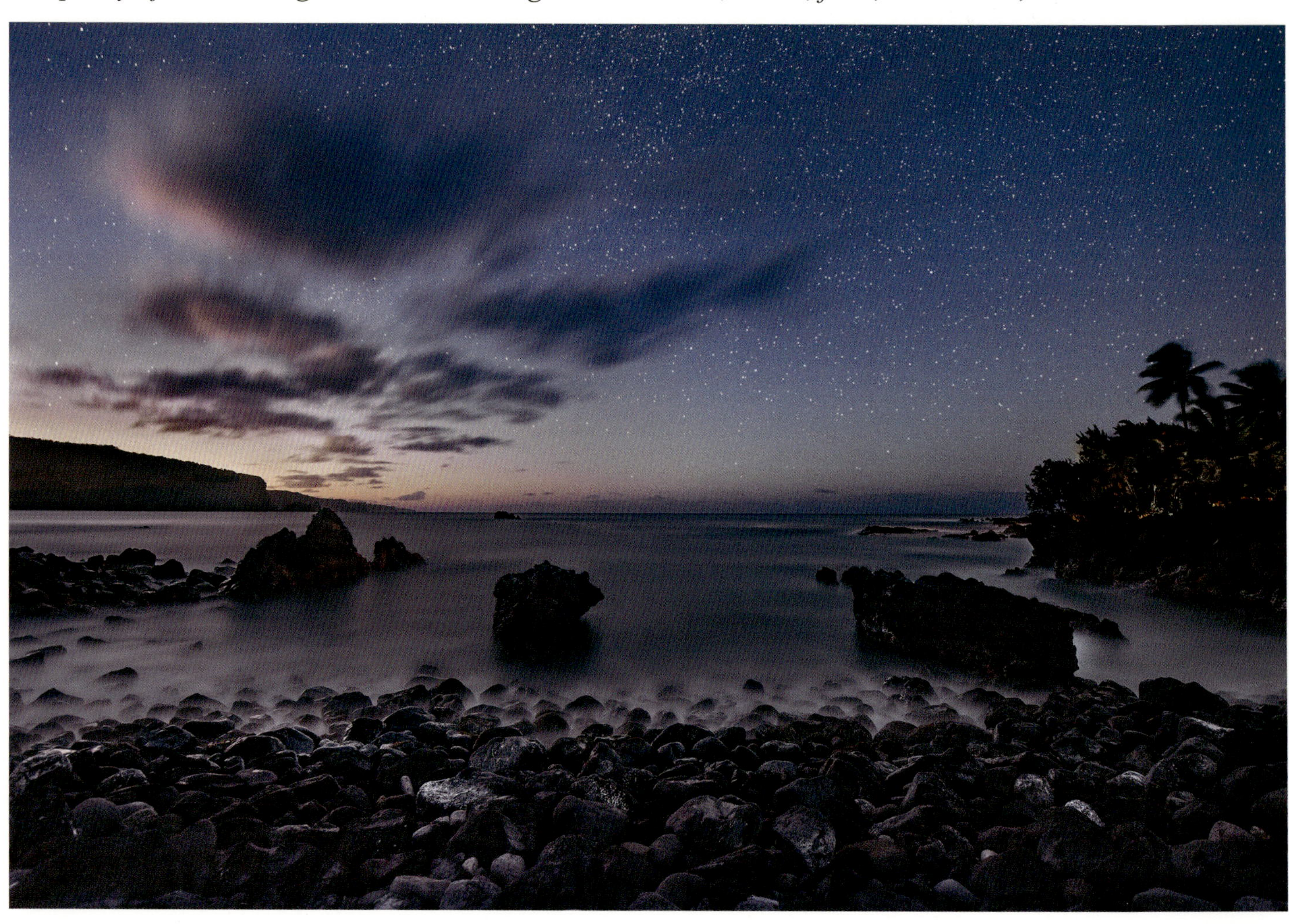

AccuWeather also has free Android and iPhone apps.

National Weather Service

To get a visual representation of expected future cloud cover, you can go to the National Weather Service website at Weather.gov. If you click on Forecast Maps and then on Sky Cover, it will show a map of the current cloud cover over the United States. If you scroll down to where it says Sky Cover on the right, you can click on a later time to see how the cloud cover is forecast to change over time.

These maps are useful if it is expected to be overcast in your area, but you are intent on getting to a location to shoot a celestial event, like a meteor shower or an eclipse. If you find a place you can drive to that is likely to have clear skies, you can give yourself a chance of getting the shot you want.

ClearDarkSky.com

ClearDarkSky.com is used by astronomers to determine when it will be best to observe stars at night. It has forecasts for many locations throughout North America. I've sometimes found it to be more accurate than most weather sites at forecasting exactly when the skies will clear up. Other times, the forecasts have been way off, probably because it's not updated as frequently as other sites. So I recommend using it in conjunction with another weather site. ClearDarkSky only forecasts two days out, so it is not useful for longer planning.

To use ClearDarkSky.com, click on Clear Sky Charts and then select a U.S. state or a territory in North America. Look for an observatory in a town close to where you will be photographing. In the charts they provide for each town, the most important thing for photographers to look at is Cloud Cover. If the squares under any of the hours are white, it means you can expect overcast skies during that hour. If they are dark blue, you can expect clear skies, and if they are light blue, you can expect partly cloudy skies. If you click on any of these squares, it will show you a map of the expected cloud cover at that time.

There is additional information available on these charts, such as Transparency and Seeing. These charts are useful for discovering just how clear the skies will be at night. However, they are more useful for astronomers trying to observe far distant objects that require ideal viewing conditions. For photographers, the most important thing is to avoid too much cloud cover.

The information found on ClearDarkSky.com is also available in an app for iPhones called myCSC.

Light Pollution Atlas

If you are photographing at night near a city or town, light pollution can be a significant issue. It can drown out light from the stars, making them more difficult to see and photograph. It can also give a murky color cast to objects you are photographing, and it can create an unnatural glow in the sky. Although I discuss techniques for minimizing the effects of light pollution in post-processing in Chapter X, your best bet is always to get far away from cities and towns. You can see a map of light pollution levels throughout the world at https://www.lightpollutionmap.info/.

Ideally, you'll want to shoot in areas that aren't colored on the map. Unfortunately, the eastern United States and western Europe have few such locations. If you are shooting in these areas, you should at least try to get to a spot that is shaded purple or green.

There's also a free iPhone and Android app called Light Pollution Map that provides similar information.

Astronomy Calendar

Seasky.org has an astronomy calendar that lists most of the major celestial events that will occur during the year. It includes dates of major meteor showers, eclipses, planetary conjunctions, and more. The calendar can be seen at http://www.seasky.org/astronomy/astronomy-calendar-current.html.

Starry Nights Wall Calendar

I produce a wall calendar that features my night photos and provides dates of many celestial events that you may want to photograph. This calendar can be found at https://www.collierpublishing.com.

MOBILE APPS

In addition to the ones I've already mentioned, numerous other mobile apps can help you plan your night photos. I won't overwhelm you with information on too many of them, as the first app I describe, called

PhotoPills, can do most things you need to plan your night photography. I've also included information on a few additional apps that can do things PhotoPills cannot.

PhotoPills

This is an amazingly comprehensive app. It has a Planner screen similar to The Photographer's Ephemeris that shows you where and when the sun and moon will set and rise each day. You can enter where you want the moon to be, and it will calculate the exact dates and times when it will be in that position. It also has a 3D Augmented Reality Viewer. This allows you to point your iPhone or iPad at a subject, and it will show precisely where different celestial objects will appear in the scene at different times of the night, including the moon and the Milky Way.

PhotoPills lets you keep track of all the places you want to photograph by saving them as Points of Interest. Plus, it has a depth of field calculator that tells the hyperfocal distance and the nearest and farthest distances that will be in focus with different camera settings. There is also a Spot Stars feature that calculates exposure times using the rule of 500 and the NPF rule that I describe in chapter IV.

This app is even useful for shooting star trails. The Star Trail Stimulator lets you see how star trails will appear when facing different directions and with different exposure times. It can also calculate the proper camera settings for very long single exposures for star trails.

There are many other useful features on PhotoPills that you can learn about by watching the tutorials on their website at https://www.photopills.com/.

Sky Safari

Like PhotoPills, you can point your phone or tablet up, and Sky Safari will give a present or future view of objects in the sky. This program doesn't have any of the planning features designed specifically for photographers, so it probably won't help improve your photos if you already have PhotoPills. However, it does give a more detailed view of objects in the night sky than PhotoPills and lets you learn more about what you are photographing.

Flashlight

There are several apps that make the flashlight found on most smartphones easier to use. The Flashlight app for iPhones made by iHandy Inc. and the Flashlight app for Android made by Lighthouse, Inc. both have a compass on the main screen. This can be useful for photos of star trails and for knowing where the Milky Way will be when it gets dark.

I planned my trip to Aitutaki around a new moon so that I could capture the Milky Way and the small galaxies known as the Magellanic Clouds. I used Stellarium to determine where the Milky Way would be during the night and reserved a bungalow that would give me the best view of the night sky. When I arrived, I used PhotoPills to confirm my planning was correct. 6 vertical images stitched: Nikon D800e,14mm, f/2.8, 15 seconds, ISO 6400.

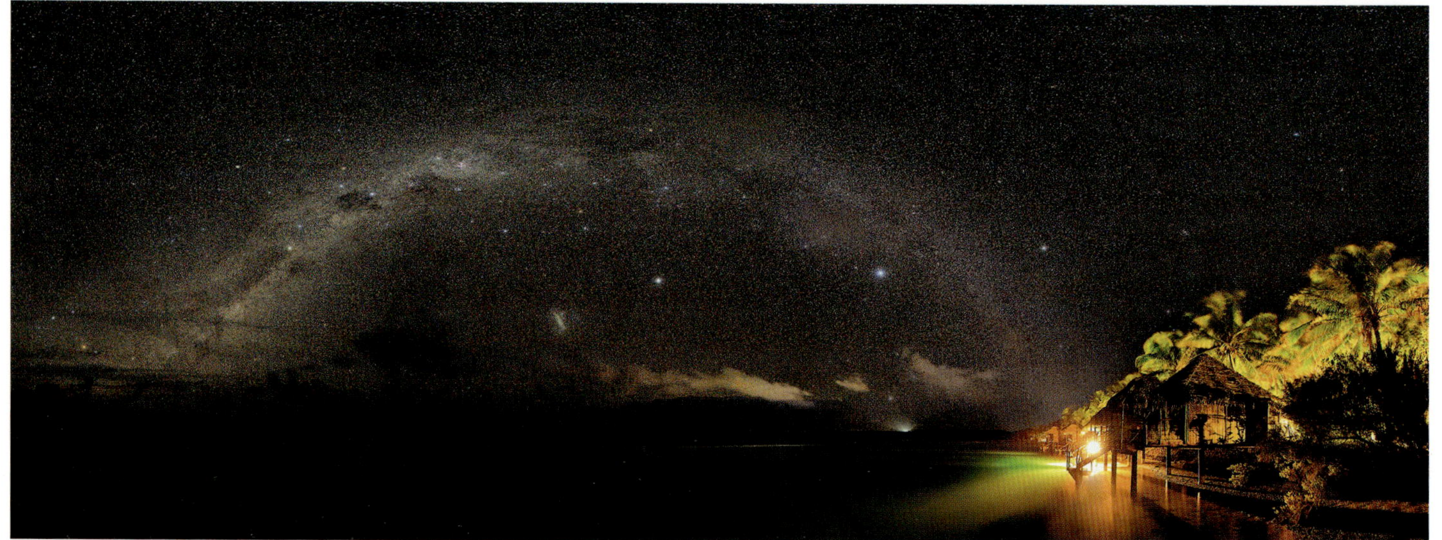

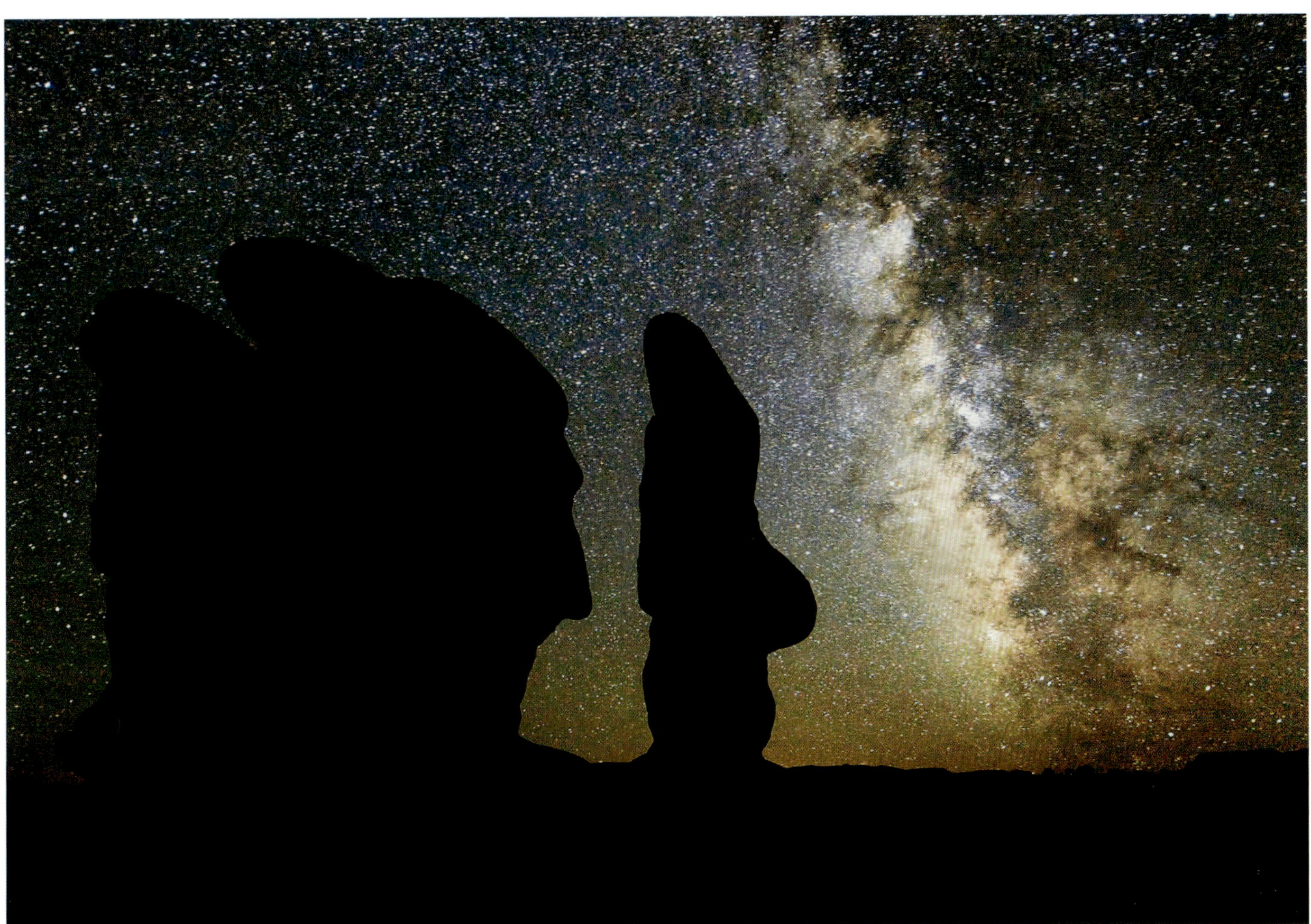

I captured this image of rock formations in Escalante National Monument under no moon so that I could get more detail in the stars and the Milky Way. I decided that the shapes of the rocks were interesting enough to work as silhouettes and that they didn't need to be illuminated by the moon or by a flashlight. Canon 5D II, 14mm, f/2.8, 30 seconds, ISO 6400.

DSLR Remote (Android only)

This free app works like a wireless intervalometer and lets you set your camera to take repeated exposures. It requires a phone with an infrared sender and a camera with an infrared receiver.

Unleashed (iPhone only)

DSLR remote doesn't work on iPhones since they cannot send infrared signals. An alternative is Unleashed, which has a lot of nice features. The app is free, but you have to purchase a Bluetooth module, which costs around $200, that plugs into a Canon or Nikon.

MOON PHASES

Knowing what the current moon phase is and where the moon will be is very important for night photography. Shooting under a full moon can produce drastically different results than shooting under no moon. While there is no right moon phase to shoot under, there are distinct advantages and disadvantages to shooting under different phases.

No Moon

The biggest advantage of shooting under no moon is that your camera can capture more stars since moonlight obscures fainter stars. This is particularly important if you want to capture dramatic images of the Milky Way.

The biggest disadvantage of shooting under no moon is that less light enters your camera, and there will be more noise visible in the photographs. The noise can be minimized by using the proper equipment and by stitching or stacking images. However, all other things being equal, a photograph taken under a full moon will have less noise than a photograph taken under no moon.

Single exposures taken under no moon and with no light painting will usually render foreground subjects as dark silhouettes. This can be good for objects with compelling shapes, like a saguaro cactus or the sandstone rock formations in the American Southwest. It probably won't work as well for things with less distinct shapes, like mountains or canyons.

Deciding whether you want to shoot under no moon is ultimately an artistic decision. I often prefer shooting under no moon because of the dramatic starscapes I can capture with no moonlight obscuring the view. Also, I think that silhouettes can emphasize how dark it is and keep the primary focus on the dramatic night sky.

If you want to do any light painting, you'll generally want to do this under no moon. You can capture dramatic dark skies while illuminating some of the foreground. You can also use some of the more advanced techniques discussed in Chapter IX to render detail in the foreground under no moon.

Full or Gibbous Moon

The advantages and disadvantages of shooting under a full or gibbous moon are the reverse of shooting under no moon. With the bright light of a full moon, you will get less noise in your images. This can be advantageous if you are using an older digital camera or if you don't have a lens with a wide aperture. In this case, you may get unacceptably noisy images when shooting under no moon. One way to avoid this is to shoot large stitched images, which will be discussed in Chapter VIII. However, if you're new to night photography, you probably won't want to start with the more advanced techniques. So you could shoot under a bright moon until you get more comfortable shooting at night or can invest in some better equipment.

It can also be good to shoot under a full moon if you shoot in an area that has some light pollution. The light pollution can create unnatural colors in the foreground and the sky, especially in the clouds. The bright white light of the full moon can drown out some of the light pollution. However, if you are too close to city lights, even the full moon will not help much. In this case, it may be best to find a darker location to shoot.

Another potential advantage of shooting under a full moon is that it will illuminate the landscape and bring out the color and detail in the scene, in much the same way as the sun would. If the foreground is an essential part of your image and you're not as concerned with capturing a dramatic starscape, you might consider shooting under a full or gibbous moon.

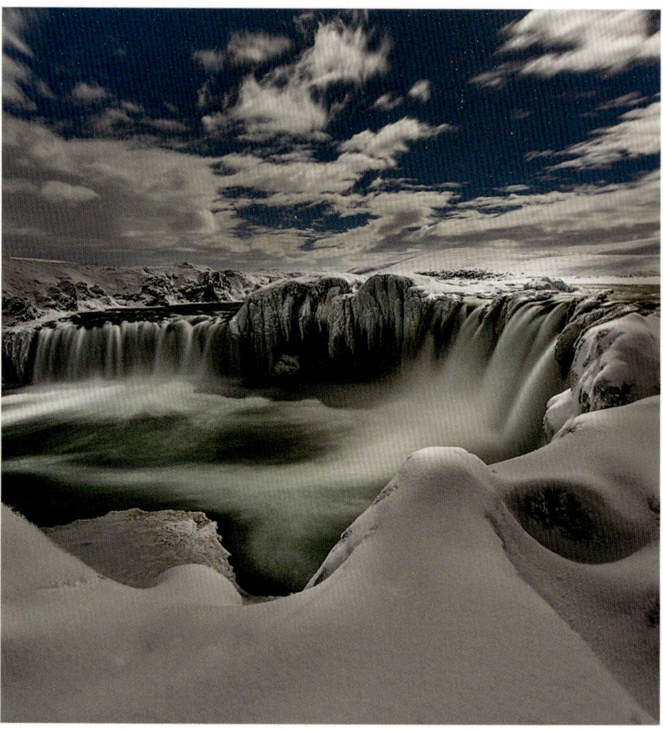

I shot this image of Godafoss waterfall in Iceland with a bright, gibbous moon behind me. The moon obscured the stars, but it didn't matter too much since the waterfall, snow, and clouds were the main focus of this image. Nikon D800e, 19mm, f/2.8, 13 seconds, ISO 1000.

A significant disadvantage of shooting under a full moon is that it obscures the light from the stars, and the skies will not look as impressive.

Another disadvantage is that it is difficult to capture long star trails under a full moon, as you can easily overexpose the image. You can get around this by combining multiple exposures on a digital camera, which I will discuss in Chapter VII. However, the star trails will be fainter than if you shot under no moon or

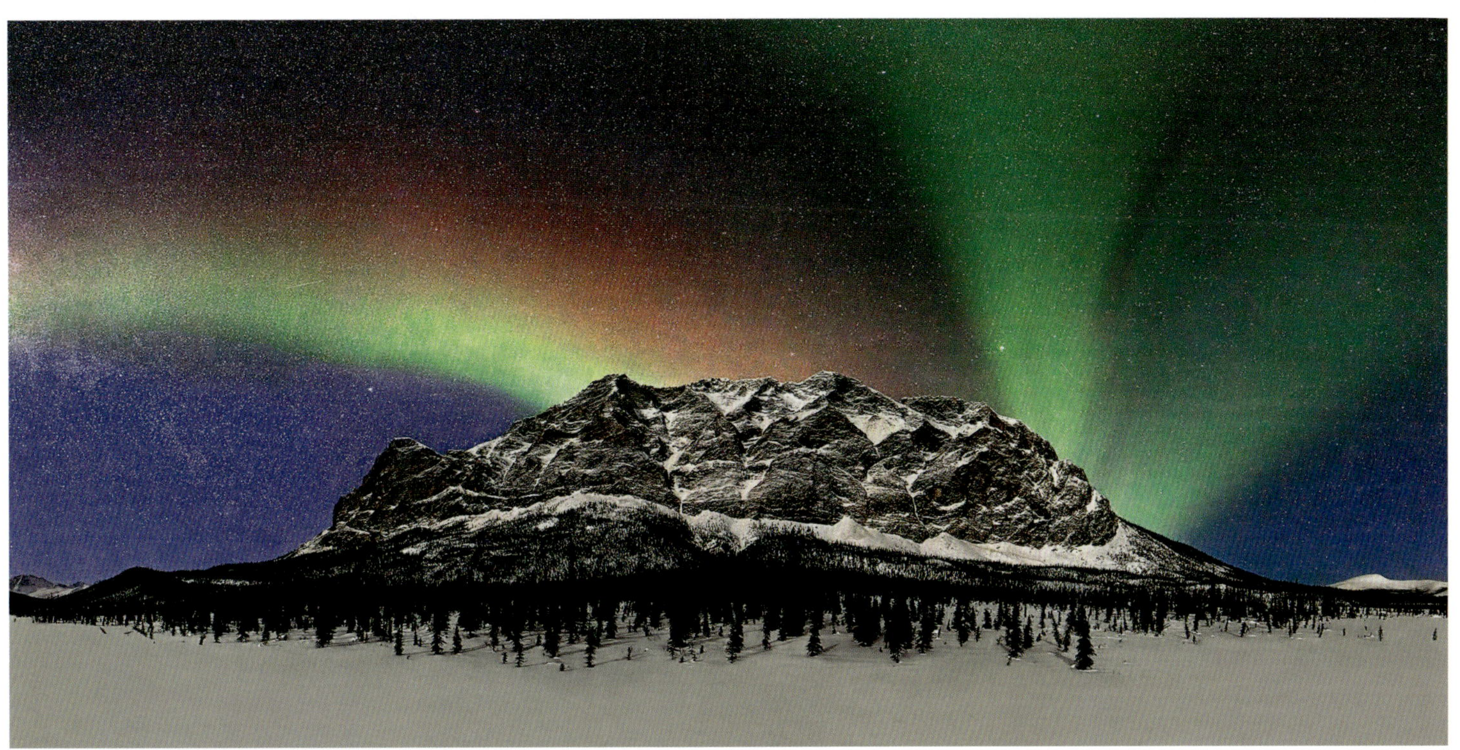

Supapak Mountain near Wiseman, Alaska would have looked like a round, dark blob under no moon. The quarter moon illuminated its jagged edges and bright patches of snow. The moon did not obscure as many stars as it would have if it had been full. It also allowed the northern lights, which were relatively dim on this night, to stand out more. Canon 5D II, 24mm, f/2.8, 10 seconds, ISO 6400, nine images stitched together.

a crescent moon.

It's generally best to photograph with the moon behind you so that it illuminates the front of the object you are photographing. Also, it is usually better to shoot with the moon low in the sky. If it is too high, it can produce harsh light, just like the sun does during the day. Shooting with the moon behind you and low in the sky will also keep the part of the sky you are photographing a little darker, and more stars will be visible.

A full moon will be up most of the night. So if you will be facing west when photographing, it's probably best to shoot early in the night when the moon is low in the sky to the east. If you will be facing east, it's generally best to photograph early in the morning when the moon is low in the sky to the west.

Crescent Moon

While there can be some advantages to shooting under a full moon, I find that the bright light usually obscures the stars too much. Also, with newer technology and proper exposures, noise is not as big of an issue as it used to be. I therefore find shooting under a crescent moon preferable if I want to render detail in the foreground and capture more stars in the sky.

An interesting fact about the quarter moon (or a 50% illuminated moon) is that it is only 9% as bright as a full moon. This is surprising to many people who would expect a quarter moon to be half as bright as a full moon. However, light from the sun reflects directly off of a full moon and straight back to Earth. Light from a quarter moon has to bounce at a 90-degree angle to reach Earth. Much of that light is blocked by irregularities on the moon's surface, like craters and boulders. The light from a quarter moon therefore obscures the stars much less than a full moon and will often result in more dramatic images.

I generally like shooting under an even fainter moon, when it is 10%-35% illuminated. This provides just enough light to illuminate the landscape, while only somewhat obscuring the stars. A moon that is 10% illuminated is just bright enough to light up the foreground if you're using good equipment that doesn't produce too much noise. You do, however, need to make sure the moon is directly illuminating the front of the foreground objects, as any large shadows will usually be too dark to render detail under such a dim moon. You could also take a longer exposure of the land or stack images of the land, as described in Chapter IX, to get more detail in the shadows.

If the moon is more than 50% illuminated, I find that it starts to drown out the light from the stars too much. I therefore usually plan my photography trips so that they end at or before the first quarter moon.

The waxing moon that occurs shortly after the new moon will appear in the western part of the sky after sunset. Thus, it is generally best to shoot under this moon when facing in an easterly direction.

The waning moon that occurs right before the new moon will appear in the eastern part of the sky before sunrise. It is generally best to shoot under this moon when facing in a westerly direction.

Throughout the year, the moon can also move from far south in the sky to far north. It wanders farther north and south than the sun does. You can plan to shoot in a southerly direction when the moon is to the north and in a northerly direction when the moon is to the south.

One exception to this is if you want to include the moon itself in the shot. In this case, you will of course want the moon in the same part of the sky that you are photographing.

MONTHS OF THE YEAR

The time of the year that you photograph is also very important for night photography. Different constellations and different parts of the Milky Way will be visible during different months of the year.

The information provided below is for shooting in the Northern Hemisphere since that is where most readers will be photographing. Different constellations will be visible from the Southern Hemisphere, and you will see different parts of the Milky Way.

The night sky may actually be more dramatic in the Southern Hemisphere. Two stunning galaxies, known as the Large and Small Magellanic Clouds, can be seen in the southern skies. Also, the brightest part of the Milky Way rises high in the sky throughout much of the year. In the Northern Hemisphere, the brightest part only rises a little bit above the horizon.

If you do plan to shoot in the Southern Hemisphere, Stellarium will provide a great preview of what you can expect to see.

December-February

Those looking to capture dramatic images of the Milky Way may be disappointed during the months of December to February. At this time, our planet is pointing away from the center of the galaxy at night, and you can only see the fainter parts of the Milky Way. It can still be photographed, but the photos won't likely be as dramatic as they are at other times of the year.

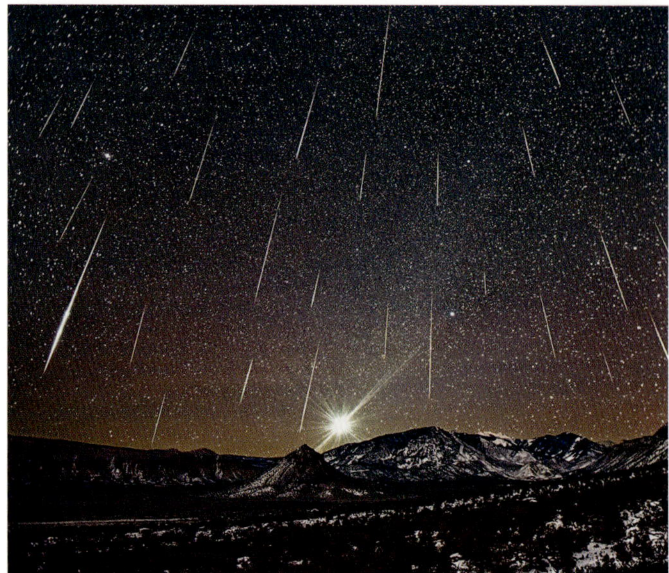

Geminids meteors streak above the La Sal Mountains in Utah, as Venus rises in the east. I combined many meteors into one image and realigned them to the radiant, as described in Chapter V. Nikon D850, 24mm, f/2.8, 15 seconds, ISO 1600.

There are still plenty of photographic opportunities during the winter months. The constellation Orion is usually visible in the southern part of the sky. This is one of the most impressive constellations, and it is made up of some of the brightest stars. Several other brilliant stars surround Orion, including Sirius, which is the brightest star in the sky.

The Andromeda Galaxy (which can be seen in the images on pages 46 and 132) is up most of the night in the autumn and winter months. It is located near the Milky Way between the constellation Cassiopeia (which looks like the letter W or M) and the constellation Pegasus (which looks like a big square).

Another tremendous photographic opportunity in winter is the Geminids meteor shower, which peaks in mid-December and is often the best meteor shower of the year.

One benefit of shooting in the winter months is that the sun will set much earlier, especially at higher latitudes. You can therefore finish shooting at a reasonable hour.

Another advantage of shooting in winter is that your images will have less dark noise when shot in cold temperatures. Of course, the cold can also be seen as a disadvantage for those not wanting to brave the frigid temperatures.

March-April

The bright, central portion of the Milky Way begins to make its return at night in March and April. It will rise in the southeast shortly before sunrise. When the Milky Way first rises, it will appear as a shallow arc stretching 180 degrees across the sky, from north to south. This can make for some stunning images if you can capture the full band of the Milky Way by stitching together multiple images.

Dates near the spring equinox are ideal for capturing zodiacal light, which appears as a faint triangular glow pointing up from the horizon. It is most visible far away from city lights about an hour after sunset or before sunrise.

May-June

For those who don't want to get up in the early hours (or stay up all night) to capture dramatic images of the Milky Way, you can wait until May or June, when it begins to rise earlier in the night.

The sun sets at its latest time on the summer solstice, so those wishing to photograph the night sky during this time will have to stay up quite late.

July-September

The Perseids meteor shower occurs in mid-August and is usually the second-best meteor shower of the year, trailing only the Geminids.

The center of the Milky Way will be in the southern part of the sky after sunset during these months. The rest of the Milky Way will appear higher in the sky each night, and it will become impossible to capture the shallow arc that is visible in the spring. Instead, the Milky Way will appear to stretch vertically into the sky.

September is another good time to see zodiacal light.

October-November

The center of the Milky Way will be located in the southwestern part of the sky after sunset in October, and it will set soon after it gets dark. By November, the center will not be visible when it is dark, but the relatively bright part of the Milky Way just above the center will be visible to the west. This is an excellent time to photograph if you want to capture the Milky Way in the western part of the sky without staying up half the night or getting up very early.

TWILIGHT STAGES

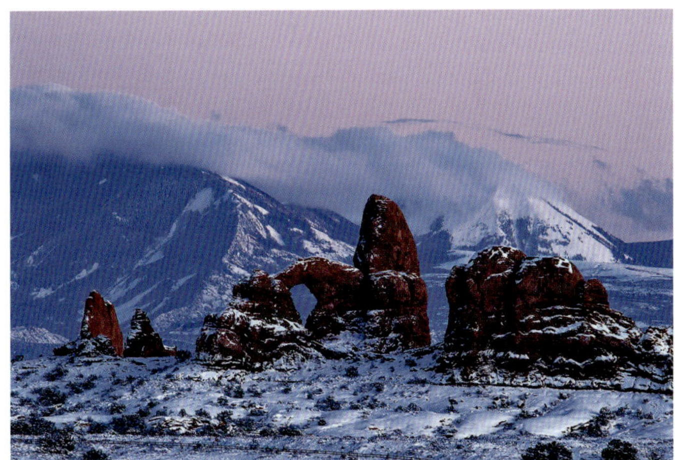

The Belt of Venus is visible above Turret Arch and the La Sal Mountains during civil twilight in Arches National Park. Earth's shadow is not visible, as it is blocked by the mountains. Nikon D800e, 300mm, f/16, 2.5 seconds, ISO 100.

It's important to understand the different stages of twilight when photographing at night. There are three stages - civil twilight, nautical twilight, and astronom-

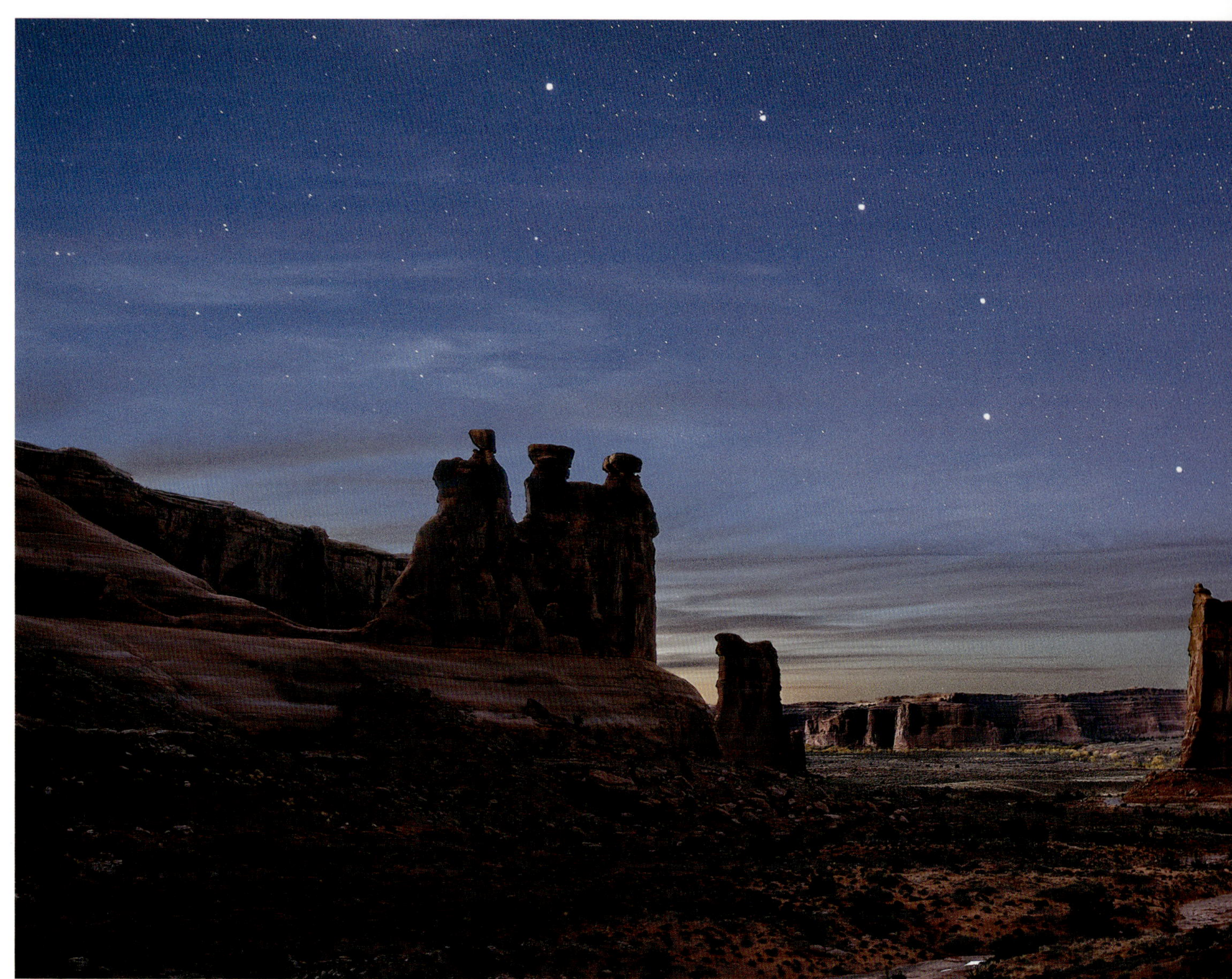

ical twilight. Each of these stages lasts about 30 minutes, though it can be longer or shorter depending on where you are on the planet and what time of year it is. You can determine the exact times each of these twilight stages occurs for your location in the Astronomy section of WeatherUnderground.com. You can also find this information on the PhotoPills app or The Photographer's Ephemeris.

I will describe how the sky changes during different stages of twilight. However, the best way to know how images will look is to take photos throughout each of the stages.

Civil Twilight

The first stage of twilight after sunset and the last stage before sunrise is known as civil twilight. It occurs during the time the sun is between 0 to 6 degrees below the horizon. During this time, you can often get vibrant colors in the sky, since a lot of light from the sun is scattered and refracted by the atmosphere. The clouds may have some of the bright orange or pink glow that you would see at sunrise or sunset. You can also capture images of Earth's shadow, which is the shadow that Earth casts on its atmosphere. This shadow will usually appear with a bright pink band of sky above it, known as the Belt of Venus or the anti-twilight arch.

Civil twilight is an excellent time to capture images of the moon and some of the brightest stars and planets. The moon will be visible throughout this time, while some stars and planets will be visible towards the end of civil twilight in the evening (or the beginning of it in the morning).

The period when the stars and planets are just visible is often referred to as the blue hour. During this time, blue wavelengths of light from the sun are more eas-

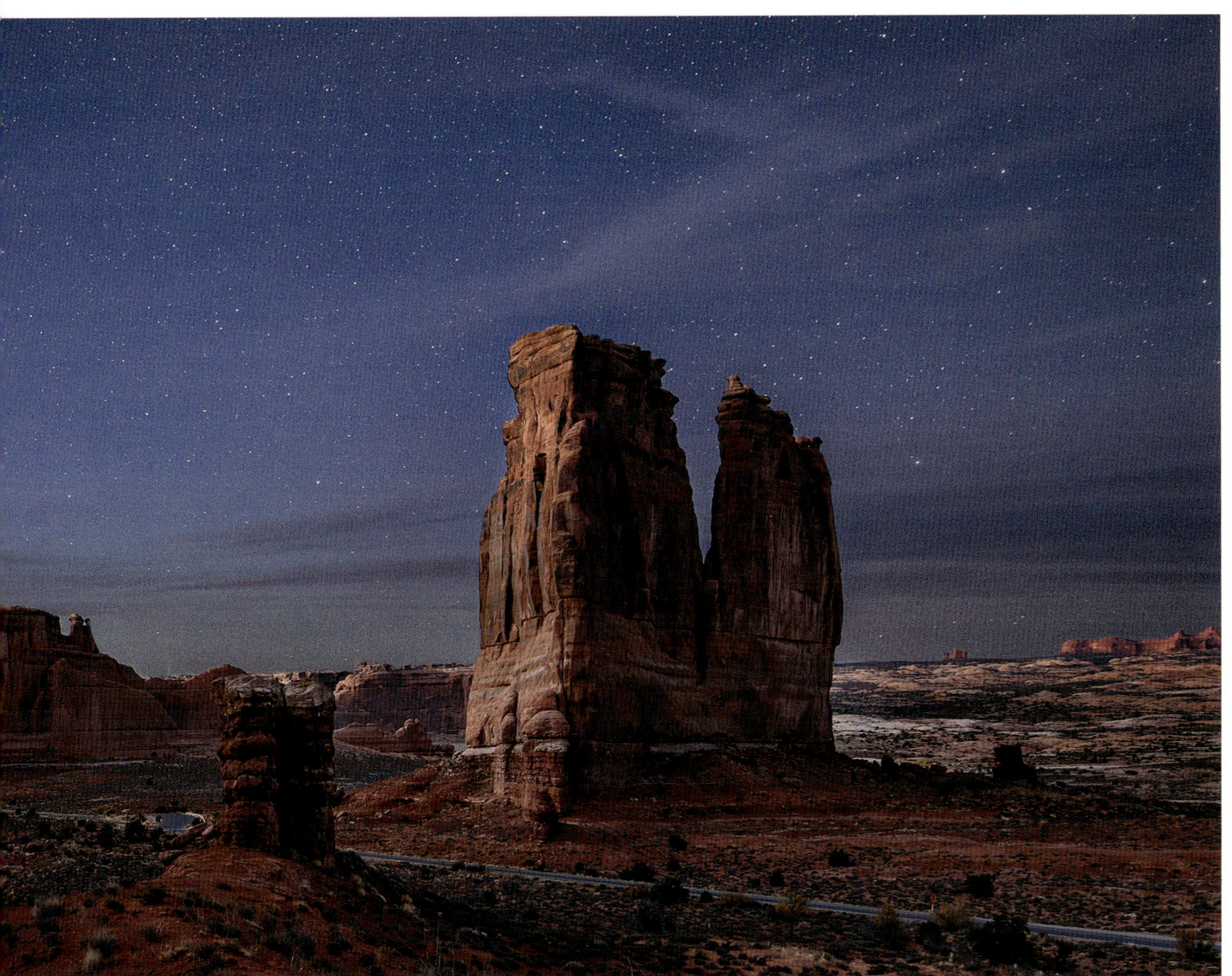

To capture this photograph, I took an exposure of the night sky over Arches National Park at the end of nautical twilight. I was facing towards the spot the sun had set, so there wasn't enough light to get good detail in the land in one exposure. I instead used a photo of the landscape taken earlier during civil twilight. Nikon D800e, 18mm; exposure for land: f/5.6, 30 seconds, ISO 400; exposure for sky: f/2.8, 20 seconds, ISO 1600.

---

ily refracted by the atmosphere back onto the land, making the scene appear bluer than usual. This effect is most pronounced near the end of civil twilight in the evening (or the beginning of civil twilight in the morning), though it is noticeable before and after this time.

You can capture some intriguing images during the blue hour. If you are photographing something that is already blue, like the ocean, it can further deepen the blues, giving a somewhat surreal effect to the photo. This may not be as desirable if you are photographing objects that aren't blue, as it can give the appearance of a color cast across the image. In this scenario, you can increase the white balance temperature until you remove the color cast.

During civil twilight, it will usually be light enough to get good exposures using your camera's exposure meter. However, you should check the histogram after you take your photos. Make sure the data extends to the right side of the histogram, without blowing out any highlights.

Nautical Twilight

After civil twilight in the evening (and before it in the morning) is a period known as nautical twilight.

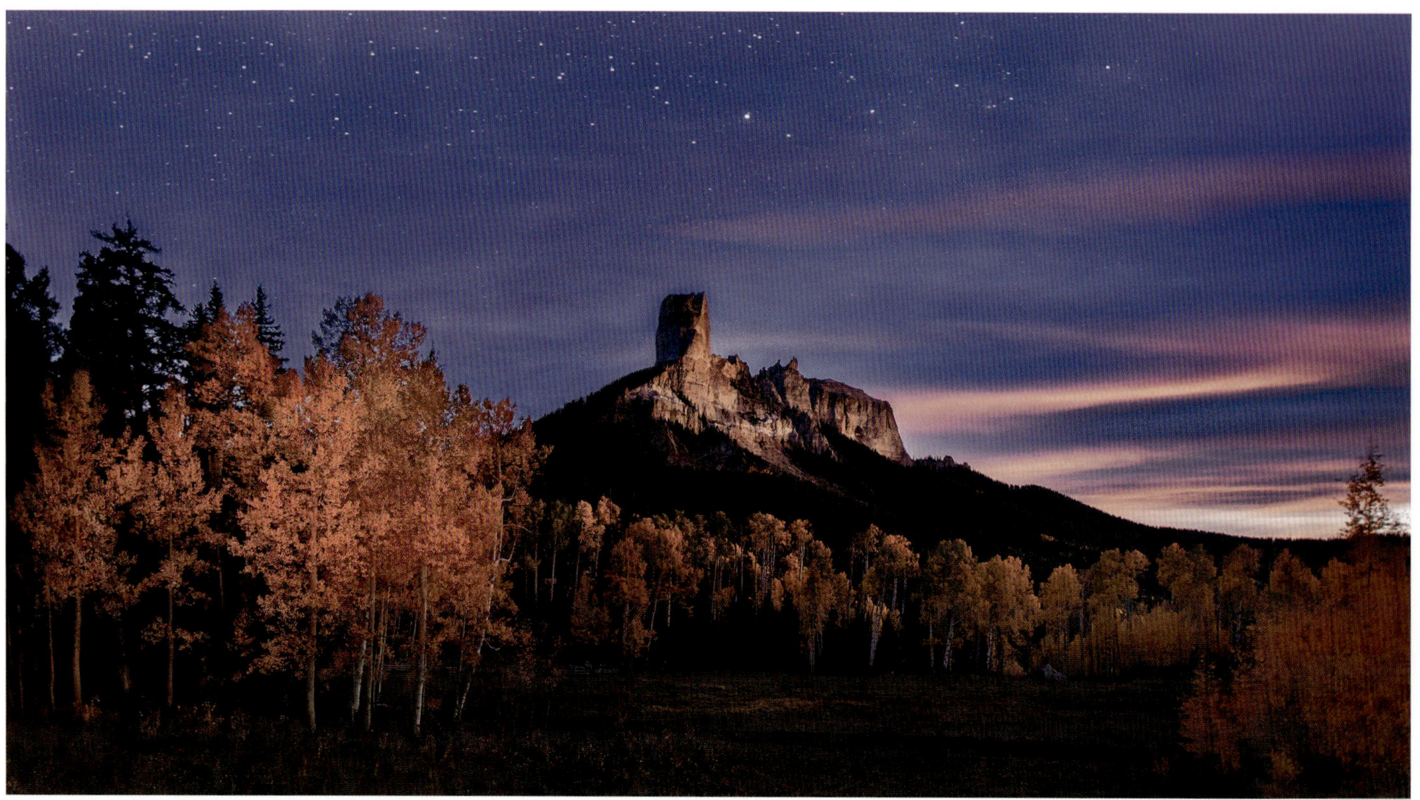

The colors from a dramatic sunset over Chimney Rock in Colorado lasted into nautical twilight. Although I could no longer see the color, the camera was able to pick it up. I stacked multiple images of both the land and sky using techniques described in chapter IX to get more detail in the photo. Nikon D800e, 24mm f/2.8, 30 seconds, ISO 100.

This stage occurs from the time the sun is 6 to 12 degrees below the horizon. During this time, you can get unique images that convey the brief moment in time between the dark of night and the light of day.

During nautical twilight, it will start to become too dark to use your camera's exposure meter. You'll need to switch to manual exposure on your camera. You should use the widest aperture you can, while still getting everything in focus. You'll need to use longer and longer exposures (up to about 30 seconds) and start raising the ISO to properly expose your image and get data extending to the right side of your histogram.

It will start to look quite dark to the naked eye during nautical twilight. However, your camera can still capture light from the sun that is refracted by the atmosphere. You'll usually get the best light on the land when facing away from the spot the sun set (or is about to rise). If, on the other hand, you face toward the direction of the sun, you can often get vivid colors in the sky above the horizon. If there was a vibrant sunset, some of the color on the clouds might last until nautical twilight.

During the beginning of nautical twilight in the evening (or the end of it in the morning), it will often be light enough to get a good exposure of both the land and the sky with a single shot. As the light fades, you'll likely need to combine two exposures to get a high-quality image. You can take a longer exposure for the land and a shorter exposure for the sky and blend them in post-processing, as I'll describe in Chapter IX.

Your camera can capture quite a few stars during nautical twilight. However, it won't be dark enough to produce dramatic images of the Milky Way.

Astronomical Twilight

Astronomical twilight occurs during the time that the sun is 12-18 degrees below the horizon. The sky will appear almost completely dark to the naked eye, but there will still be some light from the sun that can be picked up by a camera. At the beginning of astronomical twilight in the evening, the sky will still have a bluish color to it. If there is no moon out, the sky will fade to purple and then to black at the end of twilight.

There may also be some reds or yellows in the direction the sun set (or is about to rise).

If there is no moon or a thin crescent moon, the skies will be sufficiently dark that you will be able to capture many stars and the Milky Way in your images. If there is a brighter moon out, the light from it will likely overpower any light refracted through the atmosphere from the sun. Your images will look almost the same as photos taken under a moon in the dark of night (the sky will appear blue, the foreground will be lit up, and some stars will be obscured).

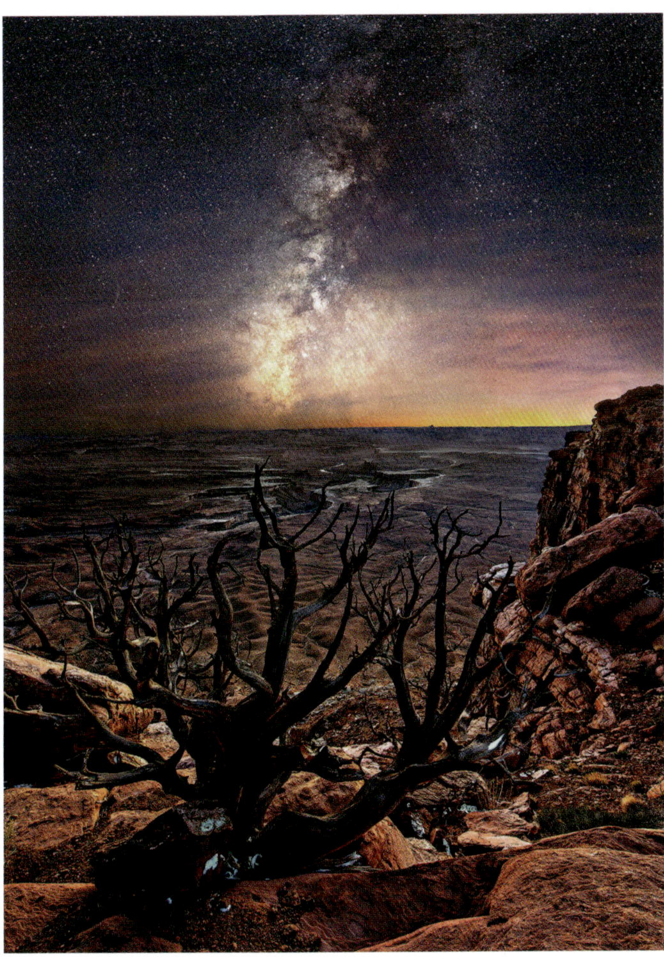

The Milky Way is seen from Green River Overlook during astronomical twilight. Some colors are still visible on the horizon where the sun had set. Nikon D800e; exposure of land during civil twilight: 14mm, f/8.0, 15 seconds, ISO 100; exposures of sky: 50mm, f/1.8, 10 seconds, ISO 6400, 28 images stitched together.

Even if there is no moon out, you can still get a little light on the foreground if you are facing away from the spot the sun set (or is about to rise). However, unless you are photographing something with a very bright, reflective surface, you'll probably need to illuminate the foreground with a flashlight or blend multiple exposures, as described in Chapter IX, to get good detail throughout the image.

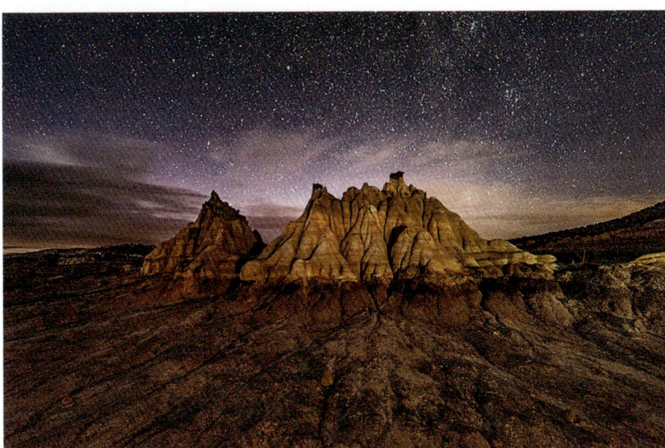

Rock formations in western Colorado are seen near the end of astronomical twilight. At this time, the sky fades from blue to purple to black. Nikon D800e, 14mm, f/2.8, 25 seconds, ISO 6400.

Astronomical twilight is one of my favorite times to shoot, and I took many of the photographs in this book during this time. I find the small amount of color left in the sky desirable for many images.

TIDES

If you will be photographing by the ocean, it's good to check the tides first, both for photographic purposes and for safety reasons. If you're in an area that can be dangerous at high tide, you'll want to make sure and visit when the tide is low. Also, some compositions may work better during different tides. It's easier to go to a place that you've already photographed during the day, so you know what tides work best for a given photo.

You can find detailed information on tides online at https://tidesandcurrents.noaa.gov/.

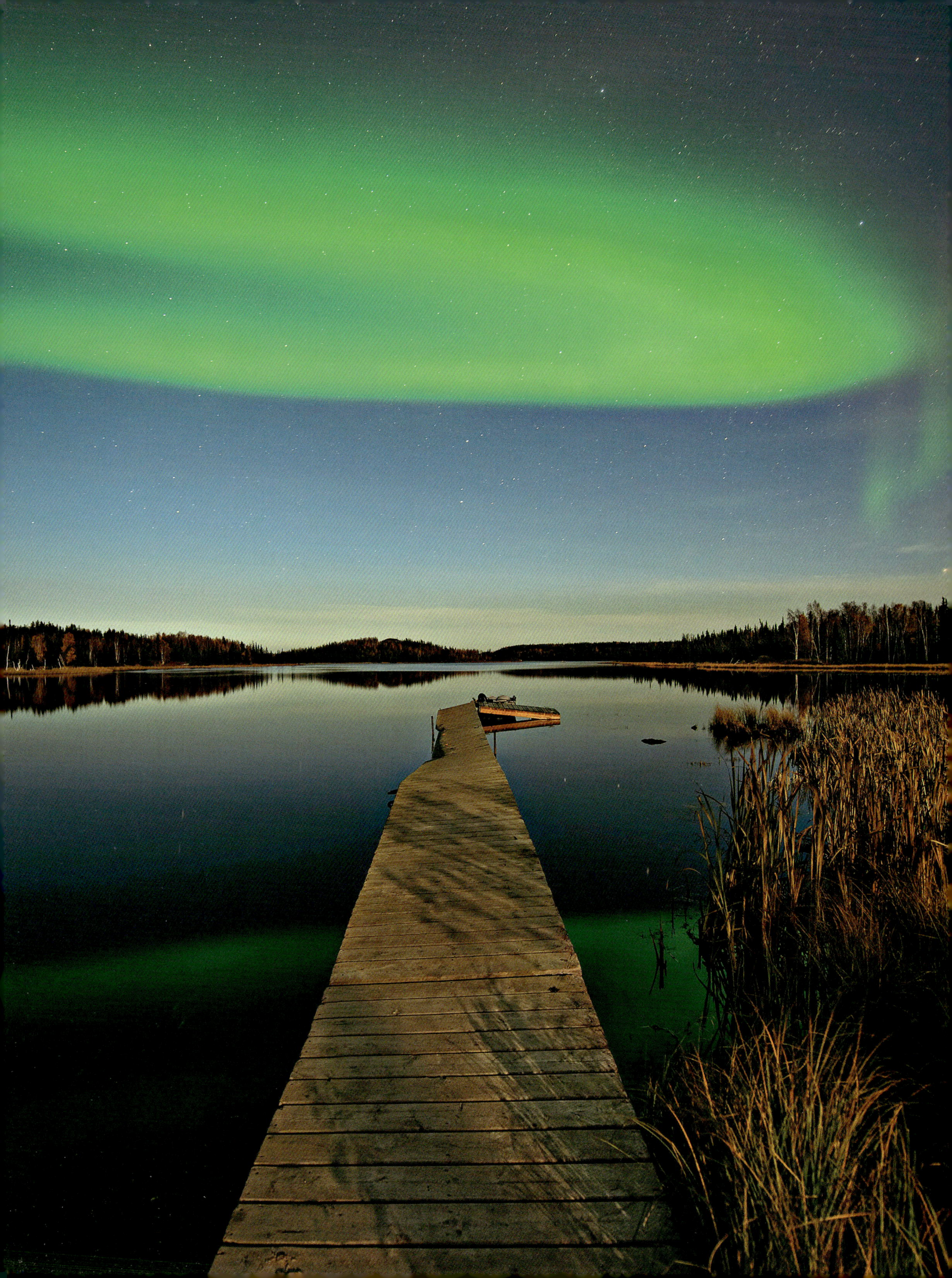

III. Composition

I believe that composition is mainly an artistic decision, and every photographer should strive to develop their own style that sets them apart from other photographers. However, it is still important to understand the factors that can make a good composition. When you take a photo, you can decide which of these factors are most important in the image and which you may choose to ignore. By consciously making decisions about what objects to include in a photograph and how to arrange them, you can begin to develop your style.

SCOUTING

Scouting an area beforehand while it is still light out is perhaps the most important thing you can do to get a good composition at night. It can be challenging to compose a shot in the dark, especially if you are unfamiliar with an area or new to night photography.

I recommend that you begin scouting a location on the computer, using programs like Google Earth or The Photographer's Ephemeris that are described in the previous chapter. Once you've decided on a location, try to arrive at least an hour before sunset to explore the area and look for an optimal composition. This will give you time to walk around and visualize compositions from many different angles until you find one that works. Always consider both horizontal and vertical compositions, and think about how the images will look with lenses of different focal lengths.

You may want to take your camera off its tripod and view different compositions through the viewfinder. You can take snapshots from various spots and with different lenses and review them to get a feel for what composition works best.

Try to previsualize where objects in the sky, especially the Milky Way, will appear after it gets dark. You can do this by checking programs like Stellarium, PhotoPills, or Sky Safari that are described in the previous chapter. If you know the Milky Way will be due south once it gets dark, you can try to find a good composition facing south. If you can't find a shot you like facing south, remember that objects in the sky will move from east to west over the course of the night. So if you find a good composition facing southwest, you can wait for several hours after it gets dark until the Milky Way moves into the southwestern part of the sky.

If you've decided on a good composition before the sun has set, you can set up your camera and set the focus. It is easier to dial in the focus while it is still light out. I recommend doing some test shots at the aperture you plan to use at night to make sure your focus is set correctly.

If you are unable to arrive early or if you want to change your shot during the night, you'll need to set up your camera approximately where you want it. You can shine your flashlight on objects in the scene while looking through the viewfinder to get a feel for what will be in your image. You can then take a test shot and view it on your camera's LCD screen. This will give you a better feel for your composition, and you can then adjust your camera position until you get it just right.

If it is windy out, this could affect your images. The wind can cause the camera to move, resulting in blurred photos. Even worse, if you leave your camera while doing long exposures or multiple exposures, the wind could topple the tripod and damage your camera. To make the tripod more stable, you can lower it and spread the legs out wider. You can also add weight to your tripod by hanging something like your photo backpack off of the center platform or center bar of your tripod.

Left: The aurora borealis is spectacular by itself, but including this old moonlit pier in the composition helped give depth to the image and provide a sense of place. Nikon D800e, 15mm, f/2.8, 30 seconds, ISO 1600.

FOREGROUND SUBJECTS

One of the most important decisions you'll need to make is what to use as your foreground subject. I've seen many night photos where there is just a flat, dark horizon with the night sky above it. While the stars may look impressive, the photographs are little different from countless other images of the night sky. What truly sets a night photo apart from the others is the foreground. It can make the photograph more original and also add depth to an image and draw the viewer into the scene.

If you're new to night photography, it is easier to choose foreground subjects that are large and far away, like a mountain or a large rock formation. This makes focusing much more straightforward. You can simply set the focus at infinity and leave it there.

If you're more experienced and want to include closer objects in the foreground, you need to be careful with the focus. You will be shooting with wide apertures at night, which will give you limited depth of field. It can therefore be easy to render part or all of the image out of focus. Always check your focus on your LCD screen after you take a shot. Zoom in on the image and look at the nearest and farthest points in the photo and make sure both are in focus.

If you want to include a very close foreground object in your image, it may be impossible to get everything in focus from the nearest point to infinity in a single exposure. The solution to this is to take multiple exposures with different focus points and later blend them in post-processing. This is known as focus stacking and will be discussed in more detail in Chapter IX.

I don't recommend focus stacking for those who are just learning night photography. It is easier to begin with more distant foregrounds and focus at infinity until you are comfortable with that. Once you are, I recommend gradually including closer subjects until you have it mastered. Using an ultra-wide-angle lens will make this easier, as it provides much more depth of field than a longer lens.

When choosing a foreground, you should also consider whether the moon will be out or not. If there is no moon, the landscape will usually be rendered as a dark silhouette. In this case, you will want to have a foreground that has a compelling shape, like a sandstone rock formation, a gnarled tree, or a saguaro cactus. If your foreground wouldn't make an interesting silhouette or if you want to keep the details and colors, there are many ways to do this. You could light paint the image, wait until the moon is in the right part of the sky to illuminate the subject, or blend multiple exposures, as described in Chapter IX.

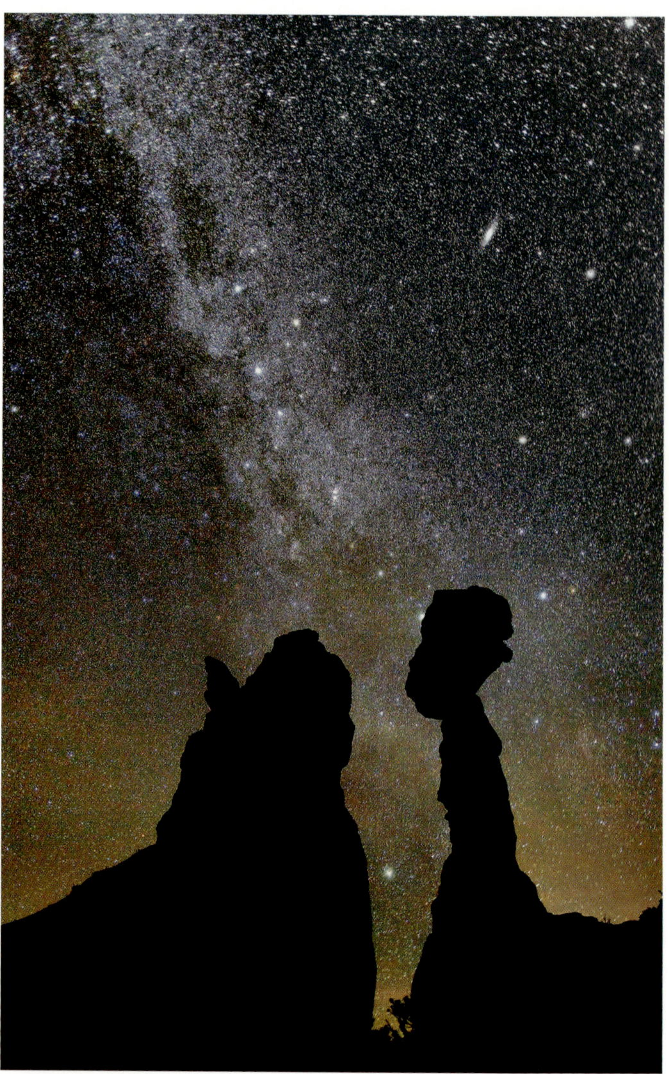

When composing this image, I decided that the shapes of the rocks were so intriguing that I could leave them as black silhouettes under no moon. Canon 5D II, 24mm, f/2.0, 30 seconds, ISO 6400.

If the moon is out, you should pay close attention to how the moonlight will affect the foreground. As with the sun, the moon usually provides better light when it is lower in the sky. However, if you are shooting under

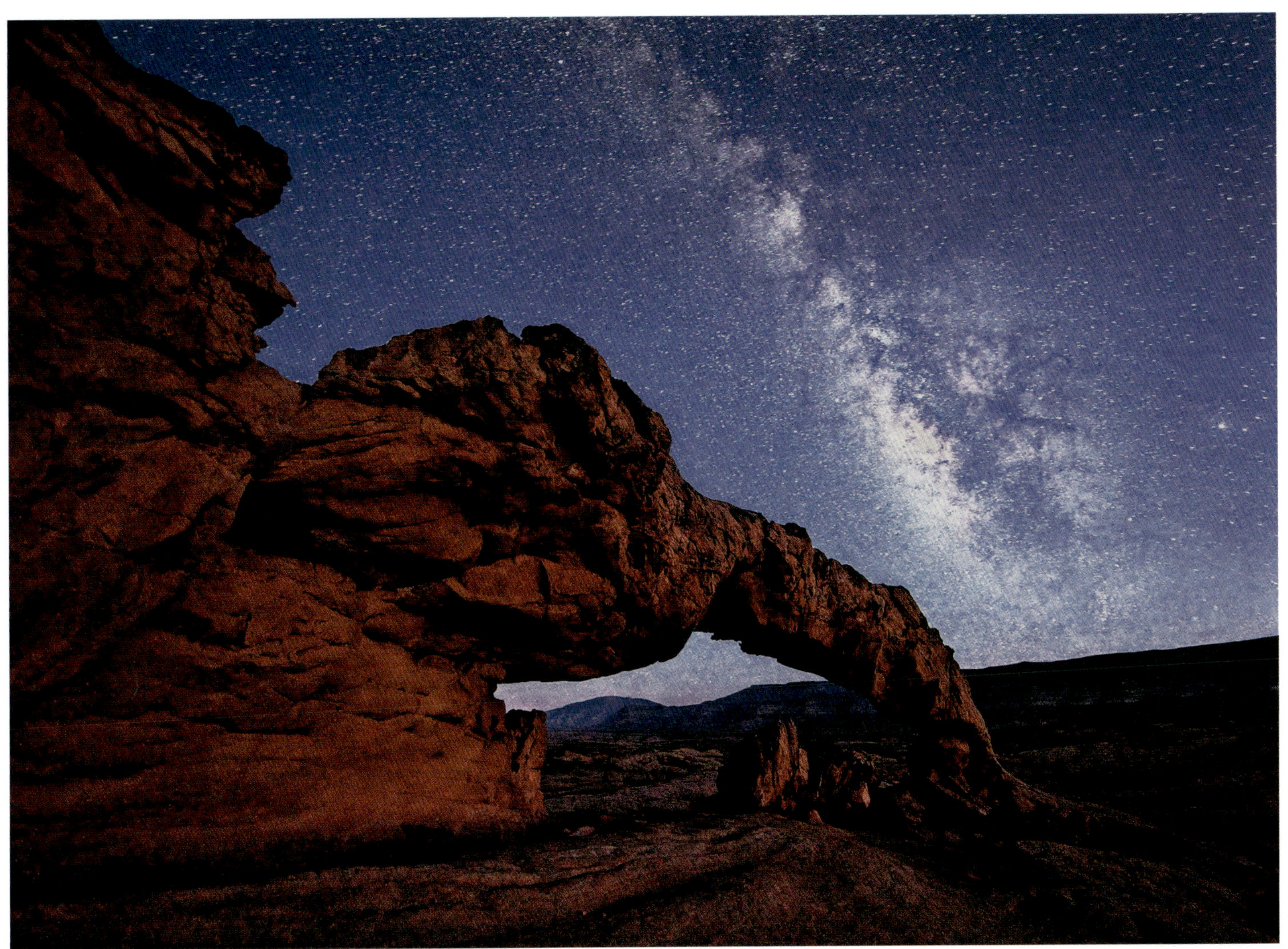

Countless stars fill the sky above Sunset Arch in Escalante National Monument. By knowing where the Milky Way would be during astronomical twilight, I was able to compose the shot and set the focus before it got dark. I made sure to keep some separation between the Milky Way and the arch. Canon 5D II, 14mm, f/2.8, 36 seconds, ISO 6400.

a crescent moon that is less than 25% illuminated, you usually won't want the moon to be so low that it is casting long shadows across the scene. Long shadows can work in images taken during the day or even with a brighter moon, as you can still capture some detail in them. However, there is so little light under a thin crescent moon that shadows can appear as black blobs with little detail when shooting single exposures. If you try to bring out detail in post-processing, you will also bring out a lot of noise.

This is not to say that you don't want any shadows when photographing under a thin, crescent moon. Small shadows can add depth to an image and bring out texture in foreground objects. You can capture these shadows by shooting with the moon behind you and a little to the left or right. If the moon is too far to the right or left or too low in the sky, it can start to cast longer, undesirable shadows. So you should check to make sure that shadows don't cover significant parts of your foreground. If they do, you can wait until the moon moves into a better position, and the shadows are diminished. Or, you can stack multiple exposures, as described in Chapter IX, to capture more detail in the shadows. Another option is to light paint the dark shadows to bring out more detail in them.

THE NIGHT SKY

You should consider how the night sky will appear in your photo when planning a composition. Do you want to capture the Milky Way in your photograph? In this case, you will want to consider how the foreground will complement the Milky Way in the image. You'll usually want there to be some separation between the landscape and the Milky Way, as opposed to having them overlap. Sometimes, you may have to wait for the Milky Way to move higher or farther west in the sky to gain separation from the landscape. Since the Milky Way is so expansive, you'll often want to use a 14mm lens to capture as much of it as possible. Or, you may prefer to stitch images together to obtain an even wider view and a higher-quality photo.

Instead of the Milky Way, you may want to capture a specific constellation or star pattern, like Orion or the Big Dipper. In this case, you'll likely want to use a longer lens so that the constellation will appear larger in the image. You'll probably want to time the shot so that the constellation is low on the horizon and you can include more of the landscape in the photo. Longer lenses have less depth of field, so you may need to use focus stacking if you want to include a close foreground subject.

There are countless other things you may want to photograph in the night sky, and I will discuss many of them in Chapter V. With each one, you'll need to consider what lens will work best and how the landscape will complement the sky.

Another thing to consider when composing images is clouds. You will often want to photograph when there are no clouds out so you can capture as many stars as possible. However, sometimes clouds can add drama to a scene at night. You will want to photograph clouds when it is partly cloudy, and some stars show through in the clear parts of the sky. If it is completely overcast, it can be tough to capture good images at night, unless there is a thunderstorm that produces lightning or a moonbow.

If you do shoot when it is partly cloudy, the long exposures will often blur the clouds and show their motion across the sky. The appearance of the clouds will

I captured this image of a ghost building in Mayflower Gulch, Colorado on a summer night under a quarter moon. The clouds added drama and a sense of movement that wouldn't have been possible on a clear night. The distant light on the mountains was cast by the moon peeking out from behind a cloud. Nikon D800e, 14mm, f/2.8, 25 seconds, ISO 6400.

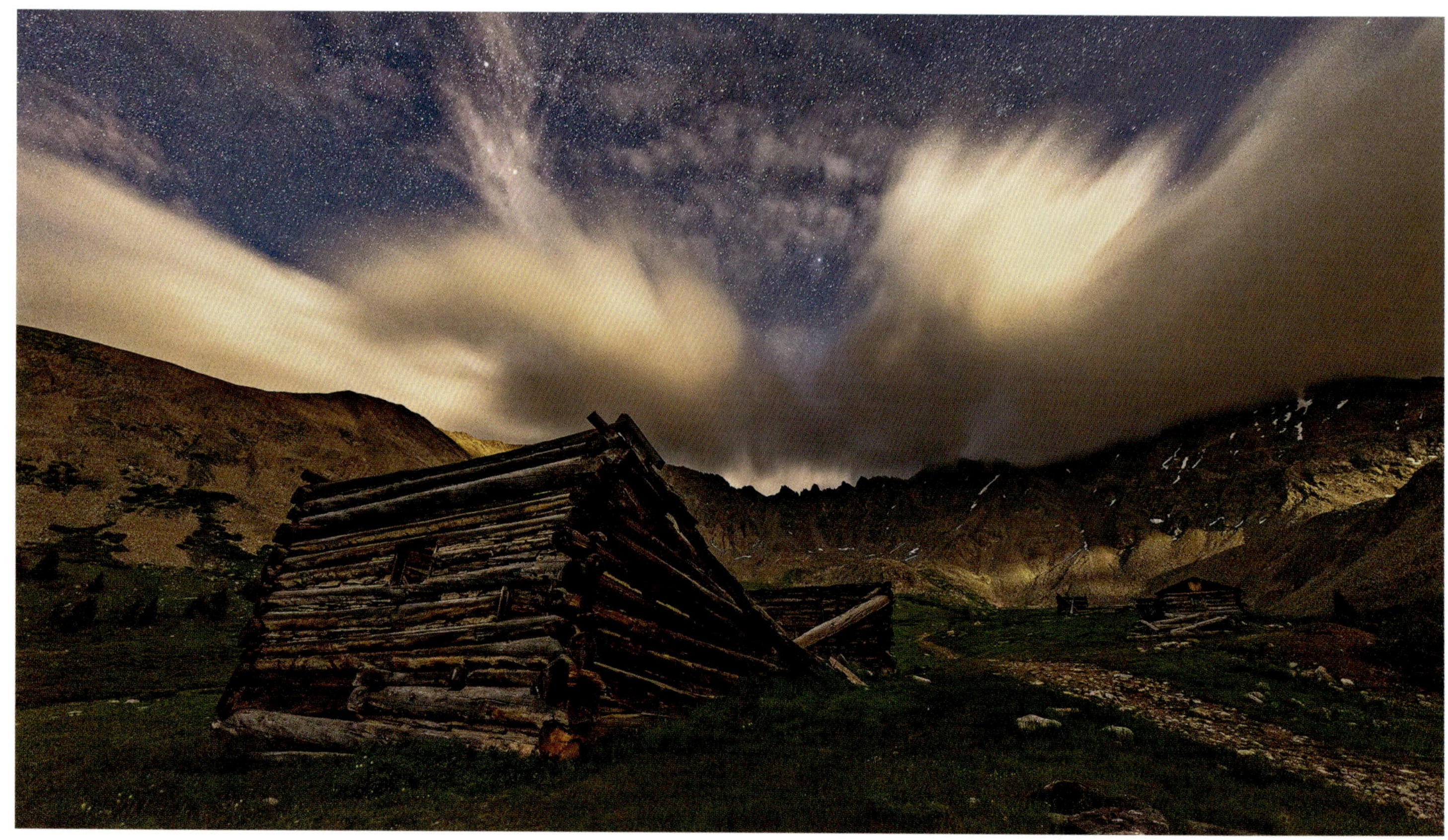

change from shot to shot, and it's difficult to previsualize these images since our eyes see the clouds as static objects. You probably won't know what you captured until you see it on the LCD screen. Many of the shots may not look too good, but every so often, you will get an image with spectacular clouds. Therefore, the key to taking good photos with clouds is to shoot a lot of exposures in a row and hope that one or more of them come out to your liking.

Clouds can also be advantageous if the moon is bright and obscuring the stars or if it is casting harsh shadows on the scene. If you wait for a cloud to cover the moon, it can diffuse the light and make the image more pleasing.

If you're anywhere near a city, you'll also want to consider light pollution when composing a photo. Occasionally, light pollution can help a shot by lighting up clouds or other objects in the photograph or adding some color to the sky. More often than not, though, you'll want to avoid light pollution and point the camera away from any city lights. There are ways to reduce or eliminate light pollution in post-processing, which I will discuss in Chapter X. However, the best way to minimize light pollution is to avoid including it in your image.

PEOPLE & MAN-MADE OBJECTS

While I don't include people or man-made objects in too many of my shots, this is something that can add drama to an image and help tell a story. This can also provide scale in a photograph.

If you include people in a shot, they will need to stay very still during the exposure, or they will appear blurry. It is easier to avoid a blurred photo if you shoot under no moon and render the person as a silhouette. Since the silhouette has little detail, any blurring won't be as noticeable. Alternatively, you can use a strobe light under no moon to illuminate the person. The strobe will put out a quick, bright burst of light, so the person will only need to remain steady at the moment you use the strobe. You'll still need a long exposure to capture the night sky, but as long as there is no other light illuminating the person, any movements they make while the strobe is not on them should not be visible in the final image.

Another option is to blend two exposures - a shorter exposure of the person and the foreground when it is lighter out and a longer exposure of the night sky once it is dark. Techniques for accomplishing this are described in Chapter IX. This can, however, be challenging, so it is easier to try and capture everything in a single shot.

You will generally want to leave space in the image in whatever direction the person is facing. The viewer's eye will usually be drawn in the direction the person is looking. If there is not much room in this direction, their eye could be drawn straight out of the photograph.

Another option for adding the human element is to include a tent that is illuminated by a flashlight or lantern from the inside. You'll want to make sure the light from the tent is not overexposing the image. If it is, you will need to dim the light or blend two different exposures - one for the foreground and the tent and one for the night sky.

Dilapidated cars or buildings can also make for captivating images. What you decide to include in the photo is really only limited by the imagination.

ARRANGING THE ELEMENTS

Once you've determined what to include in the image, you need to decide how to arrange the objects in your photograph.

Keep it Simple

Although there are exceptions, compositions that are simple and not overly chaotic are generally the most pleasing. This can be especially true at night when the main element of the image is often the dramatic, star-filled sky. You probably don't want the foreground to be so busy that it distracts from the sky. Find a primary subject to focus on, and try to exclude anything that doesn't add to the scene.

Check the edges of the frame to make sure there are no extraneous objects in the photograph that should not be there. Part of a tree branch or rock formation at the very edge of the frame might not be easily visible at night, but it can distract the eye away from the primary subject. Generally, it's best to include all of an object or none of it, rather than having part of it sticking out along the edges. If you do include all of the subject, it's usually best to have a little breathing room between the objects and the very edge of the frame, so that the image doesn't feel too cramped.

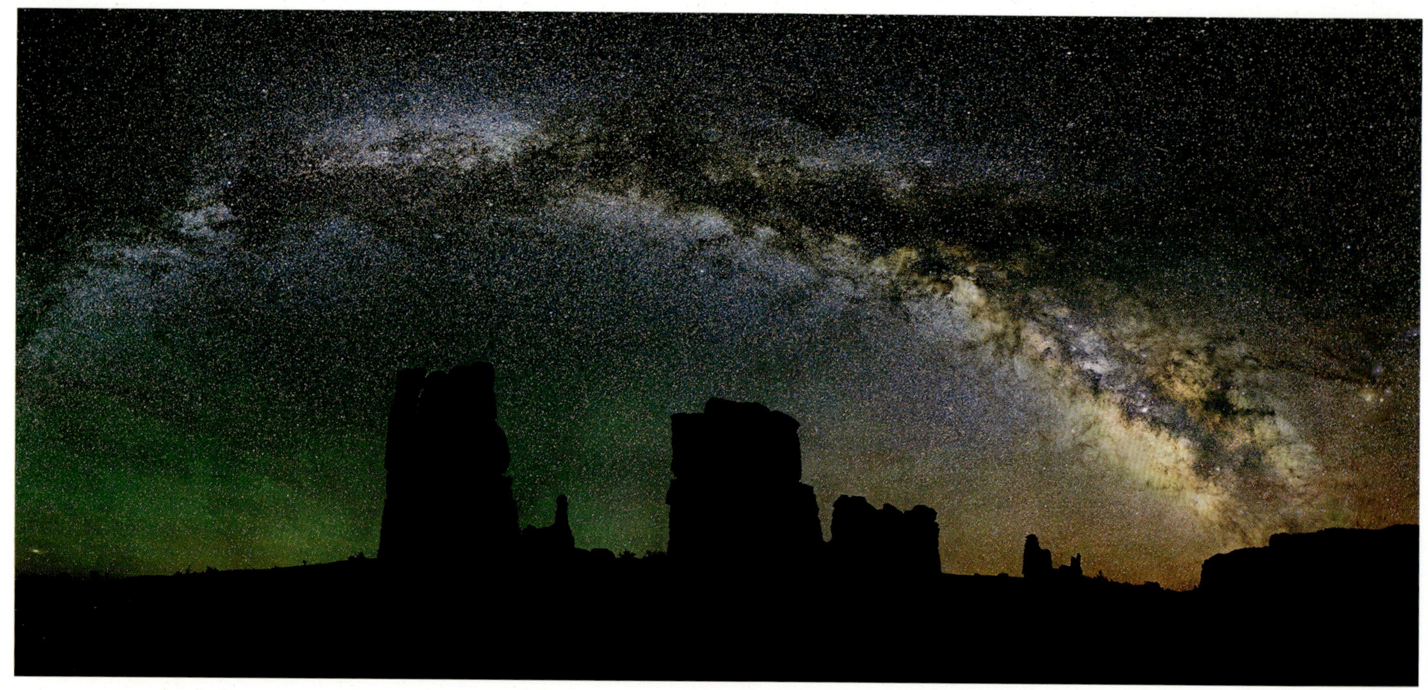

My primary goal with this composition was to keep it simple. The Milky Way was so spectacular that I didn't want anything distracting from it. I tried to position my camera so that the rock formations roughly aligned with the arc of the Milky Way. I took 50 images of smaller parts of this scene and stitched them together to create a 300-megapixel photo. The red and green colors at the bottom of the sky were produced by airglow. Canon 5D II, 50mm, f/1.6, 10 seconds, ISO 5000.

Keep it Balanced

If you have strong elements on the left side of the image and no strong elements on the right side, it can cause the image to appear too unbalanced. In this case, you may want to recompose the shot or change your lens so that the strong elements are broadly spaced on both sides of the image.

Leading Lines

Leading lines can draw the viewer into the scene and force the eye to follow a predictable path through the image. An example of this is the photograph on page 44. The converging lines from the wooden pier draw the viewer's eyes from the foreground towards the distant background and the night sky. Leading lines don't always have to be straight. Curved lines, especially those with the shape of the letter 'S,' can be appealing, as they can lead the viewer's eye on a meandering journey through the picture. Also, pronounced diagonal lines can give a feeling of movement and add interest to the scene.

It can be challenging to capture leading lines in a night photo, as you'll likely need to include a close foreground subject. Sometimes, you can accomplish this with careful focusing and an ultra-wide-angle lens. Other times it will require focus stacking.

Rule of Thirds

I don't believe there are any rules to composition, so I think this would be better referred to as the Suggestion of Thirds. If you draw two evenly-spaced vertical lines and two evenly-spaced horizontal lines across an image, the lines will intersect at four different points. The Rule of Thirds states that you should try to have strong elements of a composition located along these lines and, ideally, the strongest elements located at the four points of intersection.

The Rule of Thirds is based on the notion that we as humans tend to respond better to images that have elements that are not too firmly centered or placed at the very far edge of a photo. It tries to strike a balance between these two extremes. This rule is essentially a simplified version of the Golden Mean. The Golden Mean describes a geometrical relationship between objects that humans seem to find aesthetically pleas-

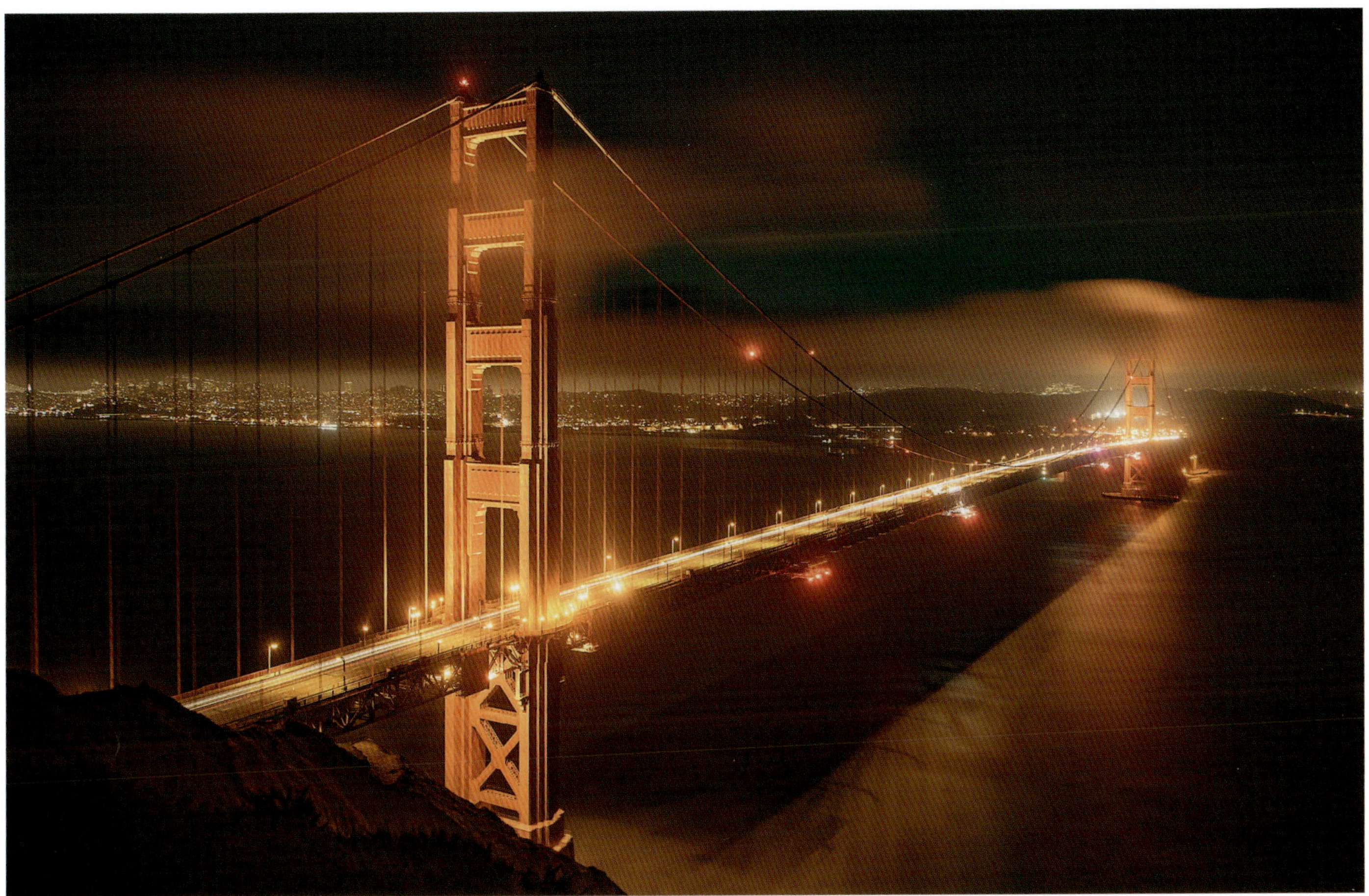

I took this image of the Golden Gate Bridge as low-lying clouds began to move in over San Francisco. This photo adheres somewhat closely to the Rule of Thirds. The large bridge tower is located along the left third of the image, and the road interests the tower along the bottom third of the image. The main cloud layer is situated along the top third of the photo. Nikon D850, 24mm, f/3.5, 10 seconds, ISO 64.

ing. It can be a bit complicated, and even if you understand it, it would be difficult to consciously incorporate it into a photograph. So the Rule of Thirds is a way to approximate the Golden Mean.

I have seen stunning images that completely ignore the Rule of Thirds and have strong central objects or strong elements closer to the edge. So this is a rule that is made to be broken.

Change the Proportions

Full-frame digital cameras have a 2:3 aspect ratio, meaning that the long edge of the image is always 1.5 times longer than the short edge. However, the scene you are photographing will not always look best with a 2:3 aspect ratio. Sometimes a wide panorama will work better, and other times a square composition will be preferable.

You can crop an image to change the proportions, but you'll want to avoid cropping night photos too much, as this will reduce the file size and image quality. It is better to take multiple images and later stitch them together, as described in Chapter VIII. You can then crop the stitched image as necessary. A panoramic photo will be of much higher quality if it is made from five images stitched together than if it is produced from a single image cropped down.

Make Sure Its Level

When setting up your shot, you may be so focused on getting your camera settings right and finding a good composition that you forget to make sure your camera is level. Always use a bubble level or your camera's built-in level to make sure that your horizons are horizontal before taking that first image.

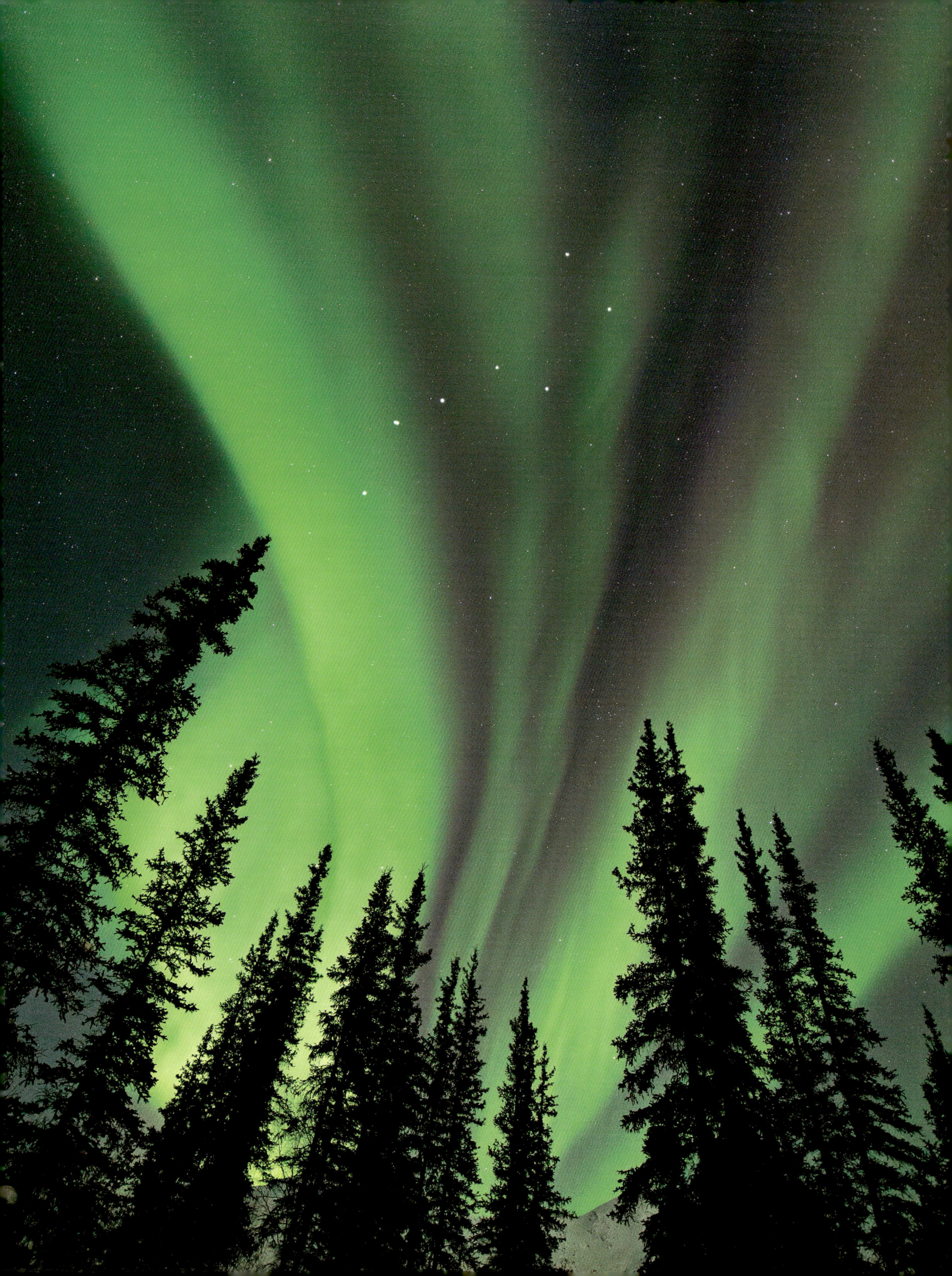

IV. Camera Settings

Using the correct camera settings is essential when shooting at night. With the proper exposure, you can capture stunning images with minimal noise and maximum detail. However, a simple mistake can cause a photograph to be very noisy or completely out of focus.

Unlike daytime shots, you can't use automatic settings on your camera when shooting at night. Your camera's light meter will not work in such dark conditions. You will almost always have to shoot in manual mode. This chapter is geared toward photographers who already have some understanding of shooting in manual. If you are new to shooting in manual, there are many instructional books that can help get you up to speed. Or, you can take a class at a local camera store, community college, or camera club.

APERTURE

When taking photos at night, you will generally want to shoot with the widest possible aperture on your lens. The widest aperture is the lowest number aperture, like f/2.8 or f/1.8. Wide apertures let more light into the camera. This is very important at night because you need to let in as much light as possible to help minimize noise.

Doubling the number of the aperture from, say, f/2.8 to f/5.6 will let in only 1/4 as much light. This can effectively make the noise in the image four times worse and is why having fast lenses is so important.

One disadvantage of shooting at such wide apertures is that you will have less depth of field in your image (meaning that it can be difficult to get both the near foreground and distant background in focus). One solution to this is to not include close objects in your image. Another solution is to use a very wide lens, like 14mm. Wider lenses allow for more depth of field. In some cases, you may want to use a slightly smaller aperture to get more depth of field, but you should avoid doing this if possible. A more advanced option is to use focus stacking, which will be described in Chapter IX.

One exception to using the widest possible aperture is if you have an extremely fast lens, like f/1.4 or f/1.2. Even with the best lenses, the corners of the image can show a lot of coma at these ultra-wide apertures. The widest aperture I generally shoot with at night is therefore f/1.8 or f/1.6.

Another circumstance where you can use a smaller aperture is if you include the moon in your photograph and want to capture a sunstar effect with the moon. This is discussed in more detail on pages 67-68.

You may also want to use smaller apertures when taking long exposures that result in star trails. This will be described in Chapter VII.

Other than these exceptions, you will almost always want to shoot at the widest aperture on your lens. This makes selecting the aperture rather easy.

SHUTTER SPEED

Determining the proper shutter speed for images that include the night sky can be tricky. A one-minute exposure will yield better-quality images than a six-second exposure because you are letting more light into the camera and therefore increasing the signal-to-noise ratio. However, during a one-minute exposure, the stars will move across the sky and create small star trails in your image. This is not ideal if you are trying to capture stars that appear as round points of light like you see them with the naked eye.

You need to get exposures that are as long as possible without producing obvious star trails. This is where the rule of 500 or NPF rule can be used.

Left: Since the northern lights in Alaska were changing rapidly, it was important to be able to quickly adjust the camera settings to get a good exposure with no blown highlights. Canon 5D II, 14mm, f/2.8, 8 seconds, ISO 6400.

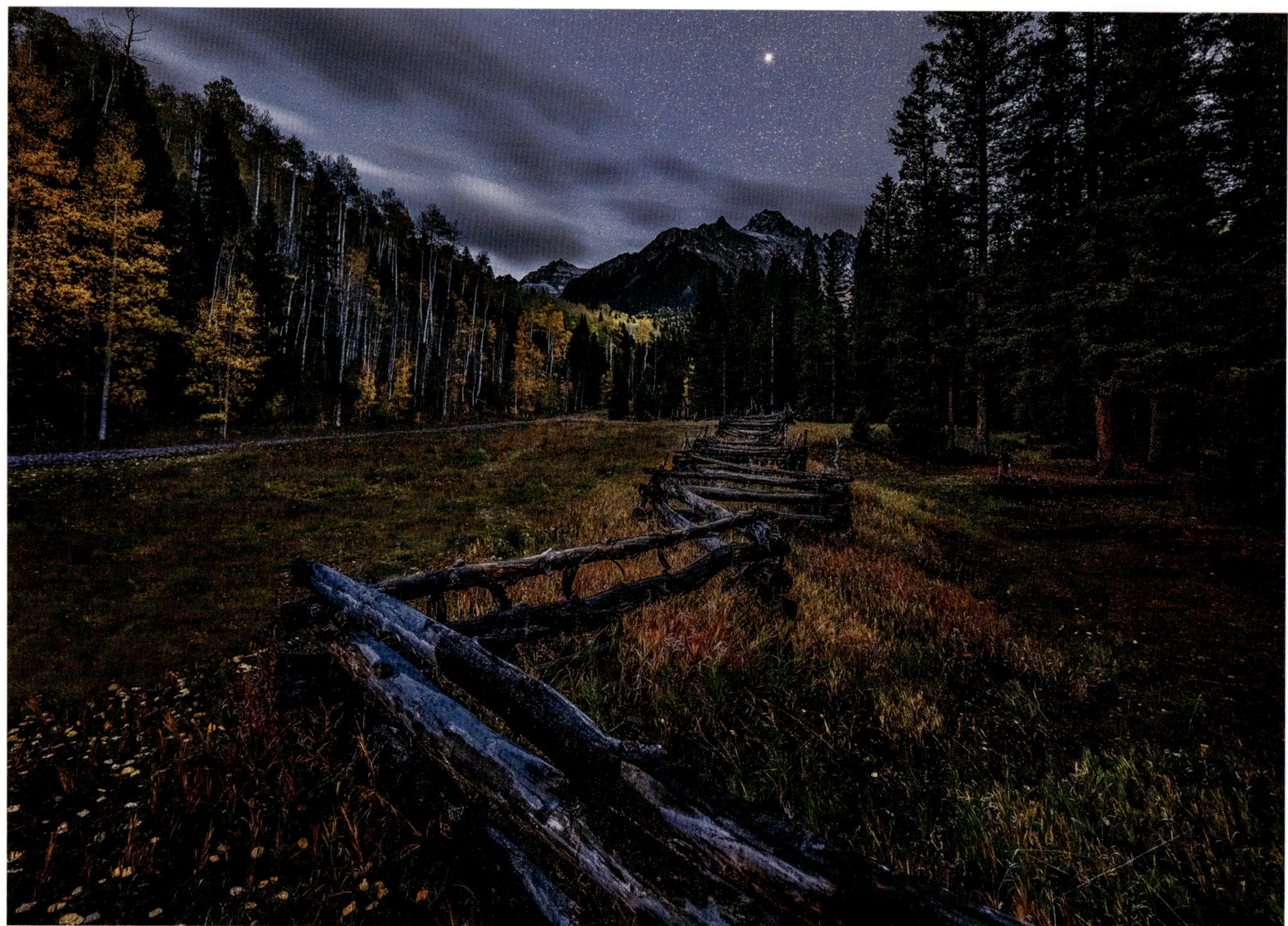

For this image of an aspen-bole fence below Mount Sneffels, the rule of 500 said I should use a 36-second exposure. However, since it was taken during astronomical twilight and I was using high-quality gear with a wide aperture, I lowered this to 25 seconds. Sony a7 III, 14mm, f/2.8, 25 seconds, ISO 1600.

Rule of 500

With this rule, you take 500 divided by the focal length of your lens to determine the shutter speed. For example, if you are shooting with a 50mm lens, you take 500 / 50 = 10. So 10 seconds would be your shutter speed. If you are shooting with a 17mm lens, you take 500 / 17 = 29.4. So 30 seconds would be your shutter speed.

If you are not using a full-frame camera, then you will need to first multiply the focal length of your lens by the crop factor before using the rule of 500. For example, if you are using a 16mm lens on a camera with a 1.5 crop factor, you will multiply 16mm x 1.5 to get 24mm as your effective focal length. Then take 500 / 24= 20.8. So 20 seconds would be your shutter speed.

While this is called a rule, it's really just a suggestion and a good starting point in determining your shutter speed. Once you've become more experienced shooting at night, you will get a feel for how different exposure lengths will look with your camera and your intended use of the images. You can then adjust the shutter speed a little to your liking.

You might consider straying from the rule of 500 and using slightly longer exposures in the following circumstances:

- If you are facing due north (or south in the Southern Hemisphere), the stars will move slower, and you can get away with a little longer exposure.

- If you don't have the optimal camera and lenses for night photography, you might want to increase the exposure time to reduce noise and improve image quality. The longer exposures will produce more elongated stars, but it may be a worthwhile trade-off when shooting with lower-quality equipment.

- When shooting with lenses that are 35mm or longer, the rule of 500 will require shorter exposure times, which will reduce image quality. In this case, it may sometimes be worthwhile to use a slightly longer exposure to get a higher quality image.

You might consider using shorter exposures in the following circumstances:

- If you are shooting under a bright moon or during twilight, the extra light could allow you to get away with shorter exposures and still get good quality images. The shorter exposure will allow the stars to appear even less elongated.

- If you are shooting with a wide lens and are using good equipment for night photography, you can often use shorter exposures. For example, if you are shooting with a 14mm lens, the rule of 500 states that the shutter speed should be 36 seconds. I usually use a shutter speed of 20-30 seconds in this situation. You can still get good quality images with these exposure times.

NPF Rule

While the rule of 500 usually does a good job of striking a balance between getting high-quality images and minimizing star trails, it will not eliminate star trails entirely. To make the star trails almost entirely unnoticeable, you can instead use the NPF Rule. This rule factors in your camera's megapixel count to determine how long you can expose an image before seeing elongation in the stars. This rule almost always gives shorter exposure times than the rule of 500. As a result, there will be more noise and lower image quality. You can offset this by stacking photos of the sky, as I describe in Chapter IX. I recommend stacking at least 2-3 images if you are using the NPF Rule. For single exposures, I still recommend following the advice in the last section on the rule of 500 for determining exposure time.

It's a lot more challenging to calculate exposure lengths with the NPF rule. I will spare you the details because the PhotoPills app I described in Chapter II will now do these calculations for you in the Spot Stars section.

The rule of 500 and NPF rule only apply if you want the stars to appear as points of light, not as star trails. The camera settings for star trails will be covered in Chapter VII.

ISO

Determining which ISO will maximize image quality and minimize noise is tricky and varies by camera model. In most cases, I recommend using the high-

To capture this stitched panorama of the aurora borealis over northern Alaska, I set my camera to its highest native ISO, which was 6400. If the northern lights had been brighter, I would have used a lower ISO to avoid overexposing them. I intentionally overexposed the moon, since it is much too bright to properly expose in a single exposure at night. Canon 5D II, 24mm, f/2.8, 10 seconds, ISO 6400, five images stitched together.

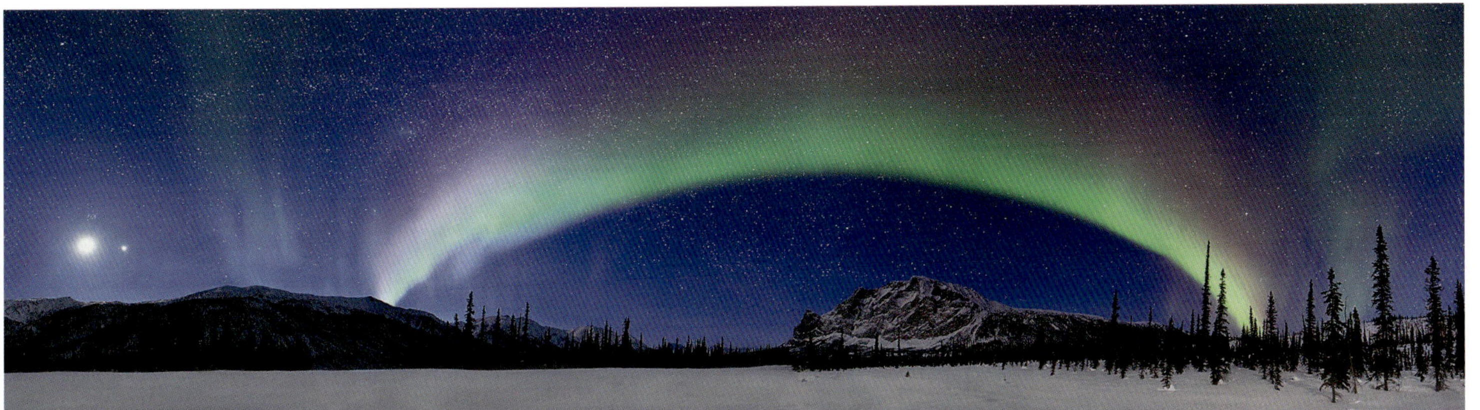

est native ISO on your camera that doesn't cause any highlights to be blown out. Native ISOs are represented by a number, such as 3200 or 6400. In tests I performed, both my Nikon D800e and Canon 5D Mark II performed best at their highest native ISO of 6400. So I left it at this ISO and only lowered it if I was overexposing the highlights.

There are some cameras that perform slightly better at lower ISOs of around 1600. However, the difference in noise between an image taken at ISO 1600 and your camera's highest native ISO will usually be minimal. The noise can start to noticeably increase at ISOs under 1600 since you'll be significantly underexposing the image. When you brighten the image in post-processing, you will also bring out a lot of noise.

One situation in which you don't need to worry much about ISO is if you are using an ISO invariant camera. These cameras are designed to generate the same amount of noise regardless of the ISO you use. However, some cameras that claim to be ISO invariant are not truly invariant at the lowest ISOs. So you should still raise the ISO to at least 800 or 1600. This will also make the image bright enough to view on your LCD screen. I typically leave the ISO on my Sony A7 III at 1600, since it is ISO invariant. That way, I usually don't have to worry about overexposing the highlights.

If you want to know exactly where your camera performs best, you can test it by taking otherwise identical images under no moon at different ISOs. Make sure you are comparing apples to apples by adjusting the Exposure slider in Lightroom so that all photos appear equally bright. For example, you should lower the exposure of an ISO 6400 image one stop (to a setting of -1.00 on the Exposure slider) to compare it to an ISO 3200 image.

You should avoid using extended ISOs. These ISOs are generally represented by letters such as H1 or H2.

I captured this image under a quarter moon on One Foot Island in the South Pacific. I first took a test shot at ISO 6400 and verified that this would not overexpose the highlights. If the moon had been any brighter, I likely would have had to lower the ISO. Nikon D800e, 14mm, f/2.8, 25 seconds, ISO 6400.

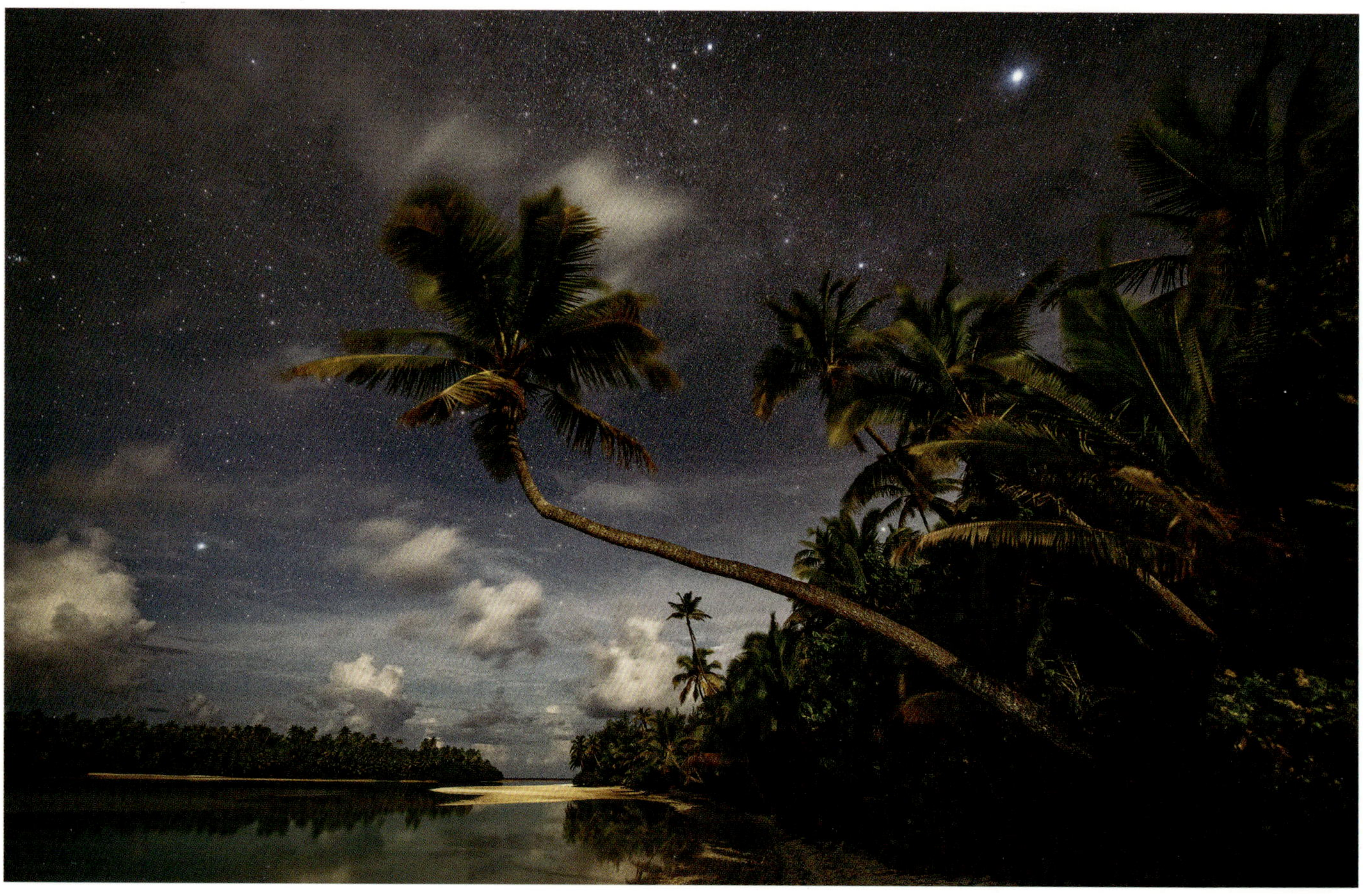

With extended ISOs, the camera software is just manipulating the data that was read from the sensors. It won't improve the image quality, and when shooting with manual settings at night, it could cause the image to be overexposed.

The only time you might want to use extended ISOs at night is if you are taking a test shot. You can use a very high ISO with a short exposure of a few seconds to get a bright image on your LCD screen. This can quickly give you a good idea of what your composition looks like. However, you should switch back to a native ISO when you are done taking your test shots.

Once you've decided on an ISO, you can take an image and check to see if any highlights are blown out. If you have the highlight alert enabled on your camera, any blown-out highlights will blink when you view the image on your LCD screen. Alternatively, if there is a spike at the very right edge of your histogram, you will know that highlights are blown out. An image with overexposed highlights will be of noticeably lower quality than an image that is slightly underexposed from the use of lower ISOs at night. So you're better off using lower ISOs if there's any chance of blowing out the highlights.

If there is a full or gibbous moon out, or if you are shooting during twilight, it can be much easier to overexpose the image. In this situation, you can start with a lower ISO of around 1600 and do the same test shots described above until you get a good exposure with no blown-out highlights.

One exception to avoiding blown out highlights is if you include the moon in the shot. It is so bright that you would have to lower the ISO and shutter speed way too much to avoid overexposing the moon. This would significantly reduce the quality of the rest of the image. You're better off letting the moon be overexposed or blending multiple exposures, as will be described in Chapter IX.

Another way you can blow out the highlights is if your image includes bright sources of light other than the moon, like lava, fire, lightning, or the northern lights. Photographing these light sources is described in detail in the next chapter.

When you use high ISOs at night, it could cause your photos to look way too bright on your camera's LCD screen. However, you should never rely on the image on your LCD screen to determine proper exposure. Only rely on the histogram or the highlight alert on your camera. If the image appears so bright that you have difficulty visualizing how the final image will look, you can change the brightness on the LCD screen to its lowest setting (assuming it has adjustable brightness). You can also do some test shots with shorter exposures to see a darker version of the photo. However, you should not use these test shots. Make sure and increase the exposure length before taking your real images.

If the photo does appear too bright out of the camera, it can be easily darkened later using the Exposure slider in Lightroom or a Levels adjustment in Photoshop. The good thing about darkening images is that it will also make the noise less noticeable in the photograph.

FOCUSING

The easiest way to get a night shot in focus is to set your camera up during the day and get your focus right before it ever gets dark. However, if you can't do this or you need to change your focus during the night, there are several ways to accomplish this.

Focusing at Infinity

If you don't have any near foreground objects in your image, you can simply focus at infinity. The easiest way to focus at infinity is to turn the focus ring on your lens to the infinity marker (∞). However, this isn't always reliable. On varifocal zoom lenses, the actual spot where infinity is will vary depending on the focal length you have chosen. Parfocal zoom lenses, on the other hand, will not alter the focus as you change the focal length. However, the infinity marker on a parfocal lens or a fixed focal length lens could be off just a little bit. One exception to this is if your lens has a hard stop at infinity, and the focus ring won't move past infinity. In this case, you should be able to reliably focus at infinity by turning the focus ring until it stops.

If the moon is out and you have an autofocus lens, there is a simple way to focus at infinity. Simply switch your lens to autofocus and center your camera viewfinder on the moon. The autofocus should work

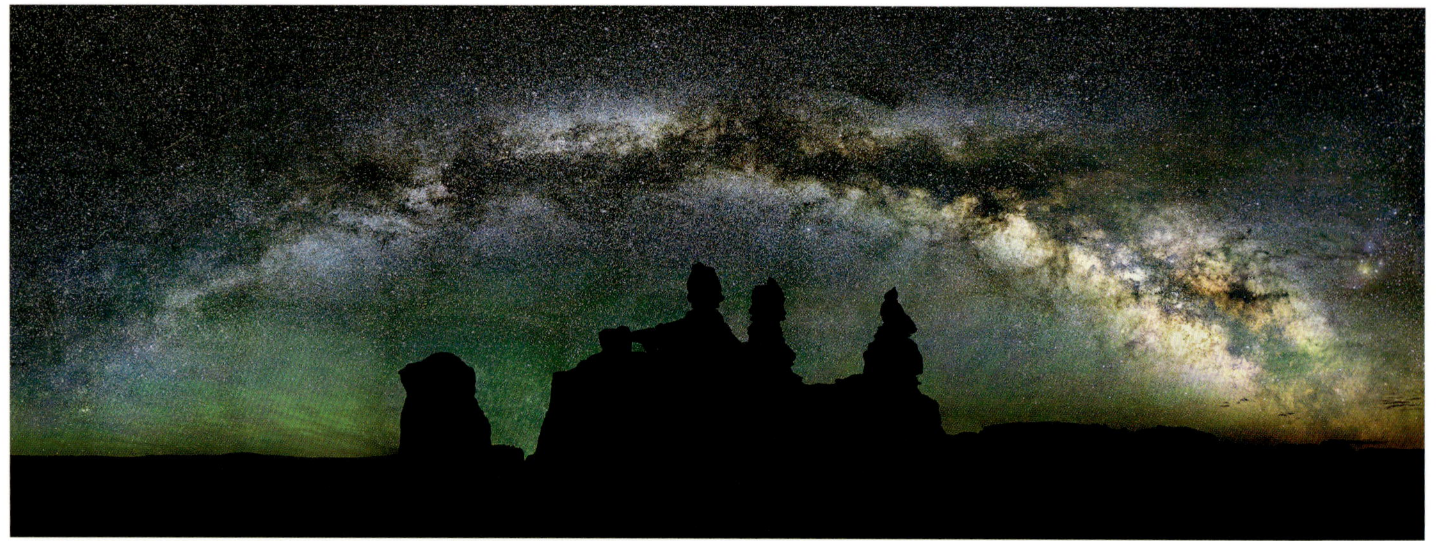

The rock formations in Goblin Valley were about 200 feet away from me, so I was able to focus at infinity. Even if the rock formations had been a little closer, I wouldn't have had to worry about focus as much as usual. Since there was no moon out and the rocks were rendered as silhouettes, they had very little detail anyway. It wouldn't have mattered much if they were a bit out of focus. Canon 5D II, 50mm, f/1.4, 10 seconds, ISO 6400, 36 images stitched together.

on an object as bright as the moon. Just push your shutter release halfway until the focus is locked in on the moon. Then switch your lens to manual focus and don't change the focus again. Some photographers like to use gaffer tape to tape down their focus ring once it is set to make sure it does not move. I personally don't find this necessary, but if you do this, you should check the focus on your LCD screen after taking a shot to confirm that you didn't accidentally move the focus ring while taping it down.

If the moon is not out or you don't have an autofocus lens, there is another way to focus at infinity, assuming you have Live View on your camera. First, manually set your focus ring near the infinity marker. Next, point your camera towards a bright star in the sky and turn on Live View. In Live View, the LCD screen will appear mostly black, but if you've pointed your camera towards a bright enough star, you should be able to see it. Center on this star, and then zoom in to about 10x magnification so you can see it clearly. The star should now be fairly bright on the screen. Gradually move your focus ring back and forth until the star appears as a small, sharp point of light.

If you have trouble with Live View or you have an older camera that doesn't have Live View, you can start by taking a shot with the focus set at the infinity marker on your lens. Then check your focus by zooming in on the image on your LCD screen. If the stars appear out of focus, you should move your focus ring slightly in one direction and take a second image. Now, compare the two photos. If the second photo appears sharper than the first, you can keep moving your focus ring in the same direction until you get the sharpest possible image. If the second photo appears less sharp than the first, you'll need to start moving your focus ring in the opposite direction until you get an image with optimal sharpness.

If you are using a varifocal zoom lens and you change the focal length of the lens while shooting, you will need to refocus your image before taking more shots. If you don't know whether your zoom lens is varifocal, you should check the image to see if it is in focus and adjust the focus if necessary.

Regardless of how you choose to focus your lens, you should always zoom in on your image on your LCD screen to check the focus. Make sure that objects in both the land and the sky are in sharp focus. It can be very frustrating to spend all night shooting only to find out later that all of your images were out of focus! Sometimes, if the image is just a little out of focus, it can produce more chromatic aberration around the stars. This will usually appear as an unnatural magenta color around the edges of stars. If you see this, you can adjust your focus slightly until the chromatic aberration is minimized or eliminated.

Focusing Closer Than Infinity

If you have a close foreground subject in your image, you can't simply focus at infinity and take the shot. You'll instead want to focus at twice the distance of the closest object in your photograph. To focus at a precise distance like this, you can simply turn on a flashlight, place it at the distance you want to focus, and use autofocus to focus directly on the flashlight. When the focus is locked in, switch back to manual focus to make sure it remains focused at this spot.

Focusing on the flashlight won't work with Rokinon lenses, as they do not support autofocus. In this case, you can again place the flashlight at the spot you want to focus on (or simply shine a flashlight on the spot you want to focus on). Then, turn on Live View and zoom in and focus on that spot in the same manner I described for focusing on the stars.

Another way to focus if you have an autofocus lens is with a laser pointer. You can shine the laser pointer at the spot where you want to focus and then center your camera on that spot and push your shutter release halfway until the focus is locked. As always, when using autofocus at night, immediately switch back to manual focus once you have the focus locked in place.

If none of these options are available to you, you will need to set the focus at approximately twice the distance of the nearest object using the focus ring on your camera.

After you've set the focus using any of the above techniques, you can take a photo and view the image on your LCD screen. Carefully check the image to see if both the nearest and most distant objects are in focus. If only the nearest object is in focus, you'll need to focus a little farther away and take another shot. If only the most distant object is in focus, you'll need to focus a little closer and take another shot. Repeat this until you have an image that is sharp throughout.

If you wind up with an image that has the middle ground in focus but both the near and distant objects out of focus, it means you can't get everything in focus with the camera settings that you are using. In this case, you have a few options. You can recompose the image so that the nearest object is farther away. Or, you can switch to a wider lens that has more depth of field. You could also switch to a slightly smaller aperture to get more depth of field. However, you should avoid this if possible, as it will let less light into the camera and result in lower-quality images. Instead, I recommend focus stacking, where you take multiple photos with different focus points and later blend them in post-processing. This will be discussed in more detail in Chapter IX.

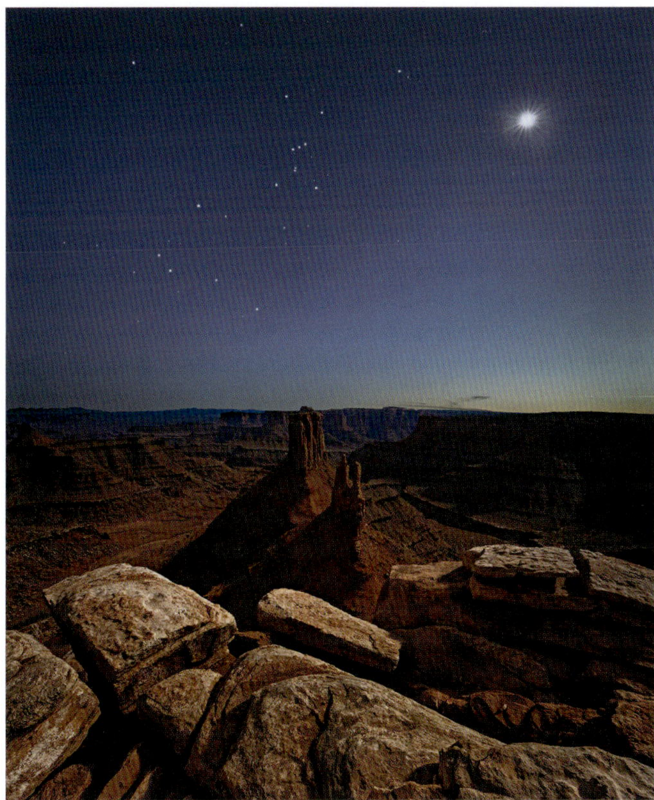

The moon and Orion are visible above an overlook in Utah during civil twilight. I was able to autofocus on the moon for the image of the sky. For the image of the land, I stacked and focus-stacked multiple exposures, using techniques described in Chapter IX. Nikon D800e, 48 exposures for foreground at f/4.0, 14mm, 30 seconds, ISO 6400; exposure for sky at f/2.8, 14mm, 15 seconds,

.

Understanding Hyperfocal Distance

Up to this point, I've avoided discussing hyperfocal distance, as it can be a difficult concept to grasp if you are not already familiar with it. Understanding hyperfocal distance can allow you to calculate whether everything will be in focus beforehand, rather than using the somewhat ad-hoc approach described in the last section.

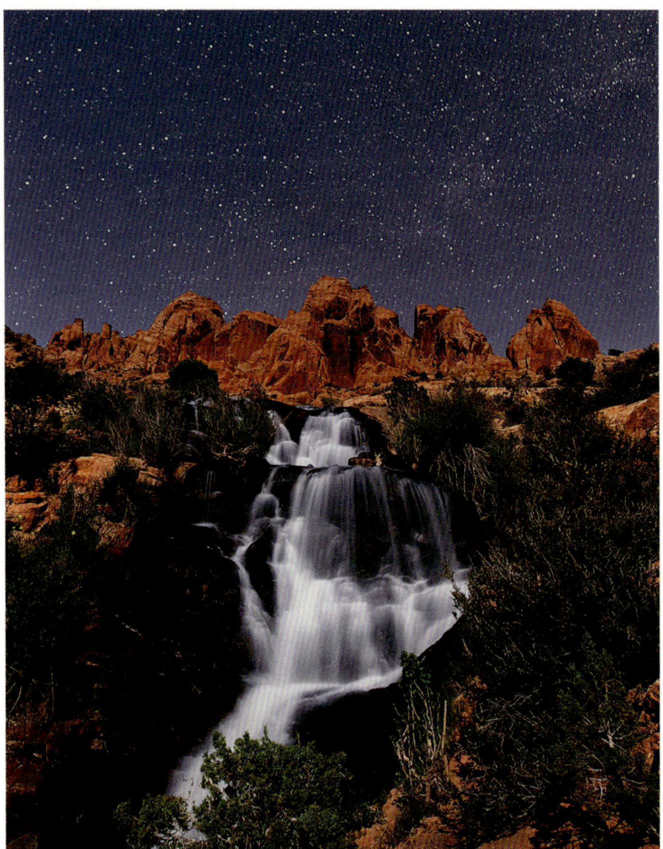

I shot this image of Faux Falls near Moab using a 24mm lens set at f/2.8. The hyperfocal distance was 22.3 feet, which would have allowed me to get everything in focus from 11.2 feet to infinity. However, the nearest object in the image was about 7 feet from me, so I had to focus stack images, which will be explained in Chapter IX. Nikon D800e, 24mm, f/2.8, 20 seconds, ISO 3200.

In the simplest terms, the hyperfocal distance is the closest distance you can focus your camera while still keeping everything at infinity in acceptable focus. When you focus your lens at the hyperfocal distance, everything from half that distance to infinity will be in acceptable focus. So if you focus at the hyperfocal distance, you will maximize the depth of field in the image. However, this does not leave you with much room for error. If you focus just a little bit in front of the hyperfocal distance, it can render the stars out of focus. Therefore, to give you the most room for error, I still recommend focusing at approximately twice the distance of the nearest object in your photograph. As long your focus point is farther than the hyperfocal distance, you can be assured that everything will be in acceptable focus.

If your focus point is closer than the hyperfocal distance, then you won't be able to get everything in the image in focus using your current camera settings and a single exposure.

If, on the other hand, the nearest object in your photograph is farther away than the hyperfocal distance, you can simply focus at infinity, and everything in your image will be in acceptable focus. Alternatively, you can still focus at twice the distance of the nearest object. This will give you a little more room for error, but since focusing at infinity is easier, this can be a good option when you don't have a close foreground.

Lens & Aperture	Hyperfocal Distance	Nearest in Focus	Farthest in Focus
14mm f/2.8	7.6 ft	3.8 ft	∞
24mm f/1.8	35.4 ft	17.7	∞
35mm f/1.8	75.3 ft	37.7	∞
50mm f/1.8	153.6	76.8	∞

Table 4.1: Hyperfocal distances with common camera settings for night photography.

I use the term acceptable focus because you won't actually be getting the maximum possible sharpness at the nearest and farthest points when focusing at the hyperfocal distance. Instead, you will get what is considered to be an acceptable standard of sharpness.

There are many software programs and websites that can calculate the hyperfocal distance for you if you enter your camera settings. One such site is DOF Master at http://www.dofmaster.com/dofjs.html. You can enter different settings to get a feel for how hyperfocal distance changes with different camera settings. It will also tell how the near and far focus points will change. When you are out shooting in the field, I recommend using an app for a mobile device that can do these calculations. The PhotoPills app that I described in Chapter II will do this.

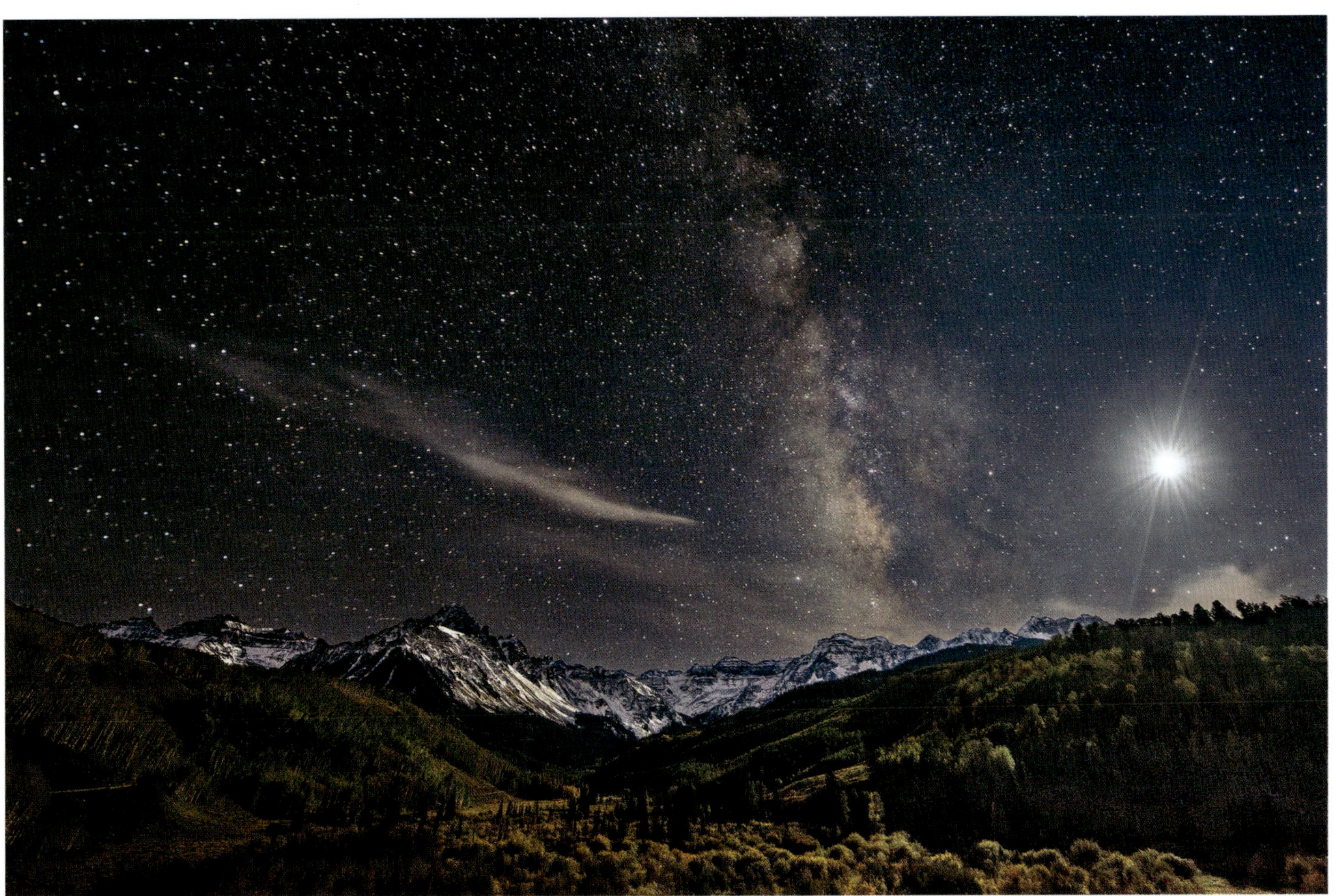

Since this scene in Colorado's San Juan Mountains was illuminated by the moon, I set the white balance to daylight and later lowered it to 4600K in Lightroom. Nikon D800e, 15mm, f/2.8, 20 seconds, ISO 2000.

I've provided a table on the previous page showing some hyperfocal distances for camera settings that are commonly used when shooting at night. These figures are for full-frame digital cameras. If you don't have a full-frame camera, most software programs should allow you to enter your camera model or the crop factor before calculating the hyperfocal distance. Remember that you need to focus your camera at the hyperfocal distance to keep the near and far distance in acceptable focus.

It is, of course, impossible to focus precisely at the exact hyperfocal distances listed in the table, so you want the nearest object in your image to be farther away than the "Nearest in Focus" point to give room for error. Then, focus at about twice the distance of the nearest object, which will be farther away than the hyperfocal distance.

If you want to be sure that your image is well above the acceptable standard of sharpness, you may want to have the nearest object be at least as far away as the hyperfocal distance, with your focus set to twice the distance of the nearest object. The numbers in the table just show the theoretical maximum depth of field with acceptable sharpness that you can get with these camera settings. You should always still check that your image is sharp by zooming in on your LCD screen after you take your first shot.

As you can see from the table, ultra-wide-angle lenses offer far more depth of field than longer lenses. So if you want a close object in the foreground, you're usually better off using a wide-angle lens.

WHITE BALANCE

When shooting at night, you'll usually need to use a lower color temperature for your white balance than you use during the day. If the moon is out, I've found that a color temperature of around 4600K works well. If there is no moon out, you'll likely need to reduce the color temperature to about 4200K to give a neutral appearance to the sky, without a blue or yellow color cast. You might need to lower it even more if there is a lot of light pollution, causing the scene to appear orange. In any of these situations, you could use a custom white balance on your camera. This can give you a better idea of how the colors will appear based on the image on your LCD screen. However, it's probably easier to keep it in daylight mode. As long as you're shooting in RAW, you can always change the white balance settings later. It's easier to fine-tune the white balance settings on a computer screen than to try to get it perfect in camera.

Twilight	Moon	No Moon
Daylight	4600K	4200K

Table 4.2: White balance recommendations.

If you shoot during nautical or astronomical twilight, I recommend setting the white balance on your camera to daylight. If you shoot about 20-30 minutes after sunset or before sunrise, during what is often called the blue hour, you may need to set it even higher.

NOISE REDUCTION

Most cameras have one or two noise reduction features built into them. Since you're constantly battling noise when taking photos at night, these features may seem very well suited for night photography. Unfortunately, while they can be useful with very long exposures, they're not quite as helpful with shorter exposures.

Long Exposure Noise Reduction

The Long Exposure Noise Reduction feature that is found in most DSLRs and mirrorless cameras helps reduce dark noise in an image. Dark noise is caused by heat from your camera's circuitry. It may also be referred to as dark current noise or thermal noise.

Dark noise increases in proportion to the length of the exposure. For exposures under one minute at night, the primary source of noise is photon noise, not dark noise. Long Exposure Noise Reduction does not target photon noise, so it will usually have only a small impact on noise levels.

When using this feature, your camera has to take a second exposure, which is known as a dark frame. This exposure takes just as long as the initial exposure. If you're shooting a rapidly changing scene, like one with the northern lights or moving clouds, you don't want to have to wait for the noise reduction after every shot, as you might miss the best photo while waiting. Also, if you are taking repeated exposures to capture star trails, meteors, or lightning, you must have the noise reduction off in order to minimize the time between exposures. The same is true if you're capturing stitched images, as you want to minimize the amount that the stars move between each shot.

The only time I recommend having Long Exposure Noise Reduction on when taking shots under one minute is when you are shooting single exposures of a slowly-changing scene. In this circumstance, you can afford to wait for the camera to take a dark frame after every shot and it will reduce the noise a little bit.

Dark noise decreases when you shoot in colder temperatures. So if you are taking photos in frigid weather, you probably don't need to worry about it. If, on the other hand, it is warm out and you can shoot in shorts and a t-shirt, dark noise may become noticeable even with exposures under one minute. You can benefit more from Long Exposure Noise Reduction in this situation.

If you don't want to wait for the camera to take a dark frame after every shot, you can instead create your own dark frame. Simply put your lens cap and eyepiece cover on (or cover the eyepiece with a cloth or hat) and take a photo. This image should be taken in similar temperatures and with the same camera settings with which you will be shooting your other photos. If you change your camera settings, you'll need to take a new dark frame. Later, when you choose a photo you like, you can open it and the dark frame in Photoshop. Stack the dark frame on a layer directly on top of the photograph. Then, change the blending mode on the layer with the dark frame to Subtract. That's it! Any dark noise captured in the dark frame will be subtracted from the image. Since the dark noise in the two photos should be very similar, it can help reduce the noise.

Since it is so easy to do, I usually take at least one dark frame when shooting at night. This way, I can use the

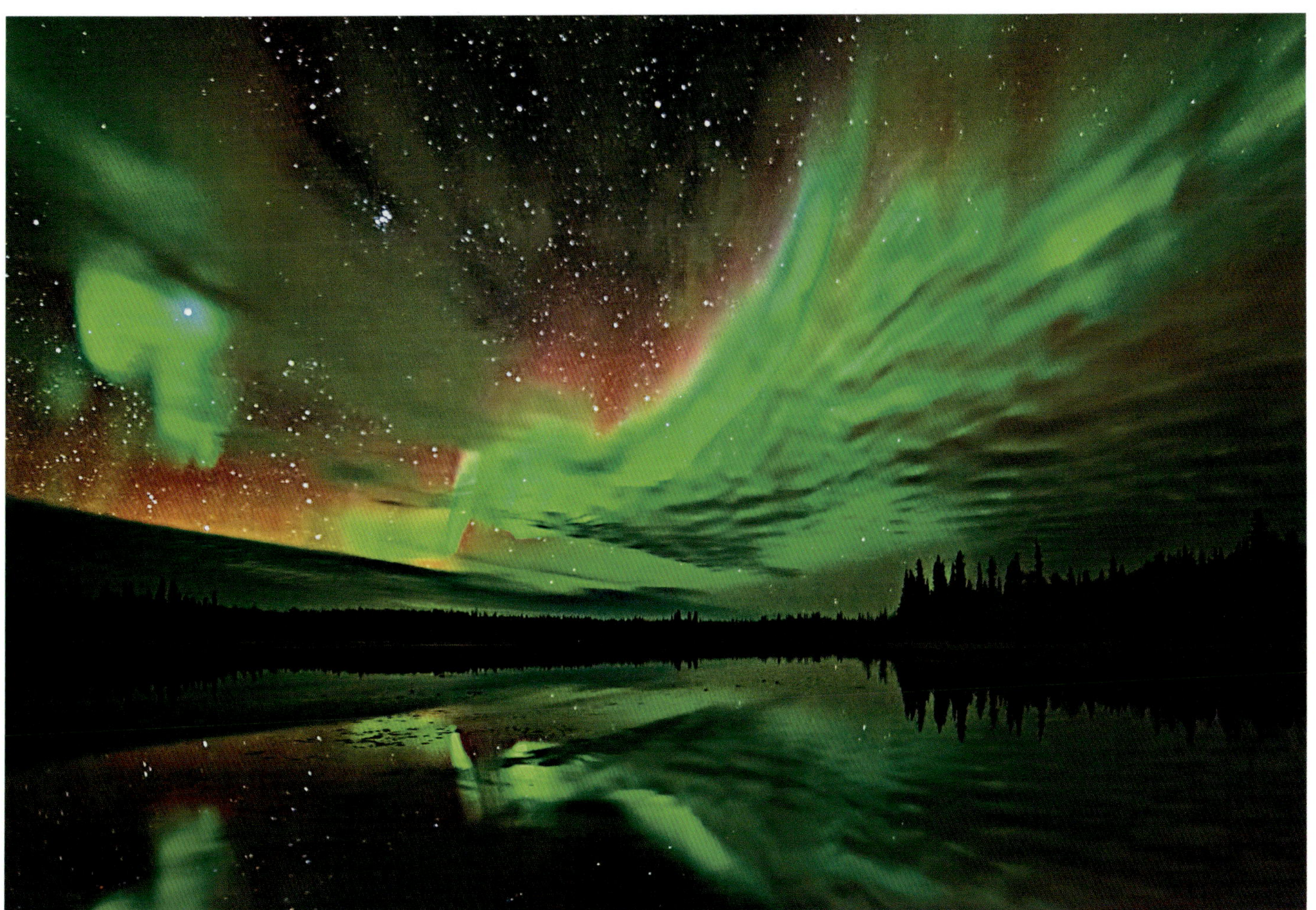

This photo shows the northern lights reflected in a pond near Yellowknife, Canada. Since there was no moon out and the image was taken after twilight, I used a white balance of 4200K. Also, it was very cold outside, so I didn't have to worry about reducing dark noise with exposures of just 15 seconds. Nikon D800e, 14mm, f/2.8, 15 seconds, ISO 6400.

---

dark frame if the need arises. It's much less time-consuming to take a dark frame that can later be applied to any image you take than it is to have the camera take a dark frame after every photo.

A disadvantage of taking your own dark frame is that it won't be quite as accurate as the dark frame taken with Long Exposure Noise Reduction. This dark frame will be taken immediately after every shot, and therefore the temperature and conditions in which you take the two images will be almost identical. However, in most circumstances, it's unlikely you'll notice the difference.

A bigger disadvantage of taking your own dark frame is that it will be less effective at reducing noise if you make too many adjustments to the image in Lightroom or Adobe Camera Raw before applying the dark frame in Photoshop. To get optimal results, you should only make adjustments to the White Balance slider and to the Highlights and Shadows sliders if you need to recover detail in these areas. Set everything else to zero in Lightroom. You'll need to apply the same settings to the dark frame as you do to the image. Then, open the image in Photoshop and apply the dark frame. You can make additional adjustments to the image in Photoshop or, if you prefer, import the image back into Lightroom and continue working on it there.

Long Exposure Noise Reduction can be a lot more useful for very long exposures (5+ minutes), as dark noise increases proportionally with the length of the exposure. However, even when shooting star trails, I rarely recommend doing exposures over five minutes at night with a digital camera. This is because you can get higher quality images by taking a series of shorter exposures and combining them in Photoshop. If you do this, you can't have Long Exposure Noise Reduction turned on, as the delay will result in gaps in your star trails. You can, however, benefit from shooting your own dark frame. I will discuss this in more detail in Chapter VII.

High ISO Noise Reduction

As mentioned in the last section, photon noise (sometimes referred to as photon shot noise or shot noise) is more problematic than dark noise for exposures under one minute. This noise is caused by the random nature in which photons hit the CCDs on the camera sensor.

Some cameras have a noise reduction feature called High ISO Noise Reduction. In newer cameras, this feature targets both photon noise and dark noise. However, unless you're using the RAW conversion software made for your camera, this feature only works on JPEG images. As I'll discuss in the next section, I strongly recommend shooting in RAW, not JPEG. If you are shooting in RAW and using Lightroom or Adobe Camera Raw, this feature will not affect your photos, so it doesn't matter if it is on or off. If you do shoot in JPEG, I recommend keeping this turned off. The in-camera noise reduction can blur details in your image, which you won't be able to recover later. You can instead reduce noise in Lightroom or using software called Topaz DeNoise, as I'll discuss in Chapter X.

Remapping Hot Pixels

Many photographs taken with long exposures at night

I shot this photo in July in Utah's Canyon Rims Recreation Area. It was over 70°F on this night, so dark noise became noticeable even with exposures of 25 seconds. There were hot pixels, and the bottom corners of the image had an unnatural red color. I therefore took my own dark frame and was able to minimize the noise in the photo. Nikon D800e, 14mm, f/2.8, 25 seconds, ISO 3200, focus stacked for increased depth of field.

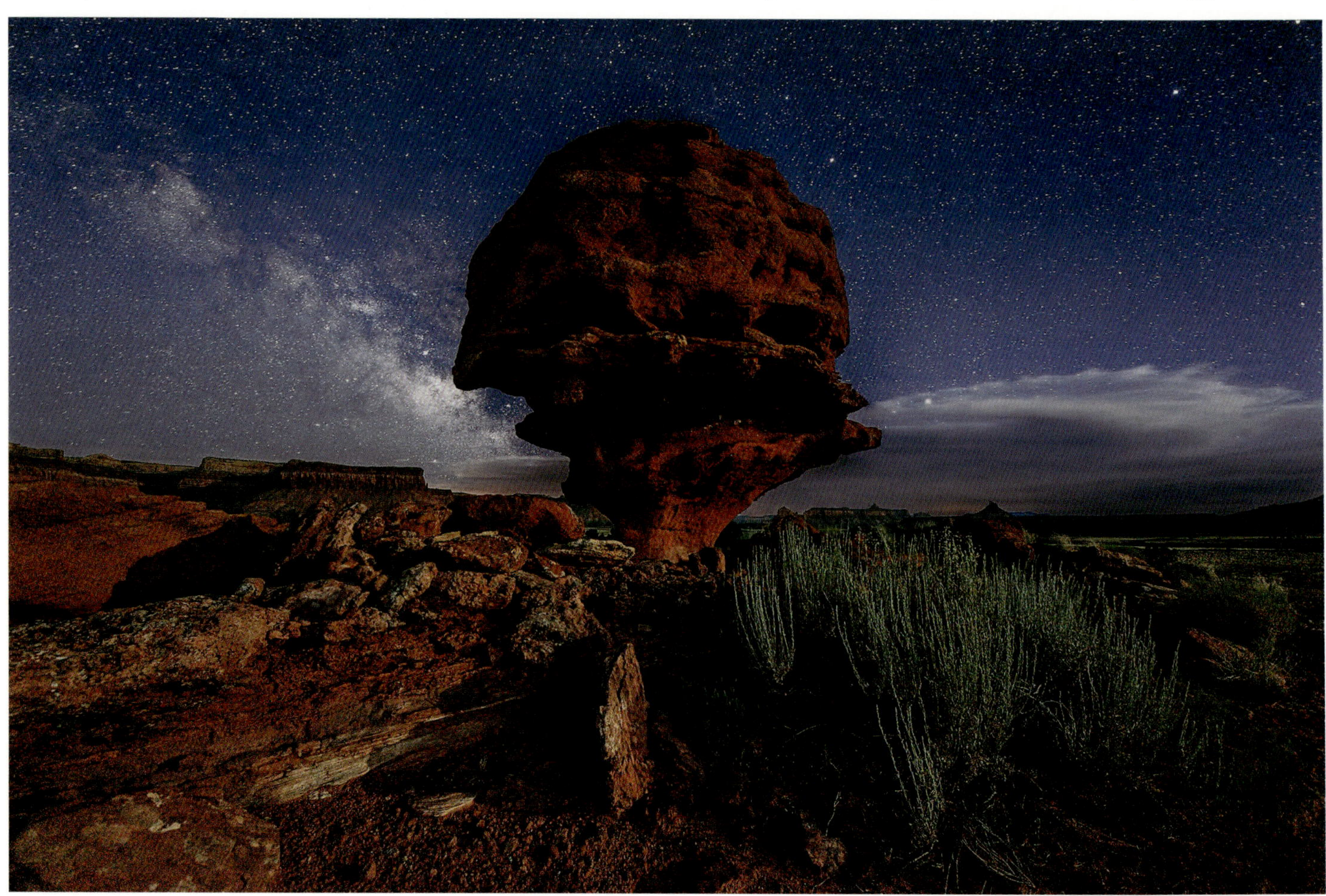

will have hot or even dead pixels, which are random, bright pixels that should not be in the photo. If you're getting a lot of hot pixels, many cameras allow you to remap the pixels so that your camera automatically corrects these pixels. With modern Nikon cameras, you can manually run sensor cleaning twice in a row to trigger the remapping. With modern Canons, you can run a manual sensor clean for 30 seconds. With a modern Sony, you can set the date on your camera to one month in the future, then turn the camera off. This works because the camera automatically does a pixel remapping every month.

Be sure to do the remapping before taking any dark frames, as described previously, as the remapping will alter the dark frames. Also, remapping only works with RAW images, which is another reason to always shoot in RAW, as described next.

RAW vs. JPEG

Since you are taking the time to read this book, you are probably serious about getting high-quality images at night. I therefore recommend that you always shoot in RAW mode with your camera. When you shoot in JPEG, the camera immediately throws out a lot of the data that is gathered by the sensors. To get the most out of your images, you should begin with as much of this information as possible. The only way to do this is to shoot in RAW.

One reason you want to keep this data is that you will often have very dark shadows when shooting at night. If you shoot in RAW, you can later recover some of the details in the shadows, something that can be difficult or impossible to do when shooting in JPEG.

Conversely, it's possible to blow out details in the brightest parts of the image at night, especially if you're shooting under a bright moon or during twilight. You can often recover slightly-overexposed highlights when shooting in RAW.

Another important reason to shoot in RAW is that you can later adjust the white balance settings in Lightroom or Adobe Camera Raw. While the daylight setting may work when shooting during twilight or under a moon, it won't often work when shooting under no moon. You could use a custom white balance on your camera, but there is no guarantee that you will get it just right. In this case, you would need to fine-tune the white balance in post-processing, and you can't do this with JPEG images.

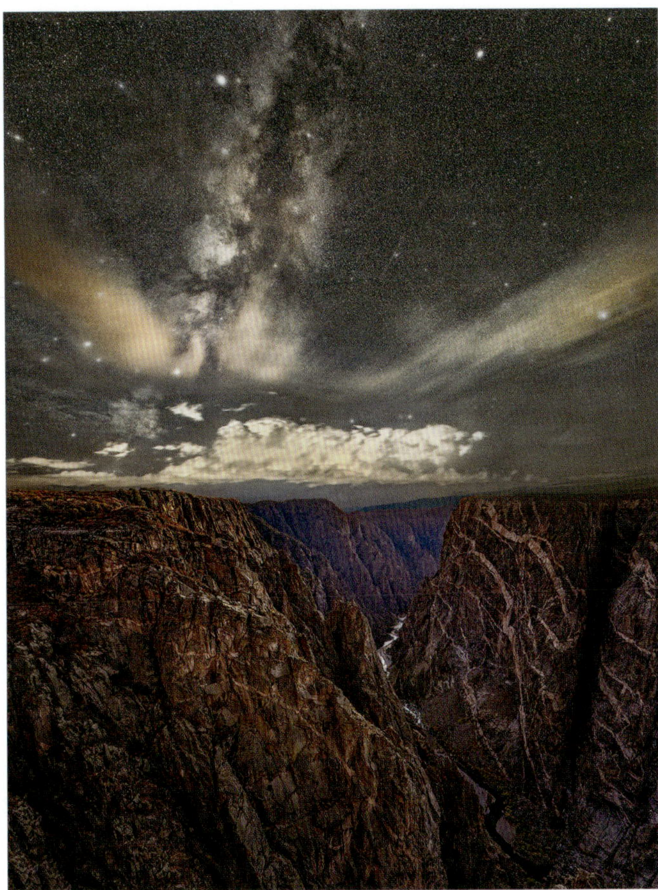

The Milky Way rises above the Black Canyon of the Gunnison in Colorado. By shooting in RAW, I was able to recover highlights in the clouds that may have been overexposed using JPEG. Nikon D800e, 18mm; exposure for land during twilight: f/10, 13 seconds, ISO 100; exposure for sky at night: f/2.8, 20 seconds, ISO 6400.

If you're not yet comfortable shooting in RAW, you can shoot RAW + JPEG. This will keep the RAW file and also produce a JPEG image. If you do this, I still recommend that you try to work with the RAW files until you're comfortable with them and no longer need the JPEGs.

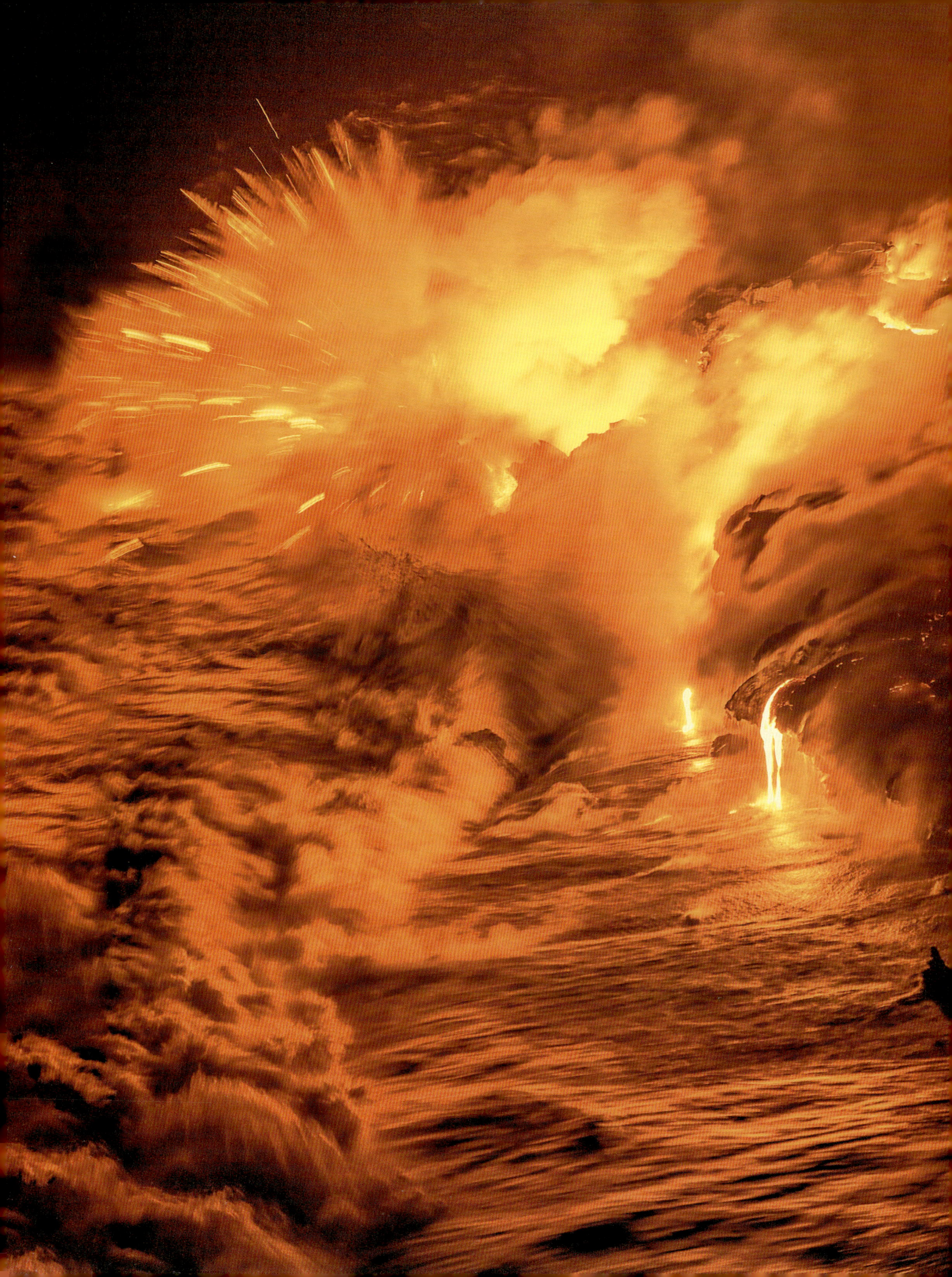

V. Natural Light Sources

When photographing during the day, the sun will usually be your only source of light. When shooting at night, you can capture many different natural light sources. This can make shooting at night a fascinating process, but it can also make it a lot more challenging. I will discuss most of the natural light sources that you can capture during the night and how to photograph each of them. Some of these light sources, like the moon, reflect sunlight off of them, but several others produce their own light.

THE MOON

The moon will often illuminate the subject you are photographing. However, it is more difficult to include the moon itself in an image. The easiest way to include the moon is to shoot it shortly before or after sunrise or sunset. At this time, it is dark enough for the moon to be clearly visible, but it's not so dark that the moon is significantly brighter than everything else. As a result, you can usually capture an image with a lot of detail in the moon and the landscape with a single exposure. However, these shots look more like daytime images, and you won't get any stars in the photo.

If you wait until it gets dark enough to see the stars, the moon will be so bright that it will be overexposed if you try to properly expose the rest of the scene. There are a few options for handling this.

You can let the moon be overexposed and render it as a round white blob in the image like it is in the photo on page 55. In this scenario, the moon won't look very interesting, but it can still produce a good image if you have other compelling elements in the photo.

Another option is to take two exposures - one short exposure that preserves the detail in the moon and one long exposure for the rest of the scene. Make sure the short exposure is one second or less; otherwise, the movement of the moon during the exposure can cause it to blur. Also, make sure you are not overexposing the moon in the shorter exposure.

You can blend these two exposures in Photoshop using techniques described in Chapter IX. It can, however, be difficult to achieve a natural-looking blend. In the long exposure, the sky around the moon will be much brighter than it is in the short exposure. You'll need to clone out the moon and the bright area around the moon in the long exposure. I only recommend this for those who are very proficient in Photoshop.

It is actually easier to place a short exposure of a moon into a night photo where no moon existed than to place it into an image where the moon existed. This is because you won't have to first clone out the moon from the long exposure. While I would never do this in a landscape photo, it is up to each photographer to decide how much artistic license to take. I just recommend that you openly disclose your techniques for creating the image.

A third option is to render a sunstar effect around the moon, as seen in the picture on the following page. To do this, you need to use a smaller aperture, such as f/9.0. This can significantly increase noise, as the lens lets much less light into the camera. However, the moon is bright enough that it can still produce acceptable results. You can use the rule of 500 to determine the shutter speed. The moon will have little detail in it, so it doesn't matter if it moves some during the exposure.

If you want to minimize noise and still capture a sunstar effect around the moon, you can take two exposures - one for the moon at f/9.0 or smaller and another for the rest of the scene at a wider aperture, like f/2.8. You can then blend the images in Photoshop. You'll probably need to darken the image taken with the wider aperture before adding in the moon from the other exposure. This is a little easier to accomplish than blending a short exposure that preserves the de-

---

Left: A dramatic steam explosion is seen on the Big Island of Hawaii as a lava bench collapses into the Pacific Ocean. Nikon D800e f/4.8, 1/8 second, ISO 400.

tail in the moon, but it still requires some experience with Photoshop.

It is easier to capture a good sunstar effect under a crescent moon than it is under a full or gibbous moon. Also, the appearance of the sunstar can vary depending on the lens that you use. So I recommend trying different aperture settings and using the widest aperture that produces an acceptable sunstar.

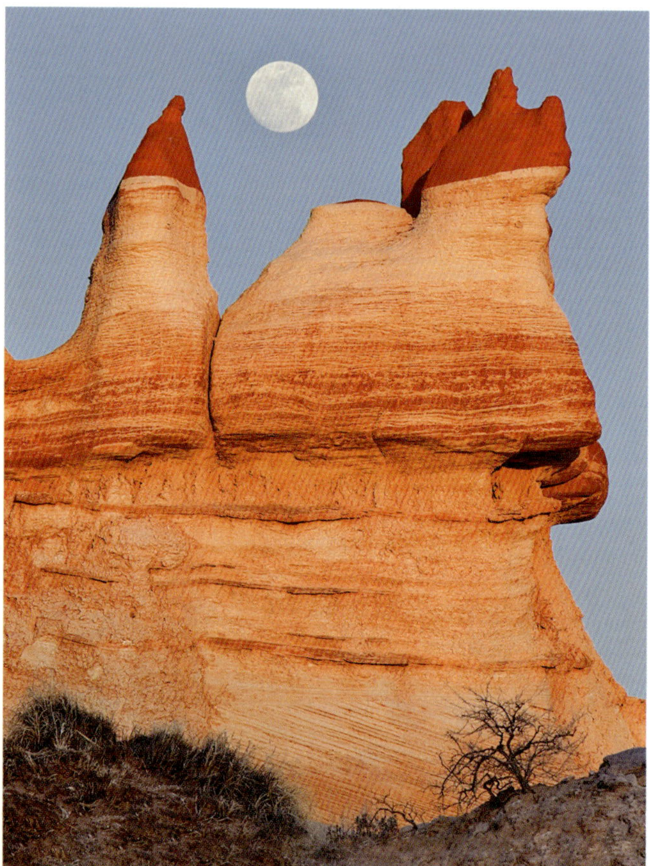

I took this image in a remote part of Arizona as the sun was setting. This was an ideal time to capture both the moon and the rock formation in a single exposure. However, it was still so bright out that it can't be considered a night shot. Canon 5D II, 200mm, f/16, 1/6 second, ISO 100.

You can capture a circular halo around the moon (as seen on page 154) when moonlight passes through ice crystals in high cirrus clouds. On rare occasions under a bright moon, you can also capture a moon dog, which appears as two bright rainbow-colored spots on the edge of the halo.

One last approach to photographing the moon is to take a very long exposure and capture a moon trail, as discussed in Chapter VII and seen on page 111. This is easier to do under a thin crescent moon.

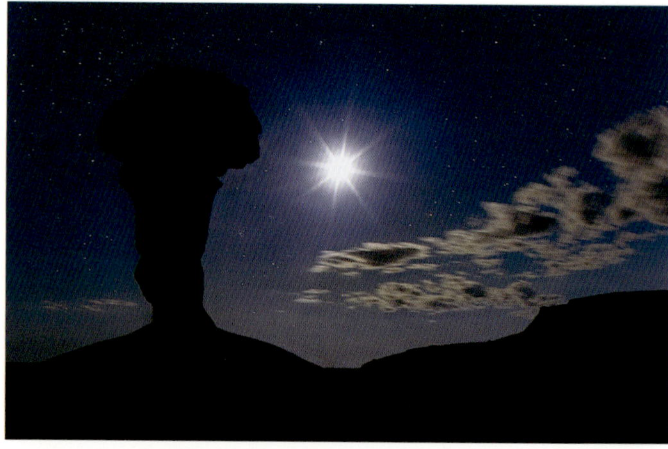

I captured this image of the quarter moon using an aperture of f/9.0. This relatively small aperture produced a sunstar effect around the moon. Canon 5D II, 24mm, f/9.0, 25 seconds, ISO 6400.

ECLIPSES

Eclipses are one of the most captivating celestial events you can witness, and you can take spectacular photographs of them. Solar eclipses only occur during the day, but I'll discuss them briefly because they are an astronomical event that night photographers may be interested in.

You can find a list of all upcoming solar and lunar eclipses and the locations where they can be viewed at https://www.timeanddate.com/eclipse/list.html.

Lunar Eclipses

A lunar eclipse occurs when Earth passes directly between the sun and the moon at night. During the first stage of the eclipse, you'll see just a small part of Earth's shadow covering the moon. If it is a total lunar eclipse, this shadow will grow until it completely blocks the moon. During totality, some light that passes through Earth's atmosphere will be refracted and still hit the moon. This refracted light will have a warm glow to it, and the moon will appear as an orange ball in the sky.

A lunar eclipse is challenging to photograph because you need to keep your exposures to about one second or less, or the moon will move too far during the exposure, causing it to blur. If you want to include foreground objects in your image, this exposure length will usually not be long enough to capture high-quality photos. You'll therefore need to blend two exposures - one short exposure for the moon and a long exposure for the rest of the scene.

Your histogram won't be too useful for the short exposure since the moon takes up a tiny part of the camera frame with most lenses. So you should zoom in on the moon to make sure it is properly exposed with a lot of detail. The exposure settings can vary a lot throughout the eclipse, especially if you photograph both the partial and total eclipse. If you are overexposing the moon, you'll need to lower the ISO and possibly use a smaller aperture during the partial eclipse.

You might be able to capture an eclipse and a foreground object in a single exposure if the eclipse occurs during civil or even nautical twilight. At this time, there may be enough light on the foreground to get good quality images with the short exposures that are required to photograph the moon.

Another time you can capture an eclipse with a single exposure is if you are using a long telephoto lens and don't include any foreground objects in the image. In this case, I recommend using a remote shutter release and mirror lock-up on a DSLR camera. When using a telephoto lens, even the slightest vibration caused by the mirror going up can cause the image to blur. With the mirror lock-up on, the first time you hit the shutter release, it will move the mirror up, and the second time you hit it, it will take the shot.

If you want very detailed images of an eclipse, you can use an equatorial mount. This device moves your camera along with the stars, moon, or sun and lets you take much longer exposures without blurring celestial objects. I discuss this in detail on pages 132-134. You can't include foreground objects when using an

A total lunar eclipse is visible over Moses and Zeus in Canyonlands National Park. To avoid blurring the moon, I blended separate exposures of the moon and the rest of the scene. I used a 600mm lens to shoot the moon so that I could also get a close-up image of the eclipse. I later down-resed the moon in the below image so that it matched the size of the moon from the longer exposure with a shorter lens. Nikon D800e; exposure for moon: 600mm, f/6.3, 0.6 seconds, ISO 6400; exposure for rest of scene: 70mm, f/2.8, 8 seconds, ISO 6400.

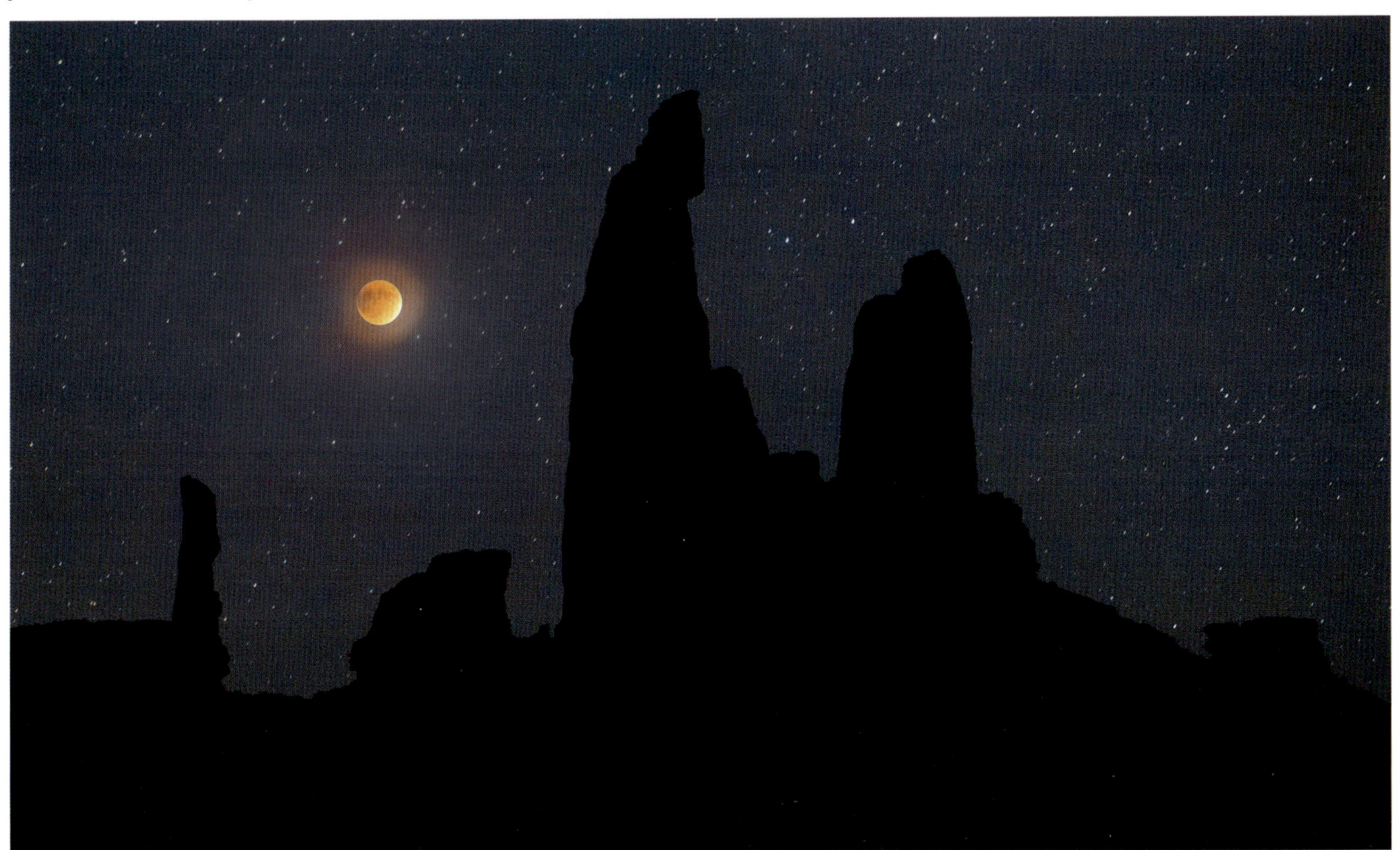

equatorial mount, as the movement will blur these objects. In this situation, you would again have to blend multiple exposures.

Another option when photographing an eclipse is to take images of many different stages of the eclipse, from the time it just begins to be covered by Earth's shadow until the time it is almost out of Earth's shadow. You can then create a composite image with many different moons at various stages. You can include the landscape with the moons arcing above it or exclude the foreground and just include the moons in the night sky. I did this with a solar eclipse in the image on page 133.

Solar Eclipses

A solar eclipse occurs when the moon passes directly between Earth and the sun, and the moon partially or fully blocks the disk of the sun. If the moon completely blocks the disk of the sun, it is called a total eclipse. If the moon's disk passes directly in front of the sun, but the disk appears smaller than the sun, it is called an annular eclipse.

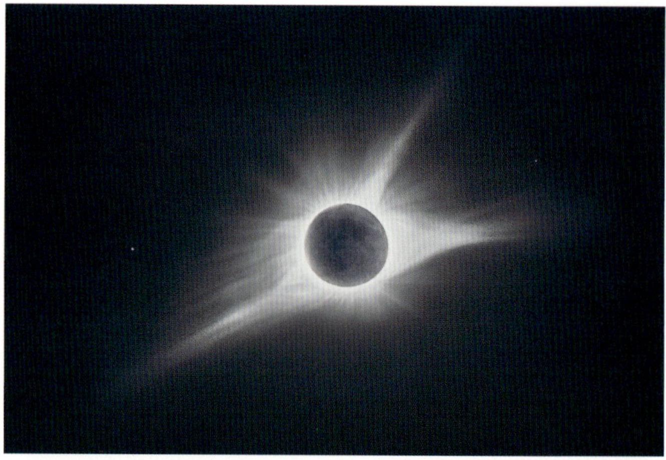

A total solar eclipse is visible over Wyoming. Nikon D8ooe, 300mm, f/7.1, ISO 100, many bracketed exposures blended.

Solar eclipses are harder to view than lunar eclipses, as they are visible over a much smaller part of Earth's surface. If there is a total or annular solar eclipse near where you live, it is worthwhile to go out and photograph it, as another eclipse may not happen for a long time.

I captured this photo of an annular solar eclipse over Cove Arch in Arizona on May 20, 2012. I took two images and blended them in Photoshop. Canon 5D II, 200mm, f/32, ISO 100 - exposure for the sun was 1/8000 second, exposure for the rest of the scene was 1/60 second.

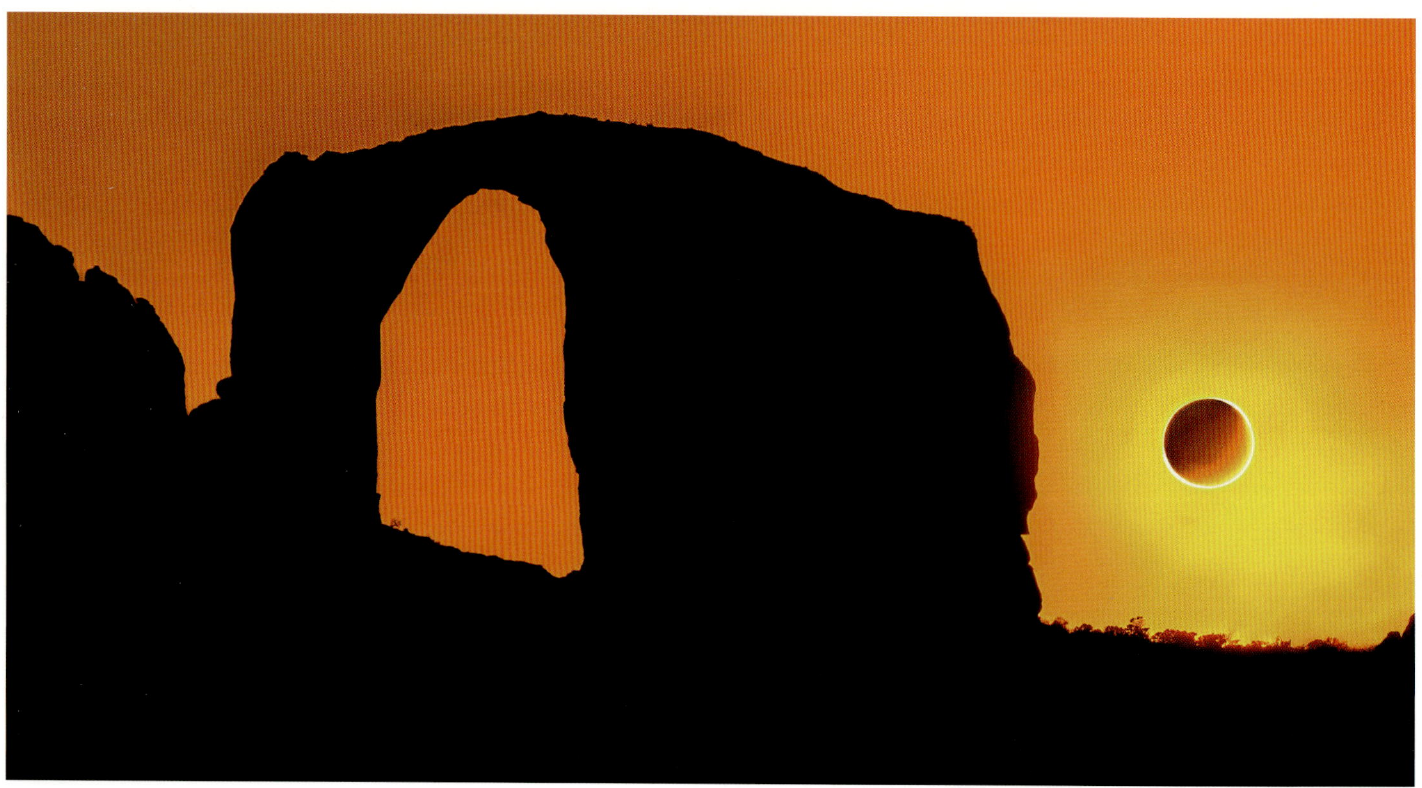

Solar eclipses can be a lot more challenging to photograph than lunar eclipses because the sun is so bright and the eclipse lasts for a much shorter time. I won't explain how to photograph them here since it is a little outside the scope of this book. However, if you want to learn more, you can read the instructional article I wrote on photographing the Great American Eclipse at https://www.gcollier.com/eclipse/.

STARS

Stars will likely be the most common objects you photograph at night. Although stars do move relative to each other, this movement is so gradual that it can take thousands of years to notice it here on Earth. Stars therefore appear to us as fixed objects in the sky. The moon and the planets are continually moving relative to the stars.

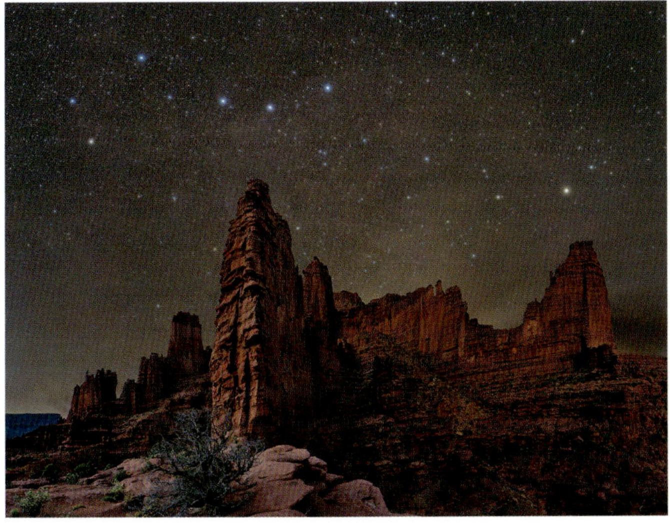

The Big Dipper is visible above Fisher Towers in Utah. Nikon D8ooe, 14mm. Exposure for land during twilight: f/4.5, 13 seconds, ISO 100, 6 images stitched. Exposure for sky at night: f/2.8, 30 seconds, ISO 6400, 6 images stitched.

Since stars appear as fixed objects, their location is very predictable. Every month, a given star will rise two hours earlier than it did the previous month. After a full year, that star will appear in the same spot in the sky as it did at that time the previous year.

The densest concentration of stars can be found in the band of the Milky Way. Our planet is located on a spiral arm far out from the center of the Milky Way Galaxy. As a result, when we look towards the center of the Milky Way, it appears much brighter. When we look away from the center, it appears fainter.

As discussed in Chapter II, you can use Stellarium to see exactly how the Milky Way will appear at any time and any location on Earth. Since the Milky Way stretches across the entire sky, you'll need to use an ultra-wide-angle lens or create a stitched image to capture more than a fragment of it.

Constellations can also be interesting objects to photograph. The two best-known constellations visible in the Northern Hemisphere are Ursa Major and Orion. The Big Dipper makes up part of Ursa Major and is more easily recognizable than the full constellation. It can be seen year-round in the northern part of the sky. Orion is visible in the winter months in the southern part of the sky. Sirius, which is the brightest star in the night sky, is visible down and to the left of Orion.

The camera can capture many more stars than the eye can see. As a result, constellations that are clearly visible to the naked eye can get lost amongst all of the other stars in a photograph. I will discuss ways to make the constellations stand out more in the section of Chapter IX called Enlarging Star Size and in the section of Chapter X called Boosting Star Size & Brightness.

PLANETS

From our vantage point, the closest planets in the night sky outshine any of the stars. Of all the planets, Venus appears the brightest. It is referred to as the Morning Star because its orbit is inside of Earth's and it always appears in the sky near the sun. It can therefore only be seen when the sun is not too far below the horizon, either in the morning before sunrise or in the evening after sunset.

Jupiter is the second brightest planet in the sky. Since its orbit is outside of Earth's, it won't always be in the same part of the sky as the sun and can appear at any time of night. Other planets that are bright and readily seen with the naked eye are Mars and Saturn. Mercury is also visible with the naked eye, but it is so close to the sun that it is usually obscured by the sun's light.

A good time to photograph planets is during a conjunction when two or more of them appear near each other in the sky. Another excellent photographic opportunity is when the moon is in conjunction with a planet. You can find dates of upcoming conjunctions at: https://in-the-sky.org/newsindex.php?feed=conjunctions. You can ignore the dates for Neptune and Uranus, as these distant planets will be very faint.

If you are able to capture two or more planets near the moon, this can be an ideal scenario. You can determine when this will occur in the above link. If two or more planets will be in conjunction with the moon within one or two days of each other, you'll likely be able to capture all of them in a single image.

METEORS

Meteor showers produce one of the most impressive displays in the night sky. They are created when Earth passes through dust particles left behind by a comet or asteroid. When the dust particles hit the atmosphere at high speeds, they burn up and briefly produce spectacular fireballs in the sky.

Meteor showers occur on about the same date each year. A list of meteor showers can be found online at https://www.imo.net/resources/calendar/. The Perseids and Geminids are typically the two best meteor showers each year. The Quadrantids in early January can also put on a dazzling show, but the peak of this shower usually only lasts a few hours. Other meteor showers may run in cycles and be incredible one year and uneventful for several years after that. For example, the Leonids are unspectacular most years, but they reach their peak every 33 years. In 1966, the Leonids produced a mesmerizing display in the night sky, reaching a peak rate that was estimated at over 100,000 meteors per hour! The next peak for the Leonids will occur in 2032.

I captured this image towards the beginning of astronomical twilight on a night when Jupiter, Venus, and the moon (seen from top to bottom) had all aligned in the same part of the sky. I used a small aperture of f/10 to render the moon and planets as sunstars. Canon 5D II, 24mm, f/10, 25 seconds, ISO 6400.

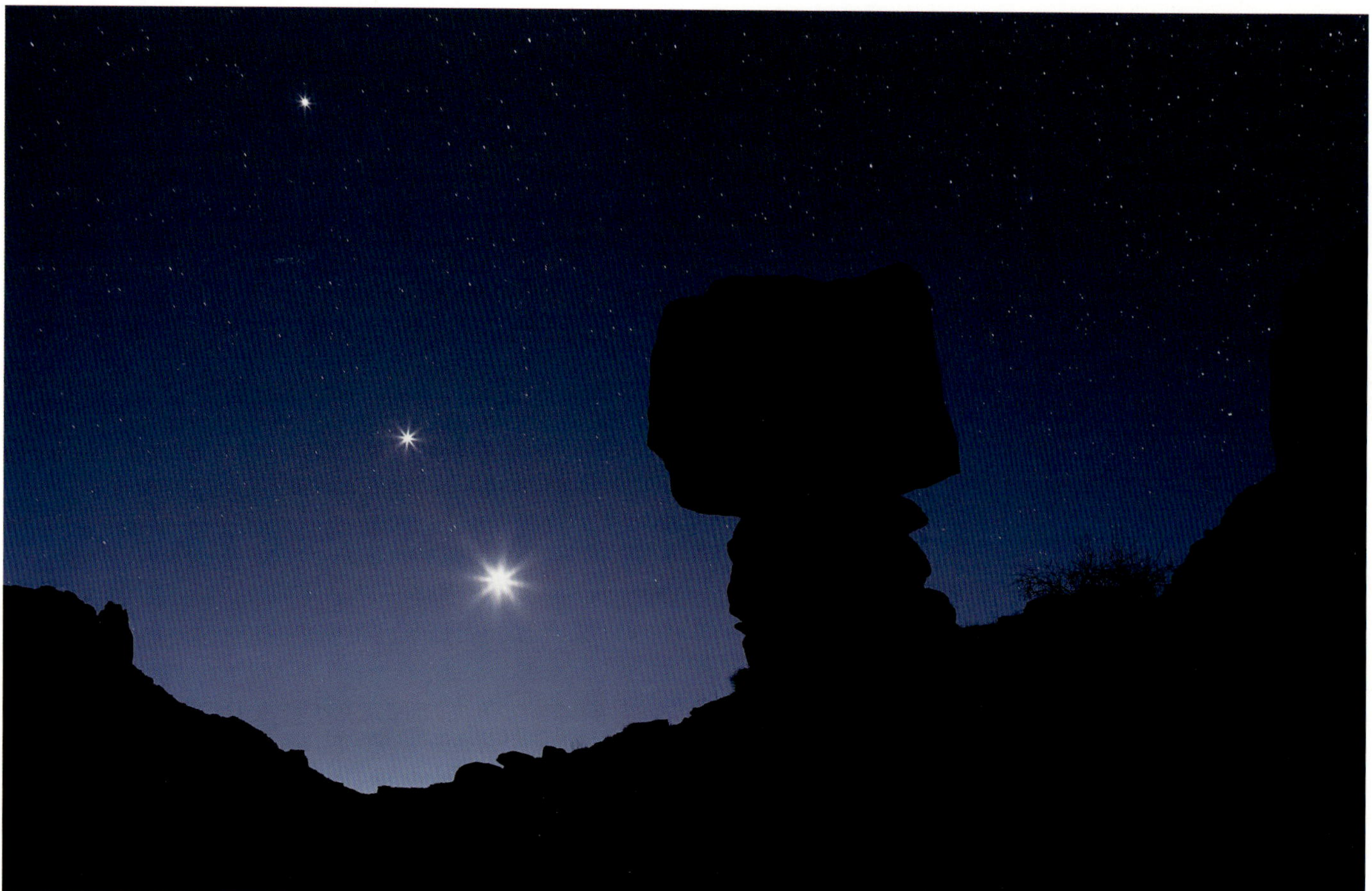

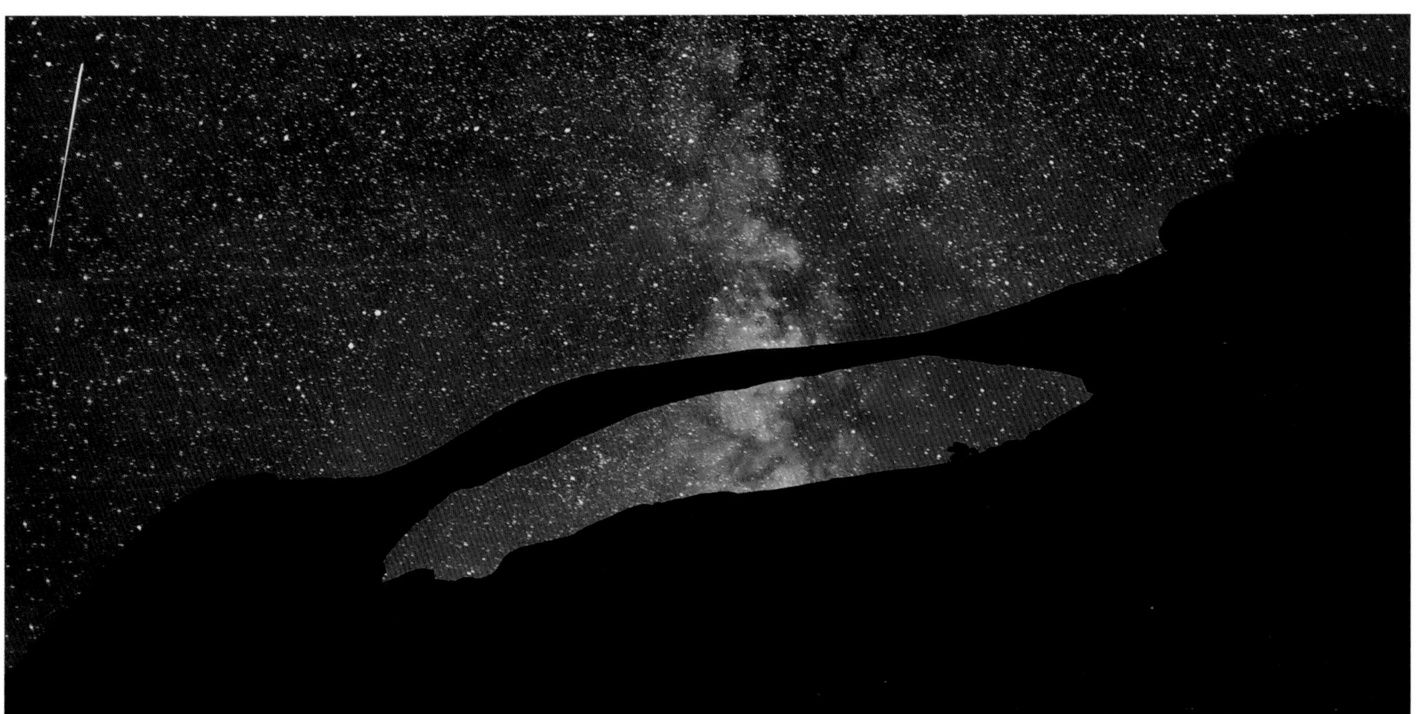

A meteor streaks above Landscape Arch in Arches National Park. I took repeated exposures of this scene in order to capture this meteor. Canon 5D, 24mm, f/1.6, 25 seconds, ISO 1600.

If the moon is out, it's light can obscure the meteors and make them even more difficult to photograph. I therefore recommend shooting meteors when there is no moon out or under a moon that is less than 20% illuminated. If there is a moon that is greater than 20% illuminated, you can wait for it to set or shoot before it rises. If the moon is full or nearly-full, it will be up most of the night, so you will probably be out of luck.

Most meteor showers tend to be more active in the early hours before sunrise. However, if you're able to photograph all night long, this will increase your chances of capturing a lot of meteors.

All meteors in a shower will originate from one area of the sky, which is known as the radiant. The meteors will not necessarily appear in this part of the sky, but they will all point back towards the radiant. Meteor showers are named after the constellation where their radiant is located. If you find this constellation, you will know where all meteors will radiate from.

You don't necessarily want to point your camera directly towards the radiant of the meteor shower. The meteors you capture near the radiant will generally be moving towards you and will therefore appear shorter. If you point your camera about 90 degrees away from the radiant, you will be more likely to photograph longer meteor trails. In fact, you can generally point your camera in any direction and capture a lot of meteors during a very active shower. This can give you more options when composing your photos.

Since meteors travel quickly across the sky, they need to be very bright to capture them in an image. To maximize your chances of photographing a bright meteor, you should take repeated exposures throughout the night and hope that a large meteor passes through the shot during one or more of the exposures. Unless your camera has a built-in interval timer, this will require a remote shutter release or intervalometer. It may also require extra batteries, as even the best batteries can die within 2-6 hours. If you buy a battery grip, you can add a second battery to your camera.

The camera settings you should use are similar to what you would use for a typical night photo, as detailed in Chapter IV. However, I recommend using an ISO of 1600 at f/2.8. Some of the meteors can be bright enough that you can overexpose them with higher ISOs or wider apertures. They will still look good if they are overexposed. However, you can often capture color in them if you avoid overexposing them.

I recommend using an ultra-wide-angle lens, like 14mm, so that you can shoot a large portion of the sky. If the composition you've decided on works better with a little longer lens, this is okay too. You won't be able to capture as much of the sky in your image, but the meteors you do capture will appear larger, and you'll be able to capture fainter meteors. The one problem with this is that the biggest meteors may travel all the way across your frame, and you'll only be able to capture a portion of them. Although these large fireballs are somewhat rare, they are usually the most dramatic meteors.

If you do catch a streak of light in your image, it is important to know if it is actually a meteor. There are a lot of things that create streaks of light, and not all of them are meteors. Airplanes will produce streaks of light, but these streaks will usually be dotted since the airplane's lights are flashing. Satellites can also create streaks of light. Many satellites look like straight lines with uniform brightness. However, some satellites produce iridium flares when light reflects off a highly reflective aluminum antenna. The satellite will get temporarily brighter and fade again, resulting in a non-uniform brightness across the streak of light. Since meteors usually have a non-uniform brightness, it can be difficult to distinguish between a meteor and an iridium flare.

Iridium flares will appear bright white, while meteors will sometimes be colorful. However, some meteors will also appear white, so this is not always a reliable way to distinguish between the two.

Meteors will usually point back towards the radiant of the meteor shower. However, a satellite could be pointing back towards the radiant by chance. Alternatively, there could be a random meteor that is not part

To capture this image during the Perseids shower, I took repeated 30-second exposures throughout the night. I combined every meteor I captured into one image and realigned them to the radiant. My camera recorded a rare meteor explosion on the right. The remnants of the explosion expanded outward over several frames, which I blended to include in this image. Nikon D800e, 18mm, f/2.8, 30 seconds, ISO 1600.

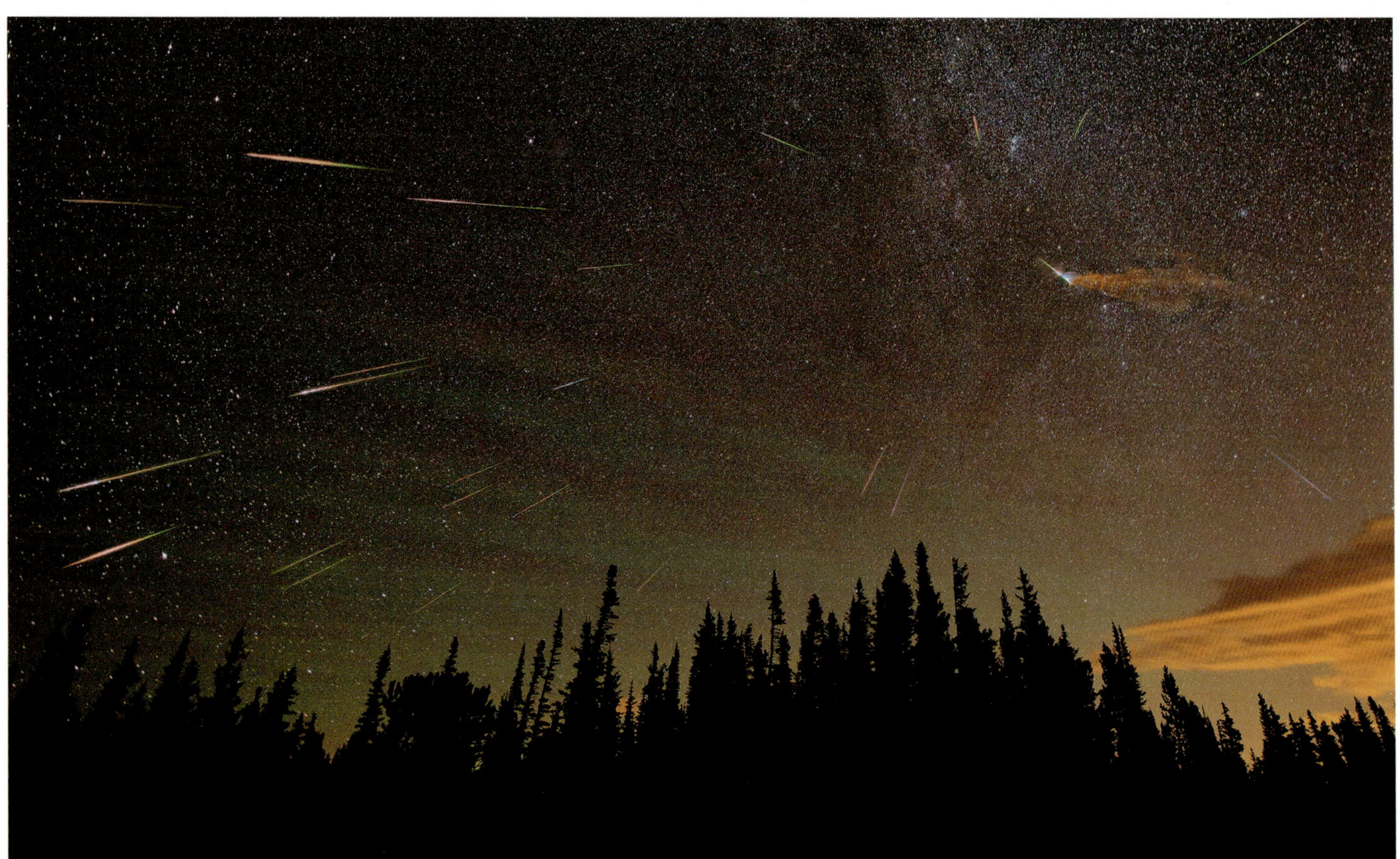

of the shower that originates from a different part of the sky.

There's a more reliable way to distinguish between a meteor and a satellite, as long as you're taking repeated exposures to maximize your chances of capturing a meteor. If you photograph something that looks like a meteor, you can check the shot before and after that one to see if the same object is also in those images. If it is, it's a satellite or airplane gradually moving across the frame of the photo. If the object only appears in that one shot and not in any before or after, it's a meteor. Meteors move so fast and die out so quickly that they'll almost always appear only in a single shot. One rare exception is if you caught a slow-moving meteor at the very end of one photo and the very beginning of the next, in which case it could appear in two images (but never three).

Even during the most active meteor showers, it's unlikely that you'll capture more than two meteors in a single frame. While a photograph with one or two meteors can be impressive, it doesn't quite capture the essence of a meteor shower, when hundreds of meteors can streak across the sky in a single night. Therefore, many night photographers like to combine every meteor they capture during the night onto a single image.

Accomplishing this is rather straightforward for those experienced with Photoshop. Simply stack every image you took that has a bright meteor in it onto one file in Photoshop. Then, on all but the very bottom layer, mask out everything except for the individual meteors.

If you do combine all of the meteors into a single image, you'll find that not all meteors point back to the same spot in the sky. This is because the radiant will be moving across the sky throughout the night. Some photographers like to reorient the meteors so that they all point back to the same spot. This is easier to do if you include the radiant in the images you shoot. First, locate the approximate location of the radiant in one of the photos. You'll then need to rotate all of the other images so that the meteors point back to that radiant. If the radiant is not in your photo, you can enlarge the canvas size of your file and draw a small dot outside of the image at the approximate spot where you think the radiant was located. Then, rotate the meteors, so they all point to that dot.

If the North Star is in your image, it is a little easier to align the meteors to the radiant. You can simply rotate every layer around the North Star until the stars in each layer line up. This will put the radiant in the same spot in each image, and every meteor from the same shower will point back to this one spot. More details on how to do this in Photoshop can be found on page 153.

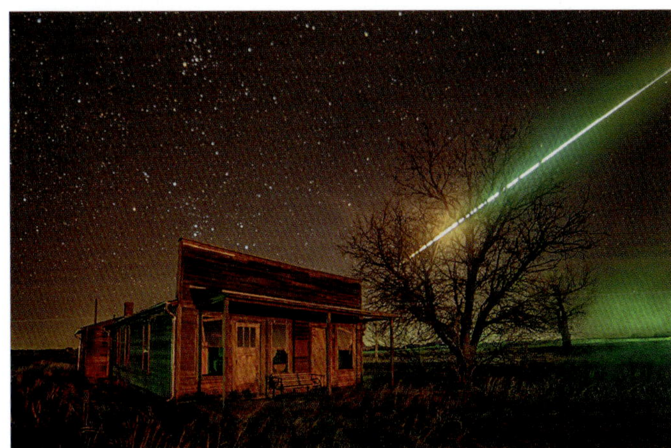

An extremely bright meteor streaks above a ghost building in Dearfield, Colorado. Nikon D800e, 14mm, f/2.8, 25 seconds, ISO 1600.

Since you'll be taking repeated exposures to capture meteors, you can stack exposures of both the land and sky to increase the quality of your base image. I explain how to do this in Chapter IX.

SATELLITES

As mentioned in the previous section, you can capture streaks of light from a satellite in an image. It might be a stretch to call this a natural light source, but since it's just reflected light from the sun, I'll include it in this chapter.

Some photographers don't want the streaks from satellites and clone them out since they are produced by man-made objects. Other photographers like to include them in the image, and some even plan ahead to try and capture satellites in their photographs.

You can predict when a satellite will be overhead

using the website https://www.heavens-above.com. This site tells you when to expect iridium flares and where some of the major satellites will be located, including the International Space Station.

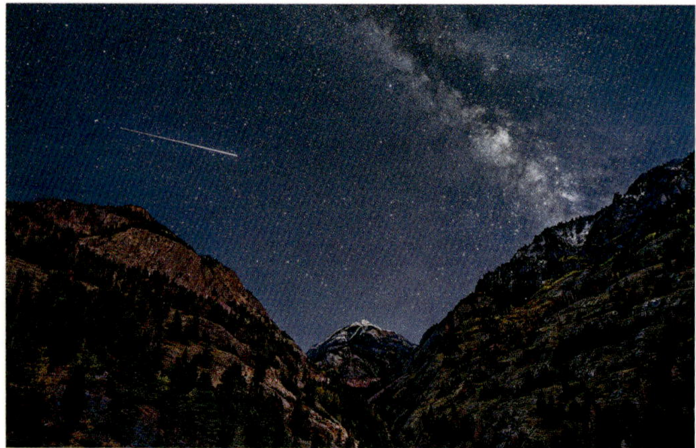

The International Space Station is seen from Red Mountain Pass in Colorado. Nikon D8ooe, 15mm, f/2.8, 25 seconds, ISO 3200.

COMETS

Comets can produce one of the most awe-inspiring displays in the night sky. Unfortunately, comets that are visible to the naked eye and easy to capture with a standard digital camera are quite rare. However, comets are notoriously unpredictable, and some that have yet to be discovered could produce a brilliant display. So if an impressive comet does become visible in the night sky, make sure and photograph it as often as you can because it could be many years or decades before you are presented with another opportunity.

You can use an equatorial mount to capture more detailed images of a comet. This is especially useful if the comet is faint. Using an equatorial mount is discussed on pages 132-134.

LIGHTNING

Lightning is an incredible natural phenomenon, but capturing it with a camera can be dangerous. I usually try to photograph lightning when the storm is a reasonable distance away and there are no storm clouds directly overhead. Occasionally, though, I will get caught in the middle of a lightning storm that I have to wait out anyway. In this case, I'll sometimes set up my tripod in the back of my vehicle, which has seats that can fold down. I'll then shoot the lightning out of a back window. Cars act as a Faraday cage, which funnels lightning around the outside of the vehicle. You are therefore much safer inside a vehicle than outside (though never 100% safe). If you're unable to set up your camera inside your car and it's not raining, you can set it up directly outside the car window and program it to do repeated exposures, while you stay in the car.

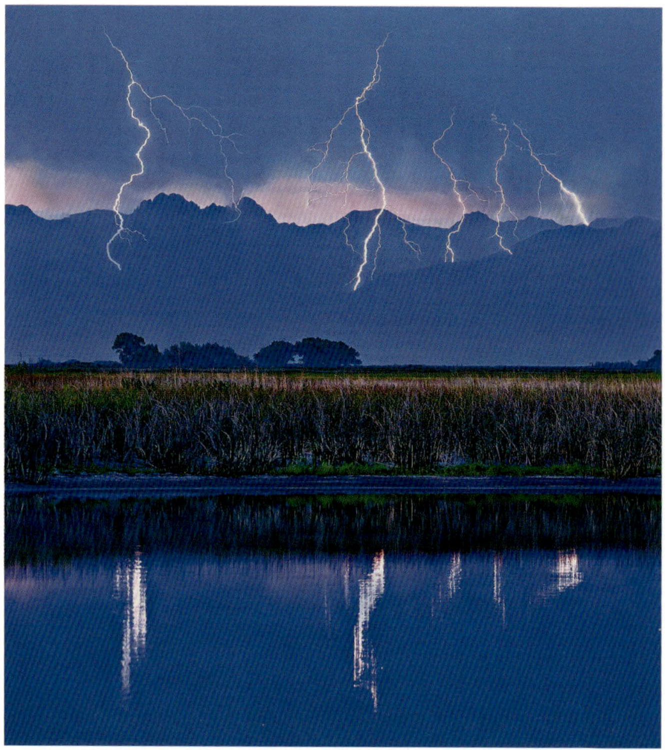

Several lightning bolts strike peaks of the Sangre de Cristo Mountains in Colorado during twilight. Nikon D8ooe, 145mm, f/8.0, 6 seconds, ISO 100, 3 exposures blended.

Lightning is so bright that it can be easy to overexpose the image. You'll therefore need to use a lower ISO and possibly a smaller aperture than you usually use at night. The exact settings you need will depend on just how intense the lightning storm is and how close you are to it. I recommend starting with ISO 100 and an aperture of f/4.0. As long as there are no stars visible above the storm clouds, you don't need to use the rule of 500 to determine exposure times. I recommend taking repeated exposures of 30 seconds to 3 minutes and hope that lightning strikes within your frame in one or more of your images. If it is still fairly light out, you will need to take shorter exposures to avoid overexposing the image.

Once you capture a bolt of lightning in your photo, be sure to check your histogram. If you are blowing out any of the highlights, you'll need to use a smaller aperture or lower ISO. If you are significantly underexposing the image, you should switch to a wider aperture or higher ISO. It is better, however, to underexpose the image than to overexpose it.

Longer exposures will increase your chances of capturing multiple lightning bolts in one shot. However, you can also blend multiple lightning bolts from different exposures taken at the same spot into a single image. Simply stack all of the photos with lightning bolts onto different layers of a single file in Photoshop. Then change the blend mode of all but the bottom, background layer to Lighten. All of the bolts will now magically appear in your image! If there are stars in your photo above the clouds, this will produce duplicate stars in the image, so you should mask out the stars in all of the layers that have the Lighten blend mode.

NORTHERN LIGHTS

Of all the light sources discussed in this chapter, the northern lights (also known as the aurora borealis) may be the most spectacular. This phenomenon is produced by charged particles from the sun interacting with gaseous particles in our atmosphere. These lights also appear in the Southern Hemisphere, where they are called the southern lights, or the aurora australis. The northern lights are more active when sunspot activity is high. For reasons that aren't entirely known, sunspot activity tends to run in cycles lasting approximately 11 years. The last peak of this solar cycle oc-

To capture this photo of a thunderstorm near Parachute, Colorado, I took repeated two-seconds exposures of the scene. I would have overexposed the clouds with exposures longer than two seconds because it was civil twilight and still fairly light out. I only captured a single bolt of lightning in all of the images I took, but it was all I needed for a dramatic photo. Nikon D800, 38mm, f/5.6, 2 seconds, ISO 100.

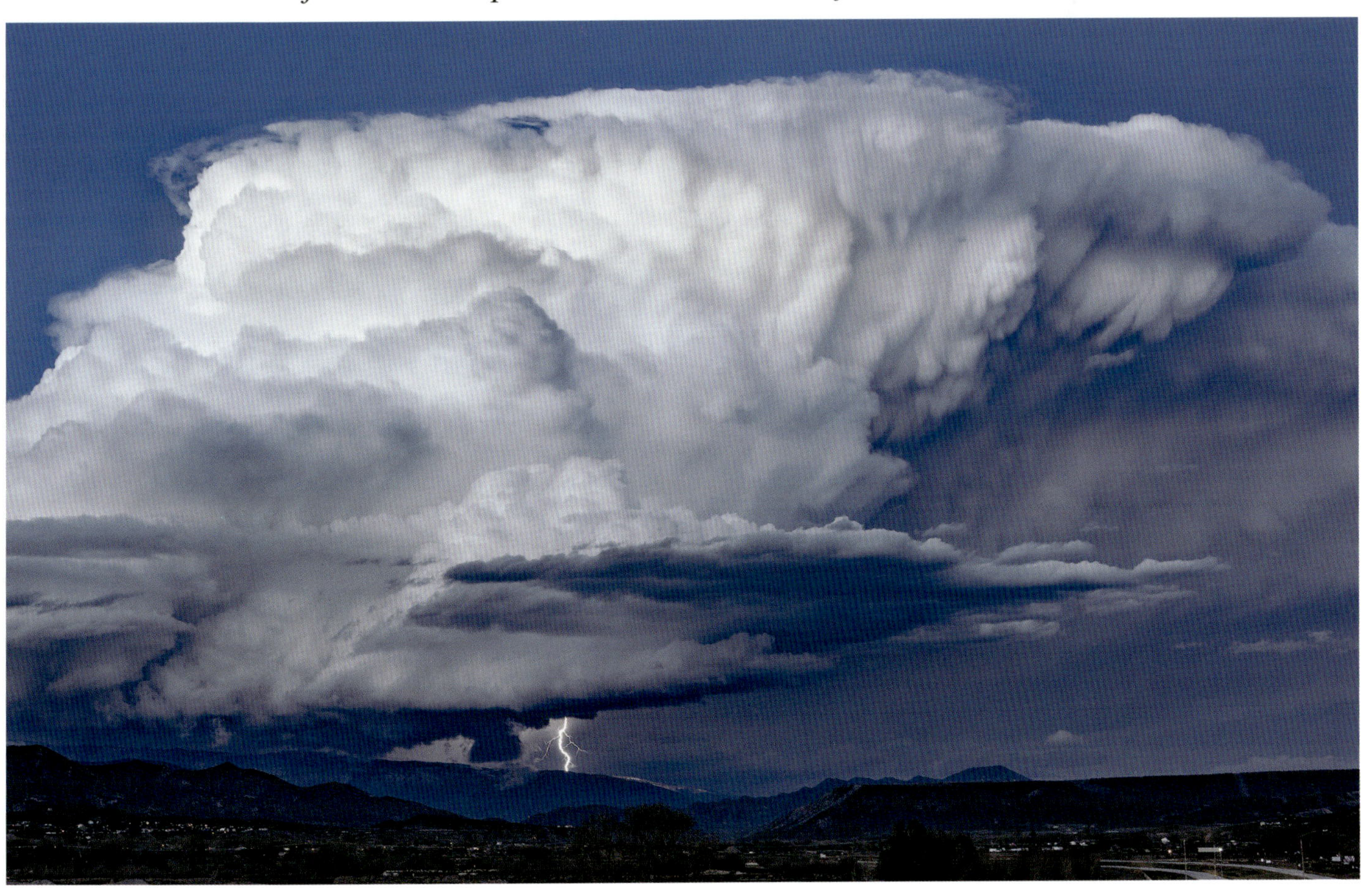

curred in 2014, and the next solar max should occur around 2025. However, you don't need to wait until peak activity to photograph the northern lights. If you travel up near the Arctic Circle, there's a good chance you will be able to see them any year.

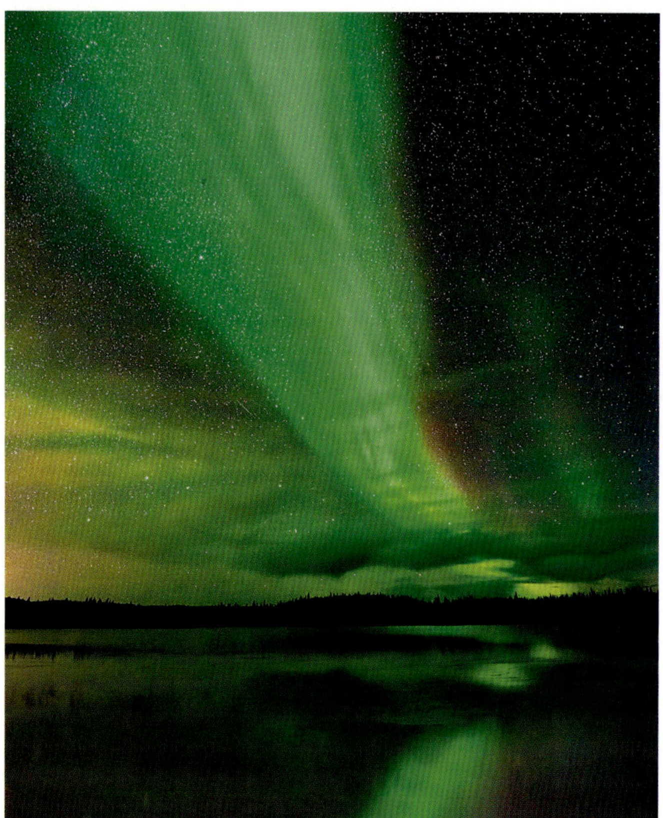

The northern lights are reflected in a lake near Yellowknife, Canada. Nikon D800e, 14mm, f/2.8, 13 seconds, ISO 3200.

There is a forecast for the northern lights at the University of Alaska Fairbanks Aurora Forecast site at https://www.gi.alaska.edu/monitors/aurora-forecast/. This website gives you a general idea of where the northern lights will be visible on any given night. For example, if you are in the northern continental United States, you might be able to see the northern lights if the forecast is 5 or higher. However, to get the best chance of viewing the northern lights, you'll need to travel even farther north. To find the best locations, look for a day when the forecast on the above website is a 1 or a 2. Anywhere within the bright green circle is a prime viewing spot for the northern lights. Some places that are somewhat easier to access in prime viewing areas are Dawson City and Yellowknife, Canada; Wiseman, Alaska; Iceland and northern Norway.

You can find another northern lights forecast on the Space Weather website at https://www.swpc.noaa.gov/products/aurora-3-day-forecast/. There is also a free iPhone and Android app called My Aurora Forecast.

In addition to short-term forecasts, there is a way to predict the aurora nearly a month in advance. If the northern lights are very active one night, there is a chance that they will be active again in 27-28 days. This is because many sunspots rotate around the sun once every 27-28 days. If the sunspot that caused the strong auroral activity is still active the next time it rotates around and faces Earth, there is a good chance the aurora will be stronger than average. This prediction is, however, far from perfect, as sunspots can fade.

While it is ideal to photograph the northern lights when they are most active, this isn't as important if you are in a prime viewing area. You may see a spectacular show even if the forecast is low. I learned this the hard way on my first night in Wiseman, Alaska. The forecast was just 1, so I decided to get some sleep after a long drive. The next day, the lodge owner told me the auroral display that night was one of the best she'd ever seen. I ignored the forecast for the rest of the trip and went out every night as long as I could. I was rewarded with a view of the northern lights every night.

You may not get as lucky as I did, and you might have to wait through a few long, cold nights to see a bright display of the aurora. But once it appears, you'll see a dazzling light show that makes the wait worthwhile. When the light show does erupt, you'll want to work fast, getting many different shots and compositions.

Since it can be very cold when shooting the northern lights, condensation could start to build up on your lens. Refer to the section on Dew Heater or Lens Muff on pages 24-25 for ways to prevent this.

To photograph the northern lights, you can rely mainly on the techniques and camera settings that I described in Chapter IV. However, if the aurora is moving rapidly, you'll generally want to limit your exposures to 15 seconds or less. Otherwise, the lights can start to blur too much with longer exposures. Also, when the

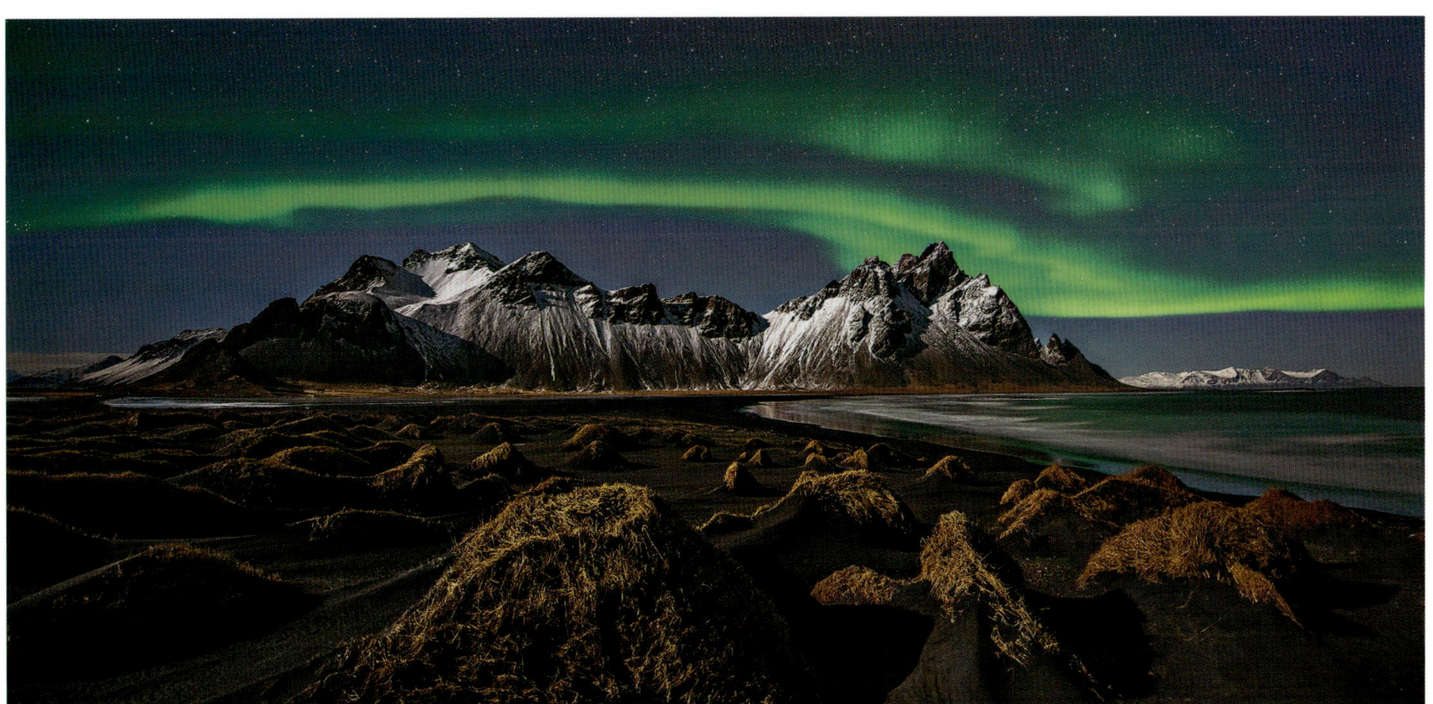

I captured this image of the aurora borealis over Vestrahorn Mountain in Iceland in February of 2015. On this date, the sun was near the peak of its 11-year cycle in sunspot activity, so my chances of seeing the northern lights were a little better than normal. Nikon D800e, 14mm, f/2.8, 10 seconds, ISO 1600.

---

aurora is especially bright, it is possible to overexpose the image. I recommend underexposing your photographs so that you won't risk overexposing the image if the northern lights suddenly brighten. You'll want to frequently check your histogram to make sure you're not coming close to clipping the highlights. If you are, you'll want to lower the ISO or exposure length.

The northern lights can fill up most of the sky, and ultra-wide-angle lenses may only capture a portion of the display. I therefore find it useful to do stitched images to capture more of the scene. If the aurora is bright and moving fast, I recommend using a 14mm lens to create a single-row stitched panorama. You'll have to take all of the images pretty quickly. Otherwise, the aurora can move so much that the photos won't stitch together seamlessly.

If the aurora is relatively dim, it doesn't tend to move as fast. In this situation, I've found it possible to do multi-row stitched panoramas with up to 20 images. These large stitched images can help minimize noise, which is more noticeable when the aurora is fainter. I usually use a 24mm lens to capture such images.

The best time of the year to photograph the northern lights is near the spring and autumn equinoxes in March and September. The aurora tends to be somewhat more active during these months than other months. Never plan a trip to photograph the northern lights between late-April and early-August. During this time, it won't got dark for very long, if at all, at the far northern latitudes. If you plan a trip in December or January, it will be dark much of the day, if not all of the day. However, it can be bitterly cold during this time, so spring and autumn are still preferable for all but the most adventurous photographers.

You can usually shoot the northern lights under any moon phase. The aurora will appear brighter under no moon, but any foreground in your image will likely be rendered as a dark silhouette. Under a full moon, the landscape will be well-illuminated and the aurora will appear fainter, but this may not matter. The northern lights are often so bright that they will be easily visible under a full moon. My favorite time to photograph the northern lights is under a moon that is 20%-50% illuminated. It will be dark enough to see the stars and aurora a little better than under a full moon, and you'll still be able to render a lot of detail in the foreground. In order to shoot under a variety of conditions, I recommend planning a trip so that you arrive near a new moon and leave near a full moon.

One mistake I've seen photographers make is to go on an expensive trip to see the northern lights without having done much night photography beforehand. They then come away with subpar images that are out of focus or improperly exposed. Unless you live in an area where you can see the northern lights, I recommend becoming proficient in night photography before paying for a trip to see them. Photographing the northern lights is more challenging than photographing most other night scenes. The lights can move fast and may not appear for very long, so you need to be able to work quickly and make the most of your time when the aurora is out. If you practice with easier subjects beforehand, you should be able to come away with some stunning images.

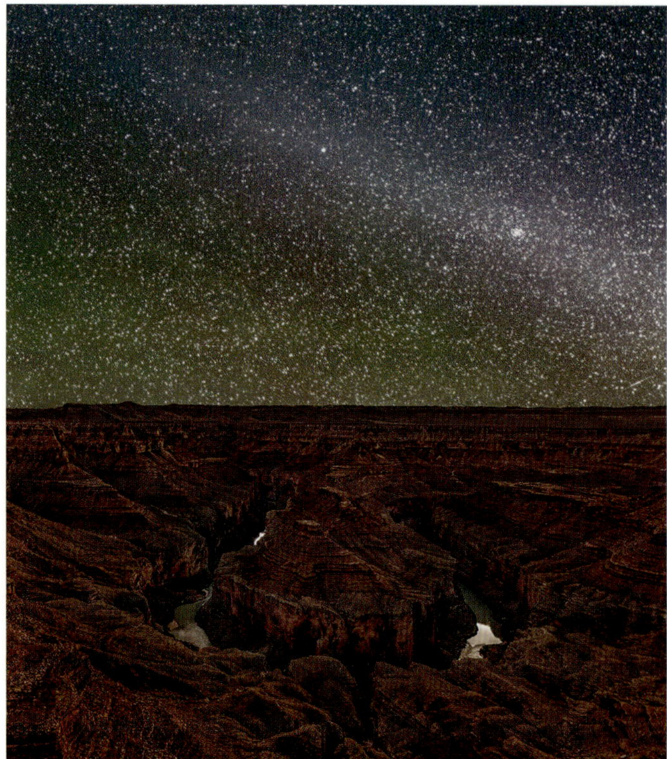

Zodiacal light and airglow are visible above the Grand Canyon. Sony a7 III, 14mm. Exposure for land during twilight: f/10, 0.8 seconds, ISO 100. Exposure for sky: f/1.8, 20 seconds, ISO 1600.

AIRGLOW

Even if you shoot outside of twilight hours when there is no moon out and no northern lights visible, you may not get perfectly dark skies. Molecules and atoms in the upper atmosphere can emit faint light known as airglow. Airglow is more prominent when the sun is near solar max and there are a lot of sunspots. You can't see airglow with the naked eye, so you will only know that it exists when it shows up in your photos. It can appear in many different colors but is usually green with smaller patches of red.

Airglow sometimes looks similar to light pollution. If you see red or yellow colors in the sky and there is a city or town in that direction, it is probably light pollution. If there are no towns in that direction and you see any green colors, it is probably airglow.

ZODIACAL LIGHT

Zodiacal light is caused by sunlight that is reflected off of space dust known as the zodiacal cloud. It appears as a thin, triangular white glow pointing up from the horizon where the sun set or where it will rise. It is easier to see during twilight around the spring and fall equinoxes, either in late March or late September. Zodiacal light is rather faint, so it is best photographed under no moon and far away from any city lights.

NOCTILUCENT CLOUDS

Noctilucent clouds are the highest clouds in the sky. They are only visible during twilight when Earth's shadow covers lower parts of the sky. They are most often seen in the summer at locations between 50 and 70 degrees north and south of the equator.

Noctilucent clouds are difficult to observe since they are quite rare. However, they can produce some surreal photographs if you are lucky enough to see them. They generally appear as thin, wispy clouds and can create intricate patterns in the sky.

LAVA

Lava is one of nature's most brilliant and fascinating phenomena. It is difficult to find, as it requires an active volcano. The Big Island of Hawaii has long been one of the best places to photograph lava. From 1983 to 2018, the Kilauea volcano erupted continuously. Although it wasn't erupting as of early 2020, scientists believe it still holds an enormous amount of magma and could erupt again at any time.

If Kilauea does erupt, lava flows can sometimes occur in very remote or dangerous places. In this case, it may be easier to photograph from a helicopter or boat around sunset or sunrise or during twilight. You may be able to take a night tour on a boat as well. The lava is bright enough that you can get acceptable results without excessive noise at night. You will, however, need to do much shorter exposures from a boat or helicopter to prevent the images from blurring.

Other places with a lot of volcanic activity include Iceland, Italy, Ethiopia, Central America, Indonesia, Papua New Guinea, and Vanuatu. Many of these places are located on the Ring of Fire, which stretches along the edge of the Pacific Ocean, where tectonic plates are colliding. You can find news on current volcanic activity at https://www.volcanodiscovery.com.

It will often be too dangerous to get close to lava, so you may be shooting from a considerable distance away. In this scenario, you'll usually want to use a long telephoto lens. I recommend having a lens of at least 200mm. Wide-angle lenses can also be useful if you're allowed to approach closer or if there are vast amounts of lava and smoke that can fill the camera frame from a distance.

When lava is entering the ocean, there can be a lot of rapidly-moving smoke in the air. You can use a short exposure of one second or less if you don't want the smoke to be blurred, or you can do a longer exposure if you prefer a blurred look.

The lava may be bright enough that you can rely on the exposure meter on your camera to determine the proper exposure. Always check the histogram after the exposure to make sure you are not blowing out the highlights.

If it's too dark to use your exposure meter, I recommend starting with an exposure of one second using ISO 100 and the widest aperture on your lens. These are very rough settings, as the lava can vary in brightness depending on how much there is and whether it is obscured by smoke. You'll need to check the histogram and adjust your ISO and shutter speed until you get an image where there is data throughout the histogram, but you are not clipping the highlights.

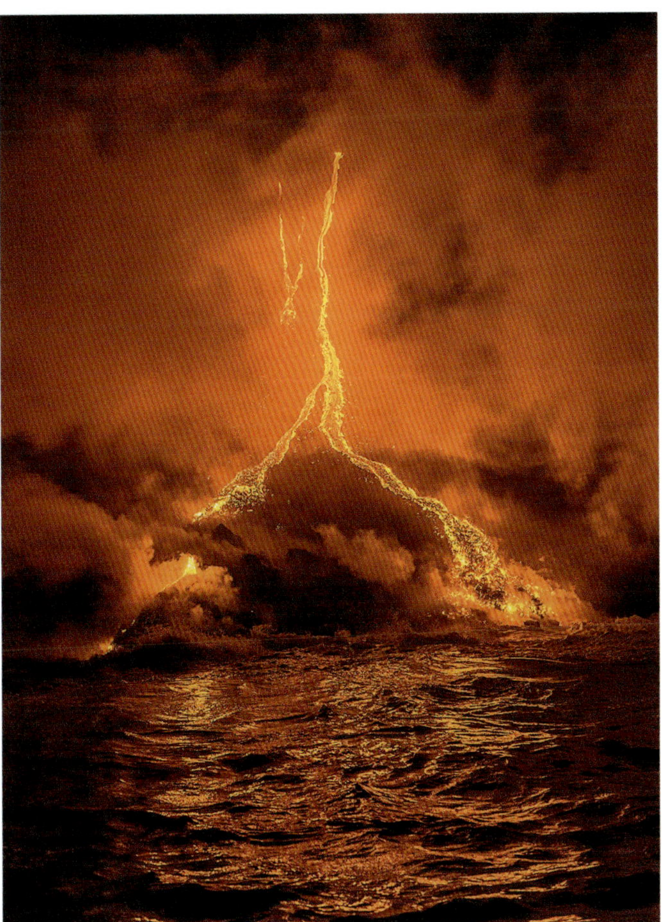

Lava pours into the ocean on the Big Island, as seen from a boat at night. Nikon D800e, 45mm, f/2.8, 1/250 second, ISO 3200.

FOREST FIRES

While forest fires can be a very destructive force of nature, they can also provide some unique photographic opportunities.

Fires can be difficult to photograph, as police and firefighters will quickly cordon off the area around them. Therefore, unless you have special access to a location, they are often best photographed when they occur on a mountainside that can be seen from a long distance away.

If you are close to a fire or using a long telephoto lens, the fire can appear very bright in your viewfinder. I recommend using the same approach to photographing it as you would with lava.

If the fire is a long distance away and appears rather faint through your viewfinder, you can use exposure settings closer to what you usually would at night. Just make sure you aren't overexposing the fire.

MOONBOWS

A little-known object that can occasionally be photographed is a moonbow. A moonbow is just like a rainbow, but it is created from moonlight rather than sunlight. When a bright moon is out, moonbows probably occur nearly as often as rainbows, but they are so little known because they can barely be seen with the naked eye.

If the moon comes out during or after a rainstorm at night, you should look in the opposite direction of the moon to see if you can spot a moonbow. It will appear as a very faint arc, and you won't likely be able to see the colors in it since you'll be using your rods to see. An easier way to find moonbows is if you photograph a misty waterfall with the moon behind you.

Since moonbows are so faint, you can use camera settings similar to those described in Chapter IV. However, if there are no stars visible, you can ignore the rule of 500 and do longer exposures from 1-3 minutes. In this case, you may need to lower the ISO to avoid overexposing the image.

If you are attempting to photograph lightning in addition to a moonbow, as I did in the image on the next page, you will need to lower your ISO a lot more to avoid overexposing the lightning.

I took this photo while a forest fire raged in Utah's La Sal Mountains. Since I was several miles away from the fire and I was using a wide-angle lens, I used only a slightly smaller aperture than I usually would when shooting star trails. Canon EOS 650 film camera, 24mm, f/4.0, 2 hours, ISO 100.

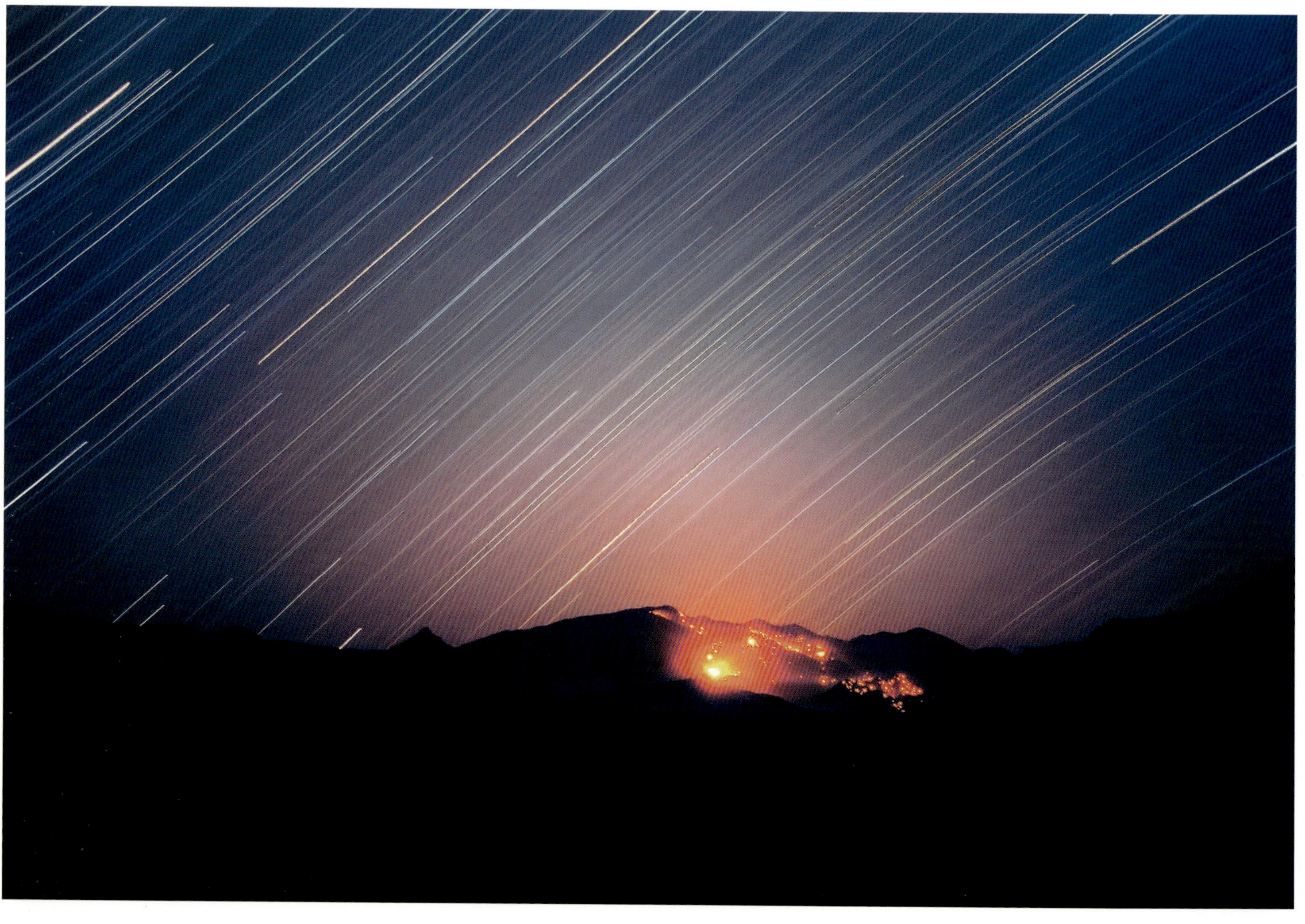

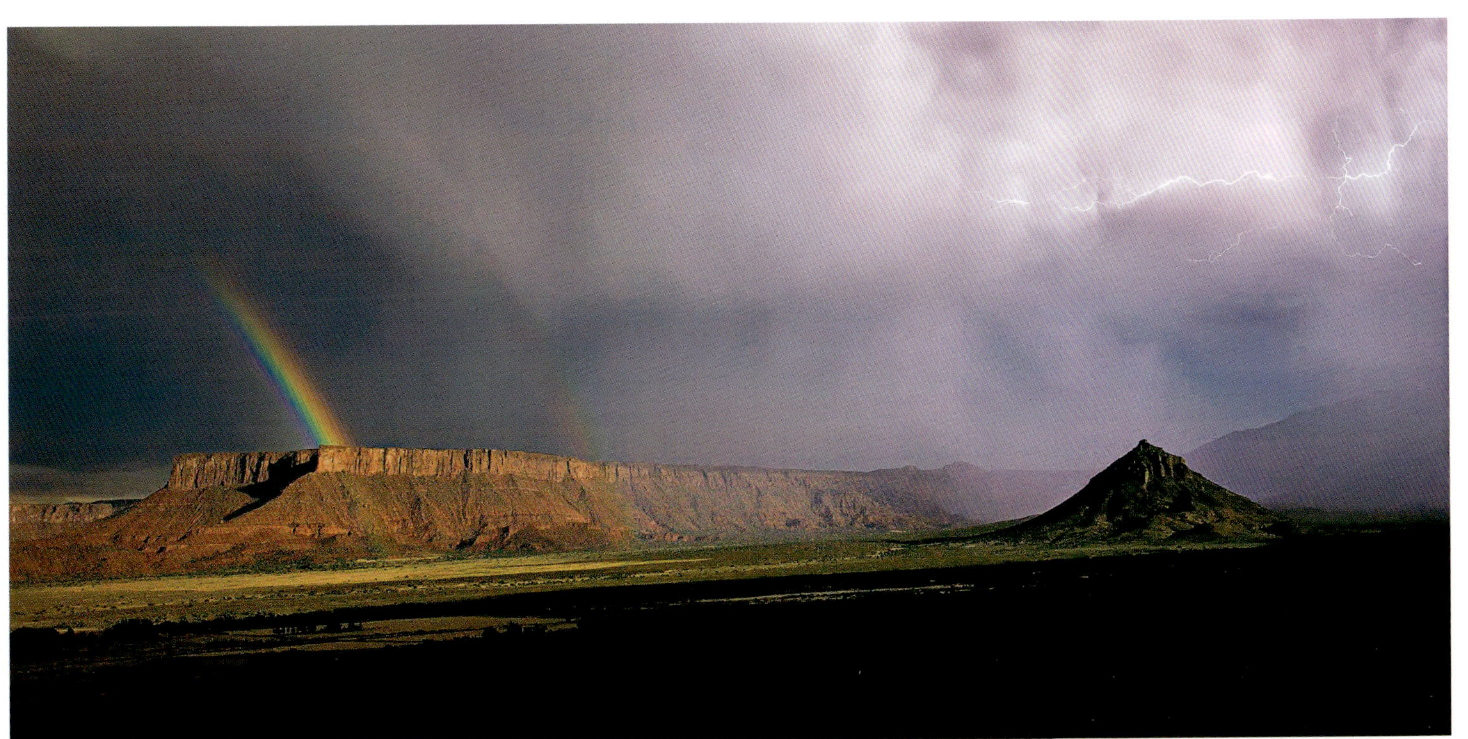

When I captured this image of a moonbow in Castle Valley, Utah, I was attempting to photograph lightning during an intense storm. I didn't actually see the moonbow until it started showing up as a faint arc on my camera's LCD screen. I used a low ISO in order to avoid overexposing any bright lightning. Canon 5D, 29mm, f/4.0, 92 seconds, ISO 200.

BIOLUMINESCENCE

Bioluminescence is the production of light by a living organism. It can be produced on land by things like fireflies, glowworms, and fungi. One of the best places to see and photograph bioluminescence on land is the Waitomo Glowworm Caves in New Zealand.

Bioluminescence occurs much more frequently in the ocean, where many deep-sea creatures produce light. These animals are very difficult to photograph, as they rarely come near the water's surface. One place where they can be seen from land is in Toyama Bay, Japan. Millions of firefly squid surface along the beach during mating season from March to June.

Perhaps the best opportunity to photograph bioluminescence is when it is emitted by phytoplankton known as dinoflagellates. Dinoflagellates can thrive in areas with a lot of algae. If the algal bloom is large enough, they can cover the ocean surface with a neon blue color at night.

Mosquito Bay in Puerto Rico is thought to have the world's largest concentration of dinoflagellates and may be the best place to photograph bioluminescence. Halong Bay in Vietnam is another good place to see this phenomenon. This is one of the most scenic bays in the world, making it a great place to photograph both day and night. Vaadhoo Island in the Maldives also has significant concentrations of dinoflagellates.

Some places to see bioluminescent waters in the United States are Manasquan Beach in New Jersey and Mission Bay in San Diego. In Europe, Norfolk, UK is a good place to view it.

Dinoflagellates shine brightest when they are in motion. So they can be easier to photograph along a breaking wave. You can also wade into the water yourself to stir them up.

The bioluminescence that is produced by dinoflagellates isn't overly bright, so you can use the camera settings detailed in Chapter IV.

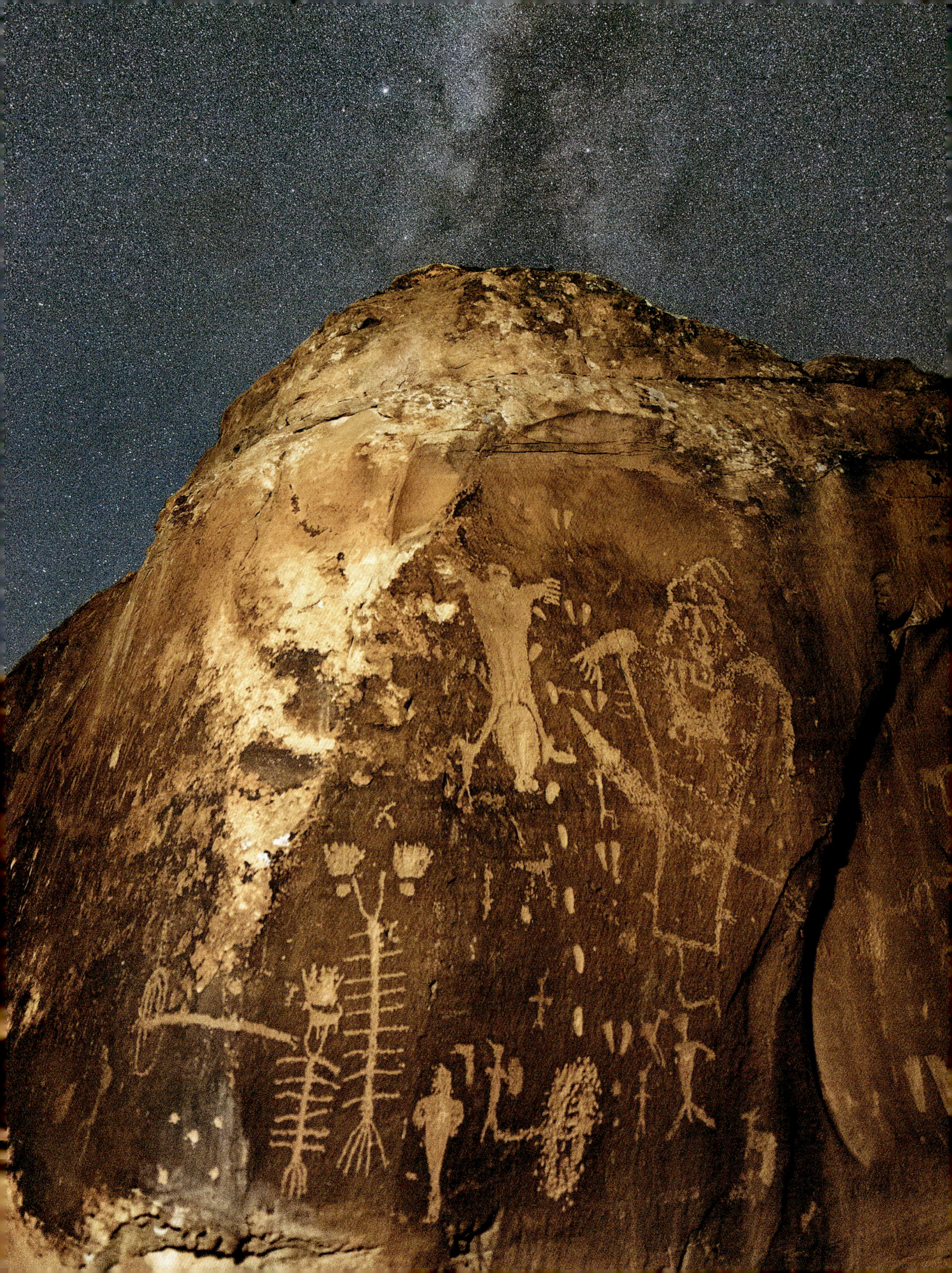

VI. Light Painting

So far, I've only discussed how to capture images at night using natural light sources. If you're unable to get the shot you want using natural light, you can illuminate the foreground using an LED panel or flashlight. This is known as light painting since you are effectively "painting" the scene with strokes of light.

Although light painting can help you capture images at night, I believe that it can be overdone. Often, when a photographer first goes out to photograph at night, they will illuminate every photograph using a flashlight. This is a natural thing to do, as humans usually need a flashlight to see at night, and therefore it may help a camera to "see" at night as well. However, modern cameras can pick up a lot more detail than humans can see with the naked eye. You can get excellent results without a flashlight.

It's also good to learn to shoot without a flashlight because some places, including Arches and Canyonlands National Park and Hovenweep and Natural Bridges National Monument, now discourage light painting. Grand Teton National Park has banned it entirely. They are concerned about the impact of the light on other visitors and nocturnal animals. It can also interfere with other photographers' images.

I very rarely use a flashlight to illuminate subjects at night anymore. As an alternative to light painting, I sometimes attempt to time a shot so that a crescent moon will be in the right part of the sky to illuminate the subject. This will generally produce more natural-looking photographs than a flashlight. I discussed this in more detail in Chapter II.

There are, however, locations, such as caves or alcoves, where the moon will never light up the foreground. There are also times when you won't want the moon to be out, as you will want the darkest sky possible to capture more dramatic shots of celestial objects, like the Milky Way, meteors, or zodiacal light. In this case, you have two main options if you want to illuminate the foreground - you can light paint the scene, or you can blend multiple exposures, which I will discuss in Chapter IX.

Blending exposures will usually produce more natural-looking results than an artificial light. However, light painting is generally easier since blending exposures requires some expertise in Photoshop. Light paintings can also benefit from extra work in Lightroom or Photoshop to make the light appear more even, but this usually won't require as much time or expertise.

Another benefit of light painting is that you can control exactly where you want the source of light to be and how the light and shadows will appear on the object you are shooting. A disadvantage is that it is difficult to illuminate both near and distant objects evenly in a photograph. The foreground will usually be it up, and the distant background (if there is any) will be dark. This can result in unnatural-looking photos.

Light painting can be used in more creative ways that are limited only by the imagination. Using light painting to create such images will not be discussed much in this chapter, as the focus of this book is on capturing photographs at night that look more natural.

LIGHTING EQUIPMENT

Before you try light painting, you'll need to decide what light source you want to use to capture your images. Since there are countless options to choose from, I've narrowed my recommendations down to five flashlights, two LED panels, a strobe, and a headlamp. If you plan to do a lot of light painting, I recommend getting an LED panel and one flashlight.

LED Panels

An LED panel can be a great alternative to a flashlight for light painting at night. It puts out a wide, diffuse beam, which can fill your entire camera frame. Since it

Left: I used a dim setting on my flashlight to illuminate a petroglyph panel in Utah known as the Birthing Scene. Nikon D800e, 17mm, f/2.8, 20 seconds, ISO 3200.

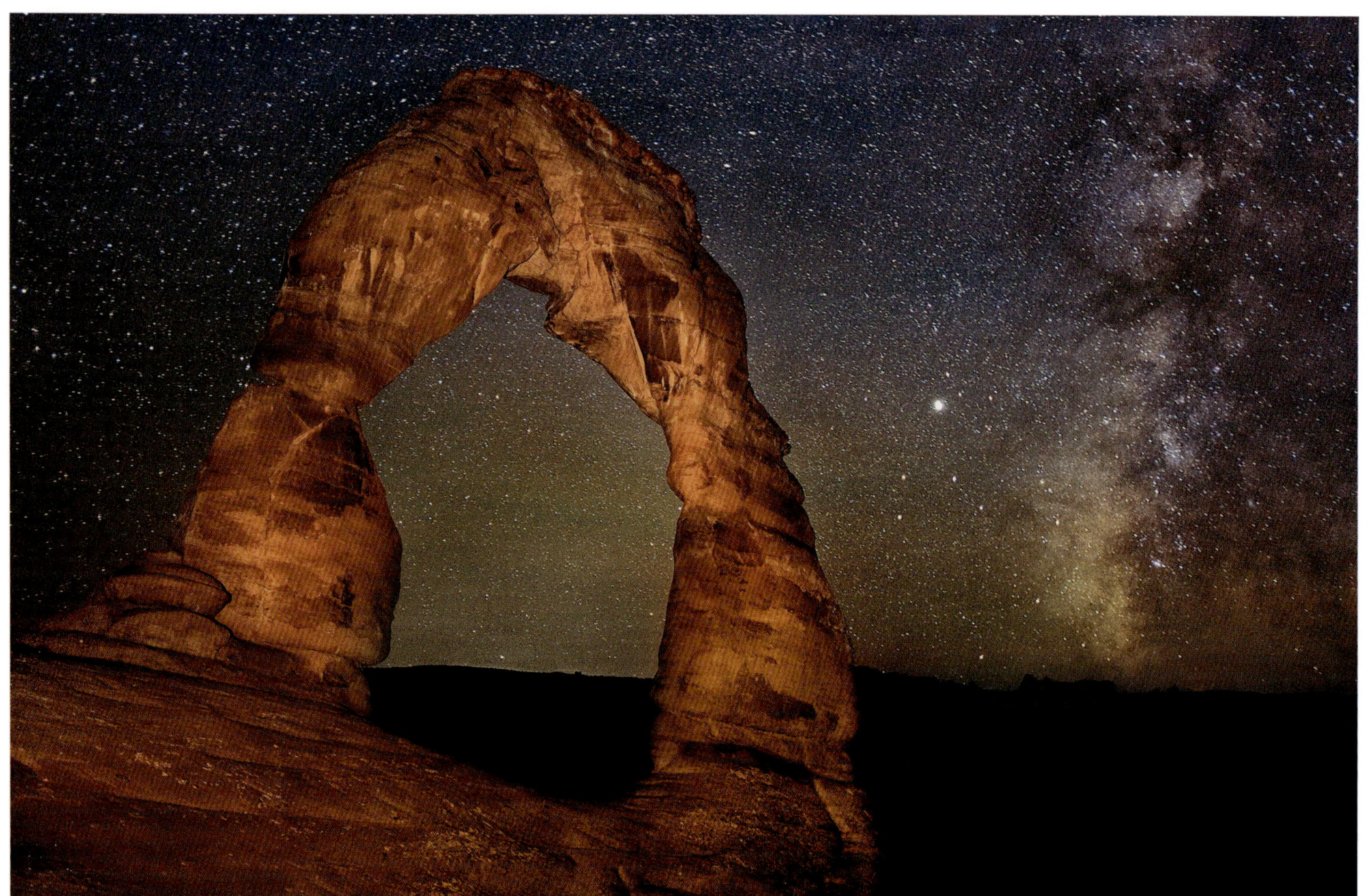

I made one of my first attempts at light painting at Delicate Arch in Utah in 2006. In order to capture a wide variety of images, I also took several shots with no light painting, where the arch appeared as a silhouette. Canon 5D, 24mm, f/1.6, 25 seconds, ISO 1600.

---

puts out such a broad light, you can use it if you want to create a stitched image or a focus-stacked image and need to make sure each frame is illuminated the same.

A disadvantage of an LED panel is that it is so diffuse that it's to difficult to control how much light hits various parts of the scene. The nearest objects may appear significantly brighter than more distant objects. A solution to this is to put the LED panel far back from your camera. This will keep both the near and distant objects in your image far away from the light source and make the lighting more even. The light will be dimmer, but since it will be illuminating the whole scene during the entire exposure, you won't need too much light on the landscape. In fact, I recommend starting with the LED panel near its minimum brightness and only increasing it if you are not getting enough detail in the foreground. This will better mimic the light from a crescent moon and can reduce light pollution.

A good, inexpensive LED panel is:

Neewer 160 LED Panel

This panel can be purchased for around $20, making it a great value. It weighs under one pound, is dimmable, and comes with filters that can make the light warmer or more diffuse.

A more expensive option is:

Luxli Viola

This panel costs around $300. It can emit any color you want by adjusting a color wheel on a phone app. This allows you to get the color just right in camera and minimize post-processing work. You can also adjust the brightness to as low as 1%, which is sometimes all the light you need.

Flashlights

Flashlights are well-suited for light painting, as they are usually light and portable. Flashlights with adjustable focus are useful, as they can put out a narrow beam or a wide, diffuse beam. A wide beam is generally more useful for light painting, but you can switch to a narrower beam if you want to shine a brighter, more concentrated light on distant objects.

If your flashlight doesn't have adjustable focus, you can use a diffuser to get a wider beam. If there isn't a diffuser made for your flashlight, just make sure the one you buy is wide enough to fit over the flashlight. If you don't want to purchase a diffuser, you can instead cut out part of a one-gallon plastic water bottle and tape this in front of the flashlight. Alternatively, with smaller flashlights, you can simply use a plastic bottle cap as a diffuser. These latter options may not be quite as effective as a real diffuser, but they cost nothing to make.

Some flashlights I recommend are:

Fenix FD45 900 Lumen Neutral White LED Flashlight

This flashlight has all the features to make it perfect for light painting. It is the only LED flashlight I have found that has adjustable focus, multiple brightness settings, and a neutral-white light. The neutral-white bulb emits a warmer light than most LEDs. You therefore won't need to adjust the colors as much, if any, in post-processing. There are five brightness settings that can emit 5, 50, 150, 350, and 900 lumens. 900 lumens will likely be too bright for most of your needs but could allow you to light paint objects up to around 1,000 feet away. The lower settings will be useful for closer subjects.

Unfortunately, Fenix has stopped producing this flashlight. However, as of this book's printing in 2020, it was still available on Amazon, eBay, and Battery Junction. The Fenix weighs 7 ounces and costs around $90.

I took this shot of a secluded arch near Moab, Utah from inside an alcove on a moonless night in autumn. I used a flashlight to illuminate the arch. Nikon D800e, 14mm, f/2.8, 25 seconds, ISO 3200.

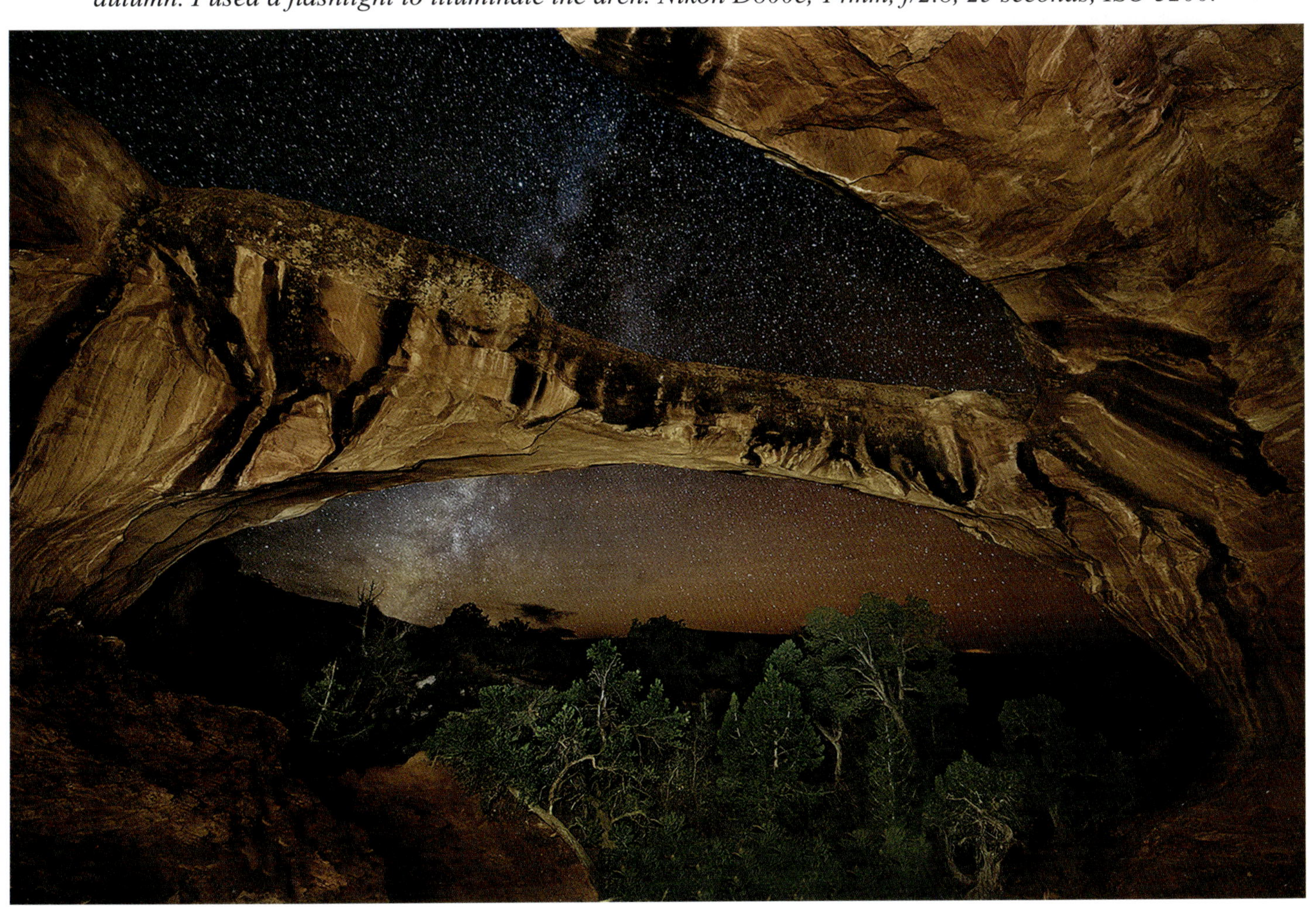

Ledlenser MT10 Flashlight

This rechargeable flashlight has adjustable focus and three brightness settings that emit between 10-1000 lumens. The dimmest setting is practical for illuminating nearby objects up to 50 feet away without overexposing the image. The medium setting is useful up to about 250 feet, while the brightest setting can be used for objects up to about 1,000 feet away.

Like most LED flashlights, the MT10 puts out a cool blue light, which will cause the photographs to have an unnatural-looking blue tint. However, if you're experienced with Photoshop, you can quickly select the part of the image that is lit by the flashlight and adjust the colors. Alternatively, you can process the photo with two different white balances - a higher temperature for the light painted part of the image and a lower one for the rest of the image - and then blend them in Photoshop.

If you want to avoid extra work in post-processing, you can put a warm filter in front of the flashlight to change the color of the light. I'll discuss these filters later in this chapter.

The MT10 weighs 6 ounces and costs around $80. There is an MT6 version of this flashlight that costs about $20 less and emits up to 600 lumens. This is more than enough for most light painting needs. Also, any Coast or Lenser brand flashlight with adjustable focus and multiple brightness settings can work well for light painting.

Coast Polysteel 400 440 lm Waterproof Flashlight

This flashlight has adjustable focus and costs around $20. Coast claims that it is waterproof, drop-proof, and crushproof. It puts out 440 lumens at its high setting and 60 lumens at its low setting. Like the Ledlenser, It does emit a cool, blue light.

This image shows the Milky Way behind Double Arch in Arches National Park, Utah. I light painted the underside of the arch with a Ledlenser flashlight to bring out some of the texture and color in the arch. In post-processing, I used Burn and Dodge layers in Photoshop to tone down any bright spots and make the lighting appear even across the arch. Nikon D800e, 14mm, f/2.8, 30 seconds, ISO 6400.

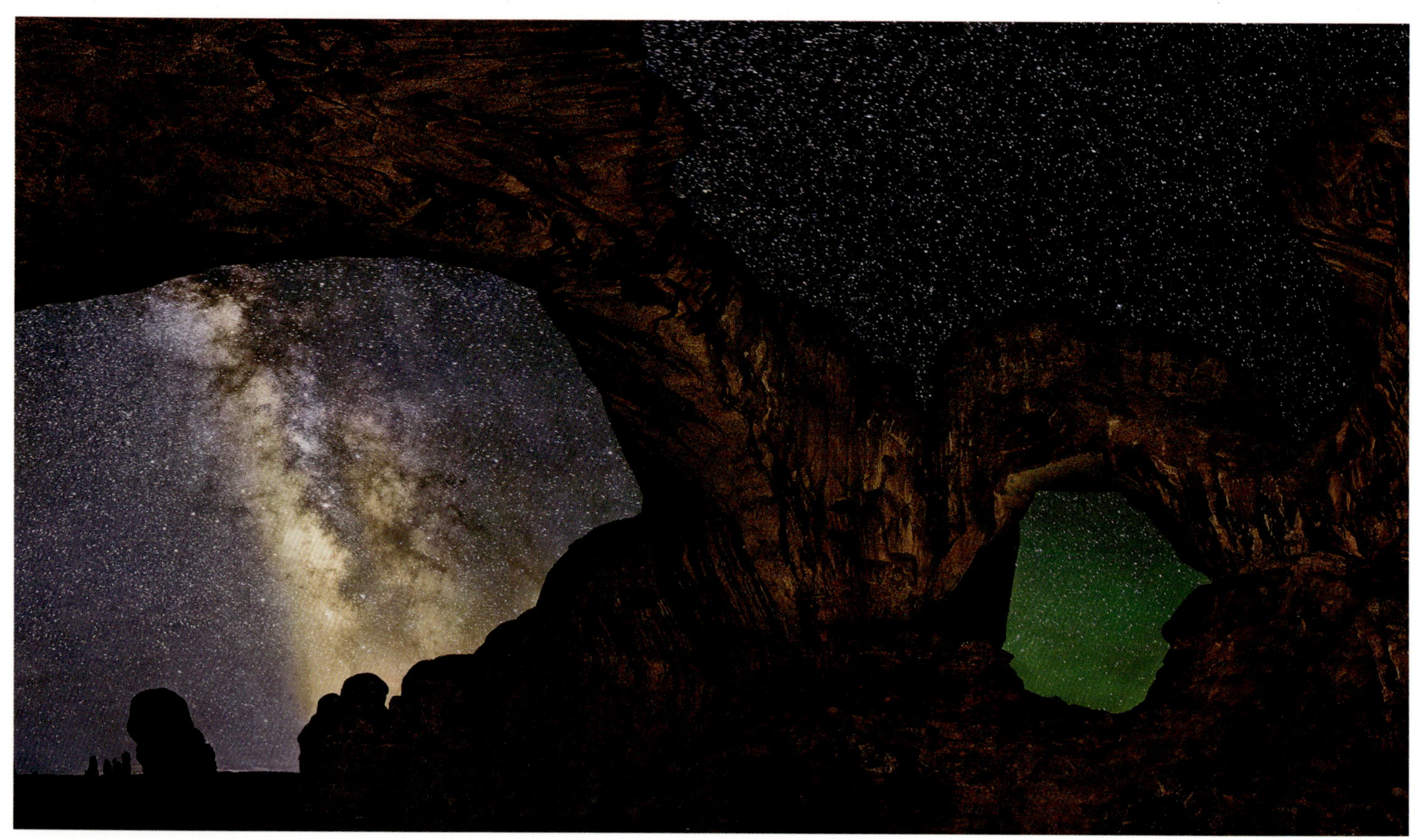

Coast HP1 190 Lumen Pure Beam Focusing LED

This is a very small, 1-ounce flashlight that has adjustable focus, and sells for $9. It also emits a cool, blue light. It can put out 190 lumens when used with a Lithium 14500 AA battery. When used with a standard AA battery, it emits 70 lumens. It doesn't have adjustable brightness settings, but you could bring both types of batteries to give some control over brightness. It's not the perfect flashlight for light painting, but for the price and size, it's hard to beat.

Eagletac Clicky Neutral White

Like the Fenix, this flashlight puts out a warmer light from an LED bulb. It is a very small flashlight that can emit a substantial amount of light. It does have multiple brightness settings, with the lower settings being more practical for light painting. It emits a fairly broad light but doesn't have adjustable focus.

Strobes

Unlike an LED panel or flashlight, which put out a continuous beam of light, a strobe puts out one quick, bright burst of light. Like the LED panel, it emits a broad, diffuse light, and you will have less control over how much light hits different parts of the scene. For most situations, an LED panel will work better at night. However, one practical use of a strobe is if you want to include people in the image and there is no moon out. Rather than having them stand perfectly still for the entire exposure, they will only need to stay still during the quick burst of light from the strobe. To even out the light in the scene, you may also want to use a flashlight to light paint more distant objects. Just make sure not to shine the flashlight near the spot the person is standing, or they could look like a ghost in the photograph. You could also blend multiple exposures - one using the strobe to illuminate the person and the second using a flashlight or a distant LED panel to illuminate the rest of the scene.

A strobe I recommend is:

Neewer Battery Powered Outdoor Studio Flash

This is a good quality strobe that costs a little under $200. Given the limited practicality for use in night photography and the much lower cost of a basic LED panel, I only recommend this strobe if you want to capture a lot of shots that include people. Even then, I'd recommend this for fairly advanced night photographers, as getting good images can be challenging. You may also want some accessories, like a light stand, diffuser, or umbrella.

Another option if you already own a flash is to use the flash off-camera. It probably won't work quite as well but is less expensive.

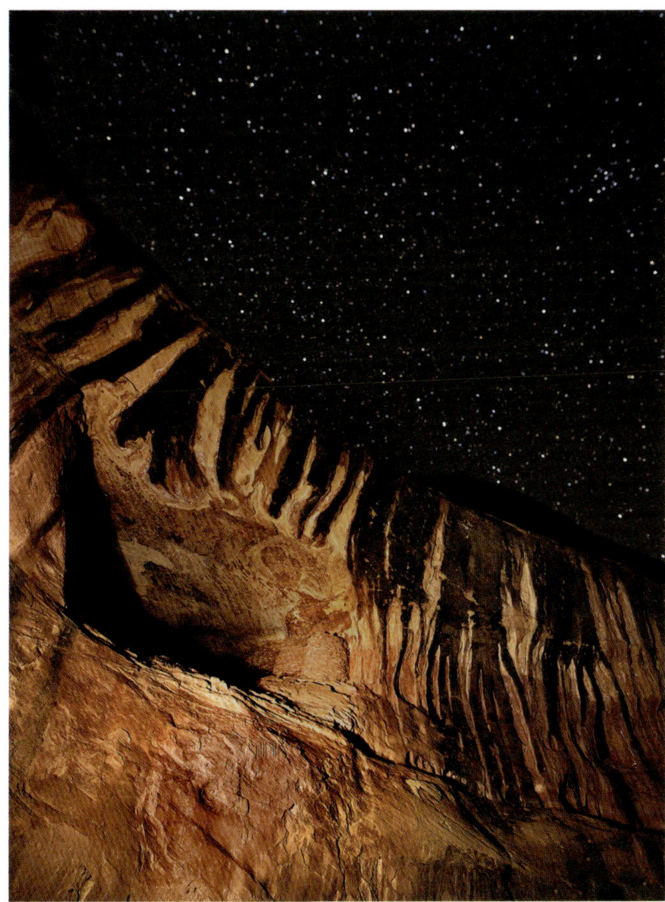

I used a Coast headlamp to illuminate an alcove in Utah containing several Anasazi Indian ruins. Nikon D800e, 16mm, f/2.8, 30 seconds, ISO 3200.

Headlamps

I primarily use a headlamp for hiking at night. However, headlamps have improved so much that they can also be used for light painting. If you expect to do a lot of light painting, you'll likely only want to use a headlamp as a backup in case your primary light stops working. However, if you don't plan to do much light painting and don't want to carry an extra light just for this purpose, a focusing headlamp can work well.

A headlamp I recommend is:

Coast HL7 Focusing LED Headlamp

This is an older headlamp, but I still like it for light painting because you can adjust the brightness to any level between 4-300 lumens. The lowest level can also be useful for preserving night vision. Many of the newer Coast headlamps just have two brightness settings.

Color Filters

Color filters can be used to change the color of your light. If you have an LED flashlight that puts out bluish light, you can use a yellow or orange filter to warm up the light. This can produce more natural-looking colors straight out of the camera. If you find a color that works best with your flashlight, you can tape the filter onto the flashlight. Some filters I recommend are:

Roscolux Swatchbook

This sample pack of color gel filters contains more colors than you could ever use and is currently available from BHPhotoVideo.com for just $2.50. These filters are 1.75" x 2.75", so they may not be big enough to cover larger flashlights.

Roscolux Designer Color Selector Swatchbook (3 x 6")

If the standard swatchbook isn't big enough to cover your flashlight, these filters may do the trick. They currently sell for $22.50 on BHPhotoVideo.com.

EXPOSURE

When light painting, you can use camera settings similar to those detailed in Chapter IV. Unless you are using a very bright flashlight or are very close to the subject, it's not likely that you'll overexpose the photograph. I recommend starting with an ISO of 3200 and your widest aperture. You will want to keep an eye on the histogram to make sure you are not overexposing the image. If you are, you can use a dimmer setting on your flashlight or spend less time painting the area that was overexposed. If neither of these options work, you can lower the ISO.

Another option when light painting is to blend separate exposures of the land and sky, using techniques described in Chapter IX. For the shot of the land, you can do a longer exposure of 1-3 minutes with a lower ISO. This will allow you to spend more time painting the scene.

If you are unable to get everything illuminated in one shot, you take can several exposures and light paint different parts of the scene in each image. You can then stack all of the exposures onto a single file in Photoshop and use masks to blend the parts of each image that are properly lit. Blending multiple exposures is discussed in detail in Chapter IX. There are even more powerful techniques for doing this with Smart Objects, which I demonstrate in depth in Volume II of my instructional videos at https://www.collierpublishing.com.

Before taking your first photo, you may want to close the eyepiece if you're using a DSLR. If light from your flashlight hits the back of the camera, a small amount could leak into the eyepiece and affect the image.

PAINTING TECHNIQUES

There are different techniques you can use to illuminate the scene. Unless you want a more artistic effect, the main goal will be to get diffuse, even light over the subject. The first three sections below are geared toward people using flashlights. If you have an LED panel, lighting the scene is straightforward, as you usually just need to decide where to place the light and leave it there for the full exposure.

Direct Light

The majority of your light paintings will likely be done with direct light. This simply means that you will shine the flashlight directly onto the object you are photographing.

I find that using small, rapid circular or side-to-side motions with your flashlight as you light paint is a good way to get even light throughout the photograph. You should move your flashlight over every part of the scene that you want illuminated while making these smaller motions. You should avoid holding your flashlight perfectly still for any period of time. This could produce uneven lighting and can cause parts of the image to be overexposed.

It's important to spend more time light painting distant subjects that you want illuminated than nearby subjects. Every time you double the distance to an object, it will

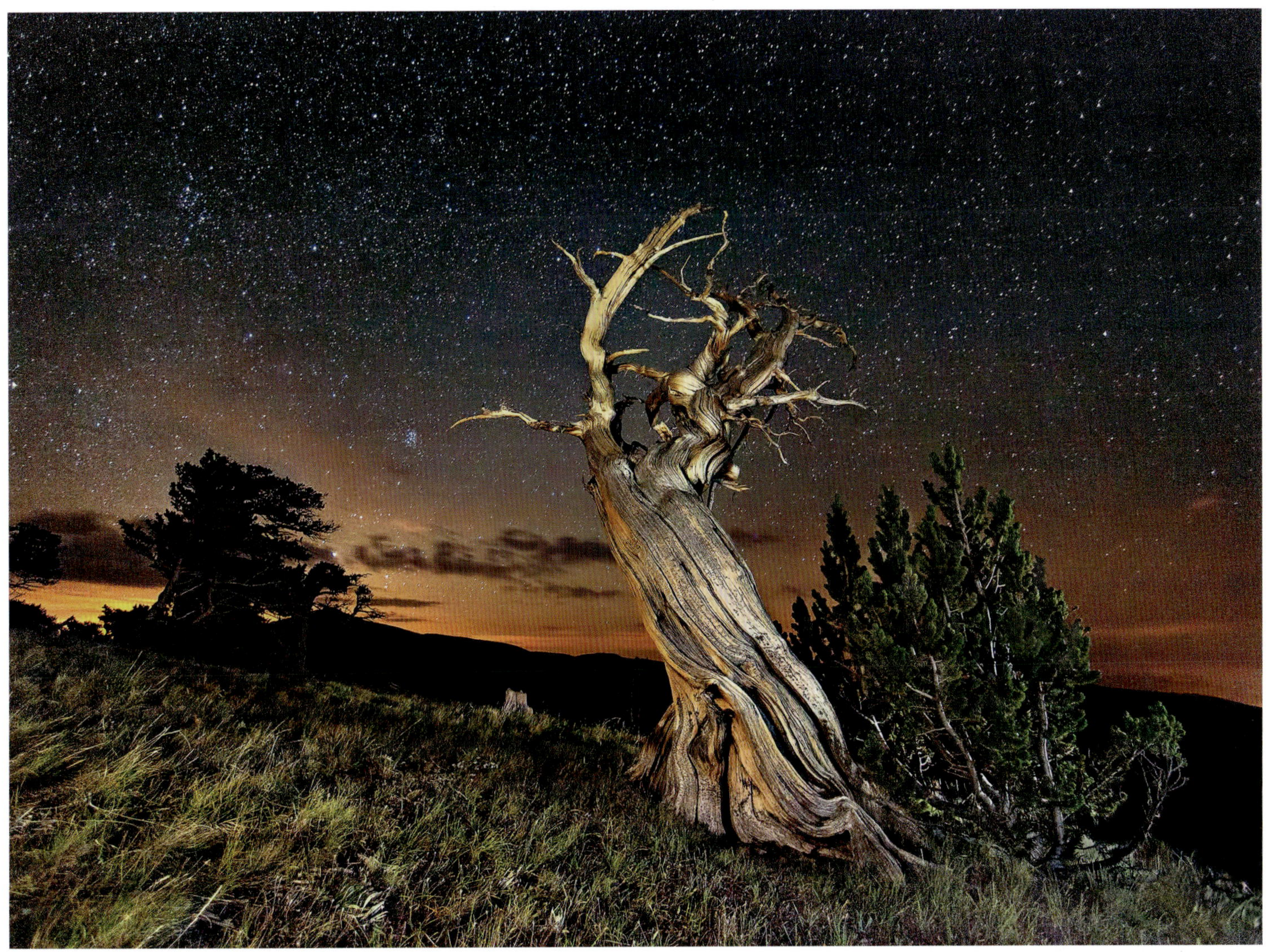

An ancient bristlecone pine stands along the slope of Mount Bross in Colorado. I created this photo from a series of images that were randomly illuminated by flashlights from students at my photography workshop. I used Smart Objects to blend multiple exposures in Photoshop and more evenly illuminate the scene. Canon 5D II, 14mm, f/2.8, 30 seconds, ISO 3200.

receive only 1/4 the amount of light. So you'll need to light paint the object four times longer than an object that is 1/2 the distance away to illuminate both objects evenly. If you have a light with adjustable focus, you can use a narrower beam to focus more light on distant subjects and a wider beam for nearby subjects.

Although this may sound complicated, you don't have to be too precise. The most important thing is to make sure that everything you want illuminated has been well lit by the flashlight. If some areas appear too bright, this is not a problem, as long as you're not overexposing the highlights. You can tone down bright spots using a Burn layer in Photoshop or the Adjustment Brush in Lightroom. I will describe how to do this in more detail in Chapter X. If, on the other hand, some parts of the scene are not well illuminated and are too dark, this is much more difficult to fix. If you try to brighten these areas later, it will bring out a lot of noise in the photograph.

It's important to check the photos you are taking on your LCD screen. Make sure you have illuminated every object you intended to light paint during the exposure and that you are not overexposing anything.

Bounce Light

One way to get more diffuse light in an image is to bounce the light off a rock or other object that is not in

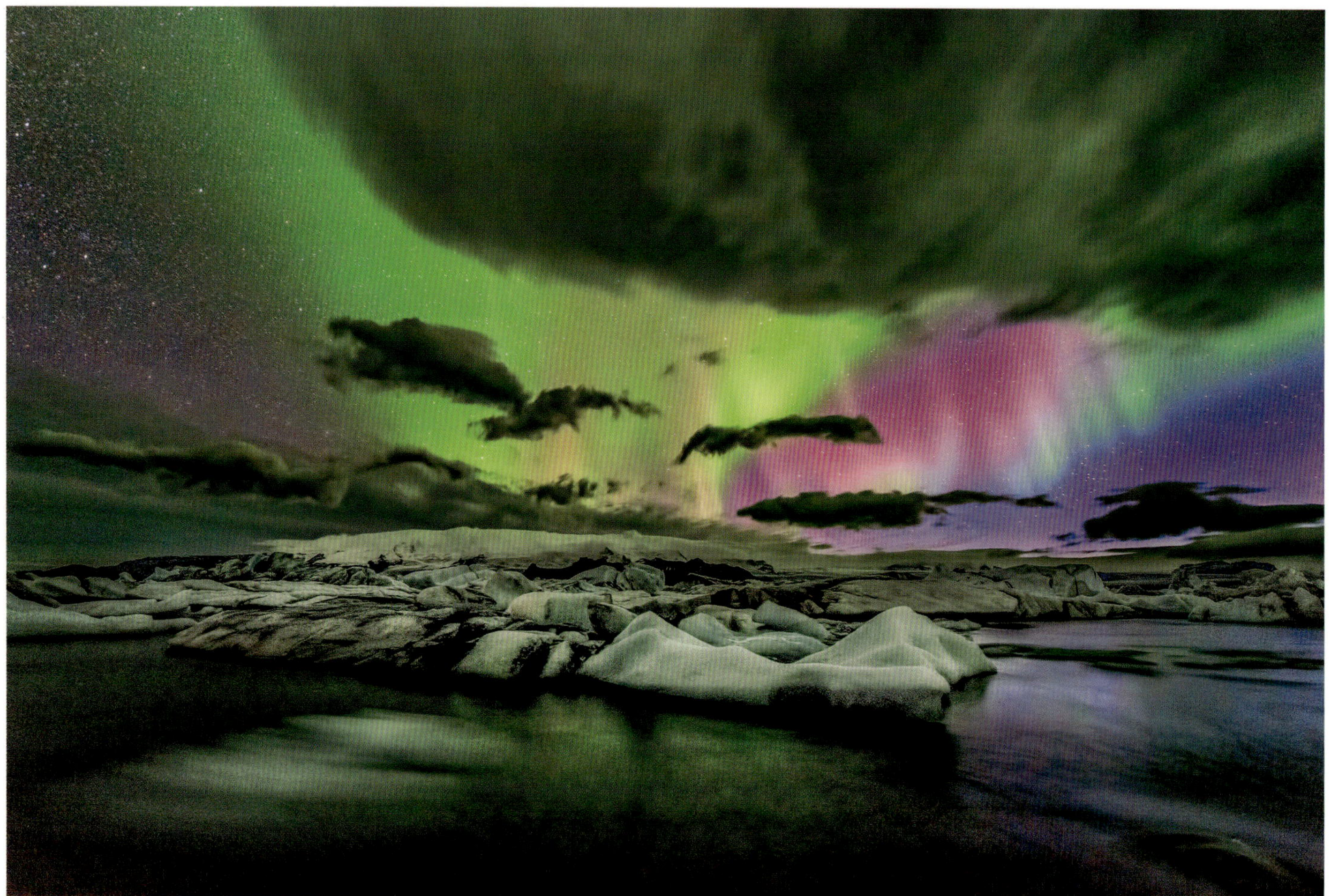

This image shows the northern lights above Jokulsarlon lagoon in southern Iceland. Even though there was no moon out on this night, the white icebergs were so bright that they reflected light from the northern lights and any other available light. I decided to use a flashlight as a fill light to add just a bit more light to the nearest icebergs. Nikon D800e, 18mm, f/2.8, 20 seconds, ISO 3200.

the photograph, rather than shining it directly onto the object you are photographing. This is usually best done when you have near foreground subjects you want to illuminate. Bounce light can significantly reduce the intensity of the beam, so it can be difficult to use bounce light with distant objects unless you have a powerful flashlight.

Using bounce light can change the color of the light from your flashlight. For example, if you are bouncing the light off of an orange rock, it will make the light warmer.

You can try bouncing light off many different things, including rocks, trees, grass, buildings, roads, or even your hand. The diffuseness and color of the beam will vary depending on what object you bounce it off.

Fill Light

You will usually want to light paint when there is no moon out, as the moon is bright enough that you won't often need a flashlight. However, sometimes the moon can cast overly dark shadows on the scene. In this situation, it can be helpful to use a flashlight to provide fill light. You won't need to shine the flashlight over the entire scene. Instead, just focus on getting some extra light in the shadow areas.

You can also use fill light if there is no moon out and the foreground is very bright or reflective. In this case, you may be able to capture detail in the landscape without a flashlight. However, you might want to use fill light to add a little more light to selective parts of the photo, as I did in the image above.

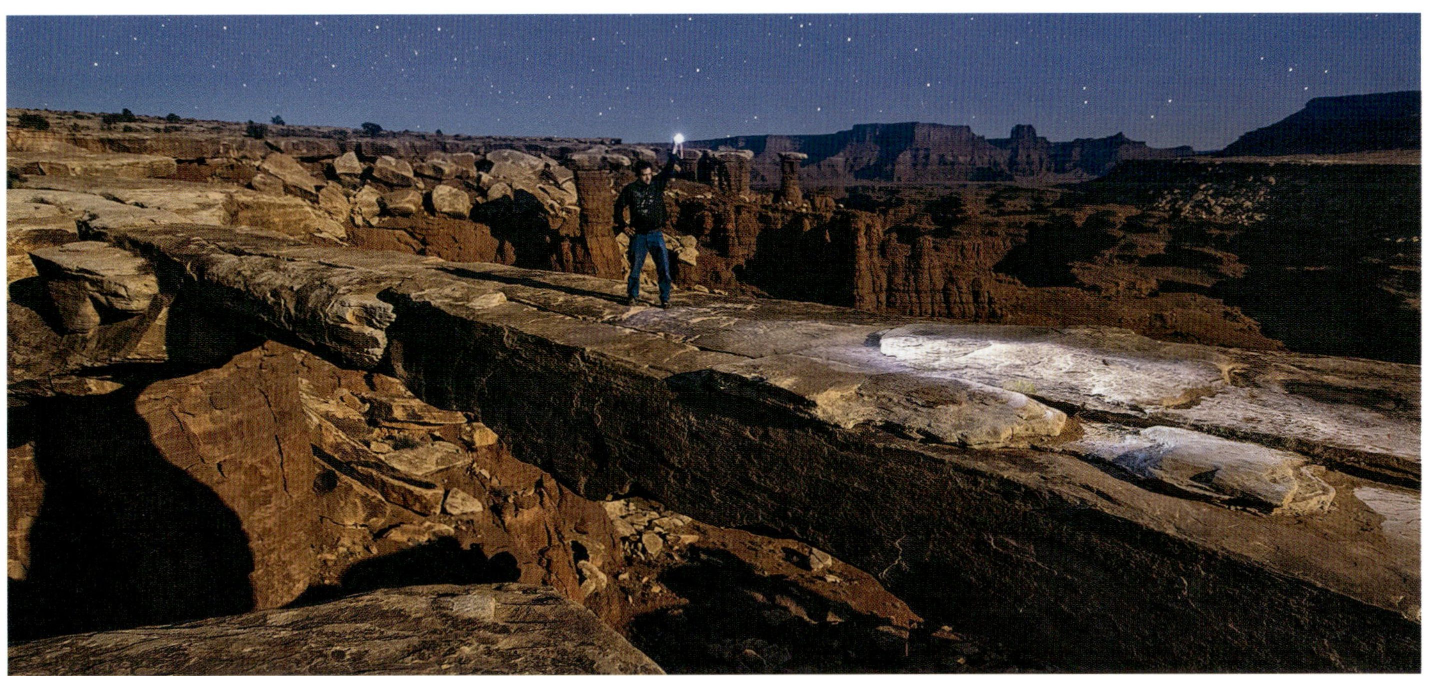

I couldn't quite get the shot I wanted of Musselman Arch in Canyonlands National Park. So I decided to stand on the arch and shine a headlamp to provide scale and add more drama to the scene. A crescent moon illuminated the landscape. Nikon D800e, 18mm, f/2.8, 20 seconds, ISO 3200.

Try Different Angles

I recommend shining your flashlight or LED panel from different angles and positions. You can take a shot with the light positioned near the camera but also take photos with the light to the left and right of the camera. This will produce some shadows and can give the appearance of more depth in the image. It can also bring out more texture in foreground objects.

If you have both near and distant objects you want to illuminate, you can try positioning the light far back from the camera. This will reduce the relative distance between the near and far objects and make it easier to illuminate the entire scene evenly.

Another thing you can experiment with is to place the light in front of the camera. You don't necessarily want the light to hit the camera directly. Instead, you can position the flashlight or LED panel behind a rock or a tree where it is not directly visible from the camera and illuminate part of the scene with it. This usually won't produce very natural-looking images, but it can produce interesting artistic effects.

If you want to shine the light far from the camera, you can use a self-timer to give yourself time to get in position before the exposure starts. If this doesn't give you enough time, you can program a longer delay if you have an intervalometer or a built-in interval timer on your camera. Or, you can simply set your camera to take repeated exposures. You can then move around as much as you want and try painting from different angles and positions, knowing that your camera will be taking shots the entire time. Another option is to purchase a wireless remote trigger that will allow you to begin an exposure from a long distance away.

Including People

One way to capture dramatic images with a flashlight is to take a shot with you or a friend standing in the photo with a flashlight or headlamp. You can shoot photos like this when the moon is out so that it illuminates the rest of the scene. Another option is to use two lights - one concentrated light that the person in the image will be holding and a more diffuse light used by the photographer to illuminate the scene. Or you can have the person standing in the shot use a diffuse flashlight to light up part of the scene under no moon and let the rest of the scene remain dark.

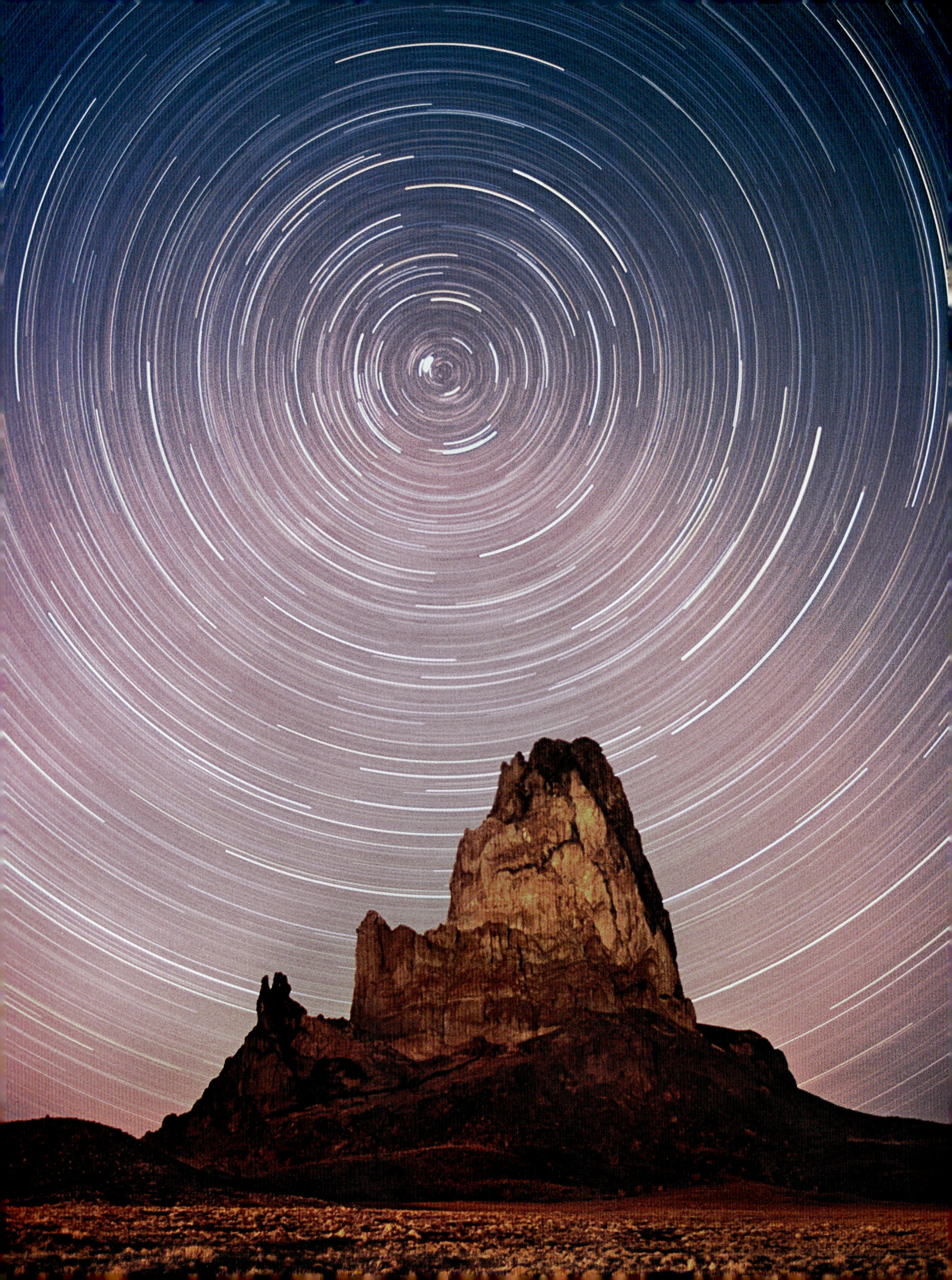

VII. Star Trails

If you take a very long exposure of the night sky using a camera that is sitting stationary on a tripod, you will capture what is known as star trails. During the exposure, our planet will rotate on its axis, and the stars will appear to move across the sky. The camera captures the light from the stars as they move, and the stars appear as curved lines in your image rather than points of light.

Some people do not like star trails because the image doesn't look like anything you would ever see with the naked eye. I find star trails intriguing because the camera provides a representation not just of the spatial dimensions but also of the dimension of time.

Since star trails take such a long time to photograph, I'll often shoot with more than one camera. With one or even two cameras, I will shoot star trails. While waiting on these shots, I'll take a lot of short exposures with a digital camera, where the stars appear as small points of light.

If you choose to set up multiple cameras, I recommend trying to find unique compositions for each image. You can even set up your cameras miles apart from one another and leave one while it is taking a long exposure. Of course, you should make sure there is no rain, snow, or strong wind in the forecast and that your camera is in a remote spot where it's not likely to be stolen.

Capturing a photograph of star trails is a seemingly straightforward process, as you just need to take a really long exposure at night. However, with digital cameras, this becomes problematic because, for reasons I will explain later in this chapter, the star trails appear fainter the longer you expose the image. Really long exposures can also produce large amounts of dark noise. This noise is minimal during shorter exposures, but it increases at a rate proportional to the exposure time. Long Exposure Noise Reduction can help reduce the noise, but the overall image quality will still be degraded.

Fortunately, there are a couple of ways around these problems. One is to take a lot of shorter exposures with a digital camera and combine them. Another option is to use a film camera.

I'll go over how to capture images with both a film camera and a digital camera later but will start with something you should consider before ever taking a photo.

PREVISUALIZING THE IMAGE

When composing an image, it's important to be able to previsualize how the star trails will appear. I've summarized below how star trails will look when you are facing different directions. This information is for photographing in the Northern Hemisphere. For photos in the Southern Hemisphere, simply point your camera in the opposite direction to capture star trails like those described below. For example, you can capture star circles when facing due south in the Southern Hemisphere rather than due north.

Facing North

If you face north when shooting a long exposure at night, you will capture star circles, as seen in the image on the previous page. The bright star near the very center is Polaris, or the North Star. Since this star is always located due north in the sky, its position will move very little during the night. All of the other stars will appear to rotate around it.

The farther north you are, the higher in the sky the North Star will be. In fact, the angle that the North Star appears in the sky corresponds exactly to the latitude from which you are taking the photo.

To locate the North Star, you first need to find the Big Dipper. The Big Dipper is one of the most prominent star patterns in the sky. As its name suggests, it looks like a giant dipper or ladle, and it will always be in the northern part of the sky. You need to locate the two

Left: By positioning my camera so that it was pointing due north towards Agathla Peak, I was able to capture the apparent motion of the stars around Polaris. Minolta 9xi film camera, 28mm, f/4.0, 2 1/2 hours, ISO 100.

stars that form the rightmost edge of the Big Dipper (or if the Big Dipper appears upside down in the sky, these stars will be on the leftmost side). These stars point almost directly to the North Star. Simply draw an imaginary line from the two stars and extend it up from the Big Dipper about five times the distance between these two stars to find the North Star.

If the Big Dipper is below the horizon or if it is obscured by clouds, you can also find the North Star using the constellation Cassiopeia. Cassiopeia looks like a big W in the sky, and it is always on the opposite side of the North Star from the Big Dipper. Take the center star in the W and the one just to the left of it (the one just to the right of it if the W is upside down), and draw a line up from the middle star at a 90-degree angle from these two stars. Extend this line about two times the width of the W, and this will lead you to the North Star. The diagram below will make it much easier to visualize this.

You can, of course, use a compass, app, or GPS unit to help you to point the camera due north. This is especially useful if you want to set up a shot before it gets dark. Unless your GPS unit has a compass built into it, it won't be able to locate due north when you are standing still. You will need to walk in the direction you think north is, and it will be able to determine your direction while you are in motion. If you use a compass, you'll need to factor in how many degrees magnetic north is off from true north at the spot you are photographing.

If you want to capture star circles, you should use a wide-angle lens to capture stars that are well above and below Polaris. I recommend a lens that is at least 30mm wide for a vertical photograph and at least 20mm wide for a horizontal photograph.

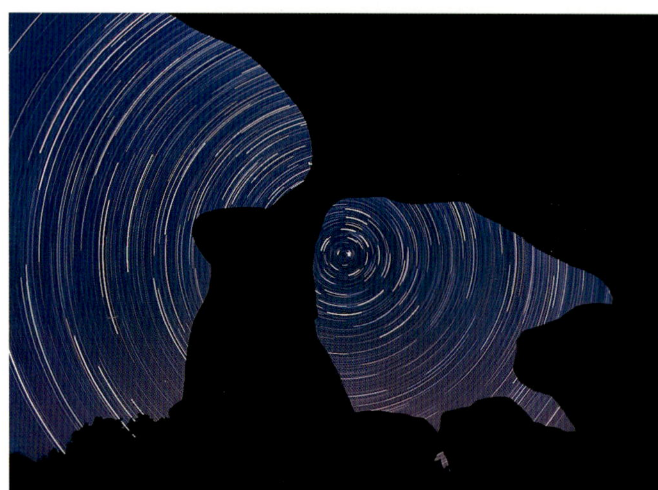

I captured this image of Metate Arch in Escalante National Monument while facing due north. I used a wide-angle lens so that I could include all of the arch and position Polaris in the center of the photograph. Canon EOS 650 film camera, 17mm, f/4.0, 2 hours, ISO 100.

When facing north, the stars will appear to move at a slower rate. You'll therefore need a longer exposure to capture sizable star trails. For most images, I recom-

You can easily find the North Star using either the Big Dipper or Cassiopeia.

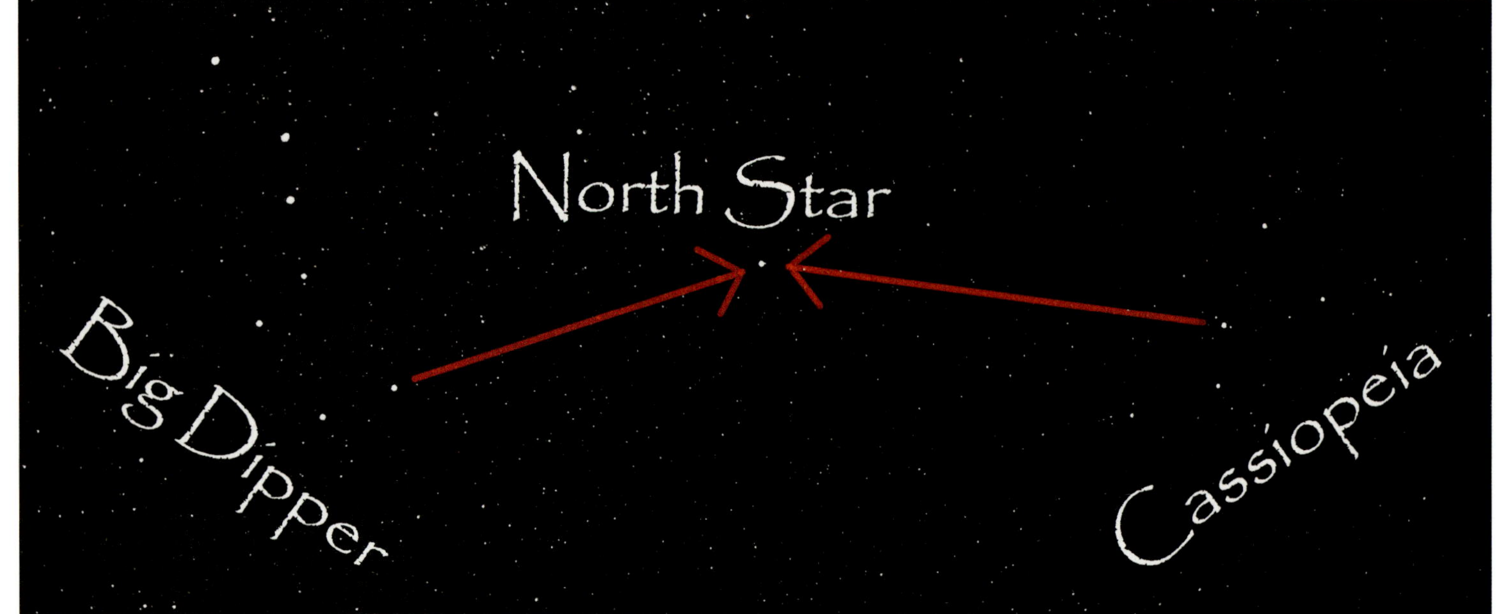

mend an exposure of at least two hours.

Facing South

If you face south when shooting star trails, the stars will move in shallow arcs above the horizon. The farther north you are, the shallower the arcs will appear.

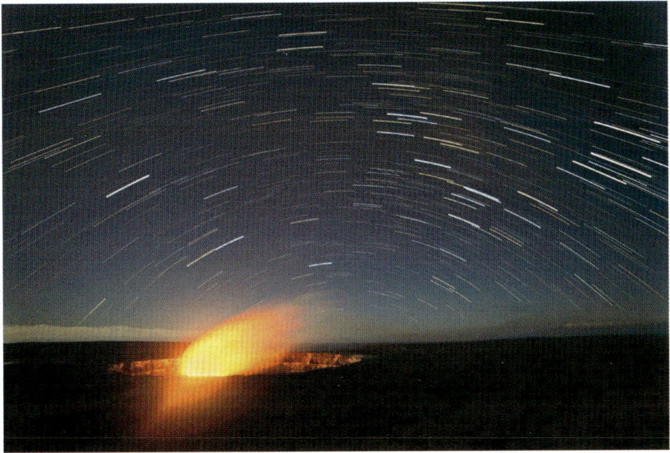

I positioned my camera so that it would be facing due south when photographing the Lava Lake on Hawaii's Big Island. Nikon D800e, f/2.8, 112 30-second exposures combined, ISO 6400.

Facing East

If you face east, the stars will move up and to your right during the exposure. The star trails will appear as curved, slanted lines. As you travel farther north, the angle of the trails to the horizon will decrease.

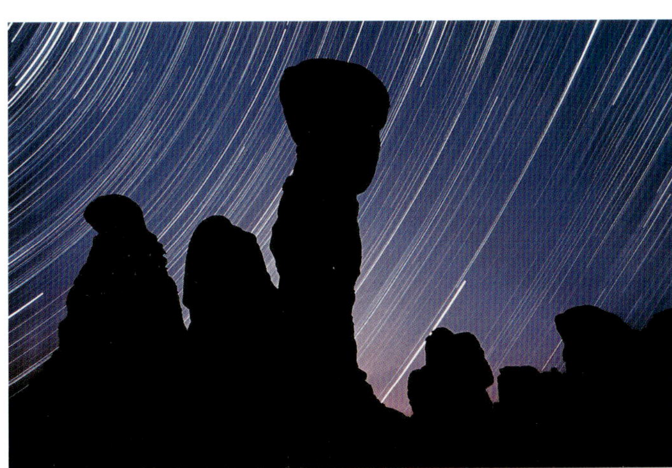

When taking this image of the Garden of Eden in Arches National Park, my camera was pointed east. Minolta 9xi film camera, 24mm, f/2.8, 2 hours, ISO 100.

Facing West

If you face west, the stars will move down and to your right during the exposure. Just like when you are facing east, the angle of the star trails to the horizon will decrease as you travel farther north.

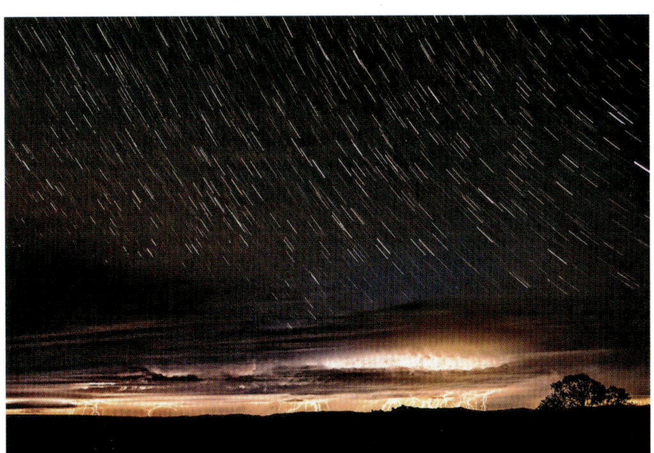

I took this image of distant lightning in Arches National Park while facing west. Nikon D800e, 35mm, f/2.8, 10 minutes, ISO 100.

Facing Southwest or Southeast

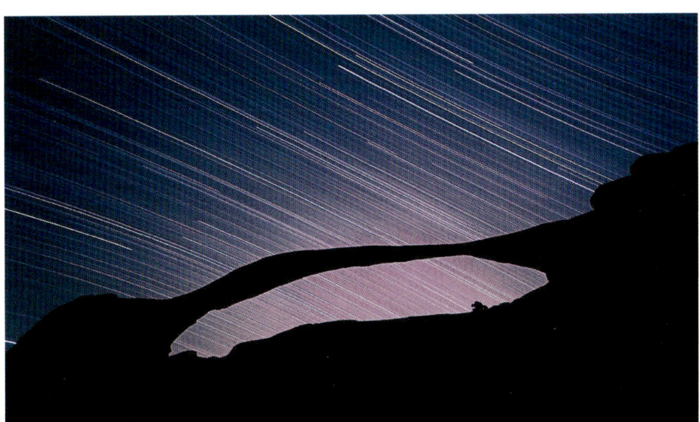

I was facing southwest when shooting this image of Landscape Arch in Arches National Park. From this direction, I was able to capture stars positioned both north and south of the equator. Minolta 9xi film camera, 28mm, f/2.8, 2 hours, ISO 100.

If you face toward the southeast or southwest in the Northern Hemisphere, you will capture the edges of two circles that are facing away from each other. A star trail located between these two circles falls along the celestial equator. This represents the division between stars positioned south of the equator and stars positioned north of the equator.

As you travel farther north, the celestial equator will become tilted more and more to the south. The point where the celestial equator touches the horizon, however, will always be due east or due west. So if you want the celestial equator to pass through the bottom corner of your image, you will need to position your camera so that the northernmost object in your frame is due east or due west of you.

At the Equator

If you take a photo from a location at or near the equator, the stars will appear as semicircles if you face north or south. If you face east or west, they will appear as nearly-straight, vertical lines. The North Star will be located just above the horizon if you are slightly north of the equator, and it will not be visible if you are south of the equator.

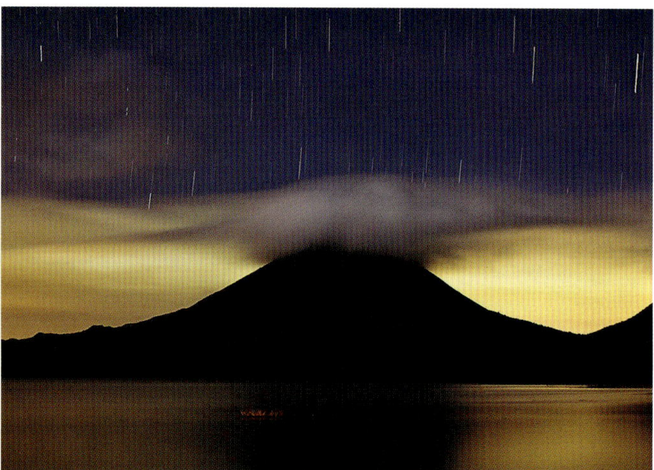

Star trails streak above Arenal Volcano in Costa Rica. Since I was near the equator and facing east, the star trails appear as vertical lines. Canon 5D, 50mm, f/2.2, 515 seconds, ISO 100.

At the Poles

It's highly unlikely that you'll ever shoot star trails from one of the poles. But if you did, all of the trails from any direction would appear horizontal and parallel to the horizon. At the North Pole, if you look straight up, you will see the North Star, and all of the other stars will be circling around it.

USING A FILM CAMERA

Once you've decided on a location to shoot and have previsualized how the star trails will appear, you'll need to choose how to capture the image. One option is to use a film camera. Perhaps the best reason to use a film camera is that it is inexpensive and can free up your digital camera to shoot shorter exposures while waiting on the very long exposures required to shoot star trails. It is also easy to shoot star trails with a film camera. You just need to take one really long exposure. However, if you own two good digital cameras, it is probably better to use one of them for star trails, as the color shift from long exposures with film cameras can sometimes be undesirable. You can skip to the section on digital cameras beginning on page 101 if you don't plan to use a film camera.

Choosing a Camera

If you don't already own a film camera, you can purchase one for a very reasonable price. Medium and large format film cameras will produce higher quality images. However, unless you already own such a camera, I recommend using a 35mm SLR film camera that is compatible with the lenses for your digital camera. You can find a lot of inexpensive 35mm film cameras on eBay. Ideally, you will want a camera that conserves battery life during the long exposure and doesn't keep a light shining on the display panel the entire time. Otherwise, you will likely be replacing the battery every few exposures. You will also need to buy a remote shutter release for the camera to shoot long exposures.

For Canon EOS shooters, I recommend the Canon EOS 620, 630, or 650 film cameras. These cameras use little battery power during long exposures, enabling you to take numerous star trail images with a single battery. Each of these cameras requires you to buy a GR20 grip to add a remote shutter release to the camera. You can usually buy the camera, the grip, and the remote shutter release on eBay for around $50.

Unfortunately, I couldn't find a Nikon film camera that works as well as the Canon cameras listed above. The F100 and N80/F80 are the only two reasonably-priced film cameras I found that are fully compatible with G lenses (G lenses are those that don't have a manual aperture ring on them). However, both of these cameras use a lot of battery power during long exposures. You can use the MC-30 Remote Shutter Release with the F100, and you will need a threaded cable release for the N80/F80.

The older, fully-manual Nikon film cameras usually don't require a battery to operate, so you won't have to worry about replacing them. Unfortunately, these cameras are not compatible with G lenses. However, every Nikon camera made since 1977 is compatible with Rokinon lenses since these have manual aperture rings. In fact, any Nikon camera made since 1959 will work with these lenses. The exposure meter won't work correctly with pre-1977 cameras, but you don't need the exposure meter for star trails. Among these cameras, I recommend the Nikon FM or FM10, since they are reasonably priced. You'll need to get a threaded cable release to take long exposures with these cameras.

If you have Sony A-mount lenses, Minolta Maxxum film cameras are compatible with these. However, the mirrorless Sony cameras that are best-suited for night photography use E-mount lenses, which are not compatible with any film camera.

Film

The film I recommend is Fuji Provia 100F. This is a super-fine grain slide film that produces more subdued colors than other films in the 100F series. This is important because high saturation films like Velvia are prone to extreme color shifts during long exposures. There will, however, be a noticeable color shift regardless of the film you use. Provia tends to produce purple and pink colors in the sky. You can adjust the colors some in post-processing if you don't like them.

Focusing

If possible, you should focus while it is still light out. It's difficult to focus film cameras when it's dark. If you use autofocus, make sure to switch your camera to manual focus once you have the focus locked in. Alternatively, if your lens has a hard-stop at infinity and you don't have any close foreground objects, you can just turn the focus ring to infinity.

If neither of these options works, it is easier to first focus the lens while it is on a digital camera, as described in Chapter IV. You can test the focus by taking a shot on your digital camera. You'll want to use the same aperture you'll be using with your film camera, but you'll need to use a much shorter shutter speed and higher ISO for the test shot. When you have the focus locked in, carefully transfer the lens over to the film camera without moving the focus ring.

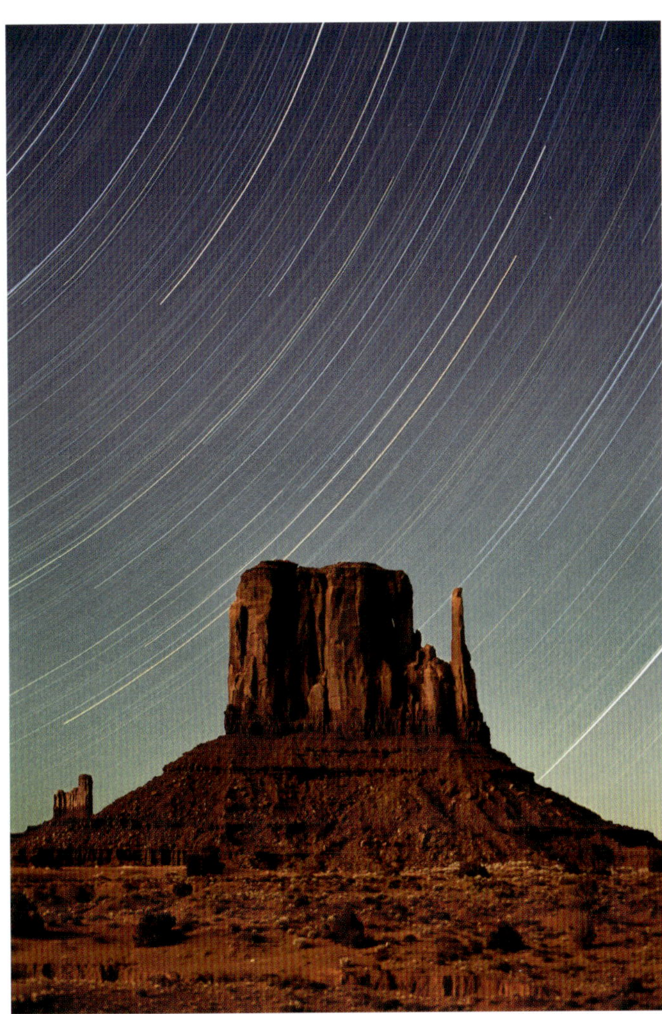

I did a 2-hour exposure under a quarter moon to capture long star trails and get a lot of detail in the West Mitten in Monument Valley. Canon EOS 650 film camera, 24mm, f/4.0, 2 hours, ISO 100.

Shutter Speed

You can expose the film as long as you want, from a few minutes for very short star trails to many hours for very long star trails. Rather than time my photos, I usually just pick out a star in the sky and note its position. I then wait for the star to move across the sky and stop the exposure when it has moved about the length I want the star trails to appear.

Alternatively, if you have an intervalometer, you can leave the camera and even go to sleep, since the camera will stop exposing when the timer expires. Intervalometers can, however, be hard to find for film cameras.

If you're using a wide-angle lens, I recommend exposing for at least two hours to capture long, dramatic star trails. You can do shorter exposures with longer lenses, as the stars won't take as long to move across the frame of your shot. However, the exact exposure length is ultimately your own artistic decision.

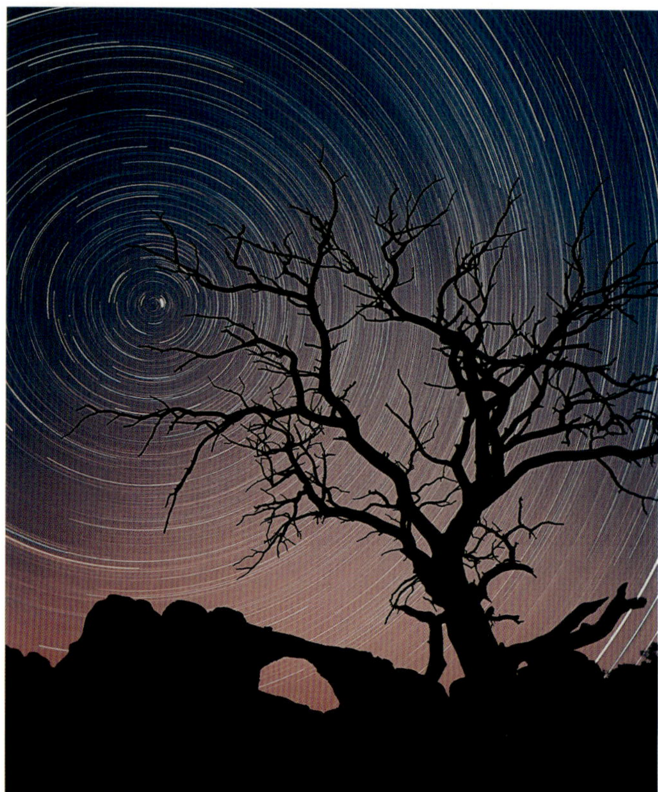

I captured this image of Skyline Arch in Utah on a night with no moon out. I was therefore able to use the widest aperture on my lens without fear of overexposing the image. Canon EOS 650 film camera, 28mm, f/2.8, 3 hours, ISO 100.

Aperture Settings

The aperture you'll use depends primarily on the phase of the moon. The brighter the moon is, the smaller the aperture you'll need. The proper settings for different moon phases are described below.

No Moon

When shooting ISO 100 film on a moonless night, you can use a very wide aperture. There is little risk of overexposing the photo if you are shooting outside of twilight hours and away from light pollution. I would, however, avoid going wider than f/2.8. Wider apertures like f/1.4 can produce more vignetting and soft corners, and there's a chance of overexposing the image. If you don't have a fast lens, f/4.0 or f/5.6 will work for star trails shot with film. The image may be underexposed, but this isn't as big of an issue with film, as you don't have to worry about dark noise.

Images shot under no moon will render the foreground as a dark silhouette. If you want detail in the landscape, you can try starting your exposure before the end of astronomical twilight. However, this can risk overexposing the image.

Crescent Moon

A better way to get detail in the foreground is to shoot with the moon out. I suggest shooting under a moon that is 20%-50% illuminated. A fainter moon may not be bright enough to fully illuminate the foreground, and a brighter moon can cause the image to be overexposed.

I recommend an aperture setting of f/4.0 and an exposure of no more than two to three hours. If you want longer star trails, I recommend an aperture of f/5.6 for exposures up to five or six hours and an aperture of f/6.7 for even longer exposures.

You'll generally want the moon behind you, so it illuminates the front of the foreground objects.

Full Moon

If possible, I recommend that you avoid shooting star trails under a full or gibbous moon with a film camera. The moon is so bright that if you set your aperture to f/4.0 or f/5.6, you will risk blowing out the highlights after just 15 minutes. One solution to this would be to use a much smaller aperture like f/13 and expose for around two hours. The problem with this is that you will get very faint star trails, and the image will look almost like a daytime shot with a blue sky and star trails that are barely visible.

You can usually get better results under a full or gibbous moon by combining multiple exposures with a digital camera. However, if you attempt to shoot with a film camera, I recommend using an aperture of f/6.7

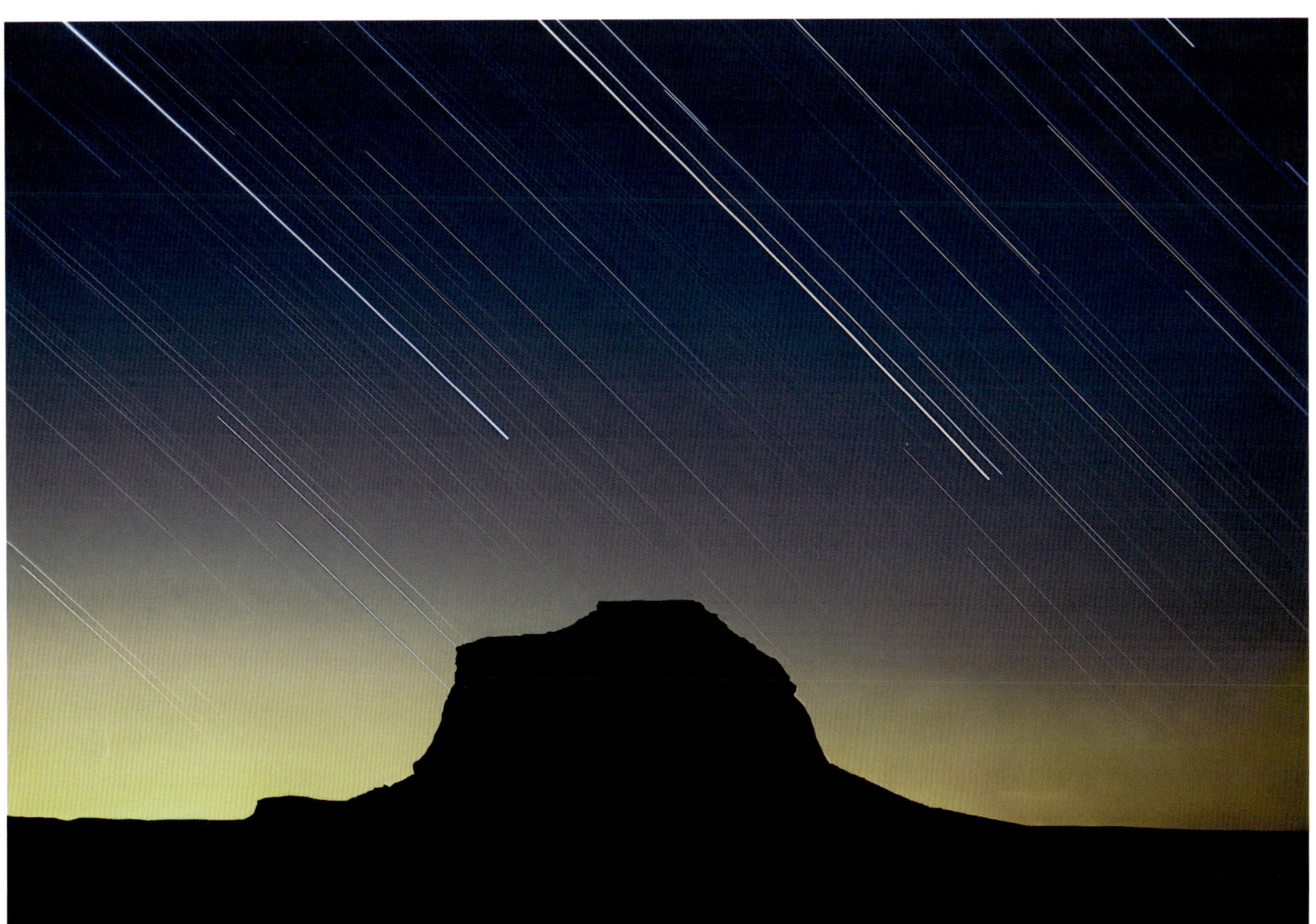

I took this image of star trails over West Pawnee Butte in Colorado using a film camera. While I took this shot, I used my digital camera to capture the image of East Pawnee Butte seen on pages 30-31. Canon EOS 650 film camera, 28mm, f/2.8, 2 hours, ISO 100.

---

and an exposure of 15 to 20 minutes. This should result in a photograph with clearly visible star trails that aren't overexposed.

Taking the Photo

Once you've decided on your aperture, you should set your film camera to Bulb mode, which allows you to take very long exposures. Then, simply lock the button on your remote shutter release in place and wait for however long you want to expose the image. If you have an intervalometer, you can set the length of the exposure beforehand.

Unless you have a darkroom and film scanner, you'll need to find a photo lab where you can develop and scan the images. Some photo labs no longer develop film, but if you live in a relatively large city, you shouldn't have a problem finding a lab that does. Alternatively, you can mail the film to a lab. You can then do post-processing work on the image, as described in Chapter X.

One issue with shooting 35mm film is that the number of exposures per roll is usually 36. You'll often only be exposing one image per night, and it may take years to shoot a full roll. So I will sometimes develop partial rolls of film.

USING A DIGITAL CAMERA

Photographing star trails with a digital camera can be more complicated than photographing them with a film camera. It can also be more expensive if you want to shoot with multiple cameras at the same time. However, a digital camera can give you the flexibility to later change the appearance of the star trails in post-processing. It will also produce more accurate colors.

When shooting these photos, you should start with a fully-charged battery, as it will drain quickly when you are taking long exposures. A battery grip that holds a second battery can be useful.

As I mentioned previously, taking a single two-hour exposure with a digital camera can result in lower-quality photographs. You will usually get better results by taking a lot of short exposures and combining them in Photoshop. I'll go over both of these options below.

Single Exposures

If you take one really long exposure with a digital camera, you'll find that the stars trails appear rather faint compared to an image taken with a shorter exposure. This is because a single star will only be located at any one point in the sky for a fraction of the length of the exposure. The camera records the light from the star when it is at that spot, but it also records much fainter light from the sky around that star. It records this light during the entire exposure. During a short exposure, that light is insignificant compared to the star, and the star will stand out brightly relative to the rest of the sky. However, over a very long exposure, the competing background light becomes more significant. The star stands out less prominently from the rest of the sky, and the star trails appear fainter.

One reason you can do longer exposures with film is because of reciprocity failure. Film becomes exponentially less sensitive to light as fewer photons hit it. So the dark areas of the sky between the stars are not eas-

I captured this image of star trails over Park Avenue in Arches National Park when there was a quarter moon out to illuminate the rock formations. I took 285 30-second exposures because I also wanted to make a time-lapse video from the images. The short exposures kept the stars looking like small points of light in the video. I didn't end up using all 285 photos for the star trails, as the increasing cloud cover would have obscured the stars too much. Nikon D800e, 14mm, f/2.8, 30-second exposures, ISO 2500.

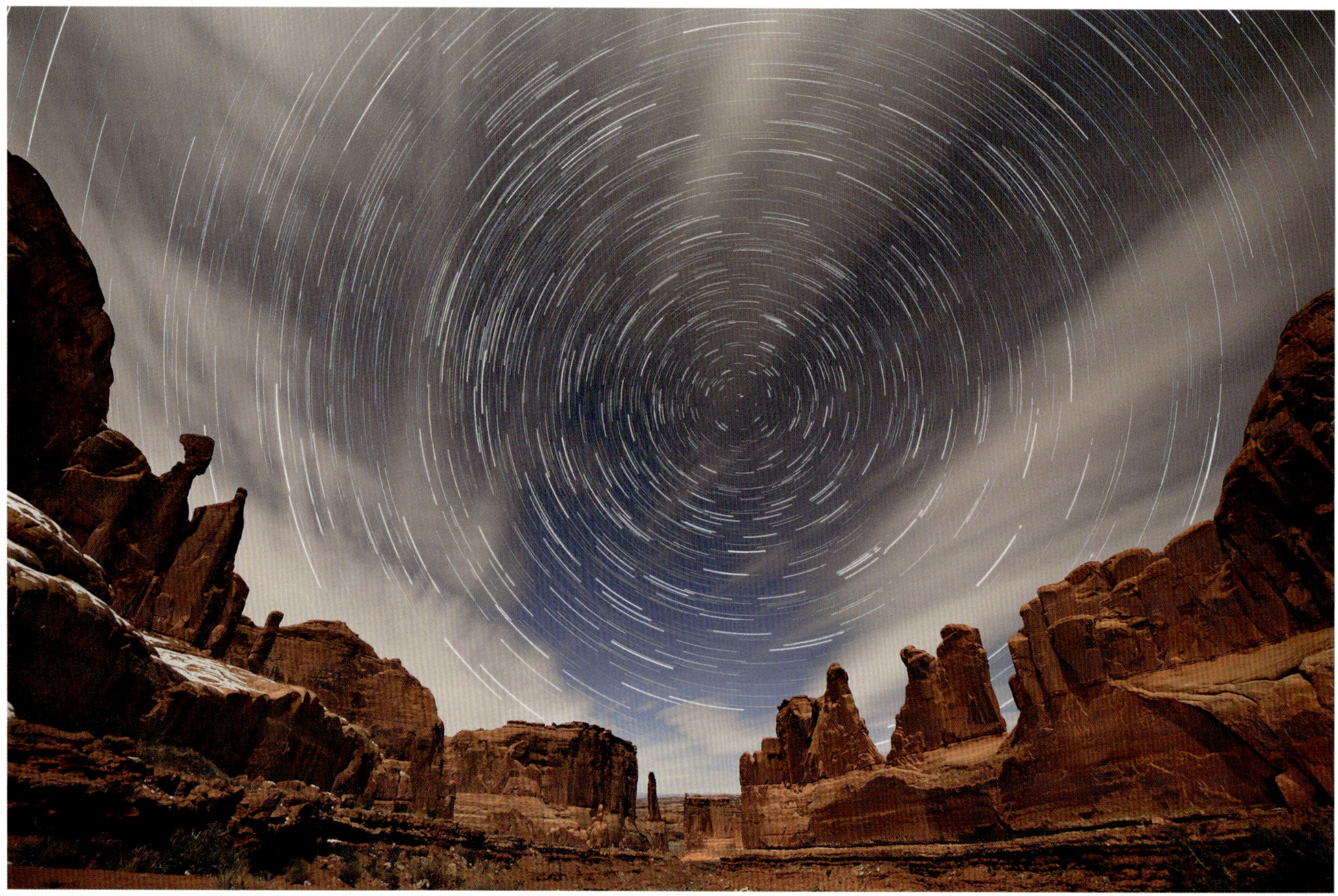

ily recorded by film, and the stars will stand out more relative to the rest of the sky.

Another issue with long exposures with a digital camera is that dark noise increases with exposure length. Long Exposure Noise Reduction can help minimize this, and it is especially useful at eliminating hot pixels. However, you may still see some red discoloration and overall image degradation that can be difficult to fix in post-processing.

You'll get less dark noise under a full or gibbous moon. This is because the moon will be so bright that the signal-to-noise ratio will be higher than it is under no moon. However, long exposures taken under a bright moon will result in even fainter star trails.

I recommend limiting single exposures on a digital camera to no more than 15 minutes. If you take longer exposures, the noise may increase to unacceptable levels when shooting under no moon. Under a bright moon, the star trails may become too faint. One exception to this is if you are shooting moon trails, as I'll describe later. In this case, you might prefer fainter trails since the moon is so bright.

You can always experiment with longer exposures on a digital camera, especially if your goal is to capture fainter star trails. Ultimately, it's up to you to decide how much noise you are comfortable with and how faint you want the star trails to appear.

If you do attempt to capture star trails with a single exposure, be sure to enable Long Exposure Noise Reduction. Your camera will take a dark frame immediately after your image is exposed, so make sure not to turn your camera off while it is taking the dark frame. The dark frame will take as long to capture as the initial exposure. You will therefore need to make sure you have enough battery power left to complete the dark frame. If you don't, you could replace the battery and then shoot your own dark frame.

To achieve the best results, the dark frame should be taken in the same conditions as the original image. Ideally, you should leave your camera at the same spot where you took the photo while it is taking the dark frame. If you don't have enough time or patience for this, you can put it in your car and drive home. The noise reduction may not be quite as effective, but it will be better than nothing. If possible, you should avoid using your heater or place your camera in your trunk in order to keep the temperature similar to the outdoor temperature.

To calculate exposure times and aperture settings for a single exposure, you can start with a test shot using a wide aperture and shorter exposures. You will then need to extrapolate the proper shutter speed and aperture for the longer exposure. For example, let's say you're able to get a good exposure with a shutter speed of 30 seconds at f/2.8 and ISO 6400. If you lower the ISO from 6400 to 100, you will be able to shoot 64 times longer. This comes to 32 minutes. So, you will be able to expose a shot for 32 minutes at f/2.8 and ISO 100. If you want to do even longer exposures, you can use smaller apertures. If you close the aperture one stop to f/4.0, you will let in half as much light. You can therefore do 64-minute exposures with ISO 100.

You can do these calculations yourself or use an app like PhotoPills. There is no reciprocity failure in digital cameras like there is with film, so you don't need to factor this in when calculating exposure lengths.

Before taking a photo, I recommend closing the eyepiece on your camera to prevent any light leak during the long exposures. If you can't close the eyepiece, you can cover it with a hat or cloth.

Multiple Exposures

Although combining multiple shorter exposures is more complicated than taking a single long exposure, it will almost always produce superior results if your goal is to capture bright, long star trails in your image. You will need to take repeated exposures with your digital camera and later combine them on the computer to create star trails. I'll go over all of the camera settings you need to use to capture these images and then discuss how to process the photos.

Shutter Speed

Perhaps surprisingly, the appearance of star trails will be affected more by the shutter speed you choose than by your ISO or aperture settings. Shorter individual exposures will yield brighter star trails than longer individual exposures. This may seem counterintuitive because it would be logical to think that combining 90 one-minute exposures would be basically the same as combining 30 three-minute exposures. However, the

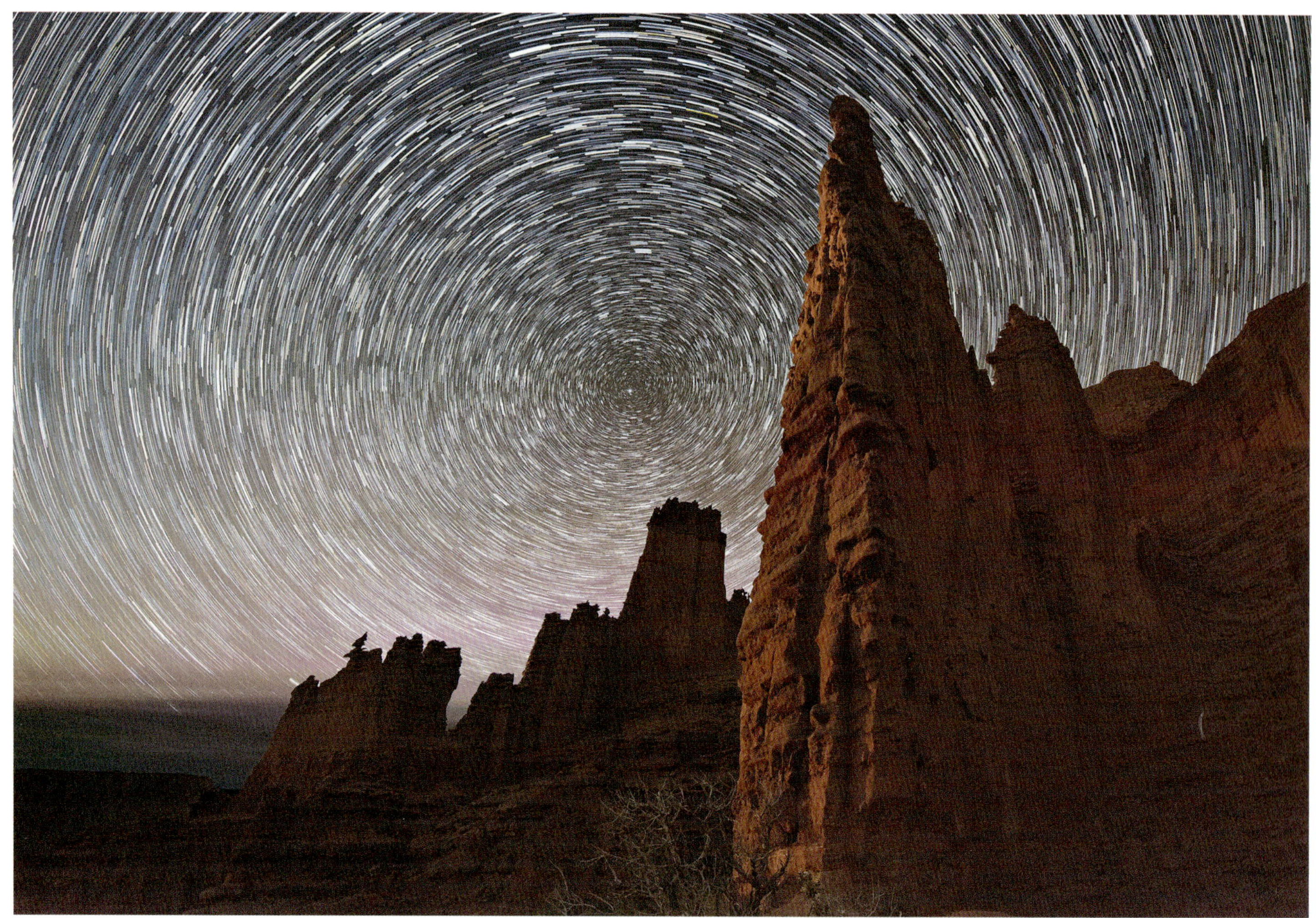

I pointed my camera due north to capture stars rotating above Fisher Towers in Utah. As with the previous image, I used 30-second exposures so that I could also create a time-lapse video. This image was taken with no moon out, and distant car headlights illuminated the scene. Nikon D800, 14mm, f/2.8, 208 30-second exposures, ISO 6400.

star trails will appear brighter in the image made from 90 one-minute exposures.

As explained in the section on single exposures, longer exposures will produce fainter star trails than shorter exposures. So the stars will be fainter in a three-minute exposure than a one-minute exposure relative to the rest of the sky. You might think that this would be offset when you combine the 90 one-minute exposures vs. just 30 three-minute exposures. In the final photograph, each star trail will have been exposed for 90 minutes, and the star trails will appear the same length in both images. This would be the case if the software you used to create the star trails simply averaged the brightness levels in each exposure, similar to how a camera records data over a period of time. However, the software doesn't work this way.

When blending two images, stacking software used to create star trails typically only uses the brightest pixels from one image and discards the darker pixels in the other image. If there is a bright star in a certain spot in one image but not the other, it will keep the data from that star and discard data from the other photo. This will make the star nearly twice as bright as it would have been if the software had simply averaged the brightness of the pixels in each image. The more photographs you combine, the brighter the stars will be compared to an image where you simply average the values of all of the pixels. This will make it look like there are more star trails in the photo, but this is mostly an illusion. It only appears this way because the faint star trails stand out more.

If this sounds complicated, don't worry. All you need

to know is that, when combining multiple images to create star trails, shorter individual exposures will produce brighter star trails than longer individual exposures.

The exact exposure length you choose is ultimately an artistic decision. 30-second exposures shot under no moon will produce a substantial number of bright star trails packed together, as seen in the image on the previous page. Some people may prefer all the streaks of light, as it can create a mesmerizing effect, especially if you are facing north. Others may feel that this makes the image look too busy and overcrowded.

If you do a short exposure based on the rule of 500 or the NPF rule, as explained on pages 54-55, you can also produce a time-lapse video with all of the images you take. Also, you can pick out your favorite single exposure and use that image with the stars appearing as points of light, rather than as star trails. You can even stack multiple photos of the land and sky to improve the quality of the image with the stars appearing as points of light. I explain how to stack images in Chapter IX.

Since there are so many ways to process consecutive short exposures, I often use the rule of 500 when shooting under no moon or a crescent moon and the NPF rule when shooting under a bright gibbous moon. I personally don't prefer the crowded look of star trails that can be produced by these short exposures. However, the ability to use the images in many different ways more than makes up for this in most situations.

If your main goal is to produce a good star trail image, you might want to do longer exposures. If you want to capture long star trails under no moon with a total exposure length of around two hours, I find that shutter speeds of 2-3 minutes work well. There won't be as many bright star trails, so they won't appear to be packed together as tightly. You can increase the length of the individual exposures to around five minutes if you want even fainter trails. I don't generally recommend doing longer individual exposures, as the dark noise can become more problematic.

If you shoot under a moon, the star trails will appear fainter, so you may want to compensate by using shorter individual exposures. I like using individual exposures of around 1-2 minutes under a quarter moon and 10-30 seconds under a full or gibbous moon.

You need to minimize the time between each exposure, so as to avoid having a noticeable gap in the star trails. On your intervalometer, you should set the interval between exposures to one second. Make sure Long Exposure Noise Reduction, mirror lock-up, and the self-timer are all off on your camera. These functions will increase the time between each exposure or prevent the camera from taking repeated exposures.

If you don't have an intervalometer, you can use a standard remote shutter release and take repeated exposures up to 30 seconds each. However, many cameras limit the number of shots you can take in continuous-shooting mode. So make sure your camera will be able to continue shooting as long as you want.

Another option for taking repeated exposures is to use the interval timer that is built into many of Nikon's DSLRs and some newer Canon models. You can add this function to older Canon EOS cameras with the Magic Lantern software and to some Sony cameras with the Time Lapse app. When using Nikon's timer for 30-second exposures, you should set the interval to 33 seconds, as explained on page 23.

Aperture Settings

The aperture you choose actually won't have too much effect on the appearance of the final image. If you use a wide aperture, you will get a brighter photo, and if you use a smaller aperture, you will get a darker photo. However, the relative brightness of the stars to the rest of the sky will stay the same. Therefore, if you adjust the brightness of the images in post-processing, so they match each other, they will look very similar.

For short exposures where you want the stars rendered as points of light, it is important to use a very wide aperture to reduce noise. This isn't quite as important when stacking images to create star trails. Since you will be combining so many photos, you will effectively be increasing the signal-to-noise ratio and can get good quality images with smaller apertures. I therefore recommend stopping down from the widest aperture to get closer to the sweet spot of your lens. The sweet spot is where your lens performs best if noise is not as big of an issue. It will produce less vignetting and can make the images a little sharper.

For a lens with a maximum aperture of f/1.4, I recommend shooting at f/2.8 or f/3.2. For a lens with a maximum aperture of f/2.8, I recommend shooting star trails at f/5.6. For a lens with a maximum aperture of f/4.0 or smaller, I recommend shooting at f/6.3 or f/6.7. An exception to this is if you are doing short exposures and want to use the individual exposures to also get images where the stars appear as points of light. In this case, you want to use a very wide aperture to maximize the quality of the individual exposures.

Smaller apertures will give you more depth of field and allow you to include closer foreground objects in the image. If necessary, you can use even smaller apertures to further increase the depth of field.

ISO

If you're shooting under a crescent moon or no moon, you will usually want to use an ISO between 1600-6400, so long as it doesn't cause you to blow out any highlights. If you're shooting under a brighter moon, you may need to lower the ISO to avoid overexposing the photo. Also, if the moon will be rising during your exposures, you will want to underexpose the initial image to ensure that it does not become overexposed after the moon rises.

As with the aperture setting, the ISO you choose won't significantly affect the final appearance of the image. Any ISO between 800-6400 will create about the same results. Higher ISOs will not produce brighter star trails relative to the rest of the sky. ISOs below 800 can start to show more noise, so you should avoid them unless shooting under a bright moon.

Taking the Photos

Before you begin your exposures, you should take a test shot with the camera settings you have decided on. Review this image on your LCD screen to make sure it is in focus and you aren't overexposing the highlights.

If the test shot looks good, I recommend taking a single dark frame with the lens cap and eyepiece cover on. Be sure to use the same settings that you will be using with all of the other images. The dark frame can help reduce noise in the image in post-processing.

You can now begin taking continuous exposures of the scene. You'll need to take the lens cap back off, but you can keep the eyepiece closed to prevent light leak. If you are using an intervalometer, you can set the exact number of exposures that the camera will take. If you're not sure how long you want to shoot, you can set this to the maximum value or to --. You can then manually stop the exposures whenever you want.

I recommend starting the exposures around the end of nautical twilight, or about 50 minutes after sunset. At this time, it should still be light enough to capture detail in the foreground, even with no moon out. If you find that the images you took during this time are too bright and cause the sky to look washed out, you can always eliminate the first several exposures when you are combining the images in post-processing. So it is better to start shooting a little too early than too late.

Another option for getting detail in the landscape is to take one exposure shortly after sunset. You can combine the foreground from this image with the star trails you capture later in the evening. I explain how to do this in Chapter IX.

Once you start taking the continuous exposures, you can just sit back and wait as long as necessary to capture the length of star trails you desire. It's better to shoot too many images than too few, as you can always shorten the star trails later. If you're using a wide-angle lens, I recommend letting the camera continue shooting for at least a couple of hours (or until the battery dies). If you are using a longer lens, you can do fewer exposures and still capture long star trails.

Post-Processing with Digital

There are many ways to create a composite image with star trails after you capture all of your photos. One way is to simply stack all of the images you took onto a single file in Photoshop and change the blending mode of the layers to Lighten. Unfortunately, because of the way the Lighten blending mode works, this will leave gaps in the star trails, and they will look like dotted lines. You can avoid this problem by using a combination of the Lighten blending mode and the Screen blending mode. This is a somewhat complicated process, but fortunately, Floris Van Breugel has created a free Photoshop script that does all of the work for you. This script can be found at https://www.artinnaturephotography.com/page/startrailstacker/.

When preparing files in Lightroom to be used with this script, you can select the first image you plan to use in the star trail sequence. First, you'll want to set

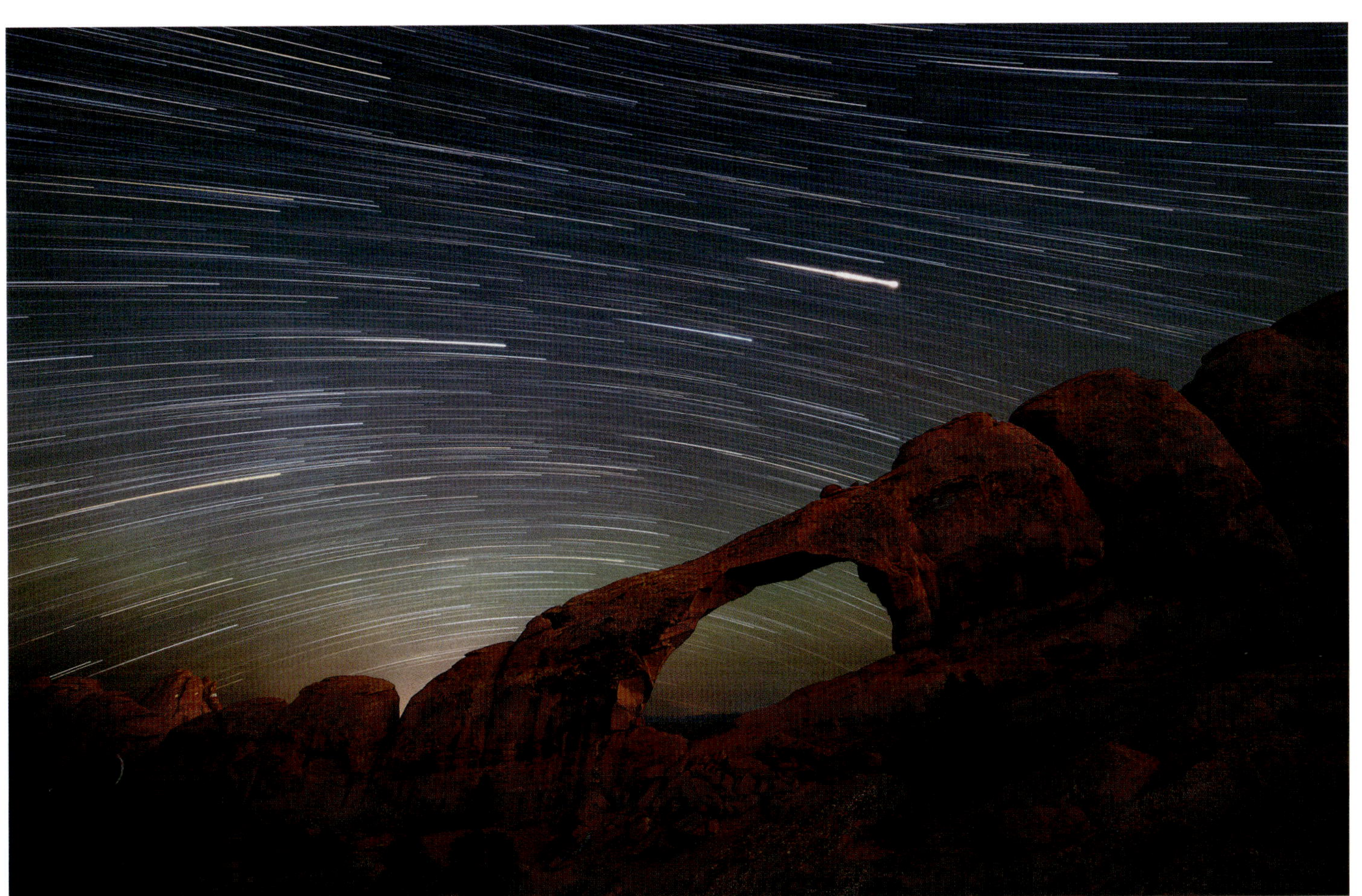

I captured this image of Skyline Arch in Arches National Park by combining a lot of shorter exposures on a digital camera. I created a comet-like effect by progressively decreasing the opacity of the layers to make the star trails slowly taper off. I did not, however, add glowing heads to these star trails. Nikon D800e, 14mm, f/5.6, 3 minutes per exposure, ISO 1600, 20 exposures combined.

the white balance at a temperature that looks natural to you. Then you should move the Exposure slider to the left to intentionally underexpose the image. You'll want to keep almost all of the data on the left half of the histogram and leave the right half mostly empty. This is an important step that isn't mentioned in the instructions provided with this script. If you don't do this, the final image produced by the stacking software may have overexposed highlights.

If you see chromatic aberration in the stars, you can try to fix this by adjusting the sliders under Defringe in the Manual part of the Lens Correction panel. All of the other adjustment sliders, including Sharpening, should be set to zero, and the Tone Curve should be set to Linear. These settings will help ensure that you get the smoothest possible star trails. You'll only want to make adjustments to contrast, saturation, vignetting, etc. after you have combined all of the images.

Once you've made the adjustments to a single image, you need to apply them to all of the photos you are using to create the star trails. Make sure the image you've made the adjustments to is selected and then hit Ctrl+Shift+C (Cmd+Shift+C on a Mac). In the dialog box that appears, click on Check All and then click Copy. Now, go to the Library module and hit G to go into Grid View. Then, select all of the images you want to use (including the dark frame if you took one) and click Ctrl+Shift+V (Cmd+Shift+V on a Mac) to paste the settings onto all of the images. Alternatively, you can use the Auto Sync feature in Lightroom. However, I prefer not to use this. If you forget it is enabled, you might unintentionally make adjustments to multiple photos at once.

If you are exporting a very large number of images or have a slower computer, I recommend exporting the images as 8-bit TIFF files. Normally, I would advise keeping the images at 16 bits to preserve as much color data as possible. However, stacked star trail images can be so big that using 8 bits can keep the size down. On rare occasions, 8-bit files can produce banding in areas of the image with subtle gradations. If you notice this, you may want to go back and reprocess the images at 16 bits.

If there are any lights from airplanes or satellites in your photographs that you want to remove, I suggest doing this before you combine all of the photos into star trails. You can do this in Lightroom before exporting the images or in Photoshop afterward. I prefer using Photoshop since it has more cloning and healing brush options. Try not to clone out any of the bright stars, as that could create a gap in the star trails. You don't have to do a very precise job with this. Since this is just one of many layers that make up the image, any small imperfections in that layer will be much less noticeable in the final image. You should, however, check the final image to see if there are any problem areas.

You can now run the script made by Floris, using the instructions found on the download page. I recommend using the script that preserves the layers, so you can shorten the star trails afterward if necessary. To shorten the star trails, just hide the first several layers or the last several layers in Photoshop. If you have a very large number of files or a slower computer, you can use the script that does not preserve the layers, as this will be much faster and produce a much smaller image file.

If you took a dark frame, you can drag this onto the very top layer of your star trail image. Then just change the blending mode to Subtract. A more precise way to do this would be to apply the dark frame to every image before creating the star trails. However, this can be time-consuming, and applying it once at the end is usually quite effective.

After you run Floris's script, you should check the histogram of the resulting image in Photoshop. If there is a spike on the right side of the histogram, it means the highlights are blown out. You'll need to start over and push the exposure slider farther to the left on all of the images in Lightroom.

Your image will likely look very flat, so you can reimport it into Lightroom or work on it in Photoshop to bring out contrast and color. I explain how to do this in Chapter X.

If you don't own Photoshop or aren't comfortable using scripts, there's a program called Startrails.exe created by Achim Schaller that you can download for free at https://www.startrails.de/. I've found that this program creates very similar star trails to those produced by Floris's script. This software, however, doesn't give you the option of preserving the layers, so you'll have to reprocess the entire image if you want to make the star trails shorter. Also, you won't be able to create special effects with this software, like the comet-like star trails described below.

Creating Comet-Like Star Trails

Some night photographers like altering the appearance of star trails so that they look like comets streaking across the sky. I personally don't like this effect as much, as I think it looks a little too unnatural. However, this can be a very eye-catching effect, and I would not discourage anyone from trying it. I'll first describe how to do this manually and then give links to some software that can do this for you.

Taking the Photos

If you want to create this effect, you'll need to take a lot of consecutive shots with your digital camera, as described previously in this chapter. You'll need to avoid exposing the individual images too long if you want to create a glowing head on the end of the star trail, as I did in the image on the next page. You can use the rule of 2000 to calculate the maximum exposure time. If you're shooting with a 20mm lens, you'll take 2000 / 20 = 100. So you would expose each photo for no more than 100 seconds. You can expose the images for shorter times if you want to produce brighter star trails. In this case, you could combine two or more of the exposures to create the glowing heads.

Manually Creating the Comet Trails

Once you've captured all of the images, you can combine them using Floris Van Breugel's script, as described in the previous section. Make sure to use the script that preserves the layers in Photoshop, not the one that flattens the image.

After you've created the star trail image, the first thing

you need to do is change the opacity of all the layers so that they are progressively more opaque. This will create a tapering-off effect with the star trails. To do this, first take 100 divided by the number of layers in your image. For example, if there are 50 layers, you'll take 100 / 50 = 2. You'll then want to change the very bottom layer to 2% opacity. This layer is the background layer, so to change its opacity, you'll first need to convert it to a regular layer by right-clicking on it and selecting Layer From Background... Next, change the opacity of the layer above this one to 4%, the layer above that to 6%, and so on until you get to the very top layer, which will remain at 100%.

You can change the direction of the tapering-off effect by starting with the top layer and moving down until you reach the bottom layer, which will remain at 100% opacity. I prefer to start with the bottom layer at 2%, as the stars will then appear to be moving in the same direction that they were in reality.

Once you've changed the opacity of the layers, you'll notice the tapering-off effect on the star trails. This effect alone is quite nice, and if you like it, you may prefer to keep this as your final image. If you want to have a glowing head on the end of your star trail, there is a way to do this in Photoshop. After a lot of experimentation, the best result I achieved was with the Paint Daubs filter. This filter can be found by going to Filter > Filter Gallery... It only works with 8-bit files, so you'll need to convert your image to 8 bits if you are working with a 16-bit file.

I produced this image of star trails over a remote arch in Arizona using a digital camera. I took 184 30-second exposures but only used 30 of the photos for this image. I created a comet-like effect with glowing heads using the Paint Daubs filter described in this chapter. Canon 5D II, 70mm, f/2.8, 30 seconds, ISO 6400.

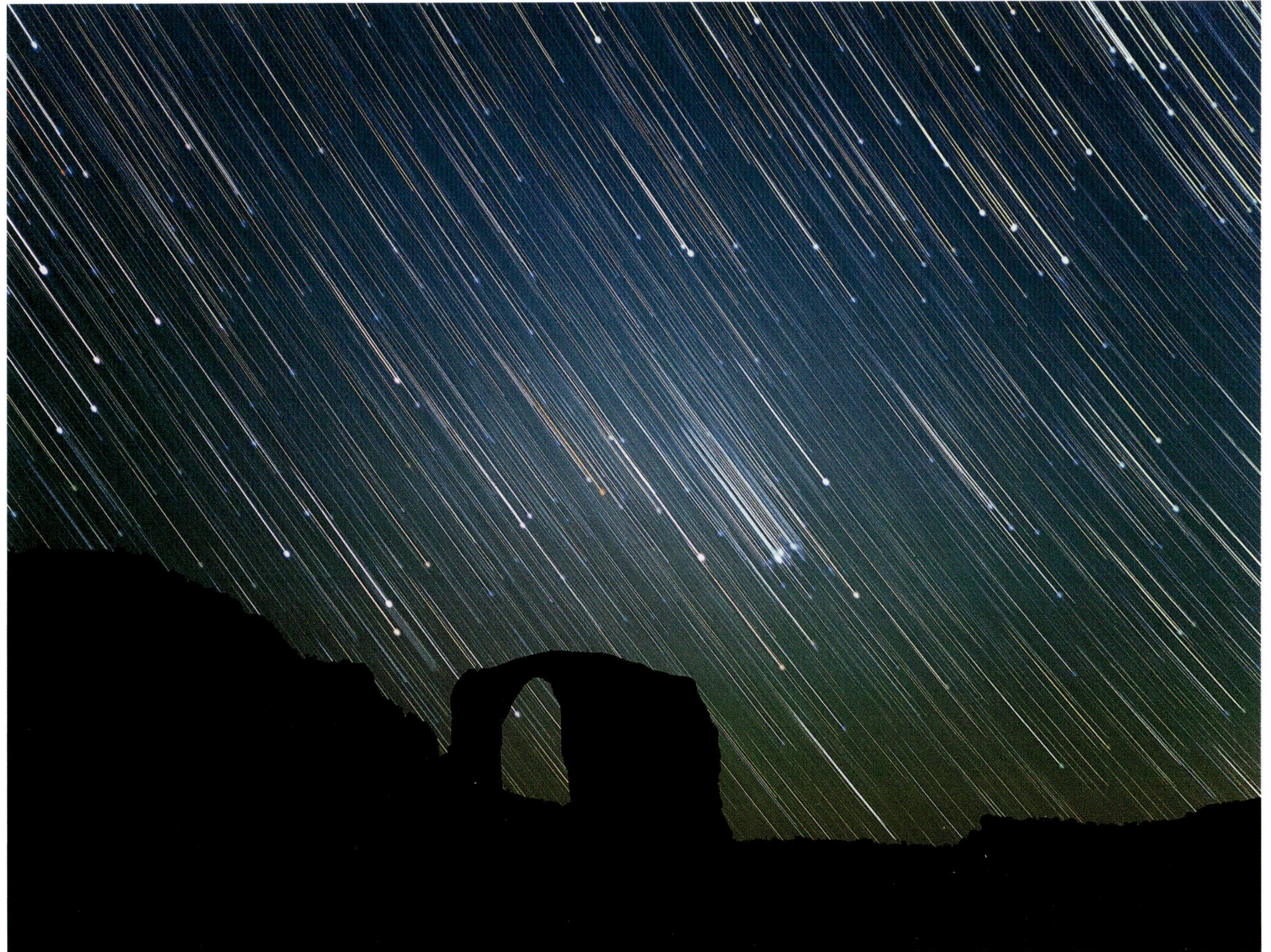

First, you'll need to duplicate the top layer on your star trail image by right-clicking on it and selecting Duplicate Layer... Now, make sure the new, duplicate layer is selected and go to Filter > Artistic > Paint Daubs. I recommend using these settings:

Brush Size: 7 to 20
Sharpness: 0
Brush Type: Light Rough

Now, click Okay, and you should see small glowing heads on the end of each star trail. This filter can blur the landscape, so you should mask out any foreground on this layer.

You can fine-tune the image and make the head glow more by selecting Filter > Blur > Gaussian Blur. You can try different radiuses and see what you like best. I recommend using a radius of 2-10 pixels.

Instead of creating the glowing head in Photoshop, you can produce it using a Photoshop plug-in called Star Spikes Pro. You'll again need to select the top, duplicate layer. To create a small glowing ball in Star Spikes Pro, you should keep the length of the spikes short and set the number of spikes to 32. This program is not available for Macintosh computers, but you can try using the Astronomy Tools Actions Set. These actions don't give you as much control over the appearance of the spikes, but they can produce interesting results.

You can also create the glowing head in-camera. Immediately after you have finished taking all of the images for the star trails, you can take a single exposure with the stars out of focus. You should add this shot to the top layer of your star trail image and set the blending mode to Lighten.

StarStaX

If this seems overly complicated, there are programs and scripts that will do much of the work for you. The best free version I have found is StarStaX created by Markus Enzweiler at https://markus-enzweiler.de/starstax/. To use this program, go to File > Open Images... and select all of the images you want to combine into star trails. If you took a dark frame, you can include this by going to File > Open Dark Frames... Next, you can set your preferences by going to Edit > Preferences... I recommend setting the Blending Mode to Gap Filling. To create a comet effect, you should check the box next to Comet Mode. The slider below this allows you to select the length of the star trails. The middle setting seems to work well, but you can experiment with other options. To make the comets appear to be moving in the opposite direction, check Process Images in Reverse Order. If you added a dark frame, select Subtract Dark Images. Now, go to Edit > Start Processing to create the star trails.

I've found that with the blending mode set to Gap Filling using the default settings, StarStaX creates images with a little more noticeable gaps than Floris's script or StarTrails.exe. You can reduce the gaps further by clicking on the wrench icon and adjusting the Threshold and Amount sliders. However, this can also widen the star trails and make them start to overlap with neighboring star trails. Also, it can cause the highlights to be blown out on some of the brighter star trails. I therefore still prefer Floris's script and StarTrails.exe. The difference will likely only be noticeable in larger prints, though, so this program can be useful for the ease of creating the comet effect.

StarStaX does not let you create the glowing heads at the end of the star trails, and it doesn't preserve the layers so you can do this yourself. You can manually add this layer in Photoshop by dragging the last image that was used in creating the star trails onto the image created by StarStaX. Then, set the blending mode to Lighten, and create the glowing head as described in the previous section.

Creative Effects UI

There is a Photoshop script created by Sathya R. that will produce the comet effect and a separate layer for creating the glowing head. It also has many other creative options for making some fascinating star trails. This script does create noticeable gaps in the star trails. I therefore don't recommend it for images that you'll be printing. It can be downloaded for free at https://liketheocean.com/night-photography/scripts-to-make-your-star-trails-awesome/. There is another script on this page that lets you create star trails from shorter, single exposures.

Moon Trails

If you include the moon in a very long exposure, it will produce a much wider trail in the sky. I recom-

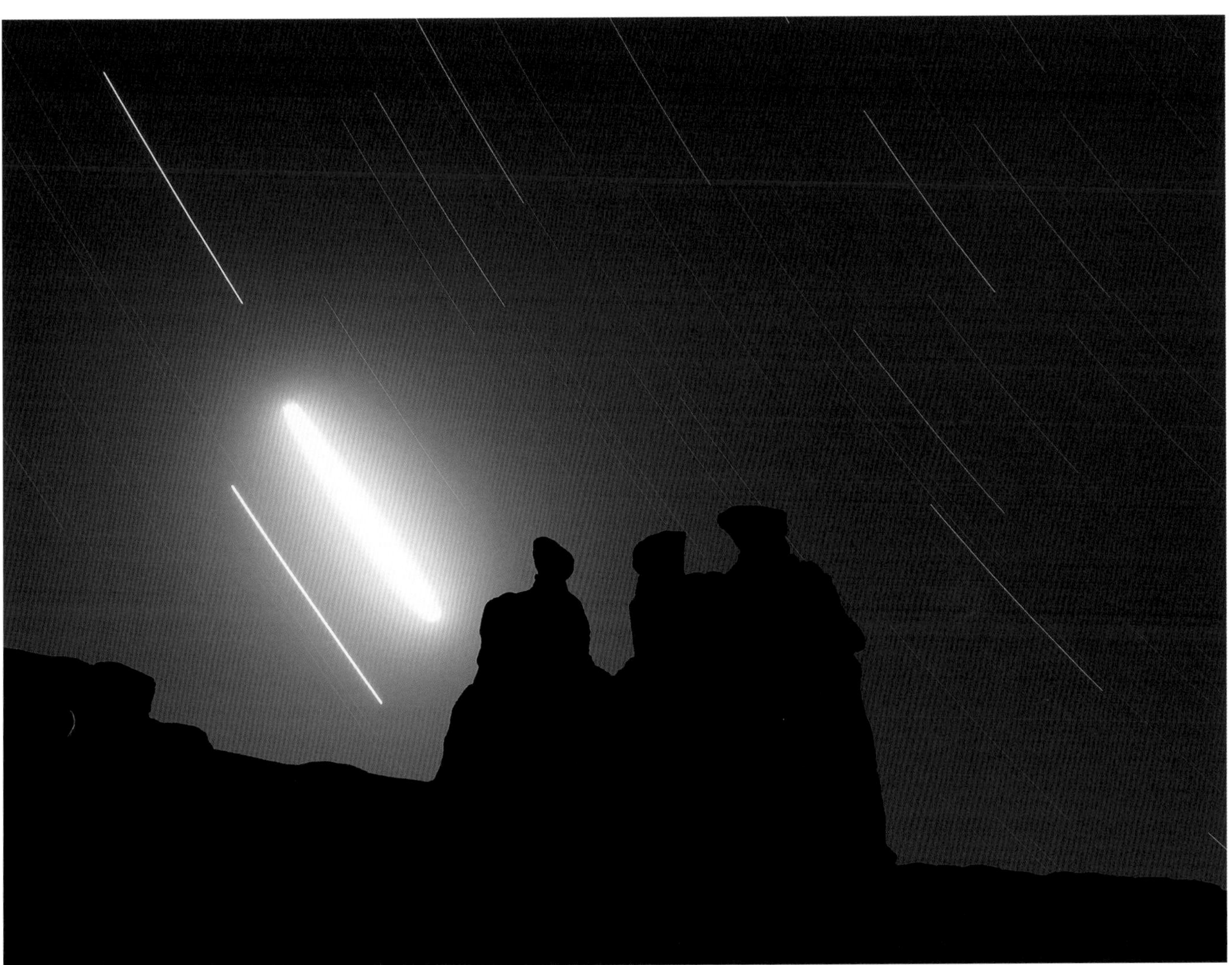

The moon, Venus, and Jupiter (all on the left side) streak above the Three Gossips in Arches National Park, Utah. I took this image when the moon was only 9% illuminated. As a result, it appeared as a fairly slender line, rather than a large blob. I did a single 40-minute exposure on a digital camera to avoid having the moon trail become too wide and bright. I also wanted the two planets to stand out and not have other bright star trails competing with them. Canon 5D II, 35mm, f/4.0, 40 minutes, ISO 100.

---

mend shooting moon trails under a moon that is just 4%-12% illuminated. If the moon is any less illuminated, it will set in the evening before it's dark enough to photograph (or it will rise too late in the morning). If the moon is more than 12% illuminated, it will start to look like a big blob and can drown out nearby stars. It is, however, still possible to get some intriguing results under a brighter moon, so you can experiment with this.

Just like star trails, you can shoot moon trails with a long, single exposure or by combining multiple exposures on a digital camera. This is one situation where a single exposure can be advantageous. The moon is so bright that you may prefer the fainter trails from a long exposure. Also, the dark noise will not be as bad as it would be under no moon. You should, however, still use Long Exposure Noise Reduction.

You can also use a film camera to capture moon trails. However, you'll likely get better results with a digital camera. Determining the proper exposure can be tricky with film since you can't take a test shot. The moon can vary in brightness significantly depending on its phase. If you want to attempt this, I recommend shooting under a thin crescent moon and using an aperture between f/4.0 and f/6.7 to avoid overexposing the image.

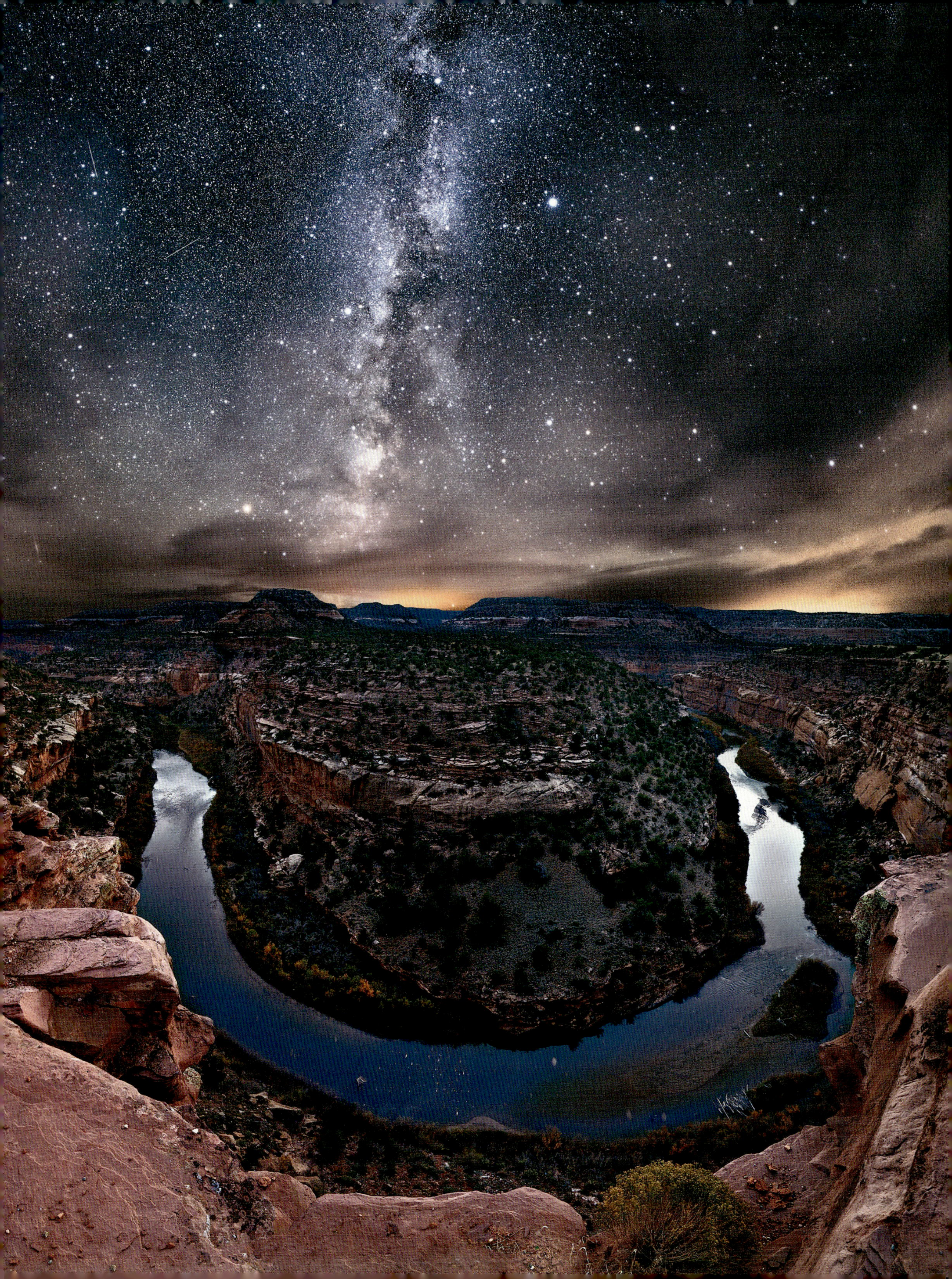

VIII. Stitching Images

Even if you have some of the best camera equipment for night photography and you properly expose all of your photographs, you will still find that there is a fair amount of noise in the images. This noise may not be very apparent when a photo is seen at small sizes. However, if you want to make a large print of the image, the noise can become more problematic. One of the best solutions I've found for this is to create large stitched images.

A stitched image is one where you take multiple shots, each comprising a small part of the scene you want to photograph. You later use computer software to "stitch" each of these images together to produce a photo of the whole scene. Since you're stitching together multiple images, the resulting file will be much larger than one from a single exposure. There will still be noise in the photo, but since the file size is so much bigger, you have to zoom in much farther to see the noise. You can therefore print the image at much larger sizes before the noise becomes noticeable.

Another advantage of a stitched image is that there is no limit to how wide your image can be. You can do a full 360-degree panoramic photo with a stitched image, something that is impossible with a single exposure with a normal camera. This is important because some things you photograph at night, like the Milky Way or the northern lights, cover a large portion of the sky.

EQUIPMENT

You don't usually need specialized equipment to create stitched images. However, if you'll be doing a lot of stitched images, some gear can make stitching a little easier.

Tripod Head

When taking stitched images, some photographers use panoramic tripod heads. These tripod heads keep the entrance pupil of the lens at a fixed spot as you turn the camera, which prevents any parallax error in the photos. This means that, as you rotate the camera, objects in the image will appear in the same relative positions in each exposure you take. This makes it easier for the stitching software to seamlessly stitch all of the photos together.

I have found that panoramic tripod heads are rarely necessary for stitching images taken at night. You have limited depth of field when taking photos at night, especially with the longer lenses that you will use for stitching images. You will therefore usually need to avoid including close foreground subjects in the photo when shooting stitched images. Parallax is much less noticeable when you don't have close foreground objects. Furthermore, stitching software has improved so much in recent years that it can still create seamless images even if there is some noticeable parallax.

A panoramic tripod head might be helpful if you use an ultra-wide lens that can provide more depth of field, and you include objects closer than 10 feet to you in the foreground. Another time it can be useful is if you have a near foreground and are focus stacking each of the individual images to increase the depth of field. However, focus stacking and then stitching images is a complicated task, and I only recommend it for those who are very proficient in photography and post-processing.

If you don't currently own a panoramic tripod head but are considering purchasing one, I recommend first using your current tripod head to stitch images at night. You may be surprised at how rare the circumstances are when a panoramic head can help improve an image.

One thing that can be helpful when creating stitched images is a tripod head with degree markings on it.

Left: The Milky Way rises above the Dolores River in western Colorado. I stitched separate images of the land and sky and blended them together. Nikon D800e; 2 stitched images of land during twilight, 14mm, f/11, 2 seconds, ISO 100; 32 stitched images of sky at night, 35mm, f/1.8, 13 seconds, ISO 6400.

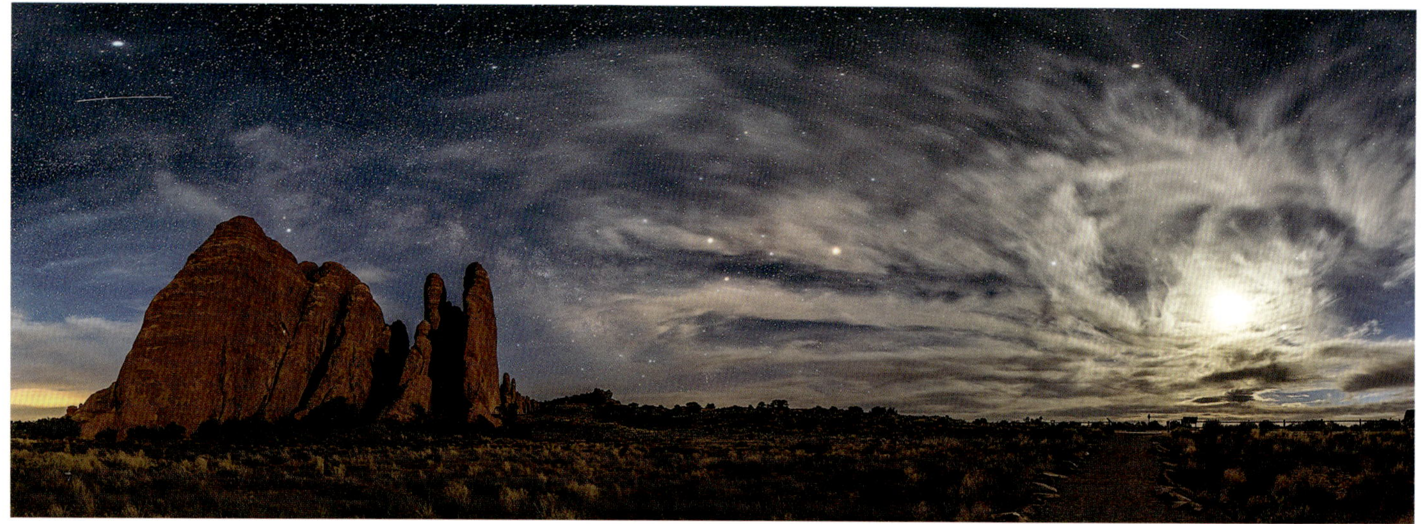

This image depicts dramatic clouds, a satellite, and the moon over sandstone fins in Arches National Park. In order to capture the stitched image quickly before the clouds moved too much, I shot a single row of seven vertical photos using my 14mm lens. Nikon D800e, 14mm, f/2.8, 20 seconds, ISO 2500.

The markings will show you how many degrees you have turned the camera between each shot. This will help ensure that you leave plenty of overlap between each of the images so that they can be stitched together without gaps.

3-way pan/tilt heads (not to be confused with panoramic heads) are a little better for stitching photographs than ball heads. However, as long your ball head has a rotating base, it is relatively easy to create stitched images with either tripod head. If your ball head doesn't have a rotating base, you will need to make sure your camera remains level as you turn it. This isn't too difficult with small stitched images, but it can be rather challenging with large ones.

The ball heads I recommended on page 21 all have rotating bases and degree markings.

Leveling Head

Another optional item you can buy is a leveling head, which is mounted between the tripod and tripod head. It will ensure that your tripod head is mounted on a perfectly level surface. This is important because as you turn your tripod head horizontally, it will remain level, and you won't have to adjust the leveling after every image you take.

If your tripod has a bubble level on top of its legs, you can use this instead of a leveling head. You just need to adjust the tripod legs until the bubble is centered in the level. If you don't have a bubble level on your tripod legs, you can remove your tripod head and place a bubble level on top of the legs where the tripod head would be. You can then adjust the legs until the bubble remains centered while you turn it. Leveling the tripod legs can be a somewhat tedious task, so if you do a large number of stitched images, a leveling head might be a worthwhile investment. However, I don't recommend purchasing one if you are just starting out doing stitched images.

Lenses

As I mentioned in Chapter I, I recommend using a 35mm or 50mm lens with a wide aperture for most of your stitched images. These lenses capture a smaller portion of the scene than wide-angle lenses, so you will need to take more shots to create a stitched image of the entire scene. This is a good thing because the more photos you stitch together, the larger the resulting image will be. The larger the image is, the larger you will be able to print it before it has noticeable amounts of noise.

If you want to include a close foreground object in your stitched image, you may need to use a wider lens to expand the depth of field and get everything in focus. You can refer to page 60 to see how much depth of field you can achieve with common lenses and aperture settings.

Another time you may want to use a wider lens is if something is moving in the scene, like clouds or the northern lights. You will want to take fewer images so that the objects move as little as possible during the time it takes to capture all of the shots. If the objects move too much, the stitching software may have a difficult time seamlessly stitching all of the images together.

Wider lenses do produce more distortion in each image, which can make it more difficult to stitch the photos together. Fortunately, stitching software has improved to the point where this is no longer much of an issue. The only lens you really don't want to use when stitching images together is a fisheye lens, as the distortion produced by these lenses is usually too extreme.

Robotic Camera Mounts

GigaPan produces the EPIC Pro Robotic Camera Mount that can automatically take all of the shots for a stitched image. I would only consider this device if you plan to create a large number of stitched images. It weighs over seven pounds, making it a little cumbersome if you plan to hike with it. Also, it takes about 15 minutes to set up, by which time you could have already manually taken a fairly large stitched image.

A robotic mount is more useful if you are using a long telephoto lens to capture hundreds or thousands of images to stitch together. This would be difficult and tedious to do manually. However, a long telephoto lens isn't too practical for stitching nightscape images. The stars will move too much relative to the foreground during the time it takes to capture the photos. The longest lens I would recommend using is 85mm.

CAMERA SETTINGS

Stitched images can be shot with any digital SLR or mirrorless camera. You need to make sure to use the same settings for every exposure you take. To do this, you'll have to set your camera to manual mode (though you'll almost always have it in manual mode when shooting at night anyway).

I usually use the rule of 500 when determining shutter speeds for stitched images. If I'm using a 50mm lens to shoot the photos, I'll take 500 / 50 = 10 sec-

The full band of the Milky Way is visible behind Broken Arch in Arches National Park, Utah. In order to render detail in the foreground, I stitched several exposures taken during twilight. I then blended this photo with a stitched image of the sky taken when it was dark. Nikon D800e; 6 images of land, 14mm, f/11, 10 seconds, ISO 1600; 30 images of sky, 24mm, f/2.8, 15 seconds, ISO 6400.

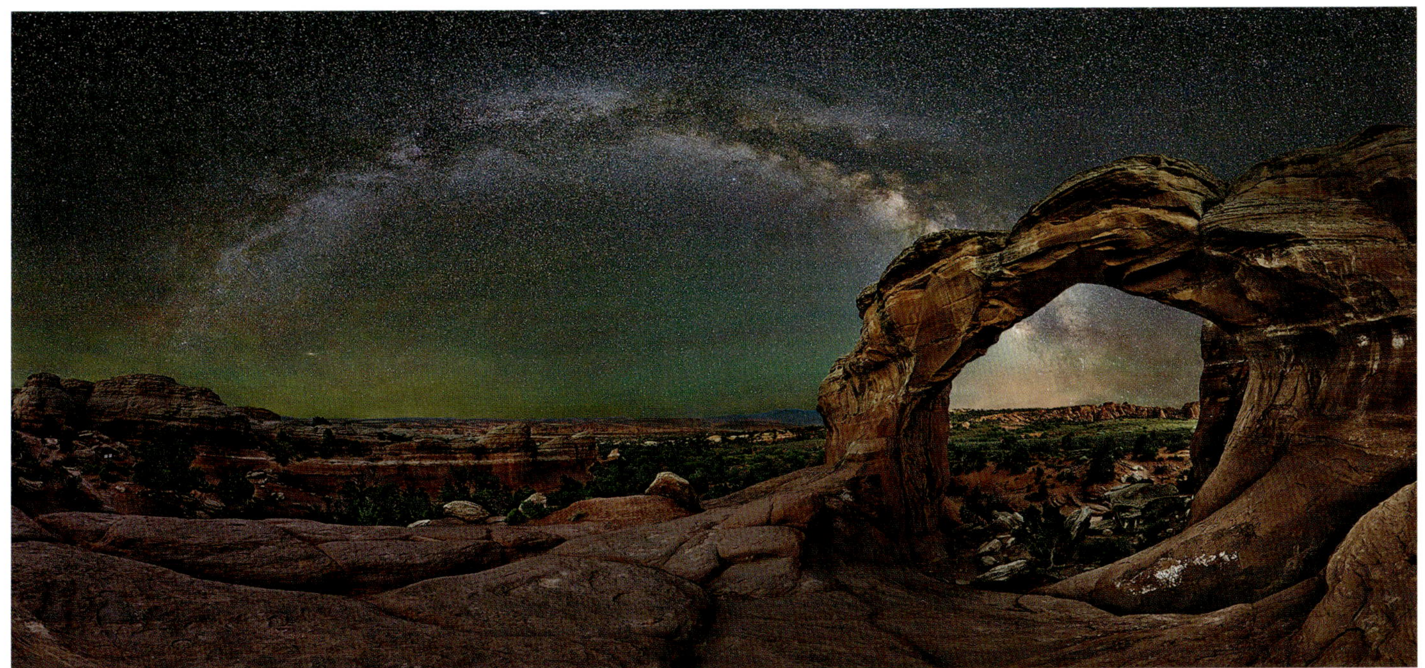

onds per exposure. This approach may seem counterintuitive because the final image is going to have a much wider field of view than a 50mm lens. It may be closer to the field of view from a 14mm lens. So you might think that you should use the same shutter speeds you would with a 14mm lens. Using the rule of 500, this would be 500 / 14 = 36 seconds. However, at 36 seconds, you can start to see star trails in the huge prints that are made possible by stitched images. I therefore find that using the rule of 500 with the focal length of the lens that I'm using to take the photos works well.

Another advantage of these shorter exposures is that the stars won't move as much in the sky while you are taking the shots. The software will then have an easier time stitching everything together.

If there is something in the scene that is moving quickly, like clouds or the northern lights, I'll sometimes use even shorter shutter speeds than the rule of 500 would suggest. This helps minimize movement between exposures.

For the aperture and ISO, you can usually use the same settings as those described in Chapter IV. One exception to this is that you can sometimes get away with apertures wider than f/1.6. There will likely be a lot of coma in the corners of these images. However, you can get around this by simply cropping off the edges of the images before stitching them.

TAKING THE PHOTOS

Once you have your camera settings dialed in, you just need to take all of the images. Make sure your tripod head is mounted on a level surface by adjusting your tripod legs or by using a leveling head. If you want to ensure that your tripod head is mounted correctly, you can turn the rotating base and see if your camera remains perfectly level.

Before beginning the stitched image, I recommend taking a test shot. Point your camera towards the brightest part of the scene you will be photographing and take an image using the camera settings you have decided on. Once you've taken the shot, check the histogram to make sure you are not overexposing the photo. If you are, lower the ISO until you are not clipping the highlights. You'll also want to zoom in on your shot and make sure everything is in sharp focus. If you have a close foreground in your image, you'll want to take a test shot of the nearest foreground and a test shot of the sky using the same focus settings. Make sure that both the near and distant objects are in sharp focus.

If everything looks okay, you can start taking your stitched image. Ideally, you will want to use a remote shutter release for all of your exposures to avoid camera shake. If you don't have one, I recommend using a two-second self-timer on your camera if it has one.

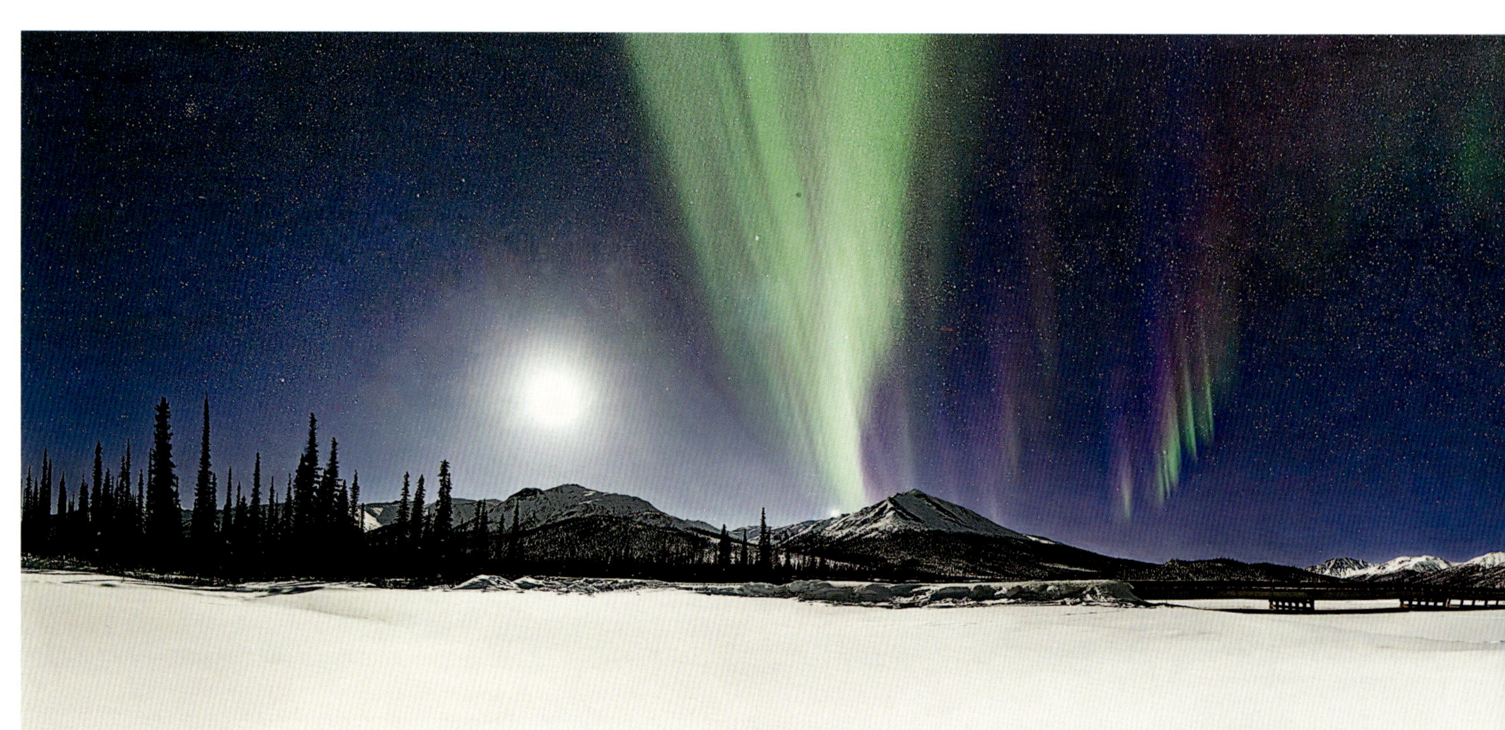

Make sure Long Exposure Noise Reduction is turned off, as it will take too long between each shot. If you want, you can take a single dark frame, which you can later subtract from all of the images before stitching them. However, stitched images are usually of such high quality, and dark noise is so low with shorter exposures that I don't find this necessary.

You should position your camera to take a photo of the far bottom corner of the scene. If you start at the far bottom left, I recommend framing the image a little bit to the left and below the scene you want to photograph. This will give you some breathing room to ensure that you capture every part of the scene. It is easy to later crop out parts of the scene that you don't want to include in the final image.

I recommend shooting all shots horizontally, even if your final image will be vertical. The camera is typically steadier when it is mounted horizontally, and it is easier to operate. Also, unless you are using an L-Bracket, the entrance pupil of the lens will move less from shot to shot, making it easier to stitch the images if you have a close foreground. One exception to this is if you are just taking one row of vertical photos. This can be easier than taking two rows of horizontal images.

You will need to make sure that your camera is level using a bubble level or your camera's built-in leveling feature. You can now take the first photograph. After you shoot this image, you will need to turn your camera to the right before taking the second photograph. Make sure to only rotate the camera horizontally, and don't change the tilt of the camera or the vertical angle. You can do this even with a ball head, as long as it has a rotating base. Just make sure to keep the ball itself tight and rotate the base of the tripod head.

You'll need to leave plenty of overlap between the images. This will make it easier for the software to stitch the photos, and it will ensure that there are no gaps in the image. You can determine the exact amount to rotate the camera using a formula I've come up with that I will call the 750 method. I'll call it a method so as not to confuse it with the rule of 500 that is used to calculate the shutter speed. For the 750 method, take 750 divided by the focal length of your lens to determine the number of degrees that you should rotate your camera between each shot. For example, if you are using a 50mm lens, you take 750 / 50 = 15. You should turn your camera 15 degrees between each shot. If you have a crop sensor camera, you'll need to first multiply the focal length

When I took this photo, the northern lights covered most of the sky in northern Alaska. I therefore spun around in circles for two hours in sub-zero temperatures, taking many 360-degree panoramas. I later picked out this one as my favorite. Canon 5D II, 14mm, f/2.8, 8 seconds, ISO 6400, eight images stitched together.

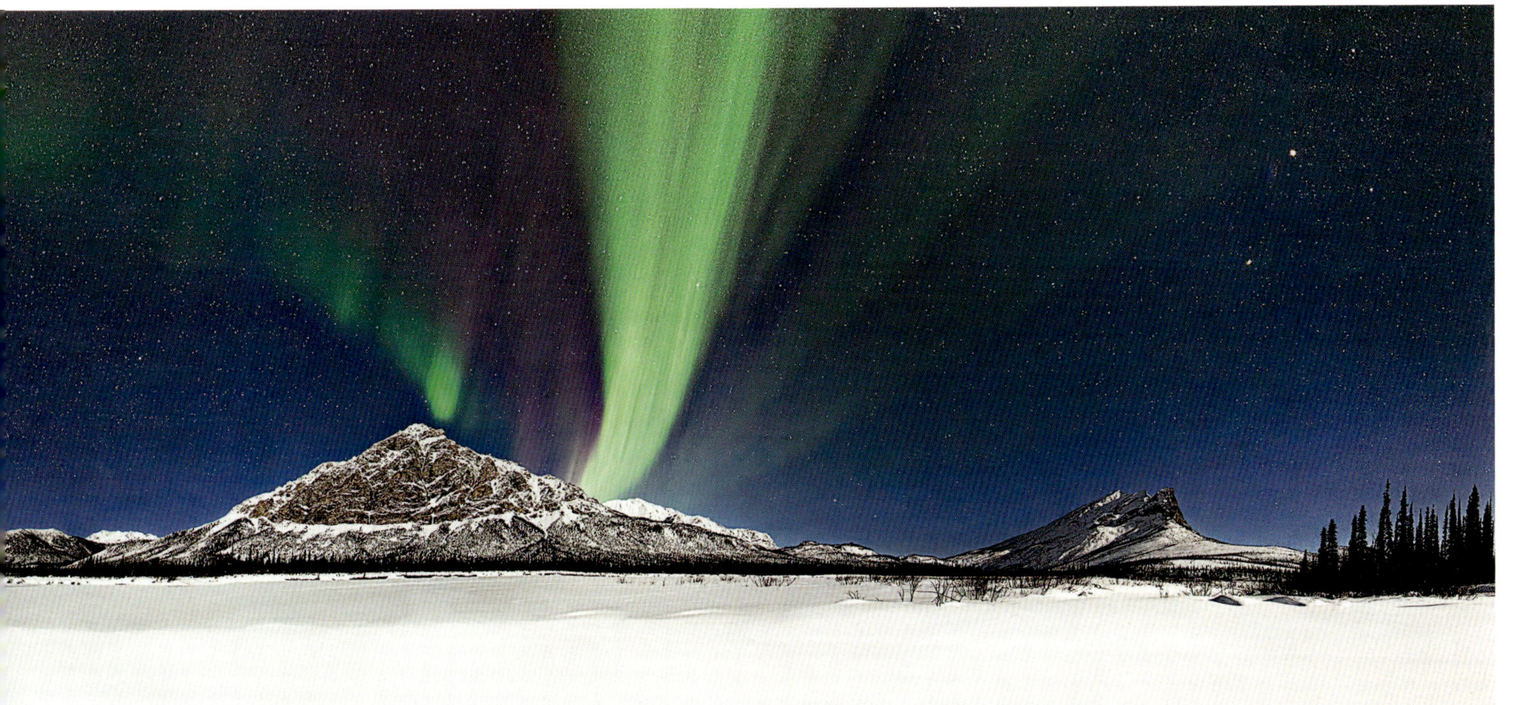

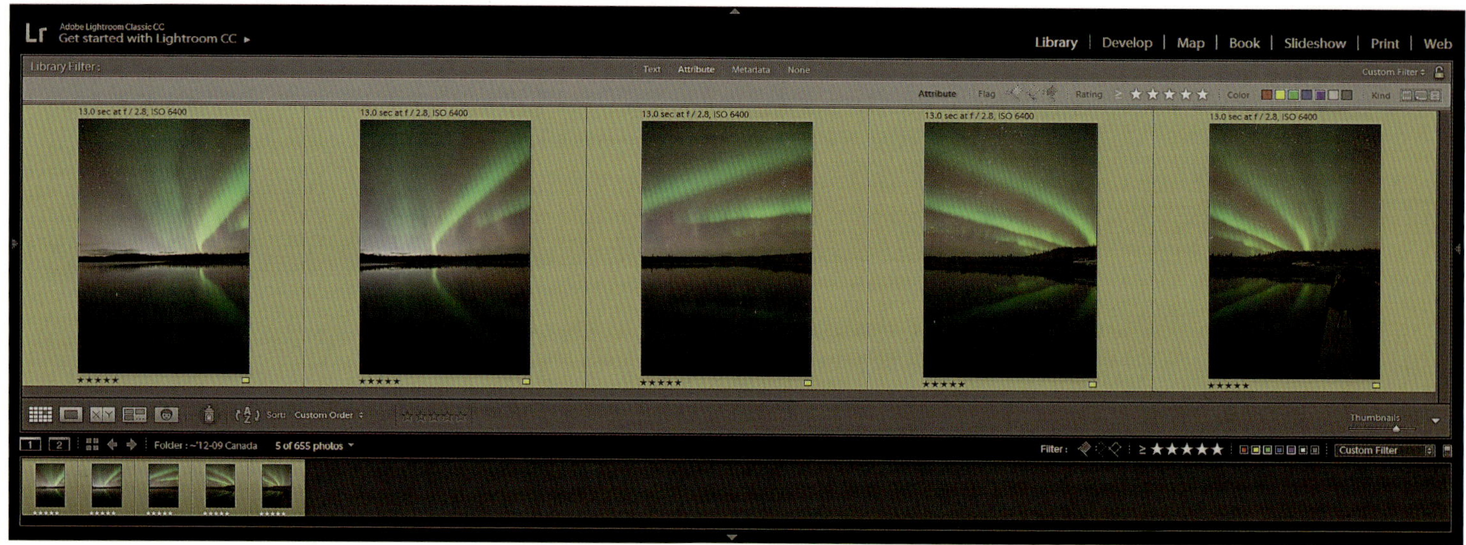

This Lightroom screenshot shows five photos I took of the northern lights over Prosperous Lake in Canada. I used Photomerge > Panorama to stitch all of the images. Lightroom doesn't always work as well if you are stitching a much larger number of exposures. In this case, you can export the photos and try a different program, like Image Composite Editor.

of the lens by the crop factor of the camera. The 750 method will leave a lot of overlap between each photo. If you are in a hurry or don't want to take so many images, you can bump this up to the 1000 method, which will allow you to turn the camera a little farther between each shot.

The 750 method will only work if your tripod head has degree markings on it, so you will know how much you are rotating the camera. If it doesn't, you'll just want to turn the camera about half of the field of view between each exposure.

Now that you know how far to turn the camera, just take a shot, quickly rotate the camera the right amount, take another shot, rotate the camera, and so on until you've captured the entire field of view that you want to photograph. Again, I recommend erring on the side of caution and capturing more of the scene than you want in your final image.

If you're taking a single-row panorama, you will be done once you've rotated the camera all the way to the right side of the scene. However, since the sky is so expansive, you will often need to do multi-row panoramas, especially if you aren't using a wide-angle lens. When you get to the end of the first row, you'll need to rotate your camera up. If you have a panoramic head or a 3-way pan/tilt head with vertical degree markings, you can use the 750 method to determine how much to rotate the camera up. If you don't have vertical degree markings, you should just try to rotate the camera up about half of the vertical field of view of your camera. You can compare the photo you take to the previous one to make sure you can see some of the same stars in each image. If you're using a ball head, you may inadvertently tilt the camera while rotating it upwards. So make sure the camera is level before starting your next row.

Now, you'll just need to take images and rotate the camera to the left until you've reached the far left side of the scene. Then, rotate the camera up again and take another row of images. Repeat this process until you've photographed all of the scene you want to capture. This process may sound complicated, but it's relatively simple once you get the hang of it.

You will want to shoot all of the images as fast as you can, as the stars will be moving while you take the photos. If the stars move too much during the time it takes to photograph the scene, it may be difficult to stitch the images together. However, stitching software has improved so much that it will usually be able to align all of the stars and create a seamless photograph.

PROCESSING THE IMAGES IN LIGHTROOM

Once you've taken all the photos, you can import

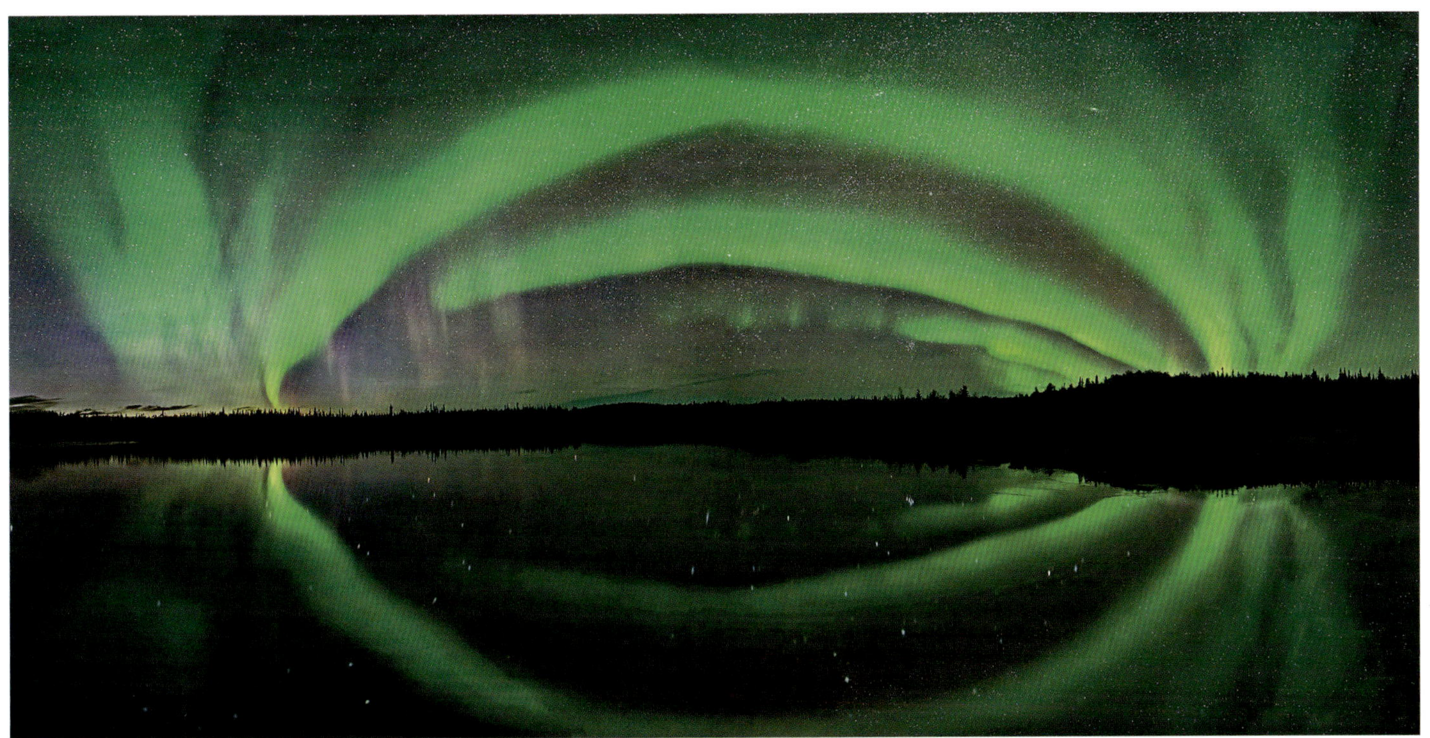

By stitching together the images seen on the previous page, I was able to create this seamless photo of the entire scene. I then optimized the color, brightness, and contrast of the image in Lightroom and Photoshop. Canon D800e, 14mm, f/2.8, 13 seconds, ISO 6400.

---

them into Lightroom. You can first attempt to stitch the images in Lightroom without making any adjustments to them. Just select the photos, right-click on them, and select Photomerge > Panorama. I go into more detail on this in the next section. If Lightroom successfully stitches the images, it will create a DNG file, which you can then work on like any other photograph.

You should check the stitched image created in Lightroom to make sure there is not a lot of coma from the corners of the photos that also appears in the stitched image. Even if you attempt to crop out the coma before stitching the images, Lightroom will ignore your crop of RAW files when stitching the photos. In this case, you could make the adjustments to the image that are described next, then export the files as TIFFs, re-import them into Lightroom, and attempt to stitch the cropped TIFF files.

If you aren't able to get a good stitch of the RAW files in Lightroom or if you want to see how the stitch will look with other software, you should initially process just one of the images in Lightroom. I recommend selecting a photo that includes the brightest part of the scene that you photographed. Then, crop off the left and right sides of this image to make it nearly square. This will help eliminate any coma that is in the corners of your image. Cropping the corners will also help to minimize vignetting and distortion, both of which can make stitching images more difficult. If you used the 750 method, there should still be plenty of overlap between the images to stitch them successfully. If your stitching software has trouble combining the photos, you can go back and crop off less of the sides. However, I have never encountered a problem with this.

You can now adjust some of the sliders in the Develop module of Lightroom. You don't have to get anything perfect, as you can always improve things further in Photoshop after you've stitched all of the images. The most important sliders to adjust for stitched images are the Highlights and Shadows and those in the Lens Corrections panel. I'll therefore describe them in more detail here. Other sliders that I frequently use will be discussed in Chapter X.

If you overexposed any highlights, you should move the Highlights slider to the left until they are not clipped. This is the reason I suggest working on an image of the brightest part of the scene. If you make sure this part isn't overexposed, you can be confident nothing else will be.

If you want to bring out detail in the dark shadows, you can push the Shadows slider in Lightroom to the right. Be aware that this will also bring out more noise in the image. Sometimes you're better off leaving the dark areas as silhouettes. If there's a specific part of the scene where you want to bring out detail in the shadows, you can select an image that contains that part of the scene and see how much of a Shadows adjustment is necessary. Then, go back to the main image you're working on and move the Shadows slider the same amount.

In the Lens Correction panel, you can go to Profile and click on Enable Profile Corrections. This will help eliminate distortion and vignetting, which will make it easier to stitch the images together. If the image still doesn't look right, you can fine-tune things using the Distortion and Vignetting sliders. If your lens profile is not found and you weren't able to select Enable Profile Corrections, you can click on Manual and adjust the sliders there.

Once you've made the adjustments to a single photo, you need to apply them to all of the images you plan to stitch together. Make sure the image you've made the adjustments to is selected and then hit Ctrl+ Shift+C (Cmd+Shift+C on a Mac). In the dialog box that appears, click on Check All and then click Copy. Now, go to the Library module and hit G to go into Grid View. Then, select all of the images you want to stitch and click Ctrl+Shift+V (Cmd+Shift+V on

In this image, Mount Baldy is illuminated in a pond at Paradise Divide in Colorado. I timed this shot so that the quarter moon would be behind me and lighting the front of the mountain. I took 30 photos and stitched them together to create a 200-megapixel image. Canon 5D II, 50mm, f/1.8, 13 seconds, ISO 6400.

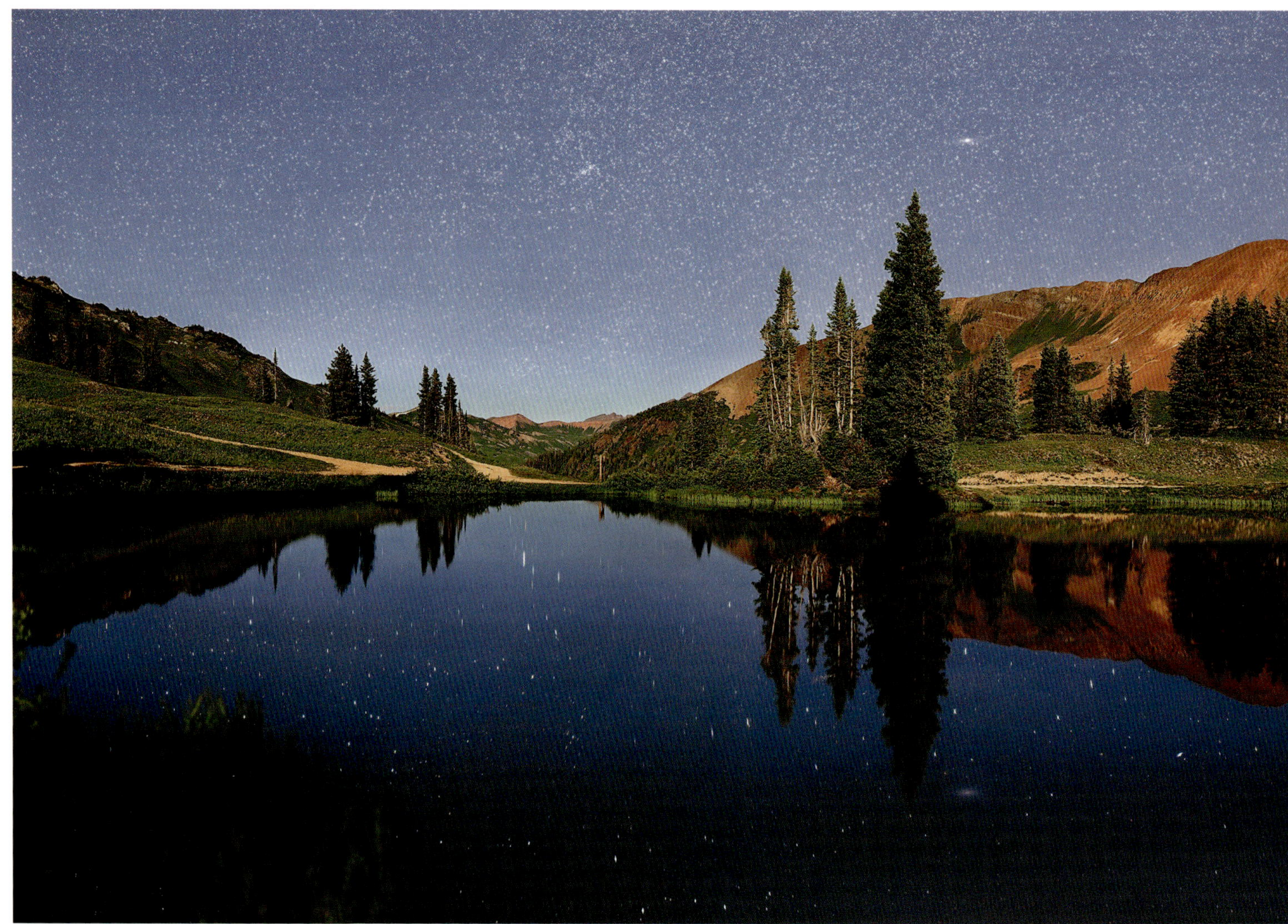

a Mac) to paste the settings onto all of the photographs.

You can now export all of the photos by selecting them and hitting Ctrl+Shift+E (Cmd+Shift+E on a Mac). If you have a slower computer that may have problems with large files, you can export the images as 8-bit TIFF files to keep the size down. If you're doing a smaller stitched image or you have a powerful computer that can easily handle huge files, you can keep the images at 16 bits. This will preserve all of the color data in your image.

STITCHING SOFTWARE

Once you've prepared the photos, you'll need to combine them using stitching software. I discuss the pros and cons of some of the popular software below.

Lightroom

As mentioned before, you can stitch images within Lightroom CC by selecting the photos, right-clicking on them, and selecting Photomerge > Panorama. Lightroom will attempt to stitch the images, and if it is successful, it will display a preview of the stitched image. If Auto Select Projection is selected, it will try to choose the best projection method. Usually, Spherical will work well, but you can try clicking on Cylindrical and Perspective to see a preview with these options. You can adjust the Boundary Warp slider to minimize distorted edges, but sometimes this will distort the rest of the image in an undesirable way. Alternatively, you can select Auto Crop to simply crop off the edges. It won't delete the cropped pixels, so you can later go back and adjust the crop if necessary. When the image looks good, click Merge, and it will create a full-sized stitched image.

Lightroom does have a file size limit of 65,535 pixels on the longest side and a total file size limit of 512 megapixels. This will prevent you from being able to stitch very large images in Lightroom, in which case you'll need to try a different program.

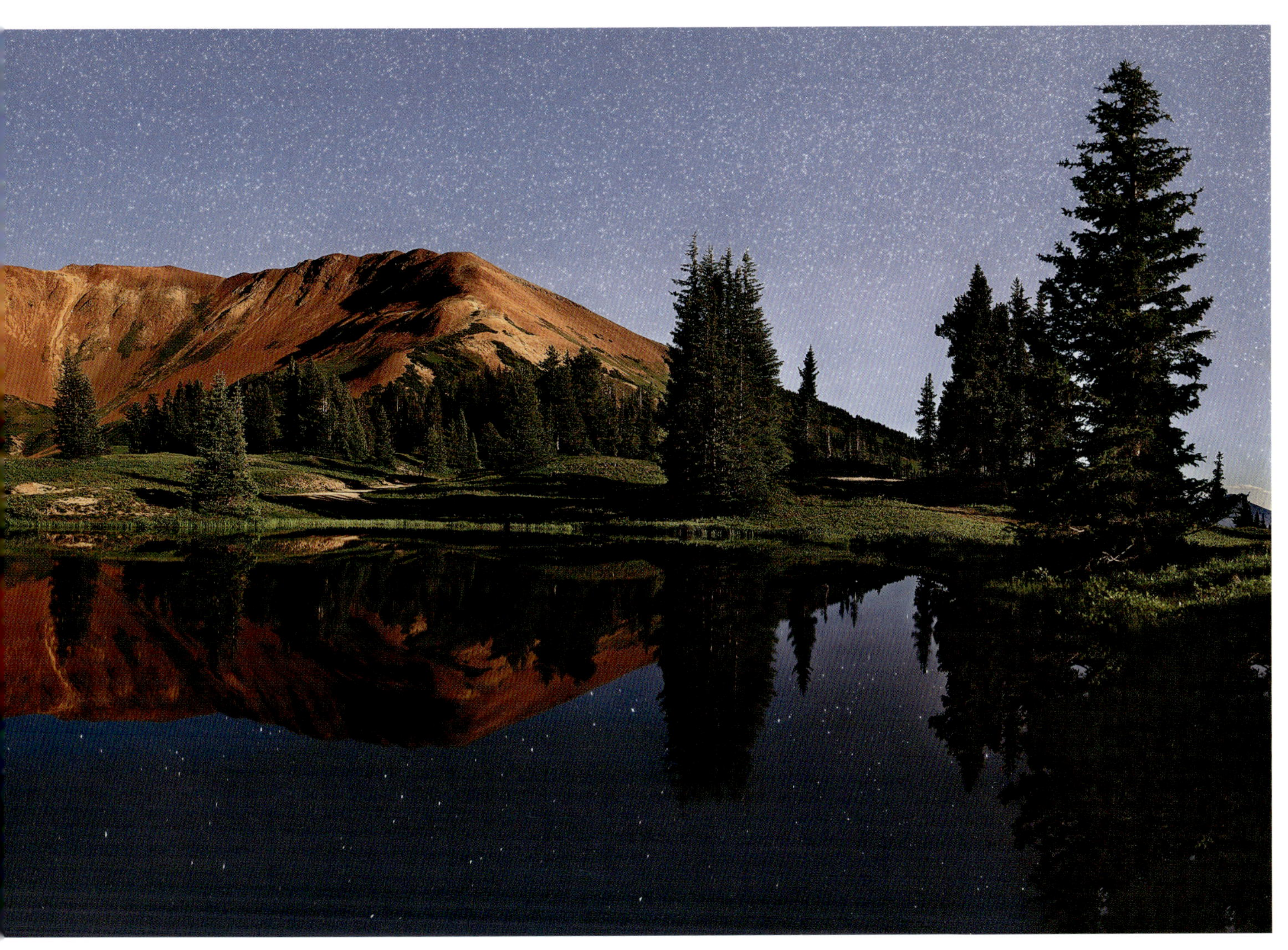

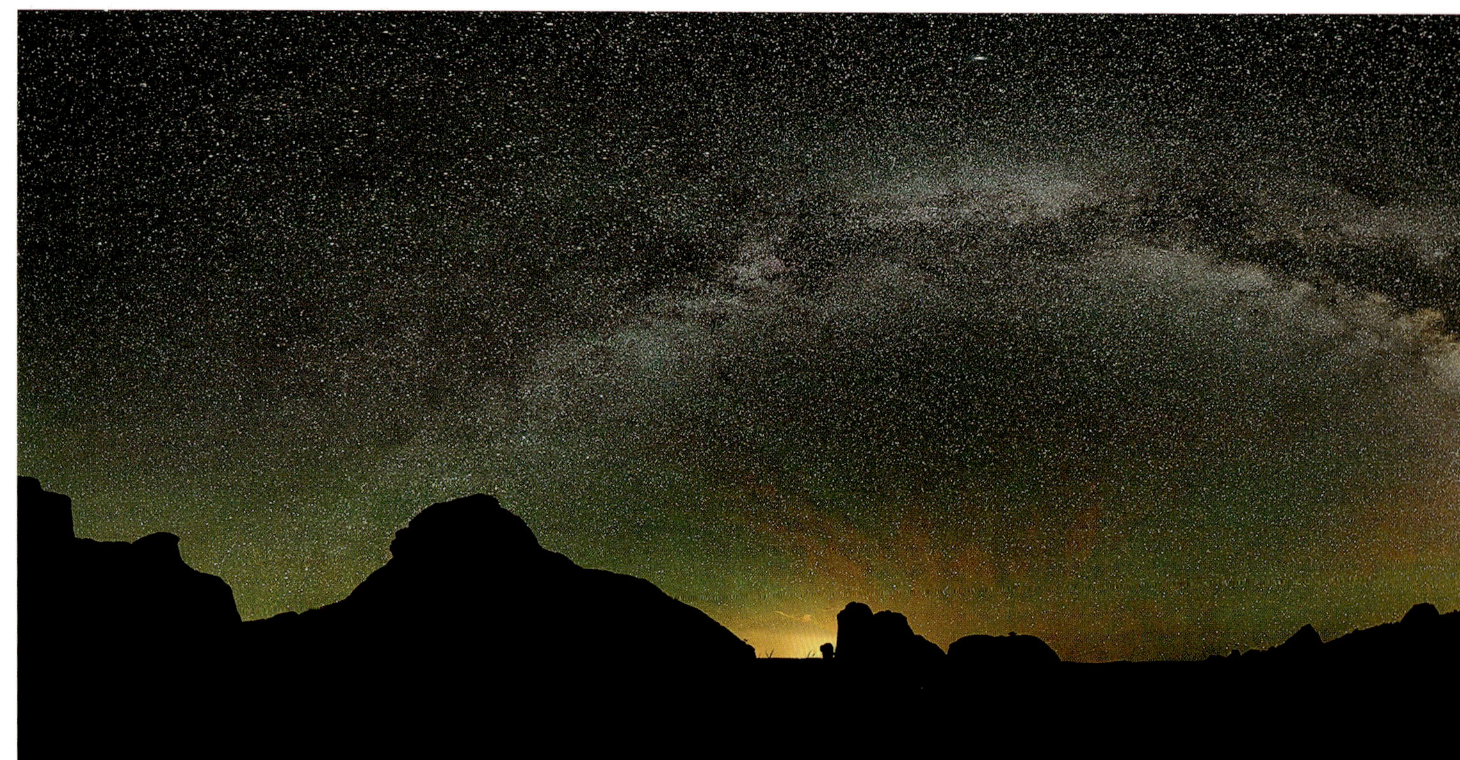

The Milky Way rises alongside Landscape Arch in Arches National Park. I used Stellarium to verify when the Milky Way would be in the correct position for this photo. I then took 44 images and stitched them together to capture a 360-degree view of the scene. Nikon D800e, 24mm, f/2.8, 15 seconds, ISO 6400.

Photoshop

I have found that Lightroom usually does at least as good of a job at stitching images as Photoshop. However, Photoshop currently has a much larger file size limit of 300,000 pixels x 300,000 pixels. You will need to save any extra-large files in the PSB format.

To stitch images in Photoshop, go to File > Automate > Photomerge. In the screen that pops up, I recommend leaving the Layout set to Auto. You can keep Blend Images Together selected and leave the other boxes unchecked. Then, browse for the images you want to stitch and click OK.

If Photoshop fails to stitch the images together or the stitch doesn't look very good, you can try clicking Vignette Removal or Geometric Distortion Correction in the Photomerge dialog box. With Geometric Distortion Correction, Photoshop can sometimes do a good job stitching a small number of images taken with an ultra-wide-angle lens. Vignette Removal can help if there is noticeable darkening around the edges of the individual photos (though it's better if you were able to minimize this in Lightroom).

Image Composite Editor (ICE)

Image Composite Editor is an exceptional software program for stitching images that is available as a free download online. Since Microsoft makes this program, it is only available for PCs. I've experienced few problems when using ICE, and it is relatively fast when creating a preview of the images. It usually does an excellent job with larger stitched images, something that Lightroom and Photoshop can struggle with. It has no file size limit, though some file formats will not be allowed when exporting larger photos.

To use Image Composite Editor, click on New Panorama From Images. Find and select every image you want to stitch and click Open. Now, click 2-Stitch, and it will attempt to stitch the photos together. If it is successful, it will show a preview of the image.

You can choose from many different projection options on the right side of the screen. I recommend trying all of them and selecting the one that looks best. Usually, Spherical will work well. Below this, you can adjust the orientation of the image. If you

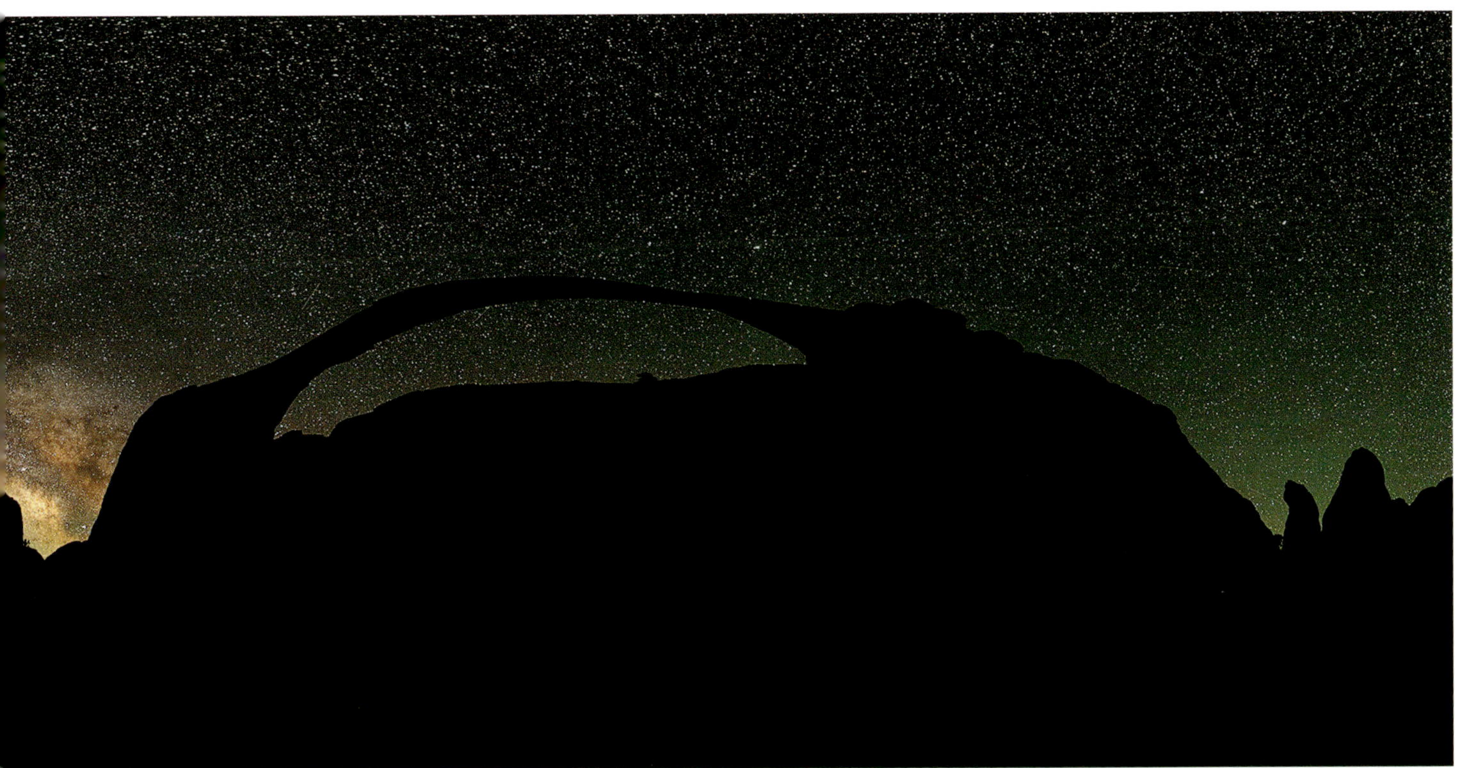

click on Auto Orientation, it often does a good job.

Next, you can click 3-Crop, and it will give you an option to crop the image. Be sure not to crop out any part of the photo that you might decide to use later. You can always adjust the crop in Photoshop.

You can now click 4-Export. The only thing I would adjust on this screen is the file format. I recommend selecting Adobe Photoshop or TIFF Image. Then, click Export to Disk..., select the folder where you want to save it, and click Save.

Hugin

Hugin is a free alternative to Image Composite Editor that is compatible with both PCs and Macs. However, I've found it to be slow and difficult to use. I only recommend it for Mac owners who haven't had success with Lightroom or Photoshop.

PTGui

PTGui is a software program you can purchase to stitch images together. Mac users might consider this if they experience problems stitching images with the other programs I've mentioned. Windows users probably won't need this software, as Image Composite Editor will usually work just as well, if not better. They do have a free trial version you can use that will create watermarked images.

PROCESSING THE IMAGES IN PHOTOSHOP

Once you've stitched all of the images together, you can open the resulting file in Photoshop. Zoom all the way in to make sure you have a seamless stitch. If you find any issues, they can usually be fixed with a clone stamp or healing brush. You can now work on the photo like you would any other image in Photoshop. I will discuss post-processing techniques I use on night photos in Chapter X.

When you start adding new layers to your image, it can increase the file size considerably. This shouldn't be a problem if you have a fast computer with a lot of RAM and a solid-state drive. If you don't, it can cause your computer to slow to a crawl. If this happens, you can flatten the image and save it with a new name. This isn't an ideal workflow for processing images in Photoshop, as it's better to use a non-destructive workflow and keep all of the layers intact. However, this can become impractical with really large images. As long as you save the file with a new name, you can always go back to the original file if necessary.

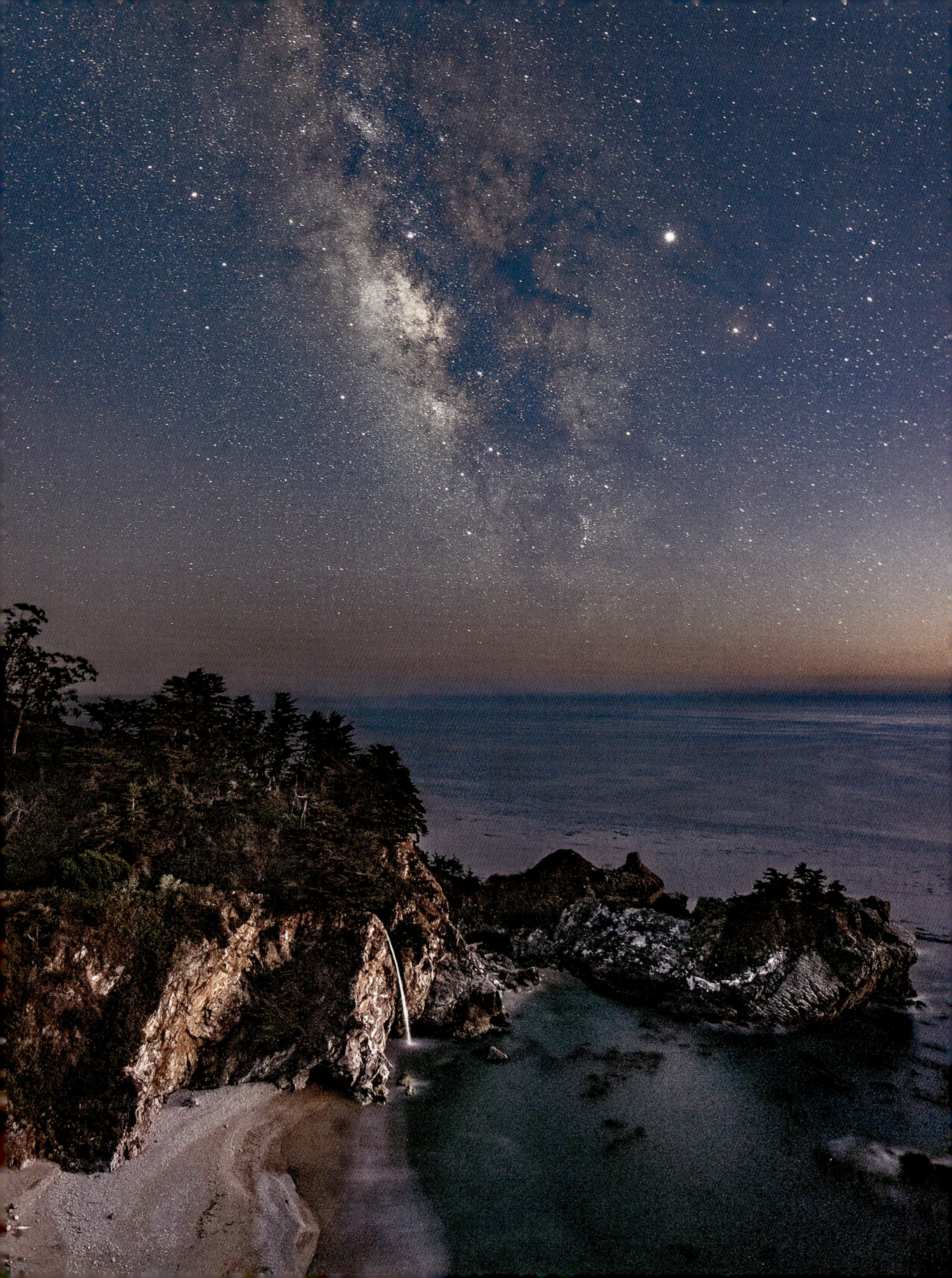

IX. Blending Multiple Exposures

Even if you use all of the techniques described so far, there will still be situations where it can be difficult to capture great night photos.

If you want to photograph a vast, sweeping landscape at night that has both a near foreground and a very distant background, it is nearly impossible to evenly illuminate the entire scene with a flashlight. Sometimes you can time the photograph so that there is a crescent moon behind you that can illuminate the scene. However, there are situations when even this will not work.

If you are shooting from inside an alcove or rock cave, the moon will never be able to fully illuminate the inside of it. If you are photographing a deep canyon or have a mountain or cliff face behind you, the moon may only be able to illuminate the scene when it is high in the sky. When the moon is too high, it can produce harsh lighting, just like the sun does during the day. Also, if you want to capture a detailed and dramatic image of the Milky Way, even a crescent moon can obscure the stars too much to capture the image you want.

Another time you may have difficulty is if you're photographing a constellation, but the camera captures so many stars that the constellation is not recognizable in the image. There will also be times when you can't get enough depth of field in a single exposure to get both the foreground and background in focus.

In situations like these, your best option will be to take two or more different exposures of the scene and blend them together in post-processing.

Blending multiple exposures can be a difficult thing to do well and often requires a lot of skill in Photoshop. When done properly, it can be a valuable skill for a night photographer. When done improperly, it can be a way to create some truly hideous photographs! So I recommend becoming proficient in other techniques in this book before attempting to blend multiple exposures.

If blending multiple exposures sounds too daunting to you, I will first discuss a way to mimic the effect of blending two exposures with a single shot.

BLACK CARD TECHNIQUE

The black card technique (sometimes referred to as the magic cloth) allows you to mimic the effect of a graduated neutral density filter. This filter is dark on one half and light on the other. It can be used if one part of the scene is significantly brighter than the other. You can hold the filter up against your lens so that the dark part of it blocks the light from the brighter part of the scene. This will even out the amount of light that hits the sensor and prevent you from overexposing or underexposing part of the image.

As mentioned in Chapter I, it's not very practical to use filters like this at night. Since there is so little light to work with, you don't want a filter to block out even more light. This can significantly increase the amount of noise in your image. If you try to compensate for this by doing longer exposures to let in more light, the stars will begin to appear as small star trails rather than as points of light.

An alternative to this is to block some of the light from the sky from entering your camera lens using a black card, mouse pad, glove, or cloth. This will allow you to expose the land for a longer duration while preventing short star trails from appearing in the sky.

You will usually want to use the black card technique when you have some light on the foreground, but it is still noticeably darker than the night sky. This can occur near the end of twilight on a moonless night when just a little bit of light is illuminating the landscape. It can also occur after twilight when only a sliver of

---

Left: The Milky Way rises above McWay Falls in Big Sur, California. I took repeated exposures of this scene during astronomical twilight and later stacked images of the land and sky to reduce noise. Sony a7 III, 18mm, f/2.8, 15 seconds per exposure, ISO 1600.

the moon is illuminating the foreground. If a brighter moon is out, the land should be bright enough relative to the sky that you won't need the black card.

Another situation in which you may be able to use the black card is when no moon is out, but you have a very bright foreground, like snow, ice, or a reflective surface like a lake.

If no moon is out and you have a darker foreground, the disparity in the brightness of the sky and land may be too extreme to use a black card successfully. In this case, you will likely need to blend multiple exposures, as will be discussed later in this chapter.

To use the black card technique, you'll first want to calculate what your exposure time would be with the rule of 500. If you're using a 20mm lens, take 500 / 20 = 25. The exposure time would be 25 seconds. This is how long you'll want to expose the sky in your image. When you take the shot, wait 25 seconds and then cover the top part of your lens with the card or cloth so that it blocks out the light from the sky. It may take some practice to block just the right part of the lens. You'll want to slowly move the card or cloth up and down just a fraction of an inch during the exposure. This will prevent a hard transition between the part of the scene that is covered by the card or cloth and the part that isn't covered.

You can continue exposing the bottom part of the scene as long as necessary to get a good, balanced exposure of the entire scene. After you take the photo, be sure to review it carefully on your LCD screen. Make sure you were holding the card in the right position so that it was covering just the sky. Also, make sure that the brightness of the sky and foreground is similar and that one isn't significantly brighter than the other. If you see any issues, you'll need to make adjustments and try another exposure until you get an image you like.

When using the black card technique, you may benefit from using a dark frame or your camera's Long Exposure Noise Reduction. With longer exposures in such low light, dark noise can become more noticeable.

Images that are taken with a black card work best when there is a flat horizon where the sky meets the land. If rock formations or mountains are jutting into the sky, it will be difficult to get an evenly illuminated image using the black card. In this case, you may need to blend two different exposures, as I'll describe next.

MULTIPLE SHOTS AT ONE TIME

Instead of using a black card, you can take two different exposures - one for the land and one for the sky. As with the black card technique, this may be necessary when the foreground isn't completely dark but is noticeably darker than the sky. Unlike the black card, you can also do this when the land and sky are more evenly illuminated, in order to get less noise or more depth of field in the foreground.

To capture these images, you should first take an exposure for the sky using the rule of 500 and the camera settings outlined in Chapter IV. For the exposure of the land, I recommend exposures of 2-5 minutes. Longer exposures can show too much dark noise, and shorter exposures can have more photon noise. If you overexpose the shot with these longer exposures, you'll need to lower the ISO. However, you only need to worry about overexposing the land. It doesn't matter if you overexpose the sky, as you won't be using that part of the image. You could also use a little smaller aperture for the shot of the land if you need to get more depth of field in the photograph.

As with the black card technique, you may benefit from using a dark frame or your camera's Long Exposure Noise Reduction. You may only need to use the dark frame on the longer exposure for the land, as this is where dark noise becomes more noticeable.

To blend the two images, open them in Photoshop. Then, select the Move tool, hold down the Shift key, and drag the image with the exposure for the sky onto the other photo. The image you drag it onto will now have two layers - the top one with the exposure for the sky and the bottom one with the exposure for the land.

Now, select both layers and click Edit > Auto-Align Layers... You can keep the default setting at Auto and click OK. This step isn't always necessary and may not work if the images are too different from one another. However, even if you took the two photos from the same spot, they may be slightly misaligned, especially if you changed the focus between the two shots.

You'll now need to mask out only the sky in the top layer. You can start by selecting the bottom layer and use the Quick Selection Tool. Just drag the tool around

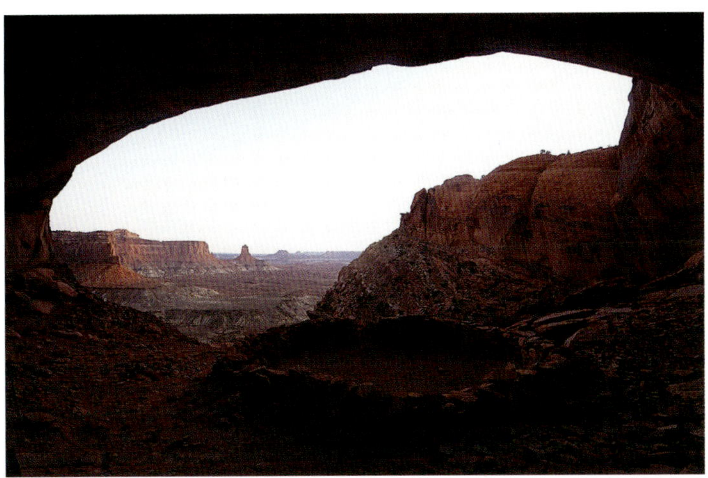

I took this image in Utah shortly after sunset. It would have been much too dark to capture detail inside the alcove at night without a flashlight. Canon 5D II, 14mm, f/8.0, 1.6 seconds, ISO 100.

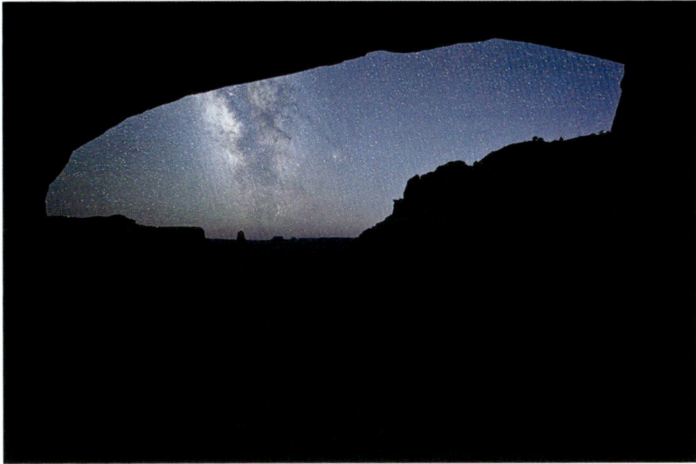

I captured this image of the Milky Way during astronomical twilight a little over an hour later from the exact same spot. Canon 5D II, 14mm, f/2.8, 30 seconds, ISO 6400.

---

the sky, and it should snap to the edges of the sky. If the selection covers part of the land, you can hold down the Alt key (Option key on a Mac) while dragging the mouse to contract the selection.

Once you have a pretty good selection of the sky, you can make it more precise and avoid halos by going to Select > Modify > Expand and expand the selection by 1 pixel. Then, go to Select > Modify > Feather and feather the selection by 1 pixel. Now, select the top layer and click on the rectangular icon with a circle in the middle of it at the bottom of the Layers panel. This will create a mask and mask out everything except the sky from that layer. The land from the layer below will show through, and you'll have combined the two images.

If the mask you create isn't perfect, you can refine it by right-clicking on the mask and selecting Select and Mask... In Photoshop CS6 and earlier, this feature is called Refine Edge... and has fewer options. To see how the image will look with the mask applied, set the View Mode at the top of the dialog box to Onion View, with the Transparency slider at 100%. To see the exact areas that are being masked out, you can try using other View Modes, like Overlay or Black & White.

You can now check Smart Radius and increase the Radius slider to see if this will automatically refine the mask to your liking. This can work well if the night sky is over a body of water, and there is not an obvious transition from sky to land. It can also sometimes work with fine details, like tree branches protruding into the sky. However, the Refine Edge Brush I describe later usually works better. Your primary focus should be on getting areas with less fine detail looking right.

You can use the sliders under Global Refinements instead of, or in addition to, the Smart Radius. Adjust each of the sliders a small amount while zoomed in on the image to see if it helps or hurts the mask. Every photo is different, so there are no set rules on how to adjust the sliders (though you will probably never want to decrease the Shift Edge slider). Just play with the sliders until you get a mask you like. Most images will only need minor adjustments if any. Once everything except areas with fine details looks good, click OK to apply the refined mask.

If you still have fine details, like tree branches, to mask out, you can duplicate the top layer by selecting it and hitting Ctrl+J (Cmd+J on a Mac). You should do this with any image that has fine details, even if you didn't need to do the Global Refinements described in the last two paragraphs. For the time being, you can hide the original, middle layer by clicking on the eyeball icon on that layer. Now, right-click on the mask in the top, duplicate layer and choose Select and Mask...

You can now use the Refine Edge Brush to mask out fine details. This brush will be the second one down on your Tool Bar, which is on the left side of the screen by default. Simply paint over the part of the image with

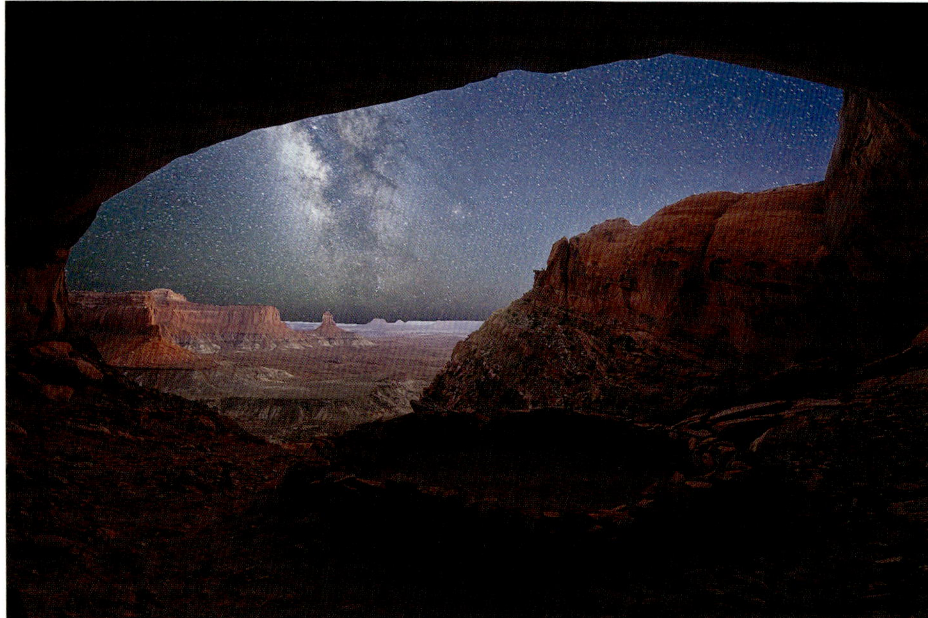

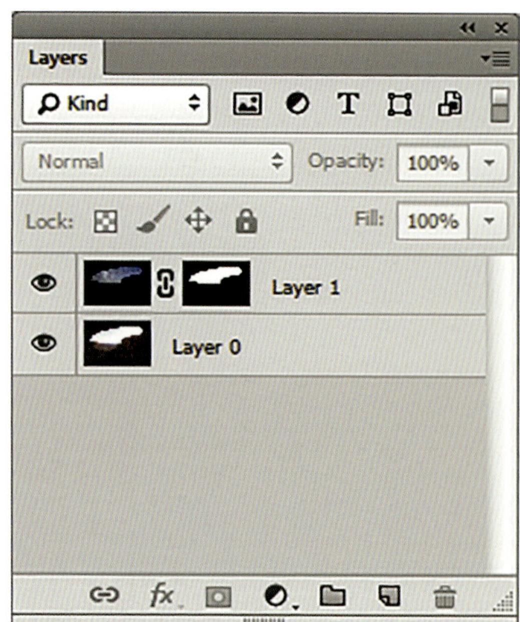

I combined the two exposures on the previous page by dragging the right image onto the left one. I then selected the sky on the top layer and masked out everything else, as can be seen in the Layers panel above. The resulting image is comprised of the land from the bottom layer and the sky from the top layer. As you can see, the blend is not perfect, especially where the distant land meets the sky. This is a common problem when blending two exposures taken at different times.

---

fine details where you want to refine the mask. After using this brush, you can adjust the Global Adjustment sliders. You'll often want to increase the Contrast slider to give the mask a harder edge and avoid having much of the sky masked out. If there is a bright halo or unnatural, bright white areas in the sky, increasing the Shift Edge slider will often work well. This can darken the tops of trees, but it will look a lot more natural than having white areas in the sky.

When the mask looks good, click OK. You can now make the middle layer visible again. Then, hide the top layer and show it again to see how it changes the image. You should use a black brush to partially or fully mask out any areas on the top layer where the photo looks better with the top layer hidden. Now, with the top layer visible, hide the middle layer and show it again to see how it changes the image. Mask out any areas on the middle layer where the photo looks better with the middle layer hidden. You should avoid masking out the same parts of both layers. Make sure to keep all layers visible once you've completed the masks.

Another way to mask out trees is with a Color Range selection. First, make sure a photo icon, not the mask in the Layers panel is selected. Then, go to Select > Color Range... Hold down the Shift key and drag on colors in the tree to select the tree. You can adjust the Fuzziness slider to refine the selection. Now, click OK, and paint on the mask with a black brush to hide the trees on the top layer. Click Ctrl+Shift+I (Cmd+Shift+I on a Mac) to invert the selection, and paint with white to reveal the sky near the trees.

If the mask isn't quite perfect, you can click Ctrl+D (Cmd+D on a Mac) to remove the selection. Then, change the brush mode on the upper left to Overlay and continue painting with black or white near the trees. With Overlay mode, dark areas aren't affected by the white brush, and light areas aren't affected by the black brush, so it's a great way to fine-tune the mask.

When the masks look good, you'll want to individually adjust the contrast, brightness, and color of both layers until they better match each other. An adjustment layer, like Levels or Curves, will affect only the layer below it if you right-click on the adjustment layer and select Create Clipping Mask. You can use techniques described in the Photoshop Adjustments section of Chapter X to fine-tune the image. This is as much of an art form as it is a science. You just need to work on the image until you get a result that you like.

MULTIPLE SHOTS AT DIFFERENT TIMES

Another approach to capturing detail in the landscape is to take two exposures at different times. You can take an exposure for the foreground around 5-10 minutes after sunset when it is still light enough to capture a lot of detail in the land. At this time, you should be able to use your camera's exposure meter to determine the proper exposure. Also, if you have close foreground objects, it will still be bright enough to use smaller apertures and get more depth of field.

You'll now need to wait until it gets dark. Make sure and leave your camera and tripod at the same spot. You can take the second exposure for the sky during or after astronomical twilight. If you plan to shoot the two exposures before sunrise in the morning rather than in the evening, you'll just need to take the photographs in the opposite order I described.

Another approach is to take an image of the land when a waxing moon is out and then wait for the moon to set to capture an image with more stars visible in the sky. Alternatively, when there is a waning moon, you can take a photo of the sky first and then wait for the moon to rise to capture an image of the land.

Both of the above approaches can help you capture good light on the landscape, with shadows that add depth to the image. However, taking exposures at different times can produce less realistic photos. Combining exposures taken at the same time will create a more natural look but can also produce noisier images. You can minimize the noise by stacking images of the land that are taken at the same time as the images of the sky. I'll describe how to do this later in this chapter. How

I refined the image on the previous page by using a Burn Layer in Photoshop to darken the land near the horizon, so it did not appear lighter than the sky. I also used Tony Kuyper's luminosity masks to bring out more detail in the shadows and increase contrast in the sky. I then adjusted the colors and saturation in the sky and land until I got a result that looked good to me. Several of the techniques I used will be described in more detail in the next chapter.

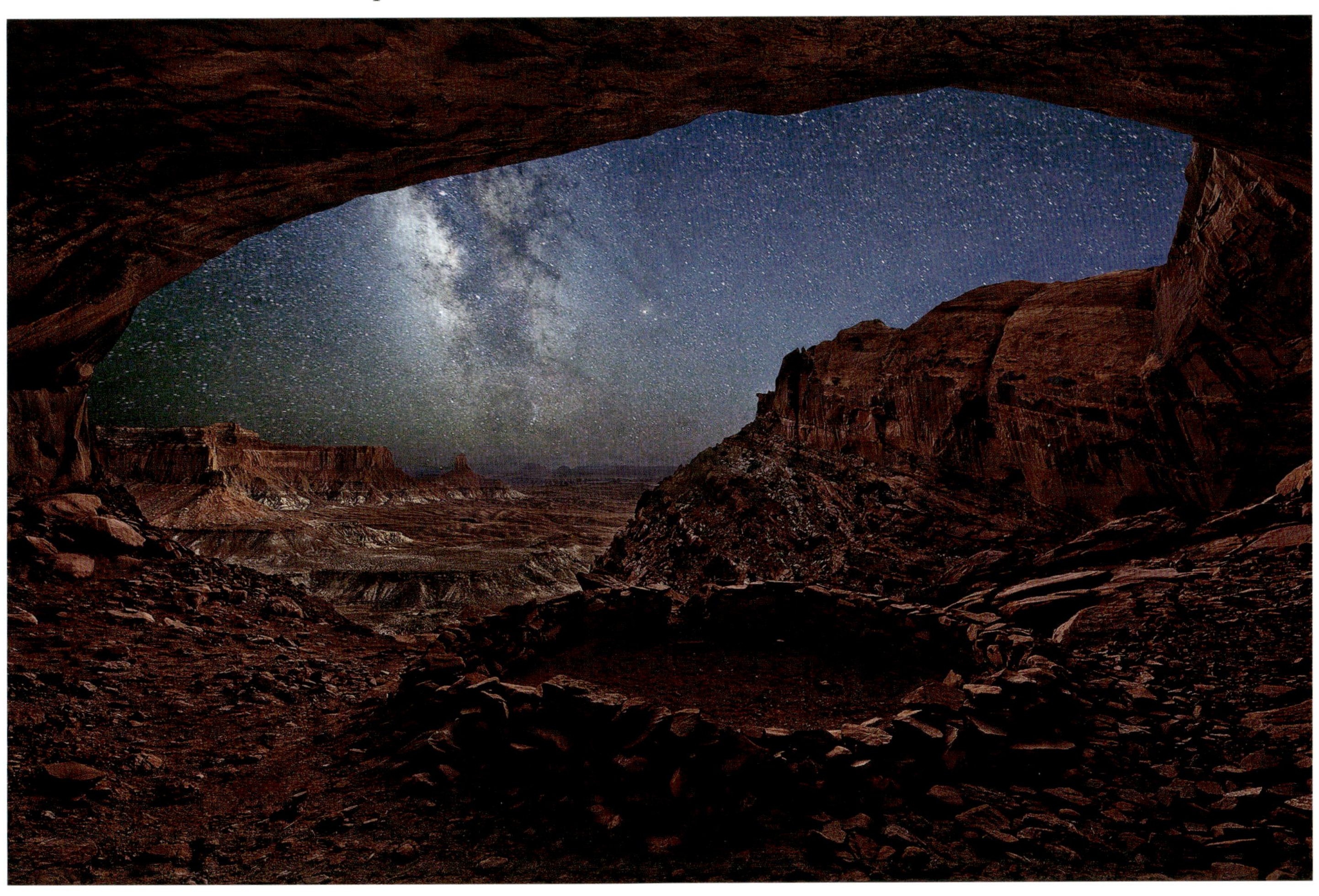

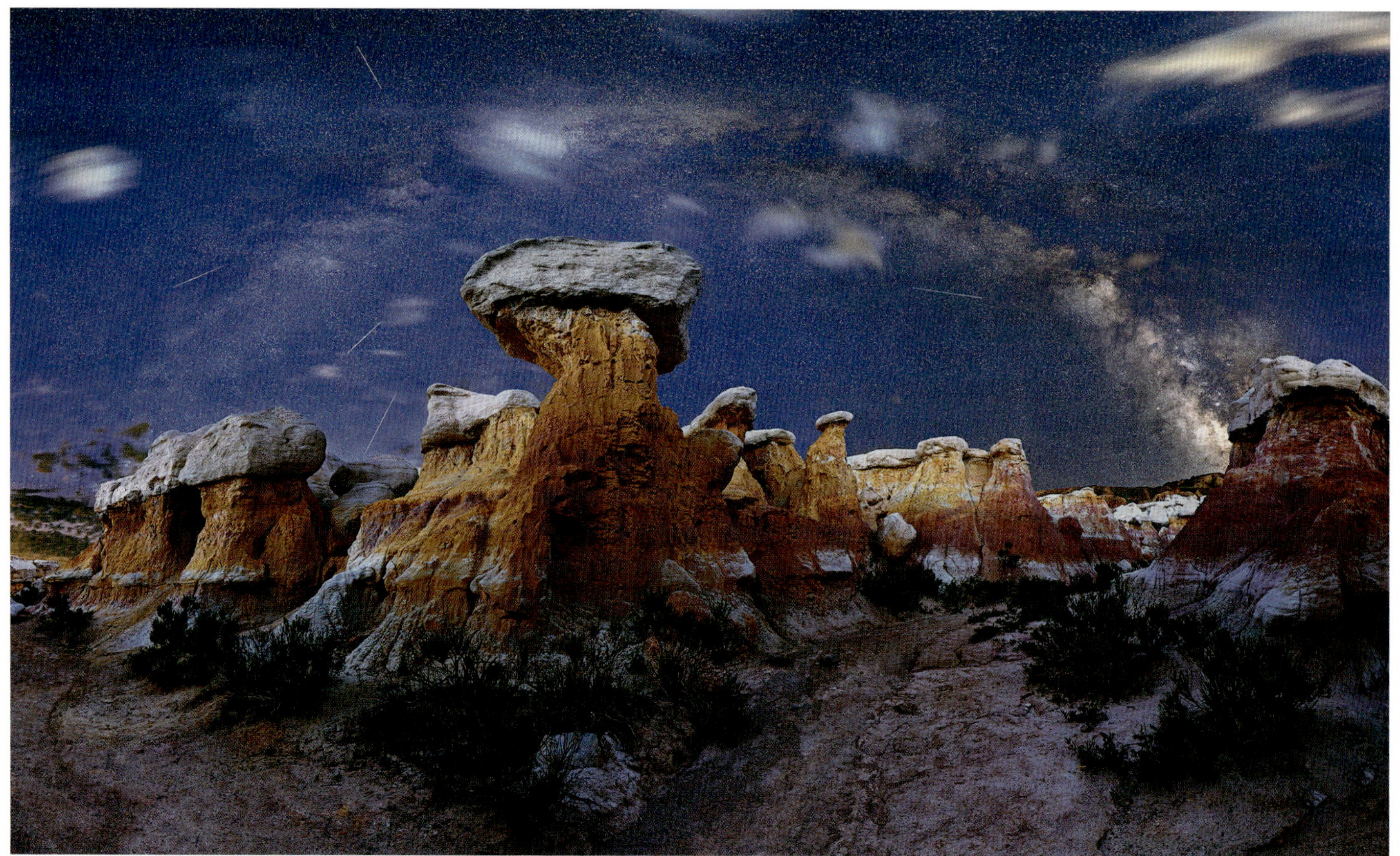

Although the image on the previous page turned out well, the sky is too noisy to print at very large sizes. To overcome this problem with this photo in Colorado, I stitched together multiple images of the rock formations taken shortly after sunset and blended them with a large stitched image of the night sky taken during astronomical twilight before sunrise. Canon 5D II; 20 exposures of land: 24mm, f/16, 0.6 seconds, ISO 100; 80 exposures of sky: 50mm, f/1.8, 13 seconds, ISO 6400.

---

you choose to shoot and process your images depends on your artistic approach and personal preferences.

If you take two images at different times, you can use the same method described in the previous section to blend the exposures in Photoshop. It is more difficult to blend these exposures than two shots that were taken one after the other. This is because the light on the scene will be different when you captured the two photos. For the white balance, you'll likely need to use a lower color temperature for the exposure of the sky than for the exposure of the land. Also, at any point where the land meets the sky in the image, you'll want the land to appear darker than the sky. Images where the land is lighter than the sky can look very unnatural. To achieve this result, you'll need to gradually darken the land as it approaches the horizon. The Burn layer described in Chapter X can be useful for this. You will likely also want to make several other adjustments described in that chapter to achieve a satisfactory result.

BLENDING STITCHED IMAGES

Once you become proficient at blending single exposures taken at night, you can attempt to blend stitched images. This will allow you to produce incredibly detailed images that can be printed at very large sizes.

To blend stitched images, you will need to shoot separate stitched images of the land and the sky using techniques discussed in Chapter VIII. You will then blend the stitched images using techniques described in the last two sections of this chapter.

You can blend a stitched image of the sky with a stitched image of the land taken about the same time using longer exposures. This will bring out additional detail in the land while keeping the stars as round points of light. I recommend exposures of around 15 seconds for the sky and exposures of around 2 minutes for the land. You can take the photo of the land right after you take the photo of the sky, then turn your camera and repeat the process to capture the stitched image. You'll then need to blend each of the pairs of images before stitching them. It can take a long time to capture these images, during which time the stars will move, making it harder to stitch the photos. As a result, I only recommend doing this with wide-angle lenses.

If you want to use a longer lens to capture a larger stitched image, you can first shoot the entire stitched image of the sky, followed by the entire stitched image of the land. Then, you'll need to stitch the two photos before blending them in Photoshop.

Another option for blending stitched images is to capture the photos of the sky under no moon and shoot the photos of the land under a moon or during civil twilight when there is more light out.

If you take the image of the land during civil twilight, you can often get away with a single exposure or a smaller stitched image taken with a wider lens. You can later up-res this image to match the size of the large stitched image of the sky taken later. Since there is a lot more light during civil twilight, I've found that the quality of a single exposure of the land with a 14mm lens taken shortly after sunset is pretty similar to the quality of a large stitched image of the sky taken after astronomical twilight with a 50mm lens. This can save a fair amount of time in post-processing, but all of the approaches in this section are still quite advanced.

Except for the first approach where you blend the images before stitching them, it can be hard to blend the two stitched images, since they will not line up perfectly. If necessary, you can distort one or both of the photos using the Warp or Puppet Warp tool in the Edit menu of Photoshop to line them up better. You can also do some cloning in areas where they don't line up well.

STACKING IMAGES OF THE LAND

Another option for getting more detail in the land than you can with a single exposure is to stack images rather than stitching them. To do this, you should take

The Three Sisters are reflected in Policeman's Creek in Canada during astronomical twilight. I stitched together four stacked images to reduce noise. Each of the stacked images was created from three consecutive exposures, with the stars manually realigned in each image. Nikon D850, 14mm, 15 seconds, ISO 1600.

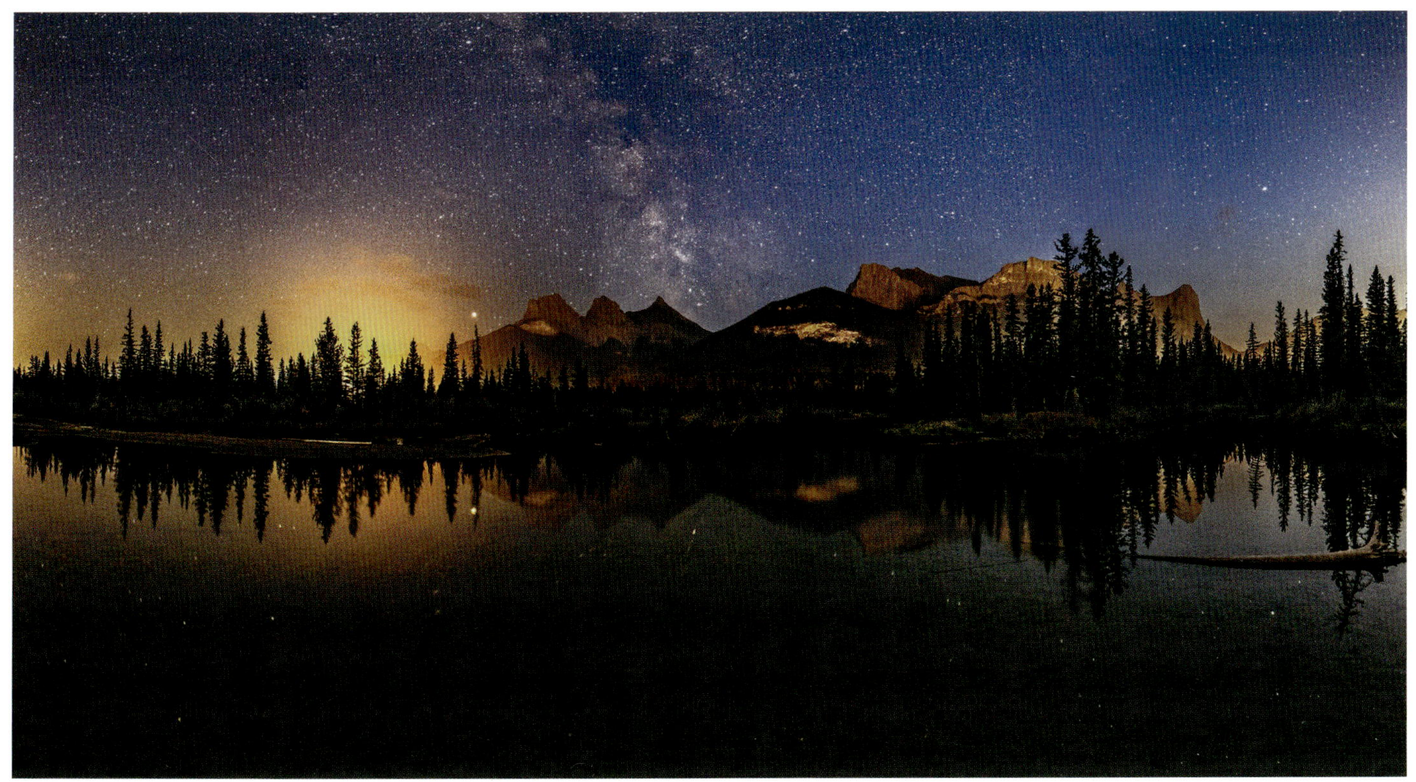

identical shots, one after another, of the same scene. I recommend using exposures of 30 seconds to 2 minutes for each of the shots and taking at least ten images, preferably more. The shorter individual exposures will help prevent dark noise while stacking multiple exposures will help reduce photon noise. You can use Long Exposure Noise Reduction or a dark frame to help reduce the dark noise even more.

To combine the images, select all of the photos in Lightroom, then right-click on one of them and select Edit In > Open as Layers in Photoshop... When the file opens in Photoshop, select all of the layers, right-click on them, and select Convert to Smart Object. Then select Layer > Smart Object > Stack Mode > Median.

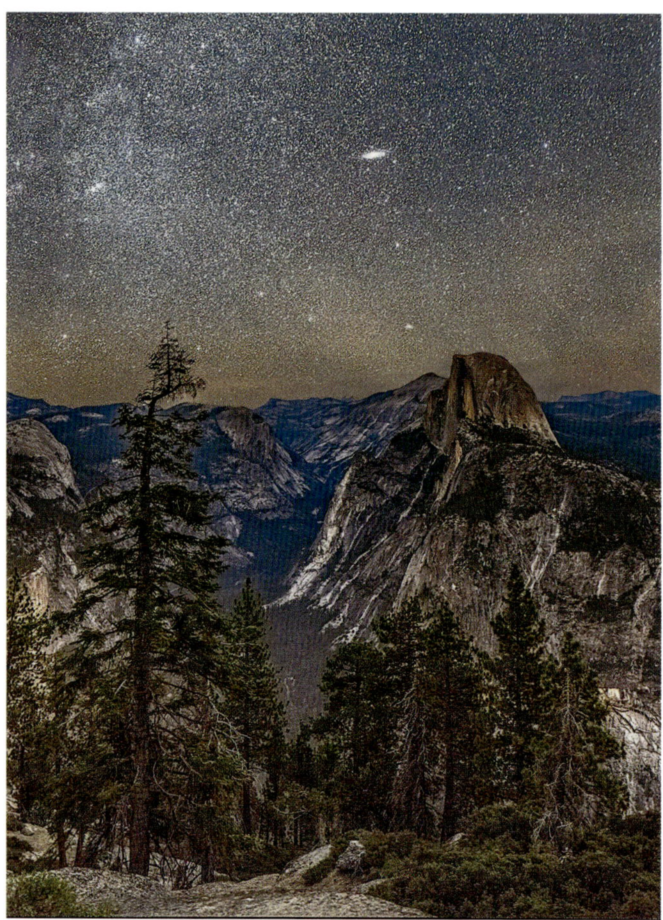

To capture this photo at Glacier Point in Yosemite, I took 65 consecutive exposures. I then stacked 5 images of the sky and all 65 images of the land to get a lot of detail on a moonless night. Sony a7 III, 14mm, f/1.8, ISO 1600, 15-30 seconds per exposure.

As long as you took all of the images with your camera firmly mounted on a tripod, you should now have a sharp image with more detail and less noise in the landscape. If the land appears blurry, the images may not all be aligned properly. In this case, you can try aligning all of them before converting to a Smart Object. To do this, first mask out the sky from each layer, then select all of the layers and go to Edit > Auto-Align Layers...

When you stack images of the land, any stars in the sky will appear blurred, since they will move during the exposures. You'll need to blend the land in this image with a separate photo of the sky. You can blend a stacked image of the land with a single exposure of the sky or with a stitched image of the sky. Or, you can blend it with a stacked image of the sky, as I'll explain next.

STACKING IMAGES OF THE SKY

You can stack images of the sky in much the same way you stack images of the land. However, since the stars will be moving during the exposure, you'll need to use much shorter exposure times to keep the stars looking like round points of light. I recommend using the NPF rule in the Photopills app (as described on page 55) to calculate the exposure time. Alternatively, you can just use the rule of 150 or 200. This will give you short exposures that will minimize star movement. The individual exposures will be of lower quality than those taken with the rule of 500. However, since you will be combining multiple images, the final image will be of higher quality, with almost no noticeable elongation of the stars.

Since the stars will be moving during the exposures, you'll have to align the images before stacking them using Photoshop or specialized stacking software. If there are any foreground objects in your photo, you'll need to mask them out in Photoshop before aligning the images. Otherwise, Photoshop may try to align the foreground rather than the stars.

Even if you mask out the land, Photoshop often still has difficulty aligning the photos. It tends to work best with images of the Milky Way, especially when the Milky Way is in the western or eastern part of the sky. It usually has the most trouble aligning stars in the northern or southern part of the sky, since these stars are rotating and moving at different speeds. In this case, you can try to manually align the stars by moving or rotating the stars in each photo in the opposite direction that they were moving when you took the shots.

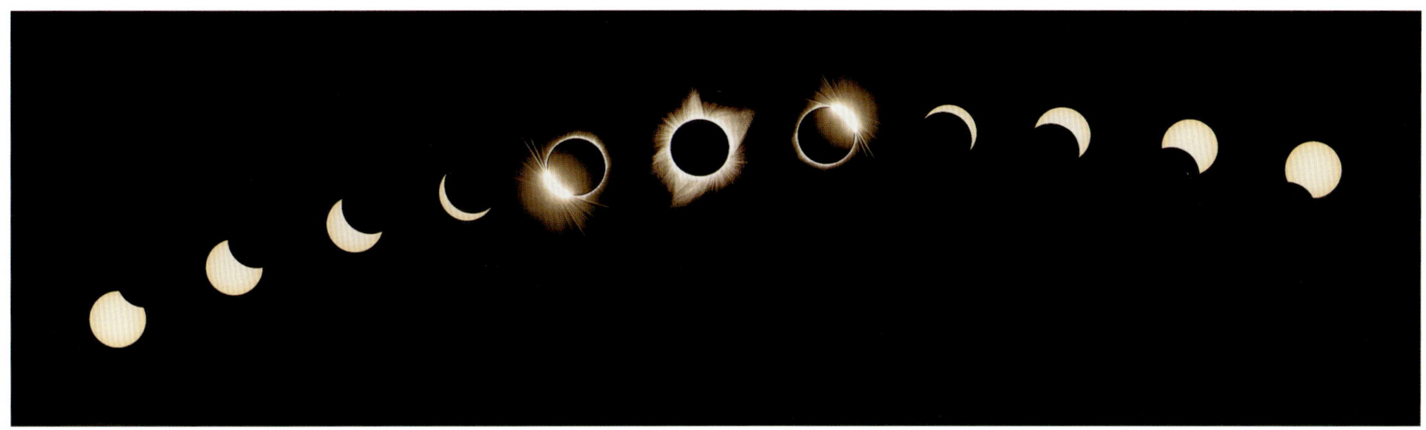

I combined all of the different stages of the Great American Eclipse of 2017 into a single image. I used an equatorial mount to help keep the moon and sun in the frame during the eclipse. This mount also let me do bracketed exposures up to 10 seconds to get detail in the moon in the image on page 70. Nikon D800e, 210mm, f/7.1, ISO 100, exposures from 1/60 to 1/1000 second, Solar filter used for images of partial eclipse.

More detail on how to rotate images can be found on page 153. This method can work for stacking 2 to 5 images. For bigger image stacks, you may need to use a star stacking program, which I'll describe later.

Another possible pitfall when using this method is that stars will move out of the frame while you are taking all of the images. This can limit your total exposure time, and it can be especially problematic if you are using a longer lens, which captures a smaller area of the sky.

You can get around a lot of the problems when stacking images of the sky by attaching your camera to an equatorial mount. An equatorial mount counteracts Earth's rotation by moving in the opposite direction and at the same rate as the rotation of Earth. This allows a camera attached to the mount to remain focused directly on the stars. Some mounts also have the option to stay focused on the moon or sun, which move slowly relative to the motion of the stars. The objects being photographed will not become blurred or elongated, even with exposures that far exceed the rule of 500.

The simplest way to capture a photograph with an equatorial mount is to take one long exposure from several minutes to several hours. If the mount is properly aligned and precise enough, it will move with the motion of the stars, and the stars will not appear elongated.

There are, however, two problems with this approach. The first is that any affordable consumer-model equatorial mount will probably not be precise enough to exactly follow the motion of the stars for a very long time. The second issue is that any long exposure over a few minutes will start to produce a lot of dark noise in the image.

The solution to these problems is to take several shorter exposures of around 1-2 minutes and stack all of them onto a single image. You can do this in Photoshop the same way you stack images of the land, or you can use specialized stacking software. You may need to align the images before stacking them.

If you get noticeable coma or other artifacts in your image, you may want to use a little smaller aperture than you usually do at night. Stacking images can reduce the extra photon noise you get with smaller apertures. I typically shoot at f/2.8 when stacking images of the sky using an equatorial mount.

You'll usually want to turn off Long Exposure Noise Reduction to avoid a long delay after each exposure. I do, however, recommend shooting one, or even several, dark frames to help reduce dark noise. The photon noise can be reduced significantly with stacking, and therefore dark noise can become a more dominant source of noise. You can use one or more dark frames in most specialized stacking software to reduce dark noise.

You can also use things like bias frames and flat frames to further reduce noise. However, this is usually only necessary for deep-sky astrophotography and is outside the scope of this book.

An equatorial mount can be especially useful if you are using a telephoto lens to photograph objects like an eclipse or a comet. Without a mount, you can only do very short exposures with a telephoto lens before these objects move too much and blur.

You can also get higher-quality photographs using a wide-angle lens on an equatorial mount than you can from a single exposure taken without one. Personally, I have found that creating large stitched images can produce photos of similar or better quality with a little less work. However, the stars can appear a bit elongated in a stitched image, whereas they should be perfectly round when photographed with an equatorial mount.

You can combine both of these techniques and stitch multiple images of the sky taken with an equatorial mount. This can be rather difficult, and I only recommend it for those who are very comfortable using an equatorial mount and stitching images. The effort may be worthwhile if you want to make huge prints, as this is a way to get extremely detailed photographs of the night sky. If you do this, you'll need to make sure none of the stars you want to photograph will set during the time it takes to capture all of the images. So you won't want to start out shooting any stars that are near the western horizon.

If you include any foreground in a stacked image of the sky, it will appear blurry. You will therefore need to blend a separate photo of the land.

Stacking Programs

Although you can use Photoshop to stack images taken with an equatorial mount, it can have difficulty aligning a large number of photos precisely. Fortunately, there are many software programs designed to stack images taken with or even without an equatorial mount. Some of these are expensive and rather difficult to use. They have more advanced options that are generally better-suited for deep-sky astrophotography. However, there is a low-cost program called Starry Landscape Stacker for Macs and a free program called Sequator for PCs. Both of these do a pretty good job and are fairly easy to learn. I recommend starting with one of these programs and consider upgrading to a more expensive one, like RegiStar, if you start doing a lot of image stacking.

Equatorial Mounts

There is now a pretty good selection of lightweight, affordable equatorial mounts that are made primarily for use with DSLR or mirrorless cameras and lenses. I've listed a couple of my favorites below. Both of these mounts have solar and lunar tracking rates, in addition to the standard tracking rate for stars. They also come with a polar scope, which you have to use to align the mount to the north star.

You will need a second tripod head (or base) for these mounts. You will then install the mount between the two tripod heads. If you don't already own a second one, I recommend purchasing one designed for an equatorial mount, like the SkyWatcher S20530 Base, as it can make polar alignment easier.

SkyWatcher Star Adventurer

This is my favorite mount, as it has more features than the other lightweight models and is rated to hold more weight. The Astro Package version of this mount is rated to hold up to 11 pounds. You can mount a longer telephoto lens or even a small telescope onto it for astrophotography. You can also get the counter weight kit to add more stability. You will need a very steady tripod that can hold all of this weight. If you don't ever plan to use long, heavy lenses, the Photo Package is a bit less expensive and easier to set up. The SkyWatcher is also nice because it has a lot of different tracking rates that can be used for creating panning movement in a time-lapse video.

SkyWatcher Star Adventurer Mini

As the name implies, this is a miniature version of the SkyWatcher. It weighs just 1.5 pounds and is rated to hold 6.6 pounds. It will be a little less stable than the larger version. It also doesn't have all the different tracking rates designed for time-lapse photography. Since it costs about the same as the larger version, I only recommend it if you plan to do a lot of hiking or airline travel with it and want the lighter weight.

FOCUS STACKING

Another situation in which blending multiple exposures can be beneficial is when you have a close foreground, and you can't get both the foreground and background in focus in a single exposure. To get around this problem, you can take two or more images focused at different distances and later blend the parts of each photo that are in focus.

As an example, if you shoot with a 24mm lens at f/1.8, the maximum depth of field you can get is from 18 feet to infinity. If you have an object closer than 18 feet in your image, you won't be able to get everything in acceptable focus. You can extend the depth of field by taking two photos, one focused at 36 feet and the other focused at 12 feet. The image focused at 36 feet will be in focus from 18 feet to infinity. The image focused at 12 feet will be in focus from 9 feet to 18 feet. You can blend these two photos to get an image that is in focus from 9 feet to infinity. In reality, you'll want to leave a lot more overlap between the areas of the image that are in focus, to leave room for error.

While I've calculated the exact focus distances above, you don't actually have to do this. You can shoot the first exposure while focused at infinity. Then turn your focus ring to slightly less than infinity, and take another exposure. Keep focusing closer and closer and shooting images until you're focused at or in front of the nearest object in your image. You likely won't need to use every photograph you take, but by shooting this many images, you can be sure that every part of the scene will be in sharp focus in at least one of the exposures. You can later choose which photos you want to use for the focus stack when you transfer them to your computer. You'll be able to zoom in on the images on a large screen and see exactly how much of the photo is in focus.

If you're doing a simple focus stack with just two exposures, you should open both files in Photoshop. Select the Move tool, hold down the Shift key, and drag the image with the distant objects in focus onto the

I took this image with a 50mm lens at f/1.8, which only allowed me to get objects from about 80 feet to infinity in focus. However, the nearest foreground object was approximately 30 feet away. I therefore had to take exposures with multiple focus points and stack them. In each of the layers below, I masked out areas that were out of focus. Nikon D800e, 50mm, f/1.8, 8 seconds, ISO 4000.

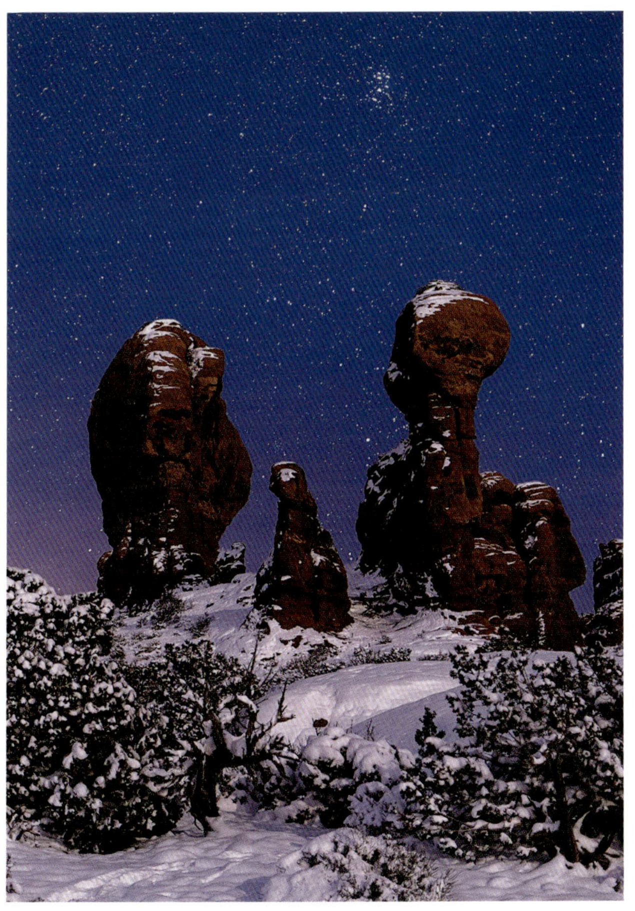

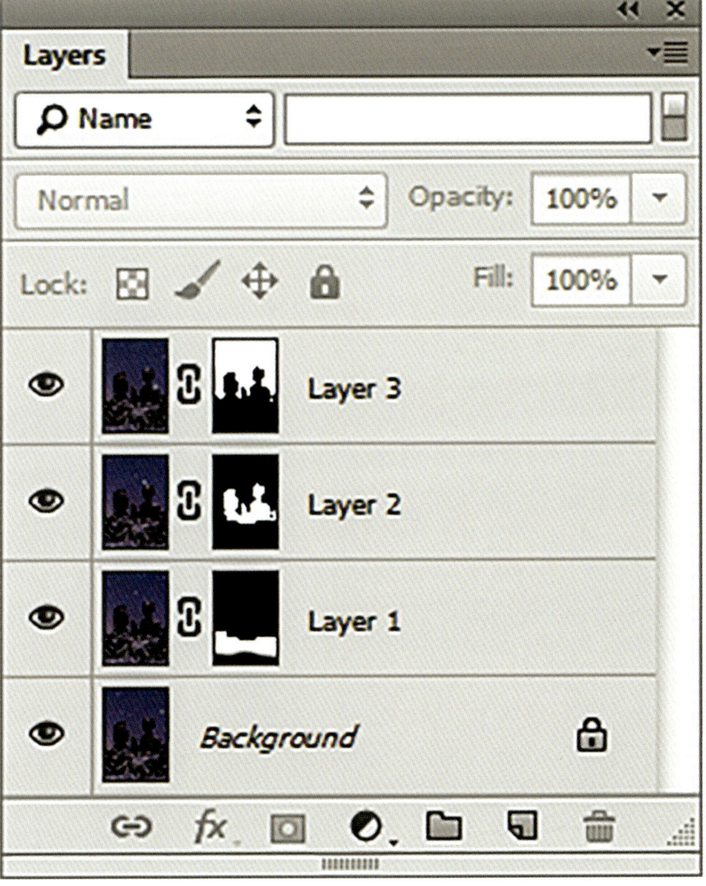

other image. Alternatively, you can select the photos in Lightroom, right-click on them and select Edit In > Open as Layers in Photoshop... Make sure that the top layer has the distant objects in focus, and the bottom layer has the near objects in focus. Now, select both layers and click Edit > Auto-Align Layers... If the layers do not align properly, you may need to first mask out the sky on all but the top layer before using Auto-Align. Sometimes the movement of stars or clouds in the sky can throw off Auto-Align.

Once the layers are aligned, select the top layer and mask out all of the foreground objects that are out of focus. Sometimes you can do this quickly with the brush tool. As long as you left plenty of overlap in the areas that are in focus, you don't have to be overly precise. However, you should check the image at 100% zoom to see if there are any out-of-focus areas. You can then refine the mask if necessary. If there are areas of the image that abruptly transition from near to far, you'll need to make a more precise mask, using a tool like the Quick Selection Tool.

If you need to blend more than two images, you'll use the same process with more layers. On the top layer, mask out everything that is not in focus. Then repeat this on all of the layers below it.

ENLARGING STAR SIZE

When shooting photos at night, your camera can capture far more stars than the eye can see. This is often a good thing, as it can produce impressive images of the Milky Way. However, this can be detrimental if you are photographing a familiar constellation or star pattern like Orion or the Big Dipper. These are easy to see with the naked eye, but they can become lost amidst all the stars that the camera can capture.

There are several ways to fix this problem. All of them involve increasing the size of the brightest stars in your image so that the constellations stand out and appear more like they do to the naked eye. A couple of these techniques involve blending multiple exposures and will be described below. There are also ways to increase star size with single exposures in post-processing. This will be discussed in the next chapter.

Shooting Stars Out of Focus

I've spent a lot of time in this book discussing how to get everything in sharp focus. However, it can occasionally be beneficial to shoot stars out of focus. When the stars are out of focus, they will appear larger in the image. Since there isn't much detail in the stars to begin with, you don't necessarily have to have them in perfect focus. If you take an image with the stars out of focus, this will cause more distant objects on the land to appear out of focus as well. So you will need to blend two exposures - one with the land in sharp focus and one with the stars a little out of focus. To really get the stars in the constellation to show up, you can add only the out-of-focus stars from the constellation to the image with everything in sharp focus.

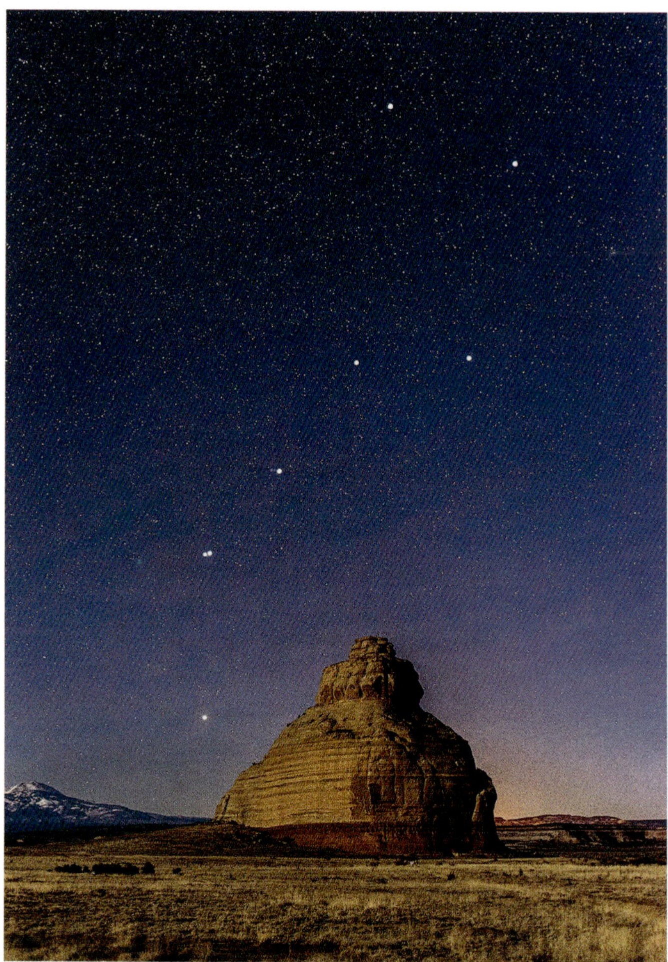

This image depicts the Big Dipper over Church Rock in eastern Utah. I took one photo with everything in sharp focus and a second shot with the stars out of focus. I then added only the out-of-focus stars from the Big Dipper to the image with everything in focus. Nikon D800e, 50mm, f/2.8, 10 seconds, ISO 6400.

To shoot the out-of-focus stars, I recommend taking

multiple exposures while gradually shifting your focus ring from infinity to closer and closer distances. This will give you stars that are more and more out of focus, and you will have a lot of options to choose from in post-processing.

Fog Filter

Another option for enlarging star size is to use a fog filter. As discussed on page 24, this filter can make bright stars appear larger and glow more. It can also make the land appear out of focus. So you will need to take an exposure for the land without the filter and blend the two exposures.

SHOOTING THE MOON

As mentioned in Chapter V, if you want to avoid overexposing the moon at night, you'll probably have to blend two exposures - one with a shutter speed of one second or less for the moon and another with a longer shutter speed for the rest of the scene. This can be difficult to accomplish, as you'll have to clone out the white blob and bright sky surrounding the moon in the second exposure. A better time to attempt this is during a lunar eclipse. During totality, an eclipse is sufficiently faint that you won't have much of a white blob and bright sky around the moon to clone out.

You could accomplish this by taking the two exposures with the same focal length lens. In Photoshop, you can place the shorter exposure on a layer above the longer exposure. Then mask out everything on the top layer except for the moon. You can also clone out some of the bright areas around the moon in the bottom layer.

While this technique seems straight forward, there is one problem with it. Celestial objects will often appear larger in an image with longer exposures. This is because you don't just capture the disk of the objects but also the glow around them. In the shorter exposure of the moon, you don't capture a glow around it, so it appears smaller. In the following image, if I had simply blended two exposures with the same focal length lens, the moon would have looked barely bigger than Mars. I therefore took the longer exposure with a 38mm lens and the shorter exposure for the moon with an 85mm lens. This made the moon appear larger in that image, and the size about matched the overexposed moon I captured with the 38mm lens. I therefore recommend taking the shorter exposure for the moon with a lens that is about twice the focal length of the lens you use for the longer exposure. This can, however, vary depending on how much glow there is around the stars and planets.

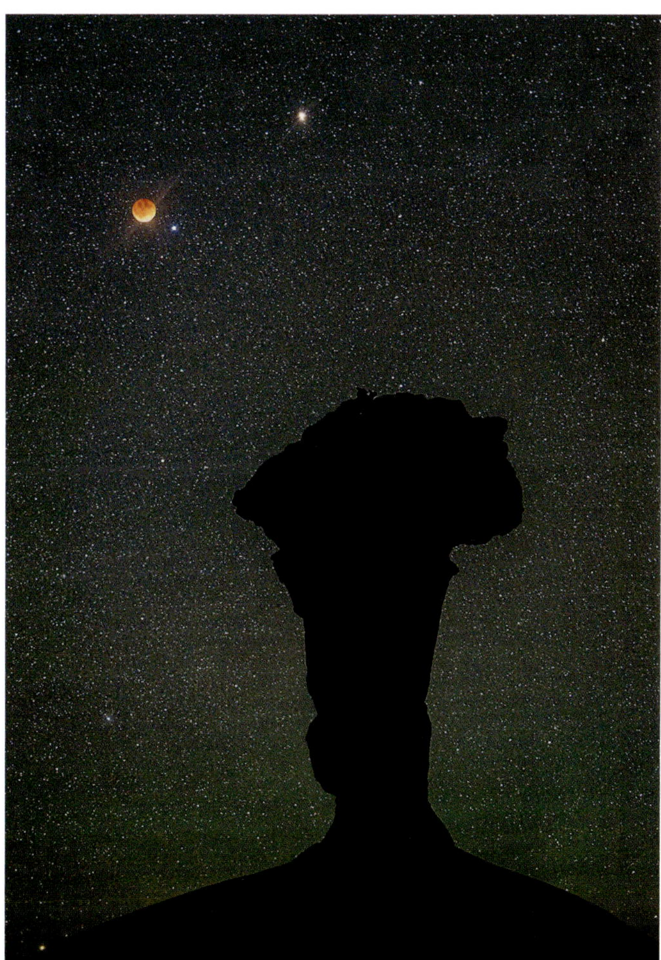

To photograph a total lunar eclipse over Utah, I blended an exposure of the moon with an exposure of the rest of the scene. Nikon D800e; exposure of moon: 85mm, f/2.8, 1 second, ISO 500; exposure of rest of scene: 38mm, f/2.8, 13 seconds, ISO 6400.

If you want the moon to appear larger, you can use an even longer lens for the shorter exposure. This can produce some dramatic images, but it can also start to make the moon appear unrealistically large.

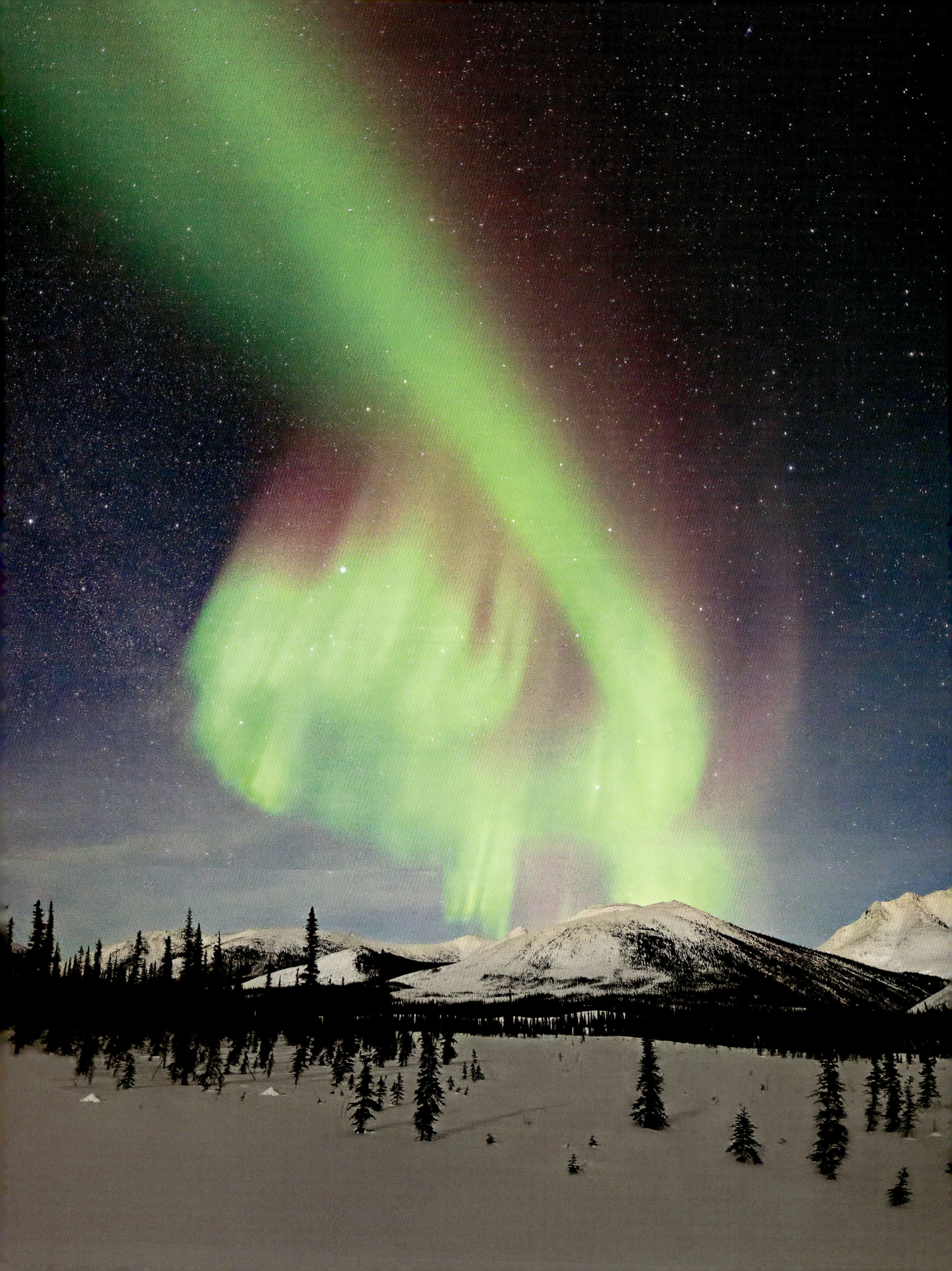

X. Post-Processing Night Photos

There is a perception among some people today that any work done on a photo in Adobe Lightroom or Photoshop will make the image "less real" and that the only "real" photographs are ones that come straight out of the camera completely unaltered.

One problem with this belief is that sensors in digital cameras convert photons of light into data that is represented by a series of 0s and 1s. If you want something that is completely unaltered from what the camera recorded, it will be a series of 0s and 1s, not a photograph.

To create a photograph, a digital camera must convert the data captured by the sensors into pixels, each of which contains one color value. There is no "right" way to convert the data into pixels. You can let the camera or computer software do all the work, or you can provide input into how you want the image rendered by adjusting the contrast, white balance, brightness, etc.

It is my belief that a photographer knows what it is that they were trying to capture in a photograph better than the default settings of a software program. By letting the camera or computer software render the photo, you are not producing an image that is "more real." You are instead allowing software to make all your artistic decisions for you. This can be especially problematic with night photos, as the software is designed to optimize images taken during the day.

There are many lengthy books devoted entirely to using Lightroom and Photoshop. I'm unable to cover all of this in one chapter. I will therefore focus more on post-processing techniques that are important to night photography but not often done with images taken during the day. You should then be able to combine these techniques with techniques you use to optimize all of your other photos.

Although there are other software programs available for preparing photographs, most photographers today use Lightroom and Photoshop. I will therefore focus on these two programs, as well as some plug-ins for these programs.

Lightroom is a software program developed by Adobe from the ground up specifically for the use of digital photographers. It is quite a bit easier to use than Photoshop, which is also intended for graphic designers and has some features that most photographers will never use. However, Photoshop is a more robust program, and you can do things with it that you cannot do in Lightroom. So I recommend using both programs, especially for processing night photos. These images are usually more difficult to process than daytime photos and may require more software tools.

I'll discuss the general workflow that I use to process my night photos. However, there is no "right way" to process images. How you want your photos to look is ultimately your decision. You should try to develop your own style of processing images and create photos that are most pleasing to you.

As stated in the introduction, I have also created a comprehensive video showing how to accomplish the post-processing techniques described in this chapter and the last three chapters. This video is available at https://www.collierpublishing.com.

LIGHTROOM ADJUSTMENTS

Many of the adjustments you make to night photos in Lightroom will be similar to adjustments you make to your daytime photos. All of the adjustment sliders I discuss can be found in Lightroom's Develop mod-

Left: The northern lights dance above the Brooks Range near Wiseman, Alaska. If I had relied on the default settings in my camera or Lightroom to process the image, it would have appeared flat and had a yellow color cast. To get the image to really stand out and convey how spectacular the northern lights are, I had to carefully process the image in Lightroom and Photoshop. Canon 5D II, 14mm, f/2.8, 10 seconds, ISO 6400.

ule. These sliders are identical to those found in Adobe Camera RAW, which comes with Photoshop. So if you don't own Lightroom, you can make the same adjustments with that software.

White Balance

White balance is one of the most important adjustments you will make to your night photos in Lightroom. The colors in your image may not look good straight out of the camera, but as long as you shot in RAW, you can now fix this.

If you took your photo during twilight, I usually recommend keeping the white balance near your camera's daylight settings. This is because light from the sun will still be giving color to the sky. If you captured your image during blue hour (which occurs around the transition between civil and nautical twilight), you might need to raise the color temperature to prevent your photos from looking too blue. Towards the end of astronomical twilight in the evening (or the beginning of twilight in the morning), you usually need to lower the color temperature a little to keep the colors looking natural.

If your photo was taken after twilight with the moon out, I recommend using a white balance between 4150K and 5000K. The light from the moon is just reflected sunlight, so it is comparable to daylight. However, since the moon isn't perfectly white, the reflected light has a different temperature than sunlight. A full moon has a color temperature of about 4150K. However, I've found that using this color temperature

This photograph shows the Milky Way and Venus rising above Turret Arch in Arches National Park. I used the Lightroom preset called Zeroed to show how this image looks with every slider set to zero in Lightroom, except the white balance, which was set to daylight. This photo needs quite a bit of work. The colors look a little too yellow, and I'll need to bring out a lot more contrast, especially in the Milky Way. The image also has quite a bit of noise. I'll be able to eliminate the noise in the foreground by making it appear as a pitch-black silhouette. Canon 5D II, 14mm, f/2.8, 30 seconds, ISO 6400.

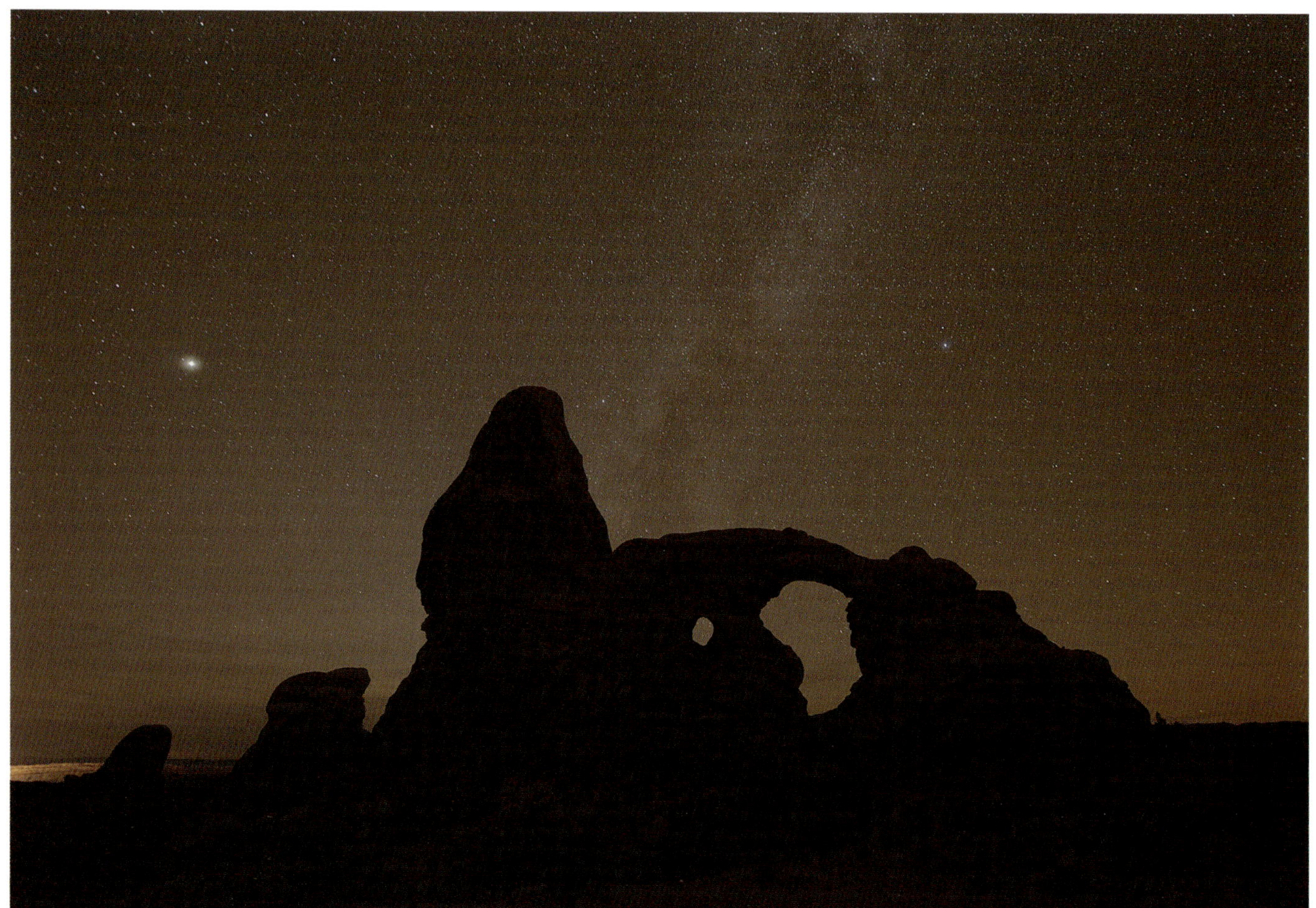

can result in skies that look almost neon blue. This might be how the sky would appear under the moon if we could see colors as well during the night as we can during the day. Since we can't, I typically use a white balance of around 4600K. This can produce skies that seem more natural. I usually keep the tint close to my camera's daylight setting.

If you took your image after twilight under no moon and used your camera's daylight setting, the photo may appear too yellow. I therefore recommend lowering the color temperature to reduce the yellow. If you have anything white, like snow or a waterfall, in your image, you can hit W and click on the white area using the White Balance Selector tool. This will often give you good colors in your photograph, but you can manually refine the white balance if necessary. If there is no obvious white area in the foreground of your image, I've found that a temperature close to 4200K will produce fairly neutral colors with limited color cast. If you reduce the temperature even more, you will start to get a bluer color to the sky. This may look more appealing since we are used to the sky appearing blue during the day. However, the sky doesn't have much blue in it after twilight under no moon.

If you prefer the look of blue skies after twilight under no moon, I don't recommend creating them by lowering the color temperature across the whole image. This will create a blue cast over the photo and make the stars and Milky Way look blue. Instead, I recommend only making darker parts of the sky bluer.

You can do this in Lightroom with an Adjustment Brush, which can be used by clicking on the far-right icon below the histogram in the Develop module. Set the color temperature to a negative value and all other sliders to zero. You can now paint over the entire sky with the brush until it appears sufficiently blue. Then, use a luminance range mask at the bottom of the brush panel to confine the brush effect to darker parts of the sky and not to the stars, Milky Way, or foreground. You can begin with a Range setting of 30/70, and then adjust the sliders until the colors look good.

Alternatively, you can do this in Photoshop with a Color Balance adjustment layer with a Midtones luminosity mask. Luminosity masks will be described in more detail later in this chapter. This mask will prevent the adjustment from affecting bright areas of the sky or dark areas of the land. You may need to manually mask out more of the land if the luminosity mask does not completely mask it out.

Personally, I believe that one of the few times you should consider adding a lot of artificial blue color to the sky is if you are combining an image of the land taken during twilight or under moonlight with a photo of the sky taken at night under no moon. Since the sky is blue under a moon and during twilight, it may look unnatural to have a landscape with a lot of detail and shadows, with a black sky overhead. Adding some blue to the sky can be helpful in this circumstance.

Rather than making the sky look blue, you may be inclined to try and make it appear black since that is closer to how it appears to our eyes at night. However, even under no moon outside of twilight hours, the sky is not always devoid of color. Molecules in the upper atmosphere can emit light known as airglow. The colors produced by airglow are similar to those from the northern lights, but they are much fainter. They can't be seen with the naked eye, but they can be picked up by the camera.

Since we can't see many of the colors in the sky at night, it can be difficult to know exactly how to render them in a photograph. I recommend adjusting the sliders until you get colors that look good to you without creating a noticeable color cast over the whole image. There is some artistic license involved here.

You can also adjust the tint until you get colors that look good to you. You don't want to alter this as much as the temperature and should generally keep it near zero. I've found that a tint of +8 often works well, but this can vary depending on your camera.

Exposure

If you used the camera settings I recommended in Chapter IV, your photograph may look too bright when you first import it into Lightroom. The Exposure slider can be used to darken the image, but I don't recommend doing this just yet. In fact, as long as you're not blowing out the highlights, I recommend brightening the image even more by moving the exposure slider to the right. You can keep moving it until you have data near the right side of the histogram but are not clipping any of the highlights. This will give you better tonal range throughout the image. You'll be able to darken the photo back up, while preserving some of the tonal range, in Photoshop.

Contrast

Your images will likely look flat when you first import them, so a big goal when processing images is to get more contrast throughout the photo. However, I don't recommend adjusting the contrast much in Lightroom, since adjustments I recommend in Photoshop will also increase the contrast. The most I suggest increasing the contrast is to +25, but you can keep it at 0 and adjust it all later.

Highlights

The Highlights slider is an excellent tool if any of the highlights are blown out in the image. It can be difficult to blow out highlights at night, but it is possible, especially when shooting under a bright moon. You can tell if any highlights are clipped by looking at the histogram. If you see a small triangle on the upper right side of the histogram, then you are clipping some highlights. You can click on the triangle to show exactly what highlights are blown out. You should move the Highlights slider to the left until the highlights are no longer clipped (or until you're clipping a minimal amount of highlights).

If you're forced to move the Highlights slider more than -25 to the left to avoid clipping the highlights, it indicates that you overexposed the photo in camera. In the future, you'll want to lower the ISO when shooting in similar conditions to avoid overexposing the image.

Shadows

The Shadows slider allows you to recover some detail in very dark shadows. This can be useful for night photos since you will frequently have very dark areas in an image. If you see a triangle on the upper left of the histogram, then you are clipping the shadows. Again, you can click on this triangle to see what areas are clipped. You can then move the Shadows slider to the right to recover some details in the shadows.

When you bring out details in the shadows, you will also bring out more noise in the image. So be careful not to push the slider too far right. It's okay to have some very dark shadows in night photos.

If your goal is to render foreground objects as silhouettes, then you won't want any detail in the shadows. In this case, you can move the Shadows slider to the left to eliminate details and render the objects pitch black. You may also need to move the Blacks slider to the left to fully darken the foreground. When adjusting these sliders, you'll want to make sure that it doesn't cause the sky to become too dark as well. If it does, you can pull back on the sliders and leave some detail in the shadows. You can later select just the shadow areas and darken them in Photoshop.

Whites & Blacks

The Whites and Blacks sliders are similar to the Highlights and Shadows sliders, but they work on a wider range of tones in the image. I don't recommend making significant changes to these sliders, as you will be able to fine-tune things in Photoshop.

Texture & Clarity

The Texture and Clarity sliders increase localized contrast in a photograph, as opposed to the Contrast slider, which increases the overall contrast. Both of the sliders can bring out more detail in the photo and make it "pop." However, increasing these sliders can also bring out more noise in an image. I therefore don't use them too often with night photos. If you find that the sliders help your image, you can increase them some, but I don't recommend pushing them past +20. If you want to increase localized contrast more, I discuss a way to do this in Photoshop with Unsharp Mask at the end of this chapter.

Dehaze

As its name implies, the Dehaze slider is intended to remove haze in an image. However, it can also be useful if you want to bring out more detail in the sky. I've found that it can do an excellent job of increasing contrast and tonal range in clouds and in the Milky Way. It doesn't affect the fine details as much as the Texture and Clarity sliders, so it doesn't bring out noise quite as much. It produces a similar effect to the Levels adjustment with a Darks luminosity mask that I describe in the Photoshop section. I do still recommend processing most images in Photoshop as well, but you can

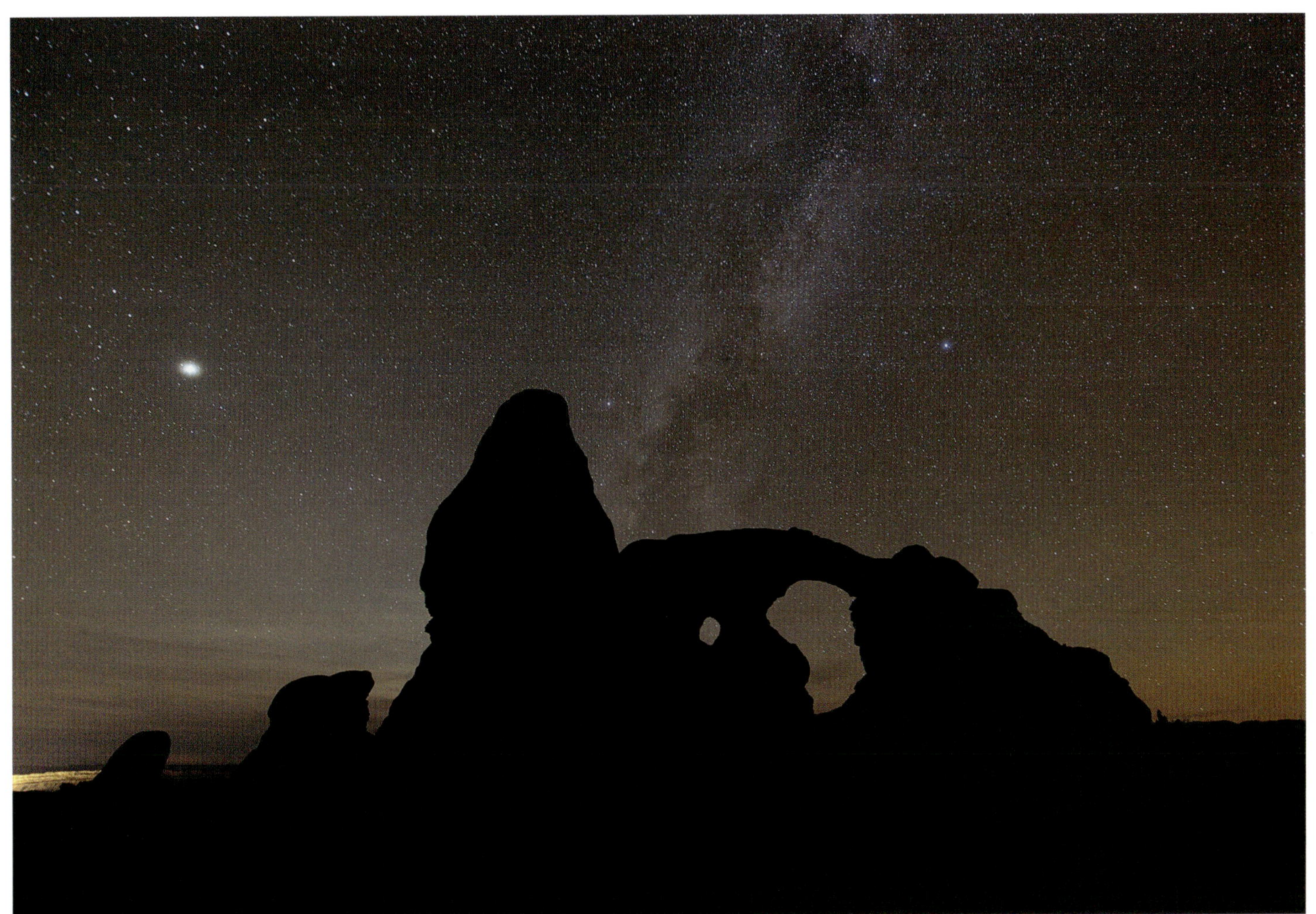

This is how the image from page 138 appeared after I finished working on it in Lightroom. I decreased the color temperature to 4200K to give the sky more of a neutral color. I increased the Exposure slider to +0.25 and the contrast slider to +25. I moved the Shadows slider to the left until the foreground appeared as a black silhouette. I also clicked on Enable Profile Corrections in the Lens Correction panel. This helped remove some of the vignetting in the corners.

---

often get closer to a final image by using this slider.

The Dehaze slider can sometimes add too much saturation to an image, so you may need to reduce the vibrance or saturation slider. It can also make the shadows too dark and the highlights too bright. You can offset this by increasing the Shadows slider and decreasing the Highlights slider.

Vibrance & Saturation

I don't recommend adjusting the Vibrance or Saturation sliders in Lightroom unless you need to reduce saturation after using the Dehaze slider. The adjustments I recommend in Photoshop will usually bring out the colors and saturation more. It's easier to wait until you've made those adjustments and then adjust the vibrance and saturation in Photoshop.

Sharpening

If you plan to use Topaz DeNoise, which I will discuss in the Photoshop section, I don't recommend doing any sharpening in Lightroom. You should set the Amount slider under Sharpening in the Detail panel to zero. Sharpening can make it more difficult to reduce noise.

If you will instead be reducing noise with the Luminance slider in Lightroom or if you won't be reducing noise, you can apply some pre-sharpening to your images in Lightroom. Since you will do final sharpening later, you don't want to sharpen your images too much at this point. I use these settings for my night photos:

Amount: 40
Radius: 1.0
Detail: 25
Masking: 20-80 (to prevent sharpening the noise)

Noise Reduction

Lightroom has some noise reduction features that can be useful for night photos, especially if you don't own other noise reduction software. There are two noise reduction sliders called Luminance and Color. The Luminance slider attempts to reduce unnatural fluctuations in the brightness of the image. This noise is often the result of photon noise, which occurs when shooting in low light. The Color slider attempts to reduce chrominance noise, which can appear as hot pixels or unnatural color variations. This noise can be the result of dark noise that is produced during very long exposures.

The Luminance slider can be effective at reducing noise, but it can also blur some of the details in the photograph. I have found that Topaz DeNoise usually does a better job of reducing this noise without blurring details. So I recommend keeping this slider set at zero. If you choose not to purchase Topaz DeNoise, you can adjust this slider. Make sure you don't blur any details too much, especially in the foreground. If you're blurring details in the foreground, you may instead want to use the Noise slider that is available with the Adjustment Brush. This will allow you to do more noise reduction in the sky, where you don't have to worry as much about blurring details.

The Color slider doesn't blur details too much, so you can use this slider in Lightroom, even if you're also using Topaz DeNoise. I usually keep the sliders at their default settings, which are:

Color: 25
Detail: 50
Smoothness: 50

This will often be effective at reducing small amounts of chrominance noise in your image. If your photo has a lot of chrominance noise, you can increase the Color slider. However, this can cause some unwanted fringing along edges in the image. So make sure the noise reduction isn't adversely affecting parts of the photo, especially in the stars and along areas where it transitions from land to sky.

Lens Corrections

The Lens Corrections panel in the Develop module of Lightroom can be very useful for night photos. Even with the best lenses, night photos often have strong vignetting in the corners and sometimes have chromatic aberration. Some of the wide-angle lenses that you use in night photography can also cause noticeable distortion in the images.

An easy way to fix vignetting and distortion is to click on Profile in the Lens Correction panel and check the box that says Enable Profile Corrections. This will attempt to fix any vignetting and distortion based on the properties of the lens that you used. If the vignetting and distortion are not properly fixed, you can fine-tune the image by adjusting the Distortion and Vignetting sliders at the bottom of the panel.

If Lightroom does not automatically bring up the lens that you used for the shot, you will have to manually enter the lens under Make and Model. If Lightroom does not have your lens in its database, you will need to manually adjust the vignetting by clicking on Manual and then adjusting the Vignetting sliders. You can also adjust the Distortion slider if you want to try and correct any distortion from the lens. This is useful if you have straight lines, like trees or the horizon, in your image that you want to remain straight.

The Lens Corrections panel can also be used to fix chromatic aberration in an image. In night photos, chromatic aberration will usually appear as an unnatural magenta color around the edges of stars. To fix this, click on Manual in the Lens Correction panel. You can then adjust the Amount sliders under Defringe to get rid of unnatural colors around stars. You should adjust the sliders the minimum amount required to remove this color. If this doesn't work, you can also adjust the Purple Hue and Green Hue sliders until you get a result you like.

Lightroom Presets

When processing night photos, you'll probably find

that you are using similar settings for a lot of images. You can save these settings as a Lightroom preset so that you can start with these settings. You can do this by selecting a photo that has the settings you want to use for the preset. Then, locate the Presets panel in the upper left corner of the Develop module. Click '+' on the upper right of this panel and select Create Preset... In the box that opens, you'll need to give a name to the preset and then select all of the settings that you want to be applied to the preset. Now click Create, and this preset will show up in the User Presets collection in the Presets panel. You can now apply this preset to any other files by selecting the photographs and clicking on the preset. You can apply multiple presets to the same image if they affect different settings in Lightroom.

You can also apply a preset when importing photos. To do this, click Ctrl+Shift+I (Cmd+Shift+I on a Mac) to import photos. Then, select the preset in the drop-down box next to Develop Settings in the Apply During Import panel.

You might start by creating your own preset for photos taken with and without a moon in the sky.

David Kingham offers some standard and advanced donationware presets for night photography. You can find these presets at https://exploringexposure.com/lightroom-presets/nightscape/. Most of these presets are designed to make the image look as good as possible in Lightroom. The settings I've recommended are designed to prepare the photo for further editing in Photoshop. So if you plan to work on the image in Photoshop, I recommend starting with the settings that I've outlined previously in this chapter.

If you don't own Photoshop or prefer to do most of the work in Lightroom, David Kingham's presets can be useful. However, I recommend that you begin without using presets. By making all of the adjustments in Lightroom yourself, you can get a better feel for how altering each slider can affect the photograph. You can also start to develop your own style for processing images.

Other Lightroom Features

There are a lot of other features in the Develop module of Lightroom, including the ability to make localized adjustments with the Adjustment Brush. I usually prefer making localized adjustments in Photoshop, but Lightroom is also a powerful tool for this. The Range Mask can be used to confine the effects of the Adjustment Brush to specific luminosity or color ranges of the image.

PHOTOSHOP ADJUSTMENTS

Once you've finished making preliminary adjustments in Lightroom, you can begin working on your image in Photoshop. To open an image in Photoshop, right-click on it in Lightroom and select Edit In > Edit in Adobe Photoshop...

In addition to adjustments in Photoshop, I'll also discuss adjustments you can make using Photoshop plug-ins. Once installed, these plug-ins can be used within Photoshop.

For some of the adjustments I discuss, you can achieve similar results in Lightroom. However, other adjustments, like Boosting Star Size & Brightness and Minimizing Star Trails, can only be done in Photoshop. Most of the post-processing work I describe in Chapter IX also requires Photoshop.

Noise Reduction

After opening an image in Photoshop, I usually attempt to reduce the noise as much as possible without blurring the details. If you took a dark frame, you can apply this in Photoshop, as described on pages 62-63. This will only reduce dark noise. To reduce photon or luminosity noise, I recommend getting a plug-in known as Topaz DeNoise AI. This software can be purchased at https://topazlabs.com/denoise-ai/. It can also be used as a plug-in in Lightroom or as a standalone app.

I've tested other noise reduction software, and many of these programs blur details in the image in addition to reducing the noise. However, Topaz DeNoise does a remarkable job of keeping the details intact while also significantly reducing noise.

Topaz says that this software will reduce noise a little better if you do the noise reduction as the first step in post-processing. However, I prefer to do it after making Lightroom adjustments so that I can work on the original RAW file in Lightroom. You get better results in Lightroom when working with the original data collected by the camera sensor, especially when using the White Balance, Highlights, and Shadows sliders.

Another advantage of using Topaz DeNoise in Photoshop is that you can do the noise reduction on a duplicate layer. This allows you to later mask out some of the noise reduction if you decide it blurred details in the land a bit too much. To create a duplicate layer, simply hit Ctrl+J (Cmd+J on a Mac).

Once it is installed, you can access DeNoise in the Filter menu of Photoshop under Topaz Labs > Topaz DeNoise AI. When the dialog box opens, you will see various options and sliders on the right side of the screen. Under Select a Model, I recommend keeping this set at Denoise AI. Under Select Mode, you can click on Auto. This will often do an excellent job of reducing noise. If it appears too blurry or if the noise isn't reduced enough, you can click on Manual, and it will show the settings that were selected by Auto. You can now adjust the sliders under Remove Noise, Sharpen, and Recover Original Detail. These sliders are fairly self-explanatory. Increasing the Remove Noise slider will remove more noise but can also start to blur the image. The Sharpen and Recover Original Detail sliders can eliminate some of the blur.

There are also sliders under Post-Processing that can be used for reducing color noise. I recommend reducing color noise with the Color slider in Lightroom before using Topaz DeNoise. If Lightroom wasn't able to eliminate the color noise, you can try reducing it further by adjusting the Chroma Noise sliders in DeNoise.

Once the preview looks good, click Save, and it will process your image and return you to Photoshop.

Pre-Sharpening

If you set the Sharpening slider to zero in Lightroom, you can now do some pre-sharpening to the image. An easy way to do this is to go to Filter > Camera Raw Filter... and add sharpening using the same sliders you use in Lightroom. When the dialog box opens, click on the small icon with two triangles to go to the Detail

After optimizing the Turret Arch photo in Lightroom, I began working on it in Photoshop. I first used Topaz DeNoise to reduce the noise in the sky. My next goal was to bring out more contrast in the image and make the Milky Way more prominent. To accomplish this, I created a Levels adjustment using the Darks 1 luminosity mask, as seen in the panels on the right.

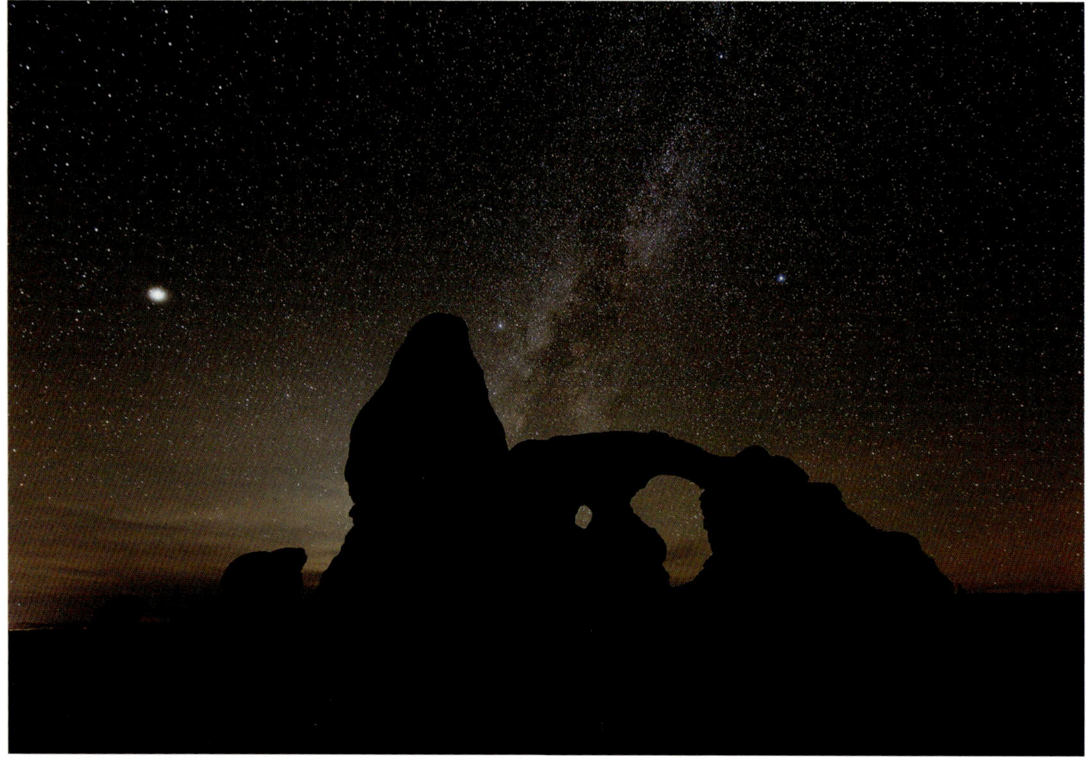

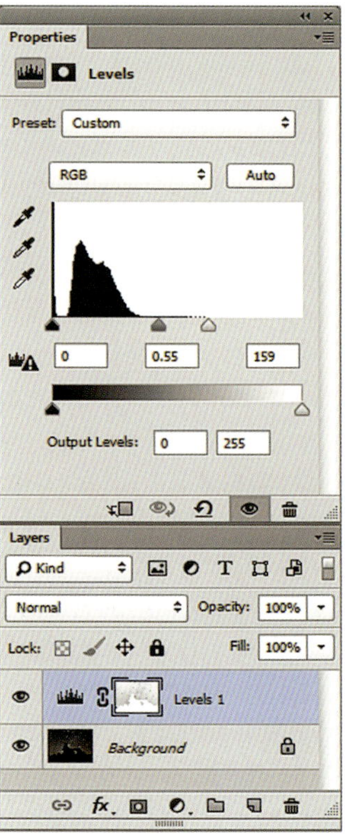

panel. Again, I recommend these settings:

Amount: 40
Radius: 1.0
Detail: 25
Masking: 20-80 (to prevent sharpening the noise)

Levels Adjustment with Luminosity Masks

You can now start optimizing the appearance of the image using adjustment layers in Photoshop. The first adjustment layer I usually create is a Levels layer. To create an adjustment layer, go to Layer > New Adjustment Layer and select the layer you want to create. Alternatively, you can click on the circular black and white icon at the bottom of the Layers panel and select your adjustment layer from there.

Once you've opened a Levels layer, you will see a histogram in the Properties panel. The histogram for many night photos, especially those shot under no moon or a faint moon, will have a lot of data on the far left side (representing darker pixels in your image) and a minimal amount of data extending to the right side of the histogram (representing lighter pixels like those from stars, planets, or meteors). A histogram like this generally means that you have a flat, low contrast image. Images that are more appealing to people usually have more data extending towards the right side of the histogram. These photos will have more contrast and stronger mid-tones.

A simple way to spread more data to the right side of the histogram is to move the right slider in the Levels palette to the left. However, this will clip the highlights in the image and cause them to be blown out. You need to be able to mask out the brightest parts of the image so that they will not be affected by the Levels adjustment and therefore not get blown out. You can do this using something popularized by Tony Kuyper known as a luminosity mask.

You can find Tony's tutorial on luminosity masks, as well as Photoshop actions and panels you can use to create them at https://goodlight.us/writing/luminositymasks/luminositymasks-1.html. There is currently a free TK Basic panel, which allows you to quickly create luminosity masks. Tony also sells the complete panel for a low price, which I think is well worth the cost. The Web Sharpening portion, which I'll describe at the end of this chapter, is only available on the full panel.

For the Levels adjustments, I often start by using a Darks 1 or Darks 2 luminosity mask. Now, you can simply drag the right slider to the left in the Levels panel, as described previously. You'll probably also need to drag the center slider a good distance to the right to make the image look darker. You can adjust the sliders back and forth until you get an image that you are pleased with. Make sure not to move the right slider so far left that it is clipping data that is seen on the histogram. The farthest you'll generally want to move it is near the rightmost edge of the part of the histogram that contains data, as seen in the sample Levels adjustment on the previous page. However, sometimes you won't want to drag it this far, as it can make parts of the image appear too bright for a night photo.

Often, a single Levels adjustment with a Darks 1 luminosity mask will significantly improve the image, and this will be the only Levels layer you need to use. However, sometimes the photo will still look too flat. In this case, you might instead try using a Darks 2 or Darks 3 mask.

If the image still appears flat, you might try creating two Levels layers with two different masks. The first mask could be a Darks 1 mask, and the second could be a Darks 3 mask, as seen in the example on the following page.

I should point out that creating multiple Levels layers like this can potentially start to degrade image quality and produce banding or an image that looks overworked. It is better if you can make the adjustments you need with a single Levels layer. However, night photos can be tricky to process, and sometimes adding a second or even third Levels layer with different luminosity masks can be worthwhile.

Curves

After you make the Levels adjustment, you should have an image that has a lot more contrast. If it still doesn't have quite as much contrast as you like, you can make a Curves adjustment. To increase mid-tone contrast, you can create what is known as an S-Curve. Click on a point on the lower left of the diagonal line in the Curves box. For night photos, you'll generally want this point to be far down and close to the bottom left of the box. Now, drag this point down.

Next, click on a point on the upper right of the diagonal line and drag this point up. For night photos, I generally recommend clicking on a point about 3/4 of the way up this line. You can then adjust these two points in the Curves box and see how it changes the photo. Keep adjusting them until the image looks good to you.

There are also some presets you can use in the Curves panel in the drop-down box next to Curves. The Increase Contrast (RGB) preset is similar to the one I just described. I recommend using the presets only as a starting point and adjusting the curve as necessary to optimize the image you're working on.

Vibrance

After you do Levels or Curves adjustments, you'll likely notice that the colors "pop" and appear more saturated. If you want to increase or decrease the saturation, you can use the Vibrance adjustment layer. This layer has two sliders called Vibrance and Saturation. The Saturation slider increases the saturation of all colors in the image the same amount. The Vibrance slider, on the other hand, increases less saturated areas of the photo more than parts that already have a lot of saturation. This helps prevent any single color from becoming oversaturated and having a "Disney" look to it. When increasing saturation, I recommend adjusting this slider first. If you can't get the look you want, you can also adjust the Saturation slider until things look right.

Dodging & Burning

Dodging and burning refers to a technique that film photographers used when they made prints in a darkroom. They would dodge parts of the image to make it lighter and burn other parts to make it darker. This technique can be easily mimicked in Photoshop.

If you bought Tony Kuyper's full TKActions Panel, you can make burn/dodge layers by clicking the B/D Layers button on the panel. If you don't have this panel, it is easy to make the layers manually. Simply create two blank layers by hitting Ctrl+Shift+N (Cm-

Although the Levels adjustment I did on the previous page helped the image quite a bit, I still felt that it looked too flat. I therefore did a second Levels adjustment, this time using the Darks 3 luminosity mask.

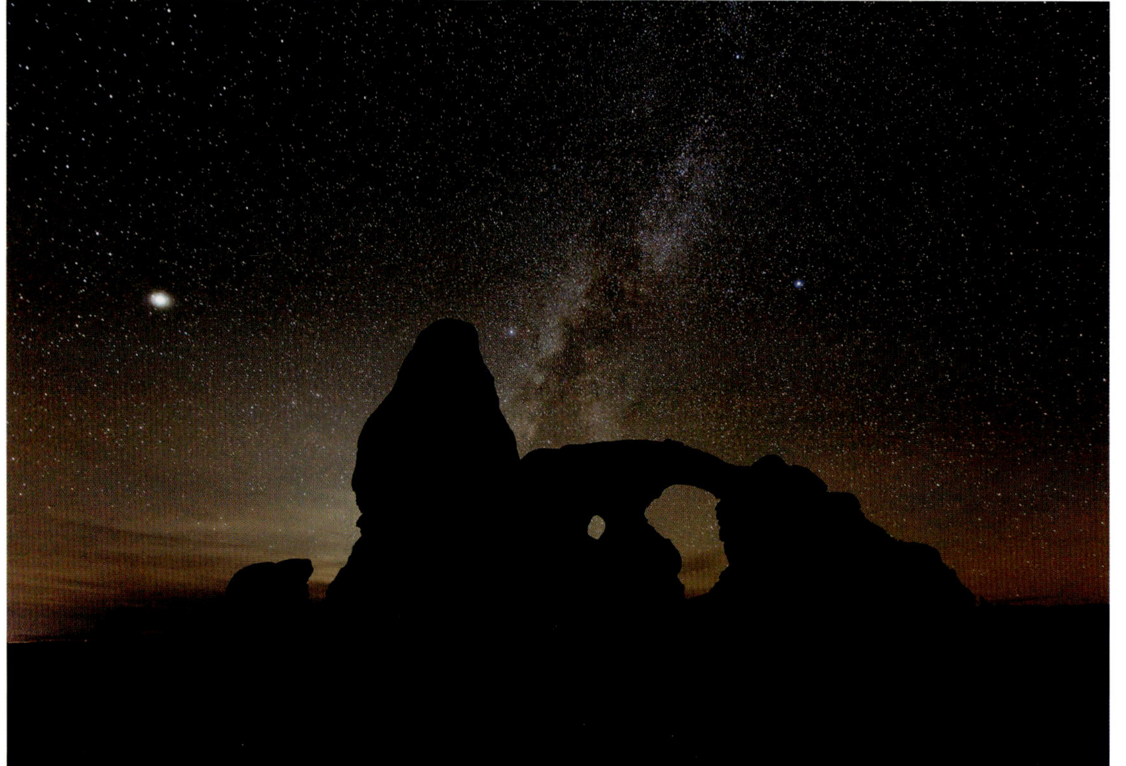

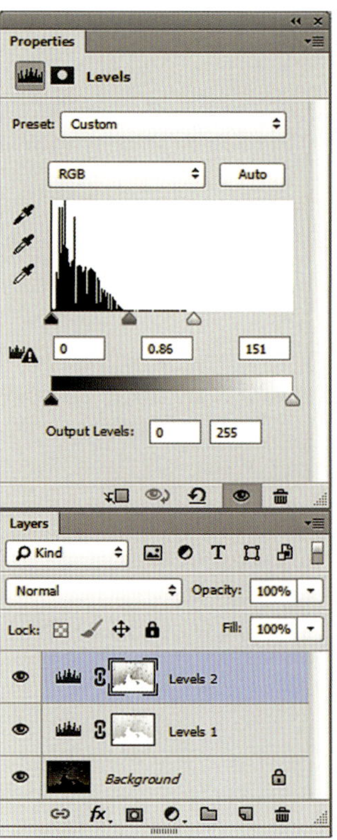

d+Shift+N on a Mac) two times. Change the blending mode of the bottom layer to Soft Light. You can name this layer Burn (Black Paint). Change the blend mode of the top layer to Overlay. You can name this layer Dodge (White Paint).

Once you've created these layers, you can paint on the Dodge layer with a white paintbrush to lighten parts of the image. You can use a black paintbrush on the Burn layer to darken parts of the image. I recommend setting the Opacity of the paintbrush to 5% and the Hardness to 0%. If the Opacity is too high, the effect can be too extreme. If the Hardness is set too high, it can produce obvious edges along areas where you did the dodging and burning.

The manner in which you use Burn / Dodge layers is largely an artistic decision. Carefully inspect your image and decide if there are parts that could benefit from darkening or lightening. Sometimes, areas of the sky will appear too light and could benefit from some burning. Alternatively, parts of the foreground may appear too dark, and you may choose to dodge them. Be careful, though, as dodging can bring out more noise in the image.

If there is still some vignetting in the corners of the image that you were unable to remove in Lightroom, you can dodge those areas to lighten them. Some photographers, on the other hand, like a little vignetting in the image and will intentionally choose to burn the corners.

Dodging and burning can be particularly useful with stitched images. Sometimes, the luminosity of the sky will appear uneven after you stitch an image. By carefully dodging and burning the sky, you can get it to look more even and natural-looking.

Dodging and burning can also be useful with light paintings. The lighting may appear uneven over the scene. You can even out the lighting and make it less evident that it was lit by artificial light.

Boosting Star Size & Brightness

If the stars don't appear large enough or bright enough to you in the image, there are some relatively easy ways to boost their size and brightness. This can be useful if you are making a small print of a photo with a lot of tiny stars. The stars may not show up in the print, unless you first make them larger. This can also be useful for selectively increasing the brightness of stars in a constellation or star pattern.

Select Stars with Lights Luminosity Masks

One way to boost the size of the stars in an image is to use the luminosity masks described previously in this chapter. You'll need to create a Levels layer with a Lights 3 or Lights 4 luminosity mask. This will mask out everything but the very brightest parts of your image. Since stars will often be the only really bright parts of your image, this is a quick way to select the stars. The Lights 3 Mask will select more stars than the Lights 4 Mask, but it could potentially select bright parts of the image that are not stars.

Now you should right-click on the mask and select Add Mask to Selection. Then, on the Photoshop menu, go to Select > Modify > Expand. Next to Expand By enter 1 pixels and hit OK. Now, go to Select > Modify > Feather, and again enter 1 pixels and hit OK.

You can experiment with slightly larger values for expanding and feathering the selection. If you expand it more, the stars will appear larger, and if you feather it more, the glow around the stars will increase. Generally, values of 1 or 2 will be the largest you want to enter. Larger values can make the stars appear unnatural.

Once you're happy with the selection, you should set the foreground color to white. You can do this by clicking on the very small black and white squares located above the larger black and white squares on the Tools panel. If necessary, click once on the arrows next to the small black and white squares to change the large top square to white. Now, with the mask still selected, hit Alt+Backspace (Opt+Delete on a Mac). This will expand and feather the mask around the stars.

Now, bring up the Properties panel by double-clicking on the Levels icon on the Levels layer. Simply drag the middle slider to the left until the stars are as bright and as large as you want them. If you end up brightening areas of the image that you don't want brightened, you can mask this out by painting on the mask with a black paintbrush.

Selecting the stars with luminosity masks may not

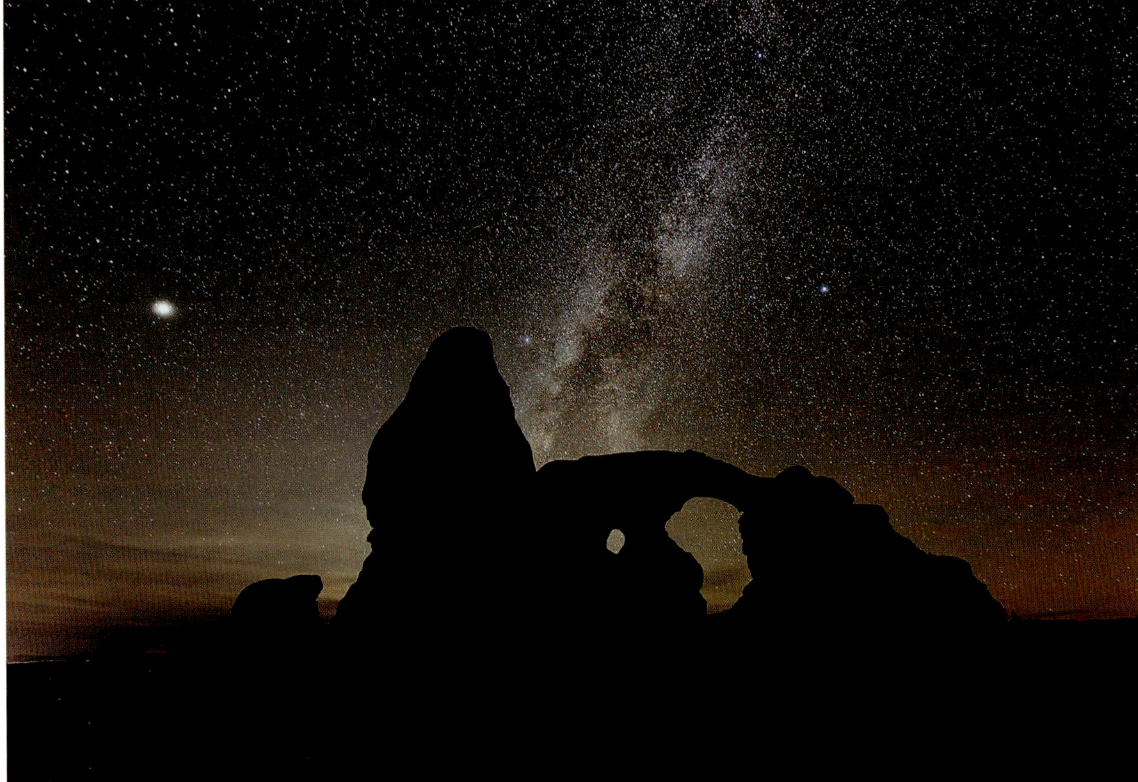

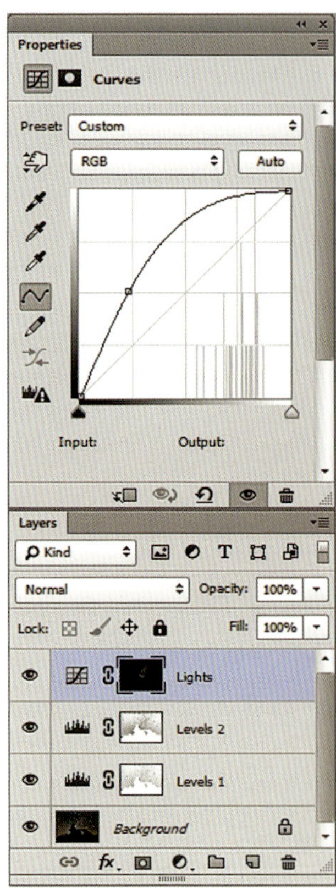

Although the Levels adjustments with luminosity masks made the Milky Way more visible, I decided I wanted to make it even more prominent. I therefore used a Lights 2 mask to select only the bright parts of the image. I then painted over everything but the Milky Way on this mask with a black paintbrush, so as to mask out everything but the bright parts of the Milky Way. I then dragged the line in the Curves panel up to brighten the lightest parts of the Milky Way. This allowed it to truly stand out from the dark sky surrounding it. This is not an adjustment I usually make, but I decided it could help this image since I had photographed a dimmer part of the Milky Way.

---

have any effect on the faintest stars in your image, as they may not get selected.

Selecting Individual Stars

If you only want to increase the brightness of the stars that make up constellations or star patterns, this can be achieved without much difficulty. You can select the individual stars in the constellation using the Quick Selection tool. Then, expand and feather the selection by 1-4 pixels and create a Levels layer. Drag the middle slider to the left to brighten the stars.

Star Spikes Pro

Another option for enlarging star size is a Photoshop plug-in for PCs called Star Spikes Pro. This program allows you to create spikes around the stars, similar to a sunstar effect. If you select a large number of spikes and make the length of the spikes short, it can enlarge the star size without creating noticeable spikes. This program has a lot of other features you can experiment with that can be useful for night photos.

Minimizing Light Pollution

If you're unable to get far away from city lights, you'll likely have light pollution in your images. Light pollution generally appears as a yellow, orange, or red hue in the sky.

If you have a large amount of light pollution in a photograph, it can be nearly impossible to remove in post-processing. But if you only have a small amount, it can be reduced or eliminated without too much difficulty.

The easiest way I've found to eliminate small amounts

of light pollution is to create a new layer in Photoshop by hitting Ctrl+Shift+N (Cmd+Shift+N on a Mac). Now, change the layer's blending mode to Color. With this blending mode, the changes you make will only affect the color of the image and nothing else. Now, you can select the Brush tool and set the Hardness to 0% and the Opacity to around 30%. Then, Alt-click (Opt-click on a Mac) on a part of the sky where the color looks good to set this color as your foreground color. On the new layer, you can paint over the light pollution to make the color of that part of the sky closer to the color you set as your foreground color. You can then alt-click on another part of the sky where the color looks good and repeat as necessary until you have minimized the light pollution.

The area of the sky with light pollution may still look brighter than the rest of the sky. If it does, you can use a Burn Layer to darken it up.

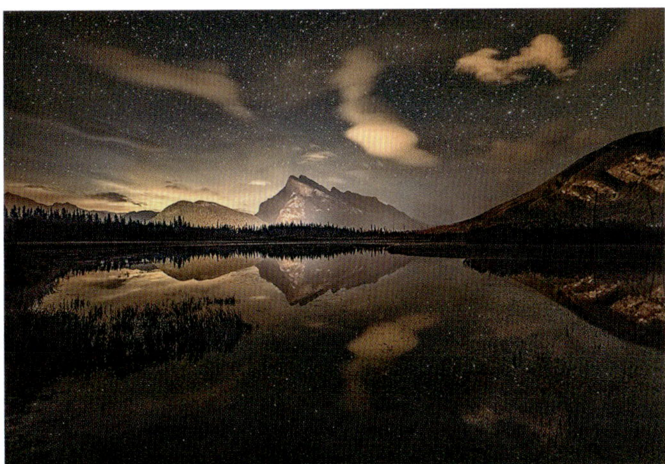

Light pollution helped illuminate the mountains in this image of Vermillion Lakes. However, I had to remove some orange discoloration on the right. Nikon D850, 18mm, f/2.8, 8 seconds, ISO 10000, 3 images stacked.

Although this is my preferred method for reducing light pollution, there are other ways to accomplish this. If you prefer to keep some of the colors from the light pollution but don't want it to stand out as much, you can use a Hue/Saturation Layer to selectively desaturate areas with light pollution. Depending on the color of the light pollution, you can desaturate just the reds, yellows, or magentas. You can do this by selecting the color you want to work on in the drop-down menu where it says Master. You can also use the Eyedropper Tool or drag the sliders at the bottom of the panel to select a different color range. If the adjustment adversely affects other parts of the image, you can create a layer mask to mask out those areas.

Minimizing Chrominance Noise

The method for eliminating light pollution can also be effective at minimizing chrominance noise in a photograph. Chrominance noise will often result from dark noise in longer exposures and can appear as an unnatural red or magenta color over parts of the image. You can attempt to minimize this unnatural color using a new layer with the blending mode set to Color, in the same way you would do for light pollution.

Chrominance noise can also appear as hot pixels, where just one or a few pixels take on a much brighter color than neighboring pixels. Noise reduction software usually does a good job of eliminating or minimizing a small number of hot pixels. If it doesn't, you can simply clone out the hot pixels using the Clone Stamp or Healing Brush tool.

If you took a really long exposure, there could be so many hot pixels that they are almost impossible to eliminate with noise reduction software or cloning. In this case, you would need to have taken a dark frame or used Long Exposure Noise Reduction to be able to further minimize the hot pixels. If you didn't do this, you could attempt to take a dark frame later. Try to shoot in similar temperatures as you did when you shot the original image and use the same camera settings as you did for the original shot. This won't work if you've remapped the hot pixels on your camera after taking the image. More information on taking dark frames was provided on pages 62-63.

Minimizing Luminance Noise

Luminance noise appears as an unnatural brightness variation, or blotchiness, in a photo. The best way to minimize luminance noise is usually with noise reduction software like Topaz DeNoise. However, there is a way to more aggressively reduce this noise if you have an area of an image with minimal detail that has a very smooth and even tone. This could be the case if you have a large field of snow in your photo or if you have nondescript clouds that are fairly uniform in brightness. In these areas, luminance noise will appear more pronounced, since your eye doesn't expect to see

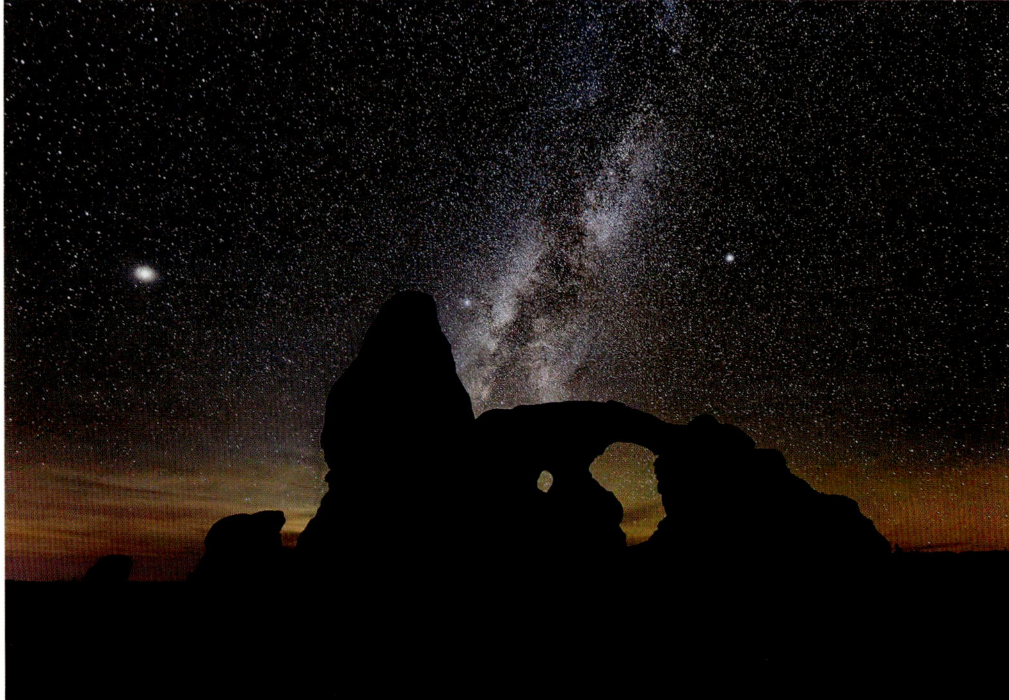

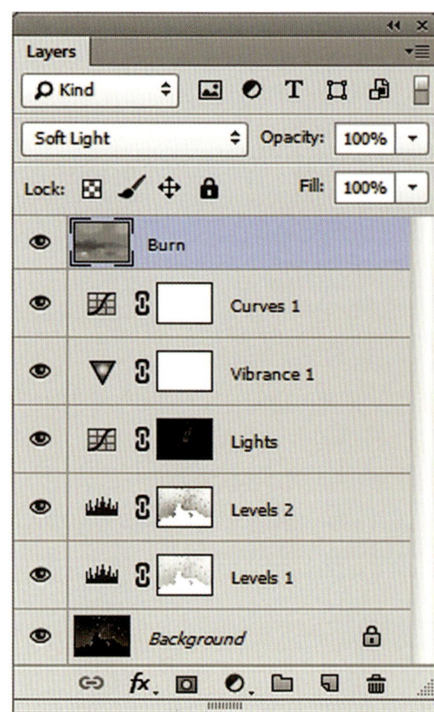

Once I had the Milky Way looking like I wanted, I focused on finalizing the image. The adjustments I had done to this point had made the bottom part of the sky look much brighter than the top. I therefore used a Burn layer to even out the brightness. I also boosted the Vibrance and Saturation a little and used a Curves layer to increase the overall contrast a bit more.

---

much variation in brightness over such smooth areas.

The method for reducing luminance noise in Photoshop is very similar to the method for minimizing chrominance noise or light pollution. For this explanation, I'll assume you're reducing noise in a field of snow. Make a new, blank layer, but change the blending mode to Luminosity instead of Color. Now, select the Brush tool and set the Hardness to 0% and the Opacity to around 20%. Then, alt-click on a part of the snow that has the brightness you want. Paint over the rest of the snowfield with the brush, and it will even out the luminosity of the snow. Paint over it a second or third time with the same brush color selected if you want to smooth it out even more.

You should avoid using this technique in any areas of the image where there is detail that you want to preserve. It can significantly blur the detail and is therefore only effective in limited situations.

Minimizing Star Trails

If you used the rule of 500 to try and render the stars as round points of light, you will usually see that the stars are still elongated when you zoom in on them. There is a remarkably easy way to shorten these star trails and make the stars look like round points of light. However, this technique can sometimes degrade the image quality, so you should check to see if it makes the rest of the sky appear noisier.

First, open the image in Photoshop and create a duplicate layer by hitting Ctrl+J (Cmd+J on a Mac). Or, if your photo has any adjustments layers, select the top layer and hit Ctrl+Alt+Shift+E (Cmd+Opt+Shift+E on a Mac) to merge all of the layers onto a new layer. Change the blending mode of the new, top layer to Darken. Then, select the Move tool and use the arrow keys on your keyboard to move the layer in the direction of the star trails. As you move the layer, you will see the star trails start to reduce in size. Keep moving the layer until the stars appear as round points of light.

If you have foreground objects that are not dark silhouettes, you will have to mask them out on the new layer. Otherwise, the foreground will appear blurred and out of focus.

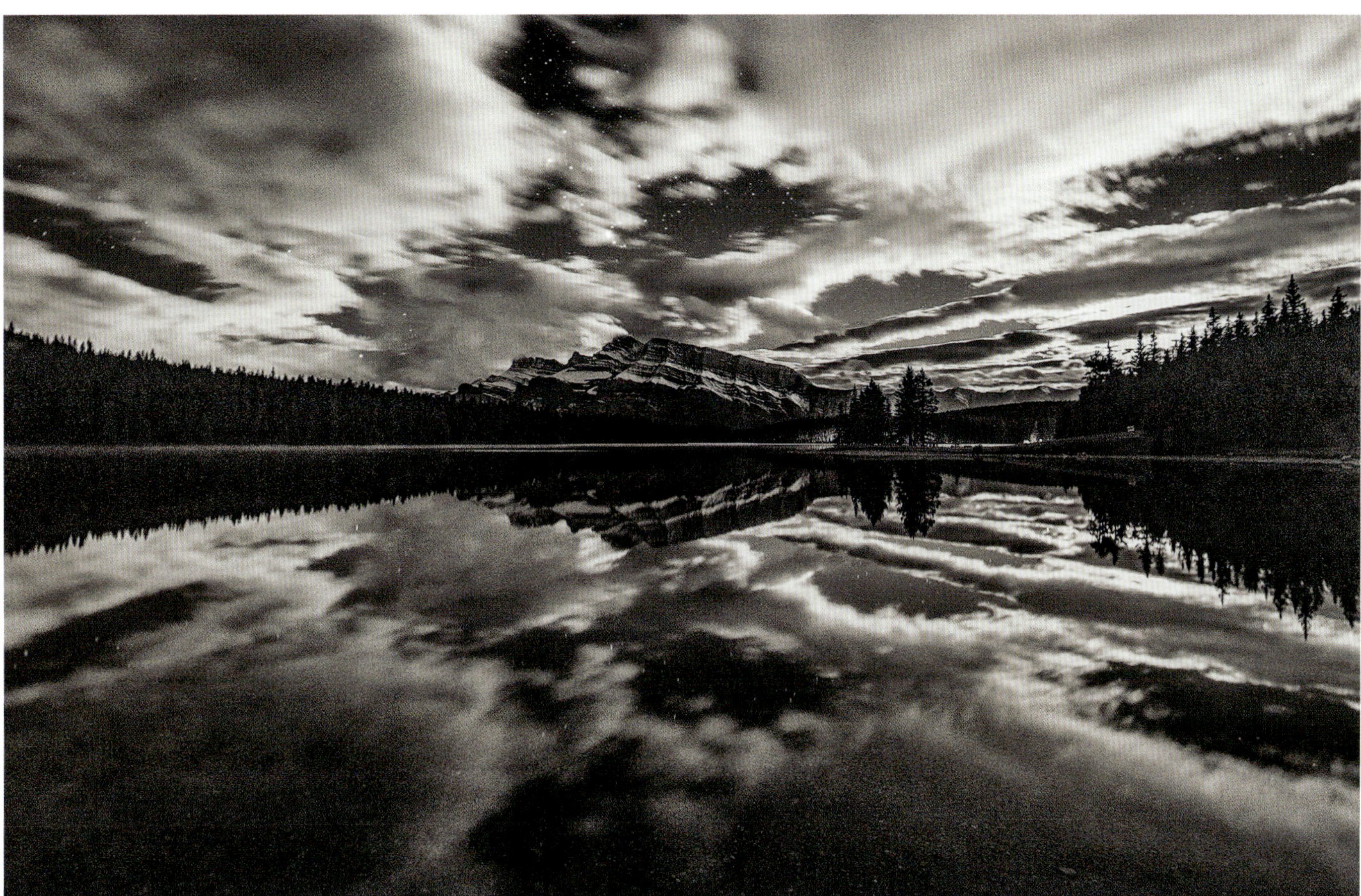

This photo from Banff National Park had discoloration from light pollution, but fortunately it had intriguing cloud patterns that worked well as a black & white image. Nikon D850, 14mm, f/2.8, 20 seconds, ISO 1000.

You may have problems with this technique if you used a wide-angle lens or the camera was pointing north or south. In this case, star trails in different parts of the sky may be of different lengths and moving in different directions. In this case, you can try rotating the duplicate layer to match the movement of the stars.

Rotating the layer is most easily done if the North Star is in your image. You can just rotate the layer around the North Star. To do this in Photoshop, you'll first need to go to Preferences > Tools and check Show Reference Point when using Transform. Now, hit Ctrl+T (Cmd+T on a Mac) to open the Free Transform tool. Click on the crosshair in the middle and move it over the North Star. Now, when you rotate the layer, everything will rotate around the North Star.

If the North Star is not in your image, you can expand the canvas size and guess where it would have been located. Or, if you were facing south, you'd have to pick a spot well below the horizon where stars over the South Pole might have been located.

This technique for rotating layers can also be used to realign meteors to the radiant (as discussed on page 75) and to manually realign stars before stacking them (as discussed on pages 132-133).

One final issue you may encounter with this method is that you may see duplicate stars at the edges of the image. Since the problem area will only be a few pixels wide, you can easily crop it out.

Converting to Black & White

Although I don't discuss black and white images much in this book, you can capture some compelling black and white photos at night. Since our ability to see color at night is very limited, black and white images can actually appear closer to what we see with the naked eye. Converting to black and white can also be useful if you have a lot of discoloration in your image from light pollution. One way to fix this is to simply get rid of the color in the photograph. You may also need to darken areas of the image that are too bright because of the light pollution.

You can convert a photo to black and white in either Lightroom or Photoshop. You can do this in Lightroom by clicking on B&W in the Basic panel. A B&W panel will then appear down below. If you click Auto, Lightroom will automatically try to convert it to a pleasing black and white photograph, and it often does a good job. However, you'll usually want to fine-tune the image by adjusting the color sliders. The color sliders let you decide how bright you want different color tones in your image to look when converted to black and white. For example, if you want areas in the photo that are red to appear brighter in the black and white image, you can move the Red slider to the right. Alternatively, if you want these color tones to appear darker, just move the slider to the left.

If you convert an image to black and white in Lightroom and then open it in Photoshop, you cannot recover the colors or adjust the conversion settings later. You'll have to go back to the original version in Lightroom. It may therefore be easier to convert to black and white in Photoshop. You can do this using a Black & White adjustment layer. As with Lightroom, if you click Auto, it will try to create a pleasing result. Again, you'll likely want to fine-tune the results.

There's also a plug-in that works with Photoshop or Lightroom called Silver Efex Pro that gives you more options when converting to black and white. It's available at https://nikcollection.dxo.com/ and comes with many other plug-ins, including Sharpener Pro.

Sharpening

The final global adjustment you should make to any image is to sharpen it. You'll need to sharpen the image differently depending on how you plan to use it. Learning how to sharpen images for different outputs can be challenging. I therefore recommend a Photoshop plug-in, like PhotoKit Sharpener, that can do advanced sharpening routines for you.

PhotoKit Sharpener

PhotoKit Sharpener is no longer being updated by the developer, but they have generously made it available as freeware at http://www.pixelgenius.com/. After you install it, you can access it in Photoshop by going to File > Automate > PhotoKit Output Sharpener 2... You will see a drop-down menu next to Set that gives you four main sharpening options - Contone, Inkjet, Halftone, and Web and Multimedia.

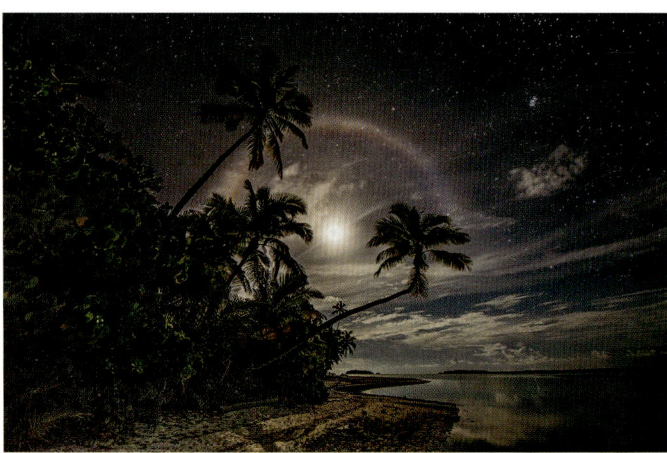

A halo is seen above the moon on One Foot Island. As with all images in the printed book, I used the Halftone option in PhotoKit Sharpener to sharpen the image. Nikon D800e, 14mm, f/2.8, 25 seconds, ISO 1250.

You will want to use Contone for most photographic prints that are not made by inkjet printers. Inkjet should be used whenever making inkjet prints. You'll need to use Halftone for most commercial printing presses, like those that produce books or magazines. Web and Multimedia can be used if you will be displaying the photo on the internet or with a projector. I do, however, usually prefer to use TK Actions for this type of sharpening, which I'll describe next.

Sharpening can make the noise in an image more noticeable. If there are areas of your image where noise is prominent when viewing the photo at 50% zoom, you can partially mask out some of the sharpening. It is preferable to mask out areas that don't have much detail, such as the sky or snow. Masking out areas that have a lot of detail can make the image appear soft, so I avoid doing this.

TK Actions Panel Sharpening

In the TK Actions Panel developed by Tony Kuyper

that I described previously in this chapter, you can also sharpen images for the web. In the TK7 panel, you can enter a horizontal or vertical pixel size and then click on Vert or Horz. It will then automatically resize and sharpen the image. You can fine-tune the amount of sharpening by adjusting the opacity of the sharpening layers that are created. I'll often reduce the opacity a little, as it can sharpen the images a bit too much for my taste. Overall, though, it does an excellent job sharpening images for the web and is the best tool I've found for this purpose. Complete information on using this panel for web sharpening can be found in the instruction manual for the panel.

Sharpener Pro

Nik's Sharpener Pro works in a similar fashion to PhotoKit Sharpener. You can sharpen the image for different output devices, and it has some creative sharpening options. I usually prefer the look of images sharpened with PhotoKit Sharpener. I think Nik Sharpener can oversharpen the image at the default settings. This can be problematic for night photos, as it can bring out more noise. To avoid this, I recommend setting the Viewing Distance to Up to 60 cm, regardless of the actual viewing distance. You may also need to reduce the Overall Sharpening Strength.

Unsharp Mask

After I use PhotoKit Sharpener, TK Actions Panel, or Nik Sharpener, I often do one final sharpening using the Unsharp Mask filter in Photoshop. If you want to try this, you should first merge all of the layers onto a duplicate layer by selecting the top layer and hitting Ctrl+Alt+Shift+E (Cmd+Opt+Shift+E on a Mac). Now, access the filter by going to Filter > Sharpen > Unsharp Mask. The settings I normally use are:

Amount: 5%-30%
Radius: 40-100 pixels
Threshold: 0 levels

The higher you set the amount, the stronger the effect will be. By using a large radius of 40 or more pixels, you will not be sharpening the fine details in the photo. Instead, you will increase the localized contrast in the image. This is similar to what the Clarity slider does in Lightroom, but I think this method produces more pleasing effects. It can, however, create halos along high contrast edges between the foreground and sky. You can create a layer mask to mask out any halos. Unsharp Mask can also cause some highlights to appear too bright or become blown out. If this occurs, you can manually mask out the highlights or apply a Darks luminosity mask, so it doesn't affect the bright areas of the image.

Smart Sharpen

If you don't use PhotoKit Sharpener or Nik Sharpener, the Smart Sharpen filter in Photoshop can be useful for sharpening night photos. It has a Reduce Noise slider that attempts to minimize any extra noise that is brought out during sharpening. You should avoid overdoing this, or it might not sharpen the details enough. You should keep the Radius at around 1 pixel to sharpen the fine details. Determining the exact settings does require some expertise, though. Some printing processes can make the image appear less sharp, so you'll often need to compensate by oversharpening the photo.

Sharpening in Lightroom

If you prefer, you can do final sharpening in Lightroom. This is a simpler option than Photoshop if you don't use PhotoKit Sharpener or Nik Sharpener. In the Export dialog box and in the Print and Web modules, you have the option to select Low, Standard, or High sharpening. Standard sharpening works well for most projects, though you might use High if you'll be doing any halftone printing.

Final Review

Once you've finished sharpening, you should do a final review of your photograph. Zoom in to 100%, and view every part of the image. Check for any dust spots on the photo or any other issues with the photo. Sharpening can bring out imperfections in the image. However, these flaws can usually be easily corrected with a healing brush or clone brush.

Appendix

RESOURCES

I've provided below a list of the apps, websites, software programs, and photography equipment that I recommend in this book. To see a regularly-updated version of this list, you can visit:

https://www.gcollier.com/gear/

Also, consider purchasing equipment from your local camera store. The prices will usually be the same, and they often provide free classes and better service.

VIDEO TUTORIALS

I've produced a 7 1/2 hour video tutorial that gives complete, step-by-step instructions on the post-processing techniques described in this book and some new ones. It can be bought at:

https://www.collierpublishing.com/

STARRY NIGHTS CALENDAR

I produce the Starry Nights Wall Calendar, which contains dates of the major celestial events that you may want to photograph. This can also be found at:

https://www.collierpublishing.com/

CAMERA EQUIPMENT

Cameras

Digital
Canon EOS 5D IV, 5DS R, 6D, 6D II, RP
Nikon D600, D800e, D850, Df, Z6
Panasonic Lumix DC-S1, Lumix DC-S1R
Pentax K-1
Sony A7 III, A7R, A7R III, A7R IV, A7S, A9

Film
Canon EOS 620, 630, 650
Nikon F100, FM, FM10, or N80/F80

Lenses

Canon
EF 50mm f/1.8 STM

Nikon
Nikkor 14-24mm f/2.8, Nikkor 50mm f/1.8D

Rokinon/Samyang
8mm f/3.5 Fisheye, 10mm f/2.8 (crop), 12mm f/2.8 Fisheye, 14mm f/2.8, 14mm f/2.4, 24mm f/1.4, 35mm f/1.4, 50mm f/1.4

Sigma
14mm f/1.8 Art, 14-24mm f/2.8 Art, 20mm f/1.4 ART, 24mm f/1.4 ART, 35mm f/1.4 ART, 50mm f/1.4 ART, 150-600mm f/50-6.3 C

Sony
FE 55mm Carl Zeiss f/1.8

Tamron
15-30mm f/2.8, SP 35mm f/1.8, SP 45mm f/1.8

Tokina
11-20mm f/2.8 DX (crop)

Tripod Legs

Bonfoto
Feisol carbon fiber
Gitzo carbon fiber
Really Right Stuff carbon fiber

Ball Heads

Acratech
Really Right Stuff
Manfrotto XPRO
Neewer Professional

Accessories

GigaPan EPIC Pro Robotic Camera Mount
Hoya or Kenko Pro Softon Type-A filter

LensMuff by Kevin Adams
Neewer, Meike, or Powerextra Battery Grip
Neewer or Vello Remote Releases & Intervalometers
Skywatch Star Adventurer & Adventurer Mini
Tiffen Double Fog 3 filter

LIGHTING EQUIPMENT

Coast HL7 Focusing LED Headlamp
Coast HP1 190 Lumen Pure Beam Focusing LED
Coast Polysteel 400 440 lm Waterproof Flashlight
Eagletac Clicky Neutral White
Fenix FD45 900 Lumen Neutral White LED Flashlight
Ledlenser MT6 or MT10 Flashlight
Luxli Viola LED Panel
Neewer 160 LED Panel
Neewer Battery Powered Outdoor Studio Flash
Proton Pro (for preserving night vision)
Rosco Cinegel Swatchbook (Large) 3x5"
Roscolux Swatchbook

CLOTHING

Heat Factory Pop-Top Mittens with Glove Liner
NEOS Overshoes
Verseo ThermoGloves

SURVIVAL GEAR

Fast Find Personal Locator Beacon
Garmin Satellite Communicators
SPOT 2-Way Messenger
SPOT Satellite GPS Messenger

WEBSITES

AccuWeather.com
ClearDarkSky.com (cloud forecast)
DofMaster.com/dofjs.html (depth of field calculator)
DPReview.com/reviews/image-comparison/
DxOMark.com (equipment reviews)
ForecastAdvisor.com
GCollier.com/eclipse (photographing a solar eclipse)
Gi.alaska.edu/monitors/aurora-forecast/
Heavens-Above.com (satellites)
Imo.net/resources/calendar/ (meteor showers)
In-The-Sky.org/newsindex.php?feed=conjunctions
LightPollutionMap.info
PhotoEphemeris.com
SeaSky.org/astronomy/astronomy-calendar-current.html
Swpc.noaa.gov/products/aurora-3-day-forecast/
TidesOnline.noaa.gov/
TimeAndDate.com/eclipse/list.html
VolcanoDiscovery.com
Weather.gov
WeatherUnderground.com

SOFTWARE PROGRAMS

Adobe Lightroom
Adobe Photoshop
Google Earth
Hugin
Image Composite Editor (ICE)
Magic Lantern
PTGui
RegiStar
Sequator
Starry Landscape Stacker
StarStaX
Startrails.exe
Stellarium

PHOTOSHOP PLUG-INS

Astronomy Tools Actions Set
Creative Effects UI
Floris Van Breugel's Star Trail Stacker
PhotoKit Sharpener
Sharpener Pro
Silver Efex Pro
Star Spikes Pro
Tony Kuyper's Basic V6 Panel & TK7 Panel
Topaz DeNoise

SMARTPHONE APPS

AccuWeather
DSLR Remote (Android only)
Flashlight
Google Earth
myCSC (iPhone only)
Photographer's Ephemeris
Photopills
Sky Safari
Stellarium
Unleashed - Camera Remote (iPhone only)
Weather Underground

INDEX

REFERENCES

Mike Berenson's Tutorials - http://www.nightphotographyworkshop.com/articles-tutorials-page
Steven Christenson's Star Circle Academy - https://starcircleacademy.com/
Nat Coalson's Nature Photography Workshop and Lightroom 5 - https://www.subjectivearts.com/books/
Phil Hart's blog - http://www.philhart.com/
David Kingham's Night Tutorials - https://exploringexposure.com/blog/night-tutorials/
Tony Kuyper's Tutorials & Luminosity Masks - https://goodlight.us/writing/tutorials.html
Mikko Lagerstedt's How to Process Star & Night Sky Pictures in Lightroom 5 & Photoshop - http://www.mikkolagerstedt.com/blog/2013/11/8/night-photography-tutorial-lightroom-5-photoshop
Ian Norman's Lonely Speck - https://www.lonelyspeck.com/
Thomas O'Brien's Meteor Shower Tips - http:// iso.500px.com/meteor-shower-tips/
Aaron Priest's NPF Rule - https://petapixel.com/2017/04/07/npf-rule-formula-sharp-star-photos-every-time/
Tony Prower's Magic Cloth - https://icelandaurora.com/blog/2010/07/20/tonys-magic-cloth-technique/
Glenn Randalls's Dusk to Dawn - https://www.glennrandall.com/books.html
Todd Salat's Predicting the Aurora Borealis - http://www.aurorahunter.com/aurora-prediction.php
Jeffrey Sullivan's blog - https://www.jeffsullivanphotography.com/
Floris Van Breugel's The Twilight Hour - https://www.artinnaturephotography.com/gallery/twilightarticle/